RICHARD HOOKER

T&T Clark Studies in English Theology

Series editors
Karen Kilby
Mike Higton
Stephen R. Holmes

RICHARD HOOKER

Theological Method and Anglican Identity

Philip Hobday

LONDON • NEW YORK • OXFORD • NEW DELHI • SYDNEY

T&T CLARK
Bloomsbury Publishing Plc
50 Bedford Square, London, WC1B 3DP, UK
1385 Broadway, New York, NY 10018, USA
29 Earlsfort Terrace, Dublin 2, Ireland

BLOOMSBURY, T&T CLARK and the T&T Clark logo are trademarks
of Bloomsbury Publishing Plc

First published in Great Britain 2023
Paperback edition published 2025

Copyright © Philip Hobday, 2023

Philip Hobday has asserted his right under the Copyright, Designs and Patents Act, 1988, to be identified as Author of this work.

For legal purposes the Acknowledgements on p. ix constitute an extension of this copyright page.

Cover image: clairevis/iStock

All rights reserved. No part of this publication may be reproduced or transmitted in any form or by any means, electronic or mechanical, including photocopying, recording, or any information storage or retrieval system, without prior permission in writing from the publishers.

Bloomsbury Publishing Plc does not have any control over, or responsibility for, any third-party websites referred to or in this book. All internet addresses given in this book were correct at the time of going to press. The author and publisher regret any inconvenience caused if addresses have changed or sites have ceased to exist, but can accept no responsibility for any such changes.

A catalogue record for this book is available from the British Library.

Library of Congress Control Number: 2023939393

ISBN: HB: 978-0-5677-0803-8
       PB: 978-0-5677-0808-3
     ePDF: 978-0-5677-0804-5
    eBook: 978-0-5677-0807-6

Series: T&T Clark Studies in English Theology

Typeset by Integra Software Services Pvt. Ltd.

To find out more about our authors and books visit www.bloomsbury.com and sign up for our newsletters.

For Hannah, Benedict, Lydia and Aidan

CONTENTS

Acknowledgements	ix
Abbreviations	x
A note on citations	xiii
Introduction	1

Chapter 1
LOCATION, LOCATION, LOCATION — 5
   Introduction — 5
   Locating Anglicanism — 5
   Locating Hooker — 7
   Locating the argument — 11
   Summary — 14

Chapter 2
KNOWLEDGE OF GOD IN AQUINAS — 15
   Introduction — 15
   Natural knowledge of God in Aquinas — 16
   Reason and its limitations — 24
   Reason and revelation — 35
   Scripture in Aquinas' theological method — 44
   Obscuring Aquinas' method — 53
   Summary — 57

Chapter 3
KNOWLEDGE OF GOD IN CALVIN — 59
   Introduction — 59
   Natural knowledge of God in Calvin — 61
   Reason and its limitations — 67
   Reason and revelation — 73
   Scripture in Calvin's theological method — 76
   Obscuring Calvin's convergence with Aquinas — 85
   Summary — 91

Chapter 4
KNOWLEDGE OF GOD IN HOOKER — 93
   Introduction — 93
   Natural knowledge of God in Hooker — 95

Reason and its limitations	99
Reason and revelation	106
Scripture in Hooker's theological method	112
Obscuring Hooker's convergence with Calvin and Aquinas	128
Summary	135

Chapter 5
TRADITION IN HOOKER, CALVIN AND AQUINAS 137
    Introduction 137
    Tradition in Aquinas' theological method 138
    Tradition in Calvin's theological method 146
    Tradition in Hooker's theological method 156
    Obscuring the convergence of Hooker, Calvin and Aquinas 165
    Summary 173

Chapter 6
POSSIBILITIES AND LIMITATIONS 177
    Introduction 177
    Faith and reason 178
    Authority in the church 188
    Summary 196

Conclusion 199

Bibliography 206
Index 221

ACKNOWLEDGEMENTS

This book is a revised version of a doctoral dissertation, and I gladly acknowledge my greatest academic debt to my supervisor Simon Oliver, who guided, encouraged and considerably improved my work over two degrees, two universities, three additions to the family, four jobs, four homes and thirteen years. For financial help towards the costs of studying I am grateful to the Barry Fund of Durham University, the Trustees of the Bayne Bequest and the Henry Smyth Charity, while for congenial working locations and help with finding material I am grateful to the staff of the following libraries: in London, the British Library; in Cambridge, the University Library and the Faculty of Divinity Library; in Oxford, the Bodleian Library, the Philosophy and Theology Faculties Library, the Libraries of Pusey House and of Blackfriars; in Reading, the University of Reading Library and Reading Central Library.

For encouragement and care over the years I owe more than I can say to Gareth Atkins, Graham Davies, Eamon Duffy, Stephen Hampton, Michael Hetherington, Ronald Hyam, John Maddicott and Kenneth Padley, as well as various groups who heard aspects of the argument and much improved it with their comments. Thanks too to colleagues, students and parishioners at Magdalene College, Cambridge; Earley St Peter's, Reading; and now Wakefield Cathedral. All have given me so much with good humour and patience. For supporting and sharpening the arguments here, I'm grateful to Paul Dominiak, Jake Griesel, Karen Kilby and Andrea Russell; and especially to my doctoral examiners, Mark Chapman and Mike Higton. Most of all I'm grateful for the support of my family and the sense of perspective which comes from Hannah and the children, to whom this is dedicated with the promise that the word count, at least for now, is done.

Festival of St Thomas Aquinas, Priest,
Philosopher, and Teacher of the Faith, 1274
28 January 2023
AMDG

ABBREVIATIONS

ACL	'A Christian Letter of Certain English Protestants with Richard Hooker's Autograph Notes', *FLE*, IV.1–80.
Antidote	John Calvin, 'Canons and Decrees of the Council of Trent with the Antidote'. In *John Calvin: Tracts and Letters*. 9 vols, III.18–188. Translated and edited by Henry Beveridge. Edinburgh: Banner of Truth Trust, 2009.
CD	Karl Barth, *Church Dogmatics*. 13 vols. Edited by G. W. Bromiley and T. F. Torrance. Edinburgh: T&T Clark, 1956–75.
Certainty	Richard Hooker, 'A Learned Sermon of the Certainty and Perpetuity of Faith in the Elect', *FLE*, V.59–82.
Commentaries	John Calvin, *Commentaries*. Translated and edited by Joseph Haroutunian. London: SCM, 1963.
CRH	*A Companion to Richard Hooker*. Edited by W. J. T. Kirby. Leiden: Brill, 2008.
CThJ	*Calvin Theological Journal*
Decrees	*Decrees of the Ecumenical Councils*, Vol. II: *Trent to Vatican II*. Edited by Norman P. Tanner. London: Sheed and Ward, 1990.
de trin.	Thomas Aquinas, *Expositio super librum Boethii de Trinitate* (*Exposition of Boethius' book on the Trinity*). The edition used is Maurer's two-volume translation: *Faith, Reason and Theology: Questions I-IV of His Commentary on the* de Trinitate *of Boethius* and *The Division and Methods of the Sciences: Questions V and VI of His Commentary on the* de Trinitate *of Boethius*. Translated by Armand Maurer. Toronto: Pontifical Institution of Medieval Studies, 1986–7.
de ver.	Thomas Aquinas, *Quaestiones disputatae de veritate* (*Disputed Questions on Truth*). The edition used is the three-volume translation, *Truth*. Translated by Robert W. Mulligan, James V. McGlynn, Robert W. Schmidt. Indianapolis, Ind.: Hackett Publishing Company, 1994.
DER	*Documents of the English Reformation, 1526–1701*. Edited by Gerald Bray. London: James Clarke, 2004.
DF	Richard Hooker, 'The Dublin Fragments: Grace and Free Will, the Sacraments, and Predestination', *FLE*, IV.99–167.
div. nom.	Thomas Aquinas, *Commentary on Blessed Dionysius's on the Divine Names*. Translated by Harry C. Marsh, 'Cosmic Structure and the Knowledge of God: Thomas Aquinas' *In Librum Beati Dionysii De Divinis nominibus expositio*.' PhD diss., Vanderbilt University, 1994.
EHR	*English Historical Review*

Fides et ratio	John Paul II, 'Encyclical Letter on the Relationship between Faith and Reason' (14 September 1998). Accessed 16 August 2020. http://www.vatican.va/content/john-paul-ii/en/encyclicals/documents/hf_jp-ii_enc_14091998_fides-et-ratio.html
FLE	Richard Hooker, *Folger Library Edition of the Works of Richard Hooker*. 7 vols. General Editor W. Speed Hill. Vols I–V: Cambridge, Mass.: Bealknap Press of Harvard University Press, 1977–90; Vol. VI: Binghamton, NY: Medieval & Renaissance Texts and Studies, 1993; Vol. VII: Tempe, Ariz.: Medieval & Renaissance Texts and Studies, 1998.
HJ	*Heythrop Journal*
HThR	*Harvard Theological Review*
IJST	*International Journal of Systematic Theology*
in Gal.	Thomas Aquinas, *Commentary on St. Paul's Epistle to the Galatians*. Translated by F. R. Larcher. Albany, NY: Magi Books, 1966.
Institutes	John Calvin, *Institutes of the Christian Religion*. 2 vols. Edited by John T. McNeill. Translated by Ford Lewis Battles. Louisville, Ky.: Westminster John Knox Press, 2006.
JAS	*Journal of Anglican Studies*
JEH	*Journal of Ecclesiastical History*
JTS	*Journal of Theological Studies*
Jude I	Richard Hooker, 'The First Sermon upon Part of St Jude', *FLE*, V.13–35.
Jude II	Richard Hooker, 'The Second Sermon upon Part of St Jude', *FLE*, V.36–57.
Just.	Richard Hooker, 'A Learned Discourse of Justification', *FLE*, V.105–69.
Laws	Richard Hooker, *Of the Laws of Ecclesiastical Polity: A Critical Edition with Modern Spelling*. 3 vols. Edited by A. S. McGrade. Oxford: Oxford University Press, 2014.
Lumen Gentium	Second Vatican Council, 'Dogmatic Constitution on the Church' (21 November 1964). https://www.vatican.va/archive/hist_councils/ii_vatican_council/documents/vat-ii_const_19641121_lumen-gentium_en.html
metaphys.	Thomas Aquinas, *Commentary on the Metaphysics of Aristotle*. 2 vols. Translated by John P. Rowan. Chicago, Ill.: Henry Regnery, 1961.
OHA	*The Oxford History of Anglicanism*. 5 vols. Gen. ed. Rowan Strong. Oxford: Oxford University Press, 2016–19.
OHST	*The Oxford Handbook of Systematic Theology*. Edited by John Webster, Kathryn Tanner, and Iain Torrance. Oxford: Oxford University Press, 2009.
Pride	Richard Hooker, 'A Learned Sermon on the Nature of Pride', *FLE*, V.309–61.
PRRD	R. A. Muller, *Post-Reformation Reformed Dogmatics: The Rise and Development of Reformed Orthodoxy, ca. 1520 to ca. 1725*. Second edition. 5 vols. Grand Rapids, Mich.: Baker Academic, 2003.

Remedy	Richard Hooker, 'A Remedy against Sorrow and Fear', *FLE*, V.363–77.
RHCCC	*Richard Hooker and the Construction of Christian Community*. Edited by A. S. McGrade. Tempe, Ariz.: Medieval and Renaissance Texts and Studies, 1997.
Romans	John Calvin, *Calvin's Commentaries: Romans and Thessalonians*. Translated by Ross Mackenzie. Edinburgh: Oliver and Boyd, 1960.
SCG	Thomas Aquinas, *Summa Contra Gentiles*. 4 vols. Translated by the English Dominican Fathers. London: Burns & Oates, 1923–9.
SJT	*Scottish Journal of Theology*
SRH	*Studies in Richard Hooker: Essays Preliminary to an Edition of His Works*. Edited by W. Speed Hill. Cleveland, Ohio: Case Western University Press, 1972.
S. Th.	Thomas Aquinas, *Summa Theologica*. 5 vols. Translated by the Fathers of the English Dominican Province. Notre Dame, Ind.: Christian Classics, 1981.
Suppl.	Walter Travers, 'A Supplication Made to the Privy Council', *FLE*, V.189–210.
Treatises	John Calvin, *Theological Treatises*. Edited by J. K. S. Reid. Louisville, Ky.: Westminster John Knox Press, 2006.
Works	*The Works of That Learned and Judicious Divine, Mr Richard Hooker*. Seventh edition. 3 vols. Edited by John Keble. Revised by R. W. Church and F. Paget. Oxford: Clarendon Press, 1888.

A NOTE ON CITATIONS

References to primary texts are generally in the body of the dissertation text, except where introductory or editorial material is being cited; in that case, there will be a footnote with reference to the appropriate volume and page number.

Hooker's *Laws* is cited by book, chapter and section number (e.g., II.2.4). These divisions were Keble's but are replicated in both the Folger Library and McGrade editions. The structure of references to Hooker's other works varies as they are laid out in different ways, but as well as the abbreviated title and any reference to a subdivision within the text, references always include details of the cited text from the Folger Library edition by volume, page and line number (e.g., V.25.22-3).

Quotations from Hooker's *Laws* are taken from the three-volume McGrade edition, which uses modernized English spelling. Quotations from Hooker's other works are taken from Volumes IV and V of the Folger Library edition, but I have modernized the spelling. Something of the complexity and elegance of Hooker's prose is admittedly lost in that process, but it makes for consistency and easier reading.

Quotations from Calvin's *Institutes* are cited by reference to book, chapter and section number (e.g., III.7.2) and from his other works by page reference to the edition cited.

Quotations from Aquinas' works follow the standard conventions, so the larger *Summa* is quoted by part, question, article and section of the article; hence I.1.1, *resp.* is a reference to the body ('*responsio*') of the first article of the first question of the *prima pars*.

INTRODUCTION

The central figure of this book, Richard Hooker (1554–1600), an English priest and theologian in the reign of Elizabeth I, was a 'loner who died comparatively young and in a country parsonage'.[1] But he wrote one of the first substantial works of non-fiction in the vernacular; C. S. Lewis called its 'style ... for its purpose, perhaps the most perfect in English'.[2] In his erudite, elegant, but sometimes elusive voice, Hooker contributed to the development of English prose style, legal theory, constitutional thought and philosophy. Most of all he is known for articulating (perhaps even creating) the Anglican way of being a Christian, describing (perhaps even inventing) the distinctive identity and character of the Church of England and of those churches around the world which grew from it.[3]

But what was the identity of the Church of England which Hooker so poetically sketched? Where, if anywhere, can we locate something coherent and distinctive to say about the Anglican Communion and the Anglican tradition which emerged from the Church of England? These are disputed questions, contested territory. Anglicans themselves, to say nothing of those from other Christian traditions, have advanced different, sometimes opposing, accounts of Hooker and of Anglicanism, appropriating Hooker to undergird an account of the tradition as a whole and/or approaching Hooker from the perspective of their account of the tradition, and challenging whether other accounts are coherent and realistic. Locating Hooker's theology more precisely will not only help us understand him more clearly but also trace one account of the identity of the Church of England and of Anglicanism.

So this book will trace an account of Anglicanism by locating Hooker's theology more precisely through looking at one theme, theological method. Theological

---

1. Diarmaid MacCulloch, *Reformation: Europe's House Divided* (London: Penguin, 2004), 508.

2. C. S. Lewis, *English Literature in the Sixteenth Century* (Oxford: Clarendon Press, 1954), 462.

3. Good overviews of Hooker's influence are Michael Brydon, *The Evolving Reputation of Richard Hooker: An Examination of Responses, 1600–1714* (Oxford: Oxford University Press, 2006), and Diarmaid MacCulloch, 'Richard Hooker's Reputation', *EHR* 117 (2002): 773–812.

method may be defined broadly as the question of how we ground theological claims, what sources yield knowledge about God and how they relate to each other. A basis for our knowledge of God is sometimes called a 'theological warrant' and normally at least three are identified: *scripture, reason* and *tradition*.[4] This study examines Hooker's theological method through a close comparative reading of Hooker alongside a representative theologian of each of the catholic and reformed traditions, Thomas Aquinas (*c.* 1225–74) and John Calvin (1509–64), respectively. This will help relocate Hooker's theological method, and therefore potentially his whole theological outlook, by showing it to be both catholic and reformed. Relocating Hooker's theological identity in this way will yield a coherent and potentially fruitful account of Anglicanism as likewise both catholic and reformed.

As working definitions,[5] 'reformed' I take broadly to mean beliefs, practices or theologians identified with churches advocating a break with the Roman Catholic Church.[6] By 'catholic' I generally mean beliefs, practices or theologians of the church in the period before the sixteenth-century divisions; and, by contrast, I use the description 'Roman Catholic' specifically for beliefs, practices or theologians of that denomination at and after the reformation. 'Anglican' and 'Anglicanism' are somewhat anachronistic when applied to the sixteenth century[7] but will serve as broad labels for beliefs, practices or theologians in the Church of England or

---

4. Good introductions to theological method and the warrants include A. N. Williams, *The Architecture of Theology: Structure, System, and Ratio* (Oxford: Oxford University Press, 2011); *The Routledge Companion to the Practice of Christian Theology*, ed. Mike Higton and Jim Fodor (London: Routledge, 2015); *Scripture Tradition and Reason: A Study in the Criteria of Christian Doctrine: Essays in Honour of Richard P.C. Hanson*, ed. Richard Bauckham and Benjamin Drewery (Edinburgh: T&T Clark, 1988).

5. On terminology, see Peter Lake, *Anglicans and Puritans? Presbyterianism and English Conformist Thought from Whitgift to Hooker* (London: Unwin Hyman, 1988), 1–7; Anthony Milton, *Catholic and Reformed: The Roman and Protestant Churches in English Protestant Thought, 1600–1640* (Cambridge: Cambridge University Press, 1995), 7–9.

6. This is quite a broad definition of 'reformed', which is sometimes used in a narrower sense to delineate Protestant denominations other than the Lutheran. However, a key insight underpinning this investigation is that the reformed were a much wider and diverse group than often supposed, though sharing many key theological concerns (such as justification by faith, rejection of the sixteenth-century papacy, insistence on vernacular worship and scriptures). Some of the reformed were also presbyterians, but others were not. It is this broader definition I adopt, following R. A. Muller, *After Calvin: Studies in the Development of a Theological Tradition* (Oxford: Oxford University Press, 2003), 7–9, and S. W. P. Hampton, *Anti-Arminians: The Anglican Reformed Tradition from Charles II to George I* (Oxford: Oxford University Press, 2008), 6–10.

7. For good discussions on the terms *Anglican* and *Anglicanism*, see Anthony Milton, 'Introduction: Reformation, Identity, and Anglicanism', *OHA*, I.6-7; Milton, 'Attitudes towards the Protestant and Catholic Churches', *OHA*, I.333-51; S. W. P. Hampton, 'Confessional Identity', *OHA*, I.210-11.

the global family of churches associated with it historically and structurally and now known as the Anglican Communion. The term *puritan*, source of much spilt scholarly ink, is avoided; I use 'presbyterian' for those, including many of Hooker's opponents, who urged further reform of the Church of England, usually including abolishing bishops and priests and replacing them with a single class of presbyters chosen by local congregations. By contrast, Hooker and similar thinkers are called 'conformist' because they argued an English Christian could in good conscience conform to the beliefs, practices and structures of the Elizabethan Church.

To trace the reformed and catholic identity of Hooker and of Anglicanism, Chapter 1 briefly sketches the different ways Anglican identity has been characterized and sets out how these often map on to readings of Hooker and of sixteenth-century Anglicanism. It then brings together recent retrievals of Calvin, Aquinas, Hooker and the Church of England in the sixteenth century to ground the plausibility of a claim that Hooker and the Church of England might be coherently both catholic and reformed. Having laid the foundation of the case in Chapter 1, Chapters 2, 3 and 4 advance the argument by considering the relationship of two of the warrants, *scripture* and *reason*. These chapters contest two key limbs of many (mis)interpretations of Richard Hooker: firstly, that Aquinas attributes too much capacity to human reason, thereby undercutting the reformation principle of *sola scriptura* or 'scripture alone',[8] and, secondly, the converse assertion that Calvin attributes too much to scripture at the expense of human reason. These chapters consider Aquinas, Calvin and Hooker in turn, asking initially what, if anything, human beings may know naturally about God by their reason and without the help of scripture before exploring the effects of the Fall on human reason and the use of philosophy in theology. While Aquinas is often characterized as very positive about, and Calvin much less optimistic about, reason, both attribute this warrant real but limited theological capacity and insist on the need for revelation to convey essential theological truths. These chapters then turn to scripture, its sufficiency and authority, again showing that despite the common interpretation that scripture is more central in Calvin's method than Aquinas' they share similar views. Both could be said to advance a *sola scriptura* theological method *if* by this we understand that God's revelation in scripture is the unique source of distinctively Christian doctrines, a source which nonetheless requires other warrants to clarify and codify. Each chapter ends by tracing reasons why this convergence has been overlooked, in particular the tendency of subsequent interpreters to misunderstand the nuance of these theologians' accounts and thereby disproportionately magnify differences.

The argument is developed in Chapter 5 which explores a third theological warrant, *tradition*. The place of tradition in official Roman Catholic theology has

---

8. As Williams, *Architecture of Theology*, 364–6, notes, the phrase, rendered 'scripture alone', appears very rarely in the sixteenth-century reformers and there is considerable dispute about its meaning. While arguing it is an appropriate way to describe the theological methods of our theologians, further definition will be needed.

been problematic for the reformed since the sixteenth century. However, Aquinas' restrained understanding of tradition is not uncongenial to reformed concerns. An account of tradition, broadly consistent with Aquinas' views, can be identified in Calvin and Hooker when a vital boundary is drawn after the first four centuries of Christian history, where tradition has a greater formative authority in the shaping of doctrine. The chapter concludes by identifying reasons why this congruence has been missed, particularly the distorting effect that official Roman Catholic theology at and after the Council of Trent had on readings of Aquinas from the late sixteenth century, and the distorting effect that John Keble's appropriation had on readings of Hooker from the late nineteenth century.

What emerges from these four central chapters is a plausible but realistic theological method which all three theologians share, albeit with some differences of tone and emphasis; and Hooker's theological identity should be relocated within the wide confluence of catholic and reformed traditions as articulated by Aquinas and Calvin. This can in turn undergird an Anglican identity which is both catholic and reformed. Chapter 6 then sketches, as worked examples or case studies, two possible applications of this understanding of theological method and Anglican identity: firstly, to debates about the place of reason in Christian theology and, secondly, contemporary ecumenical debates about authority in the church.

Locating Aquinas', Calvin's and Hooker's theological methods more precisely relocates Richard Hooker's theological identity and sustains a coherent account of Anglicanism as catholic and reformed. This will yield a fresh, comparative reading of all three theologians, generating insights into contemporary debates about each of them as well as possibilities for more informed theological and ecumenical dialogue. By reframing the debate about Hooker's catholic and reformed interlocutors, we will see how much he shares with them both. Chapter 1 will now sketch the disputes about the identity of Hooker and of Anglicanism, before situating the case for their reformed and catholic character in the context of debates about Aquinas, Calvin and the Church of England in the sixteenth century.

Chapter 1

LOCATION, LOCATION, LOCATION

Introduction

This brief chapter sets out the backdrop to the argument of the book by locating the debates about Anglicanism and Hooker. Firstly, it considers the background to contemporary disputes about Anglican identity and different ways – catholic, reformed, middle way – that the tradition has often been understood. Secondly, it shows how these different accounts map on to readings of Hooker. Thirdly, it examines how some contemporary retrievals of Aquinas, Calvin, Hooker and the sixteenth-century Church of England make it increasingly widespread and plausible to consider an Anglican theologian and the tradition itself as meaningfully both catholic and reformed.

Locating Anglicanism

Disagreements about Anglican identity are not new. In 1948, a committee of bishops asked, '[I]s Anglicanism based on a sufficiently coherent form of authority to form the nucleus of a worldwide family of churches, or does its comprehensiveness conceal internal disputes which may cause its disruption?'[1] Since then, disruption and dispute seem to prevail, driven by three trends. Firstly, Anglicanism has become less Anglocentric, with churches in different countries developing greater organizational autonomy and diversity in forms of worship, practice and belief.[2] Secondly, different Anglicans have responded differently to questions about the role of women in ministry and about the rapid legal and cultural recognition of homosexual people and relationships in many countries.[3]

---

1. *The Lambeth Conferences, 1867–1948* (London: SPCK, 1948), 84; cf. Stephen Sykes, *Unashamed Anglicanism* (London: DLT, 1995), 168–9.

2. William Jacob, *The Making of the Worldwide Anglican Church* (London: SPCK, 1997), esp. 292–3, 296–9; David Hamid, 'The Nature and Shape of the Anglican Communion Today', in *Beyond Colonial Anglicanism: The Anglican Communion in the Twenty-First Century*, ed. Ian T. Douglas and Kwok-Pui Lan (New York: Church Publishing, 2001), 85–7.

3. See, e.g., Mark D. Chapman, '"Homosexual Practice" and the Anglican Communion from the 1990s: A Case Study in Theology and Identity', in *New Approaches in History and Theology to Same-Sex Love and Desire*, ed. Mark D. Chapman and Dominic Janes (Basingstoke: Macmillan, 2018), 187–208; Kevin Ward, *A History of Global Anglicanism* (Cambridge: Cambridge University Press, 2006), 296–318.

Thirdly, Anglican dialogues with other Christian churches have often stumbled because Anglicans have seemed unwilling or unable to offer a coherent account of their tradition and its theology. As Stephen Sykes pointed out, this exasperates Anglicanism's ecumenical partners because if Anglicans cannot clearly state their own identity, it is hard to delineate areas of (dis)agreement with others.[4]

Some Anglicans assert Anglicanism has no distinctive theology because it believes only what Christians generally believe, differing only in non-essential points from other strands of Christianity.[5] Again, Sykes highlighted the incoherence of what he branded this 'no special doctrines' claim, pointing out that, for instance, there is a clear Anglican account of church order with at least implicit distinctive theological foundations: so, for example, unlike many churches, Anglicanism has retained a distinct order of bishops but has no single central authoritative figure.[6]

Of course, plenty of Anglicans *have* advanced accounts of what makes their tradition distinctive, and three broad accounts can be traced which mirror (and often claim in support) different interpretations of Hooker we will sketch in a moment. For some, Anglicanism is fundamentally *reformed*, emphasizing the Bible as source of theological truth and rejecting elements of Roman Catholicism's doctrine and structure. For others, Anglicanism is rather a local variation of *catholic* faith, looking less towards to the reformation than to the beliefs and practices it shares with the Roman Catholic Church. For yet others, Anglicanism occupies some middle ground ('*via media*') between reformed and catholic traditions, a kind of moderation or balance which avoids extremes. Each interpretation has fuelled diverse literature, organizations and movements. A representative sample might include Church Society ('maintain[ing] the character of the Church of England as … one of the Reformed Churches of Christendom');[7] Anglican Catholic Future ('embody[ing] the Catholic Faith in the Church of England');[8] and the *Via Media* blog ('the historic Anglican perspective of the "Via Media"').[9] Anglicanism's multiple self-identifications led Bishop Rowan Williams, one of the

---

4. Stephen Sykes, *The Integrity of Anglicanism* (Oxford: Mowbray, 1974), 74–5; cf. P. D. L. Avis, 'Anglican Ecclesiology', in *The Oxford Handbook of Ecclesiology*, ed. P. D. L. Avis (Oxford: Oxford University Press, 2018), 239–41.

5. For instance, H. R. McAdoo, *The Spirit of Anglicanism: A Study of Theological Method in the Seventeenth Century* (London: A&C Black, 1965), v, 1.

6. Sykes, *Unashamed Anglicanism*, x–xi, 102–9; cf. R. D. Williams, *Anglican Identities* (London: DLT, 2004), 1.

7. 'Objectives of Church Society', accessed 8 July 2021, https://churchsociety.org/docs/about_us/CS%20Objectives.pdf.

8. 'Anglican Church Future: About', accessed 8 July 2021, https://www.facebook.com/AnglicanCatholicFuture/.

9. 'Background', accessed 26 May 2020, https://viamedia.news/about-viamedia/; cf. common introductory works such as Samuel Wells, *What Anglicans Believe: An Introduction* (Norwich: Canterbury Press, 2011), 41.

tradition's foremost figures, to name a book *Anglican Identities*, a revealing plural if ever there was one.

Usually underlying these multiple accounts of Anglicanism are the different stories they tell about what happened in the sixteenth century in general and about Richard Hooker's views in particular. They see the Church of England in this period as fundamentally breaking with Rome and joining a continental family of reformed churches, severing itself from institutional relations with Rome while retaining many of its pre-reformation structures and practices, or charting a distinctively moderate Anglican course between these two poles. How Anglicanism is understood, then, often relates to how Hooker and the sixteenth-century church he served in are understood.[10]

Locating Hooker

Given his relative lack of prominence in his own lifetime, Richard Hooker's significance for English thought and for Anglican theology and identity is perhaps surprising.[11] Born in Exeter, he found a patron in John Jewel (1522–71), the Bishop of Salisbury. Studying in Oxford, he became a Fellow of Corpus Christi in 1579 and was ordained. From 1585 to 1591 he was Master of the Temple, a London church with strong links to the legal community. The Temple years were marred by a protracted and public dispute with his colleague, Walter Travers. He moved finally to be Rector of Bishopsbourne, a country parish in Kent, where he died in 1600. Respectable, well-read and erudite, Hooker never achieved high office in church, state or academy; was not a particularly prominent theologian in his lifetime and is not widely studied in other Christian traditions.[12]

If there is little clue in Hooker's biography to explain his eventual significance in the tradition, neither can it be explained, at least at first glance, by a Hooker bibliography. His principal work, weighty both literally and metaphorically, is called *Of the Laws of Ecclesiastical Polity*; the occasion for it was a seemingly dry debate about the best way to organize church structures. Only its first five books were published in Hooker's lifetime (Books I to IV in 1591, Book V in 1597). The final three books were not published until five decades after his death

---

10. See Mark D. Chapman, *Anglican Theology* (London: T&T Clark, 2012), 1–9, 12–18; Avis, 'Anglican Ecclesiology', 241–50.

11. For biography, W. Bradford Littlejohn, *Richard Hooker: A Companion to His Life and Work* (Eugene, OR: Cascade, 2015), 18–31; Lee W. Gibbs, 'Life of Hooker', *CRH*, 1–26. The only full-length modern biography is Philip B. Secor, *Richard Hooker: Prophet of Anglicanism* (Tunbridge Wells: Burns & Oates, 1999); but this work is seriously marred by the author's habit of 'reconstructing' Hooker's words by stitching together texts from different occasions and of 'imagining' different events in Hooker's life.

12. Diarmaid MacCulloch, *Reformation: Europe's House Divided, 1490–1700* (London: Penguin, 2004), 506.

(Books VI and VIII in 1648, Book VII in 1661). Alongside the *Laws* there is a handful of sermons, some fragments of incomplete works and some manuscript notes in response to various critics.[13]

Despite this lack of prominence while alive, Hooker, nonetheless, has become since his death the one indispensable thinker in Anglophone theology, almost all surveys of the Church of England and of Anglicanism pay him homage.[14] But from about a hundred years after this death, what he thought became the subject of much dispute. He is labelled an eirenic consensus-seeker on the one hand or a skilful partisan polemicist on the other;[15] his theology is regarded by some as systematic and others hopelessly incoherent;[16] and – as we now sketch – he is prayed in aid by at least three very different styles of Anglicanism.

Firstly, beginning with his presbyterian opponents, are those who think Hooker (dangerously or pleasingly) steered too close to the beliefs and practices of the Roman Catholic Church. One inquired venomously, '[S]hall we do you wrong to suspect … that you would deem her Majesty to have done ill in abolishing the Romish religion, and banishing the Pope's authority?' (*ACL* 20, IV.20-1, 24-5). Hooker's belief that Roman Catholics might go to heaven (*Just.* 9, V.117-8, condemned by Travers in *Suppl.*, V.200-2), and his argument that some pre-reformation practices such as kneeling at communion might be maintained (*Laws*, V.6.83), undermined his reformed credentials in their eyes. Later, the Oxford Movement, arguing that Anglicanism had more in common with the reformed than with Rome, appropriated this characterization of Hooker as a catholic sympathizer: 'humanly speaking, we owe it [to Hooker] that the Anglican church continues at such a distance from that of Geneva, and so near to primitive truth and apostolical order'.[17]

Such categorizations of a catholic Hooker often cite his debt to Thomas Aquinas. Hooker's opponents believed that most theologians of the medieval schools were mad, bad and dangerous to know: 'school divinity hath banished from us … sincere divinity', and in Hooker's writings they detected 'the ingenious schoolmen, almost in all points have some finger' (*ACL* 20, IV.65.5,

---

13. For the publishing history and bibliography, see *CRH*, 28–49 and 613–38.

14. So 'many would regard [Hooker] as the Anglican theologian *par excellence*': Chapman, *Anglican Theology*, 7. Diarmaid MacCulloch, 'Richard Hooker's Reputation', *EHR* 117 (2002): 811, says Anglicanism found in him 'an Anglican saint'; while W. Bradford Littlejohn concludes 'the Anglican Communion … came to see Richard Hooker as summing up everything that it admired about itself', *Hooker Companion*, 4.

15. Contrast respectively Alan Suggate, 'The Anglican Tradition in Moral Theology', in *Worship and Ethics: Lutherans and Anglicans in Dialogue*, ed. Oswald Beyer and Alan Suggate (Berlin: De Gruyter, 1996), 2, with W. J. Cargill Thompson, 'The Philosopher of the "Politic Societie": Richard Hooker as a Political Thinker', *SRH*, 14–15.

16. A debate well charted by P. A. Dominiak, *Richard Hooker: The Architecture of Participation* (London: T&T Clark, 2021), 25–7.

17. John Keble, 'Editor's Preface', *Works*, I.cxv.

13, 16, 18). More recently, this debt to Aquinas is emphasized by Munz, Marshall and Joyce; the latter asserts his distance from the reformed by arguing he 'owes much to the Aristotelian-Thomist tradition'.[18] The first strand of interpretation, then, envisages a catholic Hooker who cannot therefore be fully reformed.

Partly in reaction against this first strand, a more recent, second characterization argues that, by contrast, Hooker is thoroughly reformed. This strand includes Atkinson, for example, who argues Hooker can best be characterized as within the broad reformed spectrum of thought, and this is sometimes (though not always) taken to mean he cannot also be catholic.[19] Thus, for Atkinson, 'Hooker's aim was ... to demonstrate the Church's commitment to reformed theology and to argue that this was his commitment as well'.[20] For Atkinson, this necessarily means diverging from the catholic position embodied in, for instance, Aquinas: 'As Thomas Aquinas is regarded as Rome's chief theologian, any similarities noted between the two theologians serve, indirectly, to pull Hooker away from an explicit dependence on Reformed thought'.[21] So this second characterization is of Hooker as within the reformed spectrum and this is often defined by contrast to the catholic perspective, in particular by (in the inverse of Joyce's characterization) assuming that closeness to Aquinas must inevitably mean distance from the reformed and vice versa. Debunking that assumption is a vital basis for the argument which follows.

A third strand, perhaps most prevalent in popular Anglican thought and to some extent in more scholarly literature, conceives Hooker as advocating or even inventing a distinctively Anglican mode of Christianity: a *via media* or middle way. This usually means he is thought to take the best of Roman Catholicism on the one

---

18. Peter Munz, *The Place of Hooker in the History of Christian Thought* (London: Routledge, 1952), 49–62; J. S. Marshall, *Hooker and the Anglican Tradition* (London: A&C Black, 1963), e.g., 50-2, 55, 113, 172; A. J. Joyce, *Richard Hooker and Anglican Moral Theology* (Oxford: Oxford University Press, 2009), 240, cf. 238. However, Joyce's categorization appears confused at this point: while insisting that 'Hooker stands solidly (although neither slavishly nor uncritically) within the tradition of reformed Protestantism', she nonetheless contends 'he has no hesitation whatsoever in drawing upon the wisdom and insights of traditions that reformed Protestantism rejected out of hand', 244. Since she makes so much of Hooker's resonance with Aquinas, she may mean Aquinas' 'wisdom and insights' are among those the Protestants rejected and thus defines Hooker's Thomist sympathies over against his reformed ones, but this is a false dichotomy because many Protestants (including Calvin) did not reject Aquinas' insights.

19. Nigel Atkinson, *Richard Hooker and the Authority of Scripture, Tradition and Reason* (Vancouver: Regent College Publishing, 2005), 129–32.

20. Atkinson, *STR*, xxi.

21. Atkinson, *STR*, xvii.

hand and of reformed protestantism on the other, while avoiding the perceived extremes of both. Classically if comically, this was expounded in rhapsodic prose by the editor who described Hooker 'steer[ing] a middle way between the excesses of Romanist and Radical Protestant' theologies because of the 'love of balance, restraint, moderation, measure ... innate in the English temper'.[22] It is not too hard to imagine the next sentence attributing the moderation of Anglicanism to the temperateness of the English weather. More seriously, this reading is followed by contemporary writers such as Lake, Booty and Gibbs.[23] For the latter, Hooker advances a *'via media* theology that utilises insights derived from both the Magisterial Reformers and Tridentine Roman Catholicism, and yet which creates a genuine *tertium quid* by rejecting other teachings from both these traditions as erroneous'.[24] This third strand conceives Hooker as proponent of a middle way between catholic and reformed excesses.

The *via media* view of Hooker connects with the theme of this study, theological method, through its rhetorical cousin, the 'three-legged stool'. For, as Neelands identifies, 'it is a commonplace of Anglican self-understanding to refer to the triple authority of scripture, reason, and tradition. For at least one hundred years, Richard Hooker has been identified as a principal and original source of this position'.[25] As a theological and historiographical trope, the 'three-legged stool' is now decidedly wonky for, as this study will demonstrate, it is not a theological method Hooker would have recognized. This in turn throws serious doubt on *via media* accounts of Anglicanism, and arguments that Hooker's or Anglicanism's identity may be found there are difficult to sustain.

So there are three broad ways of categorizing Hooker: catholic, reformed, middle way. These competing interpretations, as we will see, often make assumptions about the capacity or role of the different warrants in theological method. And, as we have seen, these interpretations can both generate and be influenced by readings of the Anglican tradition more broadly as catholic, reformed or middle way. The central argument of this study is that each of these interpretations both of Hooker and of Anglican identity is fundamentally flawed because they fail to adequately account for the possibility that both Hooker and his tradition could be both catholic and reformed.

---

22. P. E. More, Introduction to *Anglicanism: The Thought and Practice of the Church of England*, ed. P. E. More and F. L. Cross (London: SPCK, 1935), xxii.

23. Peter Lake, *Anglicans and Puritans? Presbyterianism and English Conformist Thought from Whitgift to Hooker* (London: Unwin Hyman, 1998), 9, 225–30; John Booty, 'Hooker and Anglicanism', *SRH*, 208–11; Lee W. Gibbs, 'Richard Hooker's *Via Media* Doctrine of Scripture and Tradition', *HThR* 95.2 (2002): 227–35; Lee W. Gibbs, 'Richard Hooker's *Via Media* Doctrine of Justification', *HThR* 74.2 (1981): 211–20.

24. Gibbs, 'Scripture and Tradition', 234.

25. W. David Neelands, 'Hooker on Scripture, Reason, and Tradition', *RHCCC*, 75.

Locating the argument

This book argues Hooker and Anglicanism can be best understood as coherently both catholic and reformed (rather than one, or the other, or a middle way between them). It contests, in particular, the assumption there is a reformed-catholic spectrum along which Hooker and Anglicanism can be situated, by showing how much he has in common with both Calvin and Aquinas (and, indeed, how much Calvin and Aquinas have in common with each other). For while these two are often thought to diverge on key issues, such as the function and relationship of the theological warrants, which is the theme of this investigation, there is in fact much greater continuity between them.

A sustained three-way comparison between Hooker, Calvin and Aquinas is relatively unusual in the scholarship; most literature on Hooker tends to compare him principally with one or the other. To make a complex investigation manageable means setting clear limits, three of which need to be acknowledged at the outset. Firstly, other voices within the traditions are largely excluded; to take one example, a fuller study of Hooker's reformed credentials would need to engage with Luther as well as with Calvin, particularly on the role of tradition where Luther's thought was a vital springboard for the reformed.

Secondly, focusing on a single theme in systematic theology means that historical and political circumstances can only be considered in passing. This means the reader seeking detailed discussion of what Hooker might have been reading, or how his views might have been similar to or different from other Church of England thinkers in the late sixteenth century, will need to look elsewhere.[26]

Thirdly, this study argues there is substantial and surprising convergence between three theologians on questions of theological method; this is not to say they agree on everything, nor to elide all difference between the traditions. For example, as we will see, Hooker and Calvin fiercely *disagreed* with Aquinas on some issues, such as what happened to the bread and wine during the communion service. There are areas where reformed and catholic perspectives did and do diverge; my argument is not that they are wholly convergent, but that we can identify areas of unexpected agreement, even on some disputed topics where they are often thought to be at odds. So this study relocates the argument more precisely, sometimes by highlighting often-overlooked convergence, sometimes by showing that the reformed's unease might be with sixteenth-century or contemporary official Roman Catholic theology rather than with Aquinas.

The plausibility of this analysis is reinforced when we note that recent readings of all three theologians demonstrate their theologies are considerably more nuanced than many subsequent interpretations have suggested, and that they may be less antagonistic than often supposed. To use a phrase now ruined for a generation, shades of grey are often painted in sharper contrast by subsequent interpretations. So, on Aquinas, Fergus Kerr has reminded us that there are

---

26. A good starting point with references is Chapman, *Anglican Theology*, 103–25.

varieties of Thomism(s).²⁷ Theological sensibilities such as the *nouvelle théologie* in mid-twentieth century Europe,²⁸ or the strain of Anglophone Dominican interpretation identified with Victor Preller and Denys Turner, have read Aquinas as more congenial to the reformed perspective than he is often thought to be.²⁹ For example, Yves Congar offered a Thomist view of tradition intended to allay reformed concerns about tendencies in some catholic theologies which appear to rely too heavily on that warrant at the expense of scripture,³⁰ while on the reformed side theologians such as John Webster have drawn widely on Aquinas.³¹

Similarly, on Calvin, R. A. Muller and others have shown there is a wide range of reformed opinion and it is not all attributable to Calvin, thus emphasizing the possibility that there may be ways of conceiving the reformed perspective (and Calvin) as more congruent with the catholic perspective than often understood.³² And just as a number of scholars are advancing readings of Aquinas which see him as in surprising sympathy with the reformed,³³ so too reformed scholars have offered interpretations of Calvin which emphasize his continuity with Aquinas.³⁴

27. Fergus Kerr, *After Aquinas: Versions of Thomism* (Oxford: Blackwell, 2002), vi–viii, 207–10; Fergus Kerr, 'The Varieties of Interpreting Aquinas', in *Contemplating Aquinas: On the Varieties of Interpretation*, ed. Fergus Kerr (London: SCM, 2003), 27–40; cf. Mark D. Jordan, *Rewritten Theology: Aquinas after His Readers* (Oxford: Blackwell, 2006), 1–17.

28. On this sensibility, see Gabriel Flynn, 'Introduction', in *Ressourcement: A Movement for Renewal in Twentieth-Century Catholic Theology*, ed. Gabriel Flynn and Paul D. Murray (Oxford: Oxford University Press, 2014), 1–12; A. N. Williams, '"The Future of the Past": The Contemporary Significance of the Nouvelle Theologie', *IJST* 7.4 (2005): 347–50.

29. Victor Preller, *Divine Science and the Science of God: A Reformulation of Thomas Aquinas* (Princeton, NJ: Princeton University Press, 1967), vii, 22–5; Denys Turner, *Faith, Reason, and the Existence of God* (Cambridge: Cambridge University Press, 2004), 3–25.

30. Yves Congar, *Tradition and Traditions: An Historical and a Theological Investigation* (London: Burns & Oates, 1966), 142–5.

31. For instance, John Webster, *The Domain of the Word: Scripture and Theological Reason* (London: T&T Clark, 2014), where Aquinas is the most-cited writer in the index after Augustine and appears more time than Calvin or Barth, say. That Webster is clearly willing to identify areas of his disagreement with Roman Catholic theology makes his affinity with Aquinas even more revealing – see John Webster, 'Purity and Plenitude: Evangelical Reflections on Congar's *Tradition and Traditions*', *IJST* 7.4 (2005): 410–12.

32. See, e.g., R. A. Muller, *After Calvin: Studies in the Development of a Theological Tradition* (Oxford: Oxford University Press, 2003), 3–24, 63–104; the pluriform nature of reformed opinion is set out in exhaustive detail in his four-volume *PRRD*.

33. See, for instance, the essays in *Aquinas among the Protestants*, ed. Manfred Svensson and David VanDrunen (Oxford: Wiley-Blackwell, 2018).

34. There are tantalizing hints in Williams, *Architecture of Theology*, 95 fn.18, 103 fn.27. More detailed accounts of the convergence of Aquinas and Calvin include R. A. Muller, *The Unaccommodated Calvin: Studies in the Foundation of a Theological Tradition* (Oxford: Oxford University Press, 2000), 34–42, 56; Arvin Vos, *Aquinas, Calvin, and Contemporary Protestant Thought* (Grand Rapids, MI: Eerdmans, 1985).

Nathan Barczi, for instance, has demonstrated substantial similarity in their perspectives on scripture in theological method, while Rowan Williams' recent monograph highlights the similarity of their accounts of the person and work of Christ.[35]

While we cannot delve in detail into comparing Hooker with other sixteenth-century figures, the plausibility of this analysis is advanced when we note the increasing number of accounts of later sixteenth- and seventeenth-century theology in England which suggest we need not see catholic and reformed as opposite poles in this period, against the backdrop of interpretations of Aquinas and Calvin which show them as more congenial than often understood. As Hoyle reminds us, 'we now agree it is all very complicated and there is more to it than we first thought'[36] – an important caution since the nuance and complexity of theological positions is often overlooked. So, as Hampton (drawing on Muller) has shown, 'reformed' is a wide spectrum rather than a narrow monolith; 'identifying a writer as Reformed does not mean that they will hold all and only those theological views held by their predecessors within the tradition'.[37] Hampton shows that, as late as the start of the eighteenth century, there was a vibrant strand of Anglicanism which understood itself as both Thomist and reformed.[38]

Indeed, there is a growing sensibility in contemporary scholarship which identifies the potential convergence of Thomist and Calvinist theological perspectives and situates Hooker within the confluence of those streams. Some recent writers have hinted at this, and others make it explicit.[39] For instance, Kirby and Littlejohn among others agree with Atkinson that Hooker can rightly

---

35. Nathan Barczi, 'A Light to My Path: Calvin and Aquinas on the Doctrine and Metaphysics of Scripture' (MA diss., University of Nottingham, 2010), 1, 15; R. D. Williams, *Christ the Heart of Creation* (London: Bloomsbury, 2018), 142–56.

36. D. M. Hoyle, *Reformation and Religious Identity in Cambridge, 1590–1644* (Woodbridge: Boydell Press, 2007), 4.

37. S. W. P. Hampton, *Anti-Arminians: The Anglican Reformed Tradition from Charles II to George I* (Oxford: Oxford University Press, 2008), 8. Hampton's analysis converges with a range of scholarship, including, for instance, Milton, *Catholic and Reformed*; Jean-Louis Quantin, *The Church of England and Christian Antiquity: The Construction of a Confessional Identity* (Oxford: Oxford University Press, 2009); Nicholas Tyacke, *Anti-Calvinists: The Rise of English Arminianism* (Oxford: Clarendon Press, 1990), 1–8, 245–7.

38. Hampton, *Anti-Arminians*, 222–7, 267–72; cf. S. W. P. Hampton, *Grace and Conformity: The Reformed Conformist Tradition and the Early Stuart Church of England* (Oxford: OUP, 2021), esp. 1–27.

39. There are tantalizing allusions to this possibility in Williams, *Architecture of Theology*, 138 fn.3; W. J. T. Kirby, 'Reason and Law', *CRH*, 264 fn.53, 270 fn.70; Dominiak, *Participation*, 60 fn.140, 120–1; a fuller case is made in P. A. Dominiak, 'Hooker, Scholasticism, Thomism, and Reformed Orthodoxy', *RHRO*, 117–19.

be characterized as reformed;[40] but they disagree with Atkinson by insisting that Hooker's reformed stance does not mean he cannot also be catholic.[41] So Schöwbel demonstrates Aquinas' similarities with both Calvin and Hooker before concluding, 'while the influence of Thomas [on Hooker] is not to be denied, it is a mistake to set it against the influence of the magisterial reformation'.[42] Similarly, Grislis writes, '[F]or his theological framework, Hooker relied upon the thought of Thomas Aquinas and of John Calvin.'[43]

Summary

This sketch of contemporary reinterpretations of Aquinas, Calvin and Hooker therefore traces a backdrop against which it is now possible to reconceive an Anglican conformist sixteenth-century theologian like Hooker as sharing a theological perspective with both Calvin and Aquinas, rather than having to position his theology on some presumed spectrum between them. In turn, the possibility of Anglicanism being characterized as catholic *and* reformed can be seen as a more coherent claim than often recognized. Having traced this backdrop, Chapter 2 now contests the first limb of many accounts of our theologians and of Anglicanism: that Aquinas is uncongenial to a key reformed concern by affording human reason too great a capacity in his theological method at the expense of scripture.

---

40. See, e.g., W. J. T. Kirby, 'Richard Hooker as an Apologist of the Magisterial Reformation in England', *SRH*, 219–36; W. Bradford Littlejohn, 'The Search for a Reformed Hooker: Some Modest Proposals', *Reformation and Renaissance Review* 16.1 (2014): 68–82.

41. Kirby, 'Reason and Law', 251; Littlejohn, *Hooker*, 52–68.

42. Christoph Schwöbel, 'Reformed Traditions', in *The Cambridge Companion to the Summa Theologiae*, ed. Philip McCosker and Denys Turner (Cambridge: Cambridge University Press, 2016), 325.

43. *FLE*, V.631.

Chapter 2

KNOWLEDGE OF GOD IN AQUINAS

Introduction

Born in Italy to a noble family, Aquinas was sent to school at the Benedictine abbey of Monte Cassino; his father, a benefactor of the monastery, perhaps hoped his son would one day become abbot. In 1239, as war reached Monte Cassino, the putative Benedictine was sent for a liberal education at Naples, and decided instead to become a Dominican – a youthful rebellion, albeit of rather a niche short. After an abortive attempt at dissuading him through kidnapping (which he endured) and the offer of a prostitute (which he declined), Aquinas was allowed to pursue his vocation, studying then teaching in Paris and Naples. His great unfinished work, the *Summa Theologiae*, begun in the late 1260s but incomplete at his death in 1274, is central to this chapter, while drawing also on his shorter *Summa Contra Gentiles* from the early 1260s, as well as two works from the late 1250s, his *de veritate* ('Disputed Questions on Truth'), and his *de trinitate* (a commentary on a work of the sixth-century philosopher Boethius).

Characterizations of Anglicanism and of Hooker often assume catholic methodologies give reason and tradition a much greater place than reformed ones. This chapter challenges that assumption as applied to Aquinas by exploring his understanding of two theological warrants, *scripture* and *reason*, showing that, while Aquinas gives reason significant weight in theology, this is not at scripture's expense. Scripture's function and authority are unique, such that Aquinas could, if carefully defined, be said to hold a *sola scriptura* view of theological method congenial to the views of a reformer like Calvin. Reason for Aquinas is useful but limited, particularly because it can only yield general truths about God such as his existence and not distinctive Christian truths such as the Trinity – that knowledge comes only by God's revelation in Christ recorded uniquely in scripture.

This chapter begins by examining one theological warrant, *reason*, showing, for Aquinas, it can yield only limited knowledge of God. Two themes are then explored: the significance of the Fall for Aquinas' account of reason and his understanding of philosophy. These show Aquinas less optimistic about human reason (and therefore less antagonistic to key reformed concerns) than often supposed. Next, the crucial dialectic between reason and revelation is explored. Finally, Aquinas' account of *scripture* as the principal locus of divine revelation is considered, examining his view of its sufficiency and its authority. Far from being over-reliant on reason, Aquinas gives scripture a unique place in theological method as the sole source now available of the saving knowledge of God, and so he could be said to have a real (though nuanced) belief in *sola scriptura*.

Natural knowledge of God in Aquinas

Introduction

A useful starting point for a discussion of reason in theological method is the question of natural theology.[1] Topham's definition is fairly typical: 'natural theology is a type of theology which relies on reason (which is natural), unaided by any evidence derived from God's revelation through scriptures, miracles or prophecies (which is supernatural)'.[2] The phrase 'natural theology' is controversial, only entering the discourse relatively late,[3] so we adopt the less-encumbered term *natural knowledge of God*.[4] Following Topham's definition, this can be posed as the question of whether human beings can attain knowledge of God by their own natural reason without the aid of supernatural divine revelation, and if so what knowledge this might yield.

There is a widespread presumption that Aquinas is very positive about the possibility of natural knowledge of God, representing a wider optimism about human reason, and thereby differing markedly from Calvin's more pessimistic view. For example, Harrison distinguishes 'a relatively Thomistic account of human nature' in the Catholic tradition from the 'reformers' focus on human depravity' which leads to a 'mitigated scepticism' about human reason.[5] While coming from

---

1. Good introductions are *The Blackwell Companion to Natural Theology*, ed. William Lane Craig and J. P. Moreland (Oxford: Wiley-Blackwell, 2012); *The Oxford Handbook of Natural Theology*, ed. Russell Re Manning (Oxford: Oxford University Press, 2013).

2. Jonathan R. Topham, 'Natural Theology and the Sciences', in *The Cambridge Companion to Science and Religion*, ed. Peter Harrison (Cambridge: Cambridge University Press, 2010), 59; see also, for instance, Norman Kretzmann, *The Metaphysics of Creation: Aquinas's Natural Theology in* Summa Contra Gentiles II (Oxford: Oxford University Press, 2001), 3.

3. A good brief overview is A. E. McGrath, *Christian Theology: An Introduction*, 5th edn (Oxford: Oxford University Press, 2011), 158–70. There are various claims to the first use of the term (see *OHNT*, ed. Re Manning, 9–136), but certainly it became much more prominent after William Paley's 1802 work, *Natural Theology*.

4. Reformed theologians in particular seem to prefer the phrase alongside or in lieu of 'natural theology': e.g., Edward Adams, 'Calvin's View of Natural Knowledge of God', *IJST* 3.3 (2001): 282; Michael Sudduth, *The Reformed Objection to Natural Theology* (London: Routledge, 2016), 221–8.

5. Peter Harrison, *The Fall of Man and the Foundations of Science* (Cambridge: Cambridge University Press, 2007), 7.

a scientific rather than strictly theological perspective, Harrison reflects a broad range of theological and historiographical writing which has often asserted a gap between Calvin and Aquinas or their traditions more generally on this point.[6] Harrison says 'in the hands of Aquinas, a theory of cognition that evoked natural rather than divine light' emerged.[7] Even to frame the issue that way is a false step, since it supposes there is some antagonism between the two 'lights' – which, as we will see, Aquinas does not. Probing Aquinas' account of the possibility and limitations of natural knowledge of God, we see the real but circumscribed place for reason in his theological method.

The possibility of natural knowledge of God

Aquinas certainly believes human reason can naturally attain some truths about God.[8] In particular, Aquinas thinks humanity can by reason alone discern that God exists. Aquinas starts (as Calvin does) with Rom. 1.20: 'Ever since the world began, God's invisible attributes, that is to say his everlasting power and deity, have been visible to the eye of reason in the things he has made' (Revised English Bible) (*S. Th.* I.2.2, *s.c.*). Because we can proceed from effects to causes, since things exist we can infer that something caused their existence (*resp.*), and (as we will see) rather more than that. Drawing on Rom. 1.20,[9] Aquinas holds 'the existence of God … can be known by natural reason' (*ad.* 2); hence, 'the existence of God could be demonstrated through the things that are made' (*s.c.*). (Later, Aquinas will put this even more explicitly: 'God is known by natural knowledge through the image of his effects' (I.2.2, *ad.* 2).) Aquinas next turns (I.2.3) to the (in)famous 'Five Ways' in which he suggests God's existence could be demonstrated rationally. The 'fifth way', for example, infers the existence of a creator from the motion of a harmonious universe with multiple, complex working components. Aquinas returns to Rom. 1.20 elsewhere; for instance 'we come through knowledge of temporal things to that of things eternal' (I.79.9, *resp.*), and 'we can easily perceive that God exists by means of principles implanted in us by nature' (*de trin.* I.1.3, *ad.* 6). Reasoned reflection on our surroundings can help us know something about God.

---

6. See for instance Manfred Svensson and David VanDrunen, 'Introduction: The Reception, Critique, and Use of Aquinas in Protestant Thought', in *Aquinas among the Protestants*, ed. Manfred Svensson and David VanDrunen (Oxford: Wiley-Blackwell, 2018), esp. 2–4.
7. Harrison, *Fall and Science*, 41.
8. See Brian Davies, 'God', in *The Cambridge Companion to the* Summa Theologiae, ed. Philip McCosker and Denys Turner (Cambridge: Cambridge University Press, 2016), 85–9; Rudi te Velde, *Aquinas on God: The Divine Science of the* Summa Theologiae (Aldershot: Ashgate, 2006), 2–5.
9. See Eugene F. Rogers, *Thomas Aquinas and Karl Barth: Sacred Doctrine and the Knowledge of God* (Notre Dame, IN: University of Notre Dame Press, 1995), 124–46 for a close reading of Aquinas on this key passage.

Aquinas makes this same point – that observation of the relationship between (divine) cause and (created) effect yields knowledge of the former which is what we call 'God' – at the outset of the *Summa Contra Gentiles*. Thus, 'sensible things, from which the human reason takes the origin of its knowledge, retain within themselves some sort of trace of a likeness of God … effects bear within themselves, in their own way, the likeness of their causes'. Therefore as it considers the divine action 'human reason … can gather certain likenesses of the divine truth' (*SCG* I.8.1).[10]

This knowledge of God is accessible naturally not just because it is inferred from evidence which is accessible to everyone on the basis of humanity's senses but also because it is accessible to anyone whether or not they know anything of the Christian apprehension of God. Quoting Augustine approvingly, Aquinas says, '[T]he knowledge of God by natural reason can belong to both good and bad … "many who are not pure can know many truths"' (I.2.3, *ad*. 3). Whether or not a person has access to the supernatural evidence of God's existence such as the Christian scriptures, they have access to the natural evidence of God's existence, namely the caused effect of the creation. As Helm concludes, 'by reason alone, starting from self-evident principles, any sufficiently intelligent rational person may demonstrate that God exists. This is what Aquinas thought Paul was teaching in Rom. 1'.[11]

Human reason starts by speaking of God as we encounter God's effects; this is the way of causality or *via causalitatis*, the first of Aquinas' threefold way, *triplex via*, of knowing God, drawing on the earlier language of the sixth-century theologian Pseudo-Dionysius.[12] This first way gives rise to two others. We must then take away from what is said about God any attribution of something which is not, in fact, godly: for instance, we cannot speak of him as being changed because this would subject God to time. This is the way of removal or *via remotionis* (see, especially, *SCG* I.14.4).[13] Finally, what remains must then be magnified or conceived perfectly; so 'the perfection of all things must pre-exist in God in a more eminent way' (I.4.2, *s.c.*); for example, he must be perfect life and perfect wisdom (*ad*. 3). This is the way of eminence or *via eminentiae*.

The *triplex via* shows Aquinas' chain of natural reasoning yielding truths about God, beginning with, but going substantially beyond, the assertion of God's existence. The *via causalitatis* tells us more than that God exists; it yields the knowledge that God *creates*, and more:

---

10. R. D. Williams, *The Edge of Words: God and the Habits of Language* (London: Bloomsbury, 2014), esp. 6–10.

11. Paul Helm, 'Nature and Grace', in *Aquinas among the Protestants*, ed. Manfred Svensson and David VanDrunen (Oxford: Wiley-Blackwell, 2018), 231.

12. See Simon Oliver, *Creation: A Guide for the Perplexed* (London: Bloomsbury, 2017), 166–7 fn.26; cf. te Velde, *Aquinas on God*, 76–9.

13. Brian Davies, *The Thought of Thomas Aquinas* (Oxford: Clarendon Press, 1992), 40–57.

> Our natural knowledge takes its starting point from the senses. Hence our natural knowledge can go as far as it can be led by sensible things ... because they are his effects and depend on their cause, we can be led by them so far as to know of God whether he exists, and to know of him what must necessarily belong to him, as the first cause of all things, exceeding all things caused by him.
>
> (*S. Th.* I.1.12, *resp.*)

The scope of what we might know as 'what must necessarily belong' to God is quite broad.[14] For example, God's engagement with creation is not just in making it but in governing or guiding it towards its ultimate purpose: 'some intelligent being exists by whom all natural things are directed to their end' (I.2.3, *resp.*) And, as *SCG* Book I describes, many of God's characteristics and attributes can be demonstrated logically by reasoned inference alone (I.15-I.102).[15] So, says Aquinas, by reason we can know not just that God creates and guides the creation but also that he has no body (I.20), is good (I.37-42) and loves (I.91). As Chapter 3 will show, there is not a significant gap between Aquinas and Calvin on this point; for Calvin too asserted humans could know much about God on the basis of reason alone.

The limits of the natural knowledge of God

Human beings can therefore know naturally many things about God: his existence, creativity and so on. But, against those who characterize Aquinas' account as somehow optimistic about human reason, compared with a more negative view typical of reformed theology, we will see that the scope of this natural knowledge of God through reason, though real, is tightly circumscribed.

To see this we return first to the opening questions of the larger *Summa*, which Williams aptly calls 'essentially a miniature treatise on theological method'.[16] Aquinas, at the outset of the *Summa*, insists there are strict limits to the natural knowledge of God:

> Man is directed to God, as to an end that surpasses the grasp of his reason ... but the end must first be known by men who are to direct their thoughts and actions to the end. Hence it was necessary for man's salvation that certain truths which exceed human reason should be made known to him by divine revelation.
>
> (I.1.1, *resp.*)

Here, Aquinas sets out a key limitation of natural knowledge of God: reason cannot learn the truths which are essential for human salvation. There is a central distinction between the truths about God humanity can discover by natural reason

---

14. Te Velde, *Aquinas on God*, 75–7.
15. Kretzmann, *Metaphysics of Creation*, 4.
16. A. N. Williams, *The Architecture of Theology: Structure, System, and Ratio* (Oxford: Oxford University Press, 2011), 118.

and those truths about its salvation it cannot. Truths in this second category can only be learned by divine revelation.[17]

Again, the *triplex via*, while conceptualizing ways in which humans can naturally know God, serves itself as check on reason's place in our knowledge of God. For while we can certainly generate knowledge of God by our own reason, that knowledge has to be refined. For example, by *causation* we can say that God creates; this is genuine knowledge of God yielded by reason. However, by *remotion* we must refine that knowledge; for instance, we must consider what it might mean to speak, on the basis of creation, of a subject which is not part of that creation. Hence, for example, if time is created, the creator cannot be subject to time so cannot be prone to change (which entails a 'before' and an 'after'). And *eminence* then requires us to consider what it might mean to say that the creator possesses perfectly any good thing which exists imperfectly in the creation. Thus, a human being may be wise but only imperfectly and not all the time, but the wisdom which exists imperfectly in the creature must subsist perfectly in the creator. This demonstrates an intrinsic limitation to reason's usefulness; the knowledge yielded by reason has to be refined, 'purified' even, if it is to be as true as it can be to the subject of the discourse. Even where Aquinas sounds confident about what reason can yield, he is profoundly aware of its limitations.

Aquinas' caution about what reason can deliver, demonstrated in the careful conceptualization of the *triplex via*, is underpinned by a more foundational principle. It emerges, for instance, a few questions later during a rather dense discussion of whether humans can naturally see the divine essence. Aquinas says, '[T]o see the essence of God is possible to the created intellect by grace, and not by nature', and 'it is impossible for any created intellect to see the essence of God by its own natural power' (*S.Th.* I.12.4, *s.c.*, *resp.*). What is important here is the reason underlying this conclusion. Aquinas holds that 'the knowledge of every knower is ruled according to its nature', and if 'the mode of anything's being exceeds the rule of the knower, it must result that the knowledge of that object is above the nature of the knower'. Since God is his own nature, and only God is God's nature, it follows that no other being can know him fully. Hence, just as the sun is supremely visible but the bat cannot see it because of the excess of solar light, so too humans cannot see God who so exceeds their nature (I.12.1, *resp.*). Knowledge yielded by the *triplex via* is therefore limited both by the need to refine the language but also by its fundamental inadequacy to speak of its subject.

Aquinas elsewhere argues that, because God's nature so far exceeds ours, it is not possible for our nature to know his: 'by its immensity, the divine substance surpasses every form that our intellect reaches. Thus we are unable to apprehend it by knowing what it is. Yet we are able to have some knowledge of it' (*SCG* I.14.2). Thus, 'however much a rational creature knows … God, it can never know him as perfectly as he can be known' (*de ver.* 20.4, *resp.*). The ontological gap between

---

17. Thus, for instance, Brian Davies, 'Is *Sacra Doctrina* Theology?', *New Blackfriars* 71 (1990): 141–2.

the human and the divine is a fundamental boundary to our reason's natural knowledge. For there to be knowledge, 'there must be some proportion between the knower and the knowable' (*de trin.* I.1.2, *obj.* 2), but this knowledge is 'as the effect to the cause'; so there is 'no proportion ... such that the creature ... knows [the creator] perfectly' (*ad.* 2). Thus, Davies concludes, '[T]his divine nature is something that Aquinas holds to be knowable *up to a point*';[18] and te Velde highlights Aquinas' 'constant conviction ... that the human intellect cannot in any way penetrate or grasp the essence of God by means of concepts which it forms in knowing the natures of sensible reality'.[19]

So, for Aquinas, there is natural knowledge of God accessible to human reason. But it is less extensive than Harrison suggests, being tightly circumscribed in its scope. While undoubtedly Aquinas believes that reason can know God, Aquinas repeatedly emphasizes reason's limits, restricting what it yields to fairly generic attributes such as existence, creativity and so on, and always with the caution that in treating something far beyond our grasp, our language, even when refined through the *triplex via*, will be limited and inadequate.

At the outset of his *de trinitate*, Aquinas emphasizes the profoundly limited reach of humanity's natural knowledge of God to explain the need for another source of knowledge of God using the metaphor of illumination and contrasting two kinds of light, natural and divine. Thus, 'the intellectual light that is connatural to the mind also suffices to know some truth' (*de trin.* I.1.1, *s.c.*),[20] he writes, but it 'cannot know ... the truths of faith which transcend the facility of reason ... without being divinely illumined by a new light supplementing the natural light' (*resp.*).[21]

As Whidden describes, where the *de trinitate* uses the imagery of different kinds of light revealing different kinds of truths, the larger *Summa* similarly evokes the concept of the *imago Dei*. Thus, 'man possesses a natural aptitude for understanding and loving God; and this aptitude consists in the very nature of the mind, which is common to all men', but this natural aptitude is distinguished from 'the image [which] consists in the conformity of grace' (*S. Th.* I.93.4, *resp.*) by which we might truly know and love God. In other words, there is a hierarchy of knowledge of the divine, with humanity's natural knowledge ascending only to the lowest level. Its natural aptitudes are limited; as Whidden goes on, 'the cognitive limitation imposed on humans by the requirement that knowledge comes through our corporeal senses ... restricts our ability to know things about God'.[22]

18. Davies, 'God', 86, emphasis added.
19. Te Velde, *Aquinas on God*, 74.
20. This is what Whidden, in an outstanding study of the theme of illumination in Aquinas, categorizes as the natural light of the intellect: David L. Whidden, *Christ the Light: The Theology of Light and Illumination in Thomas Aquinas* (Minneapolis, MN: Fortress Press, 2014), 25–6.
21. Whidden, *Christ the Light*, esp. 1–36.
22. Whidden, *Christ the Light*, 26.

This careful distinction between two kinds of light or two aspects of the *imago*, with different sources illuminating humanity with different kinds of knowledge, undermines notions that reason's natural light might equal or supplant the light of divine illumination. Elsewhere, Aquinas couches this as a distinction between 'two modes of truth' (*SCG* I.3.2) or 'twofold truth concerning the divine being, one to which the inquiry of the reason can reach, the other which surpasses the whole ability of the human reason' (*SCG* I.4.1).[23] Rather, divine illumination is needed to show us what natural illumination cannot: 'truths we can know under our own power, without divine illumination' are limited.[24] Something else, divine light, is needed to extend our natural knowledge to reach the higher truths.[25] Nonetheless, these are not two separate truths, or truths about a different subject; they are rather dual aspects of the single truth of the same divine subject.[26]

Returning to the opening questions of *de trinitate*, where Aquinas begins to discuss the kind of truth which requires divine illumination, we read:

> All natural reason gets its power from the first principles which it knows naturally. But the fact that God is three and one cannot be deduced from naturally known principles, which are drawn from the senses, because in the sensible world we find nothing similar to there being three persons with one essence.
>
> (I.I.4, *s.c.*)

In other words, reason can only know what reason can know, in particular what it can infer from the evidence of human senses; 'the human understanding of itself is sufficient for knowing certain intelligible things, viz., those which can come through the senses' (*S.Th.* I-II.109.1, *resp.*). This includes, as we have seen, some key insights such as God's existence, creativity and so on. But supernatural enlightenment is needed for 'such things as surpass natural knowledge' (*ad.* 3). The natural knowledge of God accessible to the senses remains rather generic,

---

23. Kretzmann, *Metaphysics of Creation*, 11–13.

24. Whidden, *Christ the Light*, 7.

25. Whidden, *Christ the Light*, 26. This reading of Aquinas on the need for revelation to supplement the limited natural knowledge of God is shared, for instance, by Bruce D. Marshall, '*Quod Scit Una Uetula*: Aquinas on the Nature of Theology', in *The Theology of Thomas Aquinas*, ed. Rik van Nieuwenhove and Joseph Wawrykow (Notre Dame, IN: University of Notre Dame Press, 2010), 4–5; Rudi te Velde, 'Understanding the Scientia of Faith: Reason and Faith in Aquinas's Summa Theologiae', in *Contemplating Aquinas: On the Varieties of Interpretation*, ed. Fergus Kerr (London: SCM, 2003), 60–2; Davies, *Thought*, 11–12; Norman Kretzmann, *The Metaphysics of Theism: Aquinas's Natural Theology in Summa Contra Gentiles I* (Oxford: Oxford University Press, 1997), 35–6; Mark D. Jordan, *Ordering Wisdom: The Hierarchy of Philosophical Discourses in Aquinas* (Notre Dame, IN: University of Notre Dame Press, 1987), 197–200.

26. Cf. Rogers, *Aquinas and Barth*, 185.

disclosing God's existence and some divine attributes, but it cannot reveal the distinctive Christian truths about God (such as God's triune nature) which are not disclosed through the evidence of the senses.[27] Those truths, variously called doctrines or truths of faith, are learnable only from another source, divine revelation received by faith. Hence, Aquinas says, '[T]hose things which are above nature ... are made known to us by Divine authority' (*resp.*).

The 'things above nature', which natural reason cannot disclose, are those distinctively Christian insights about God. Thus, for example, 'one may know by demonstration the unity of the godhead, and, by faith, the Trinity' (II-II.1.5, *ad.* 4). This distinction, between generic truths about God knowable by reasoned reflection and specific truths of the Christian faith knowable only by revelation (II-II.1.5, *resp.*), recurs repeatedly in Aquinas. For instance, as well as God's triunity, Jesus' incarnation and resurrection are discernible only by faith through revelation (e.g., II-II.1.6, *resp., ad.* 1).[28] Aquinas elsewhere couches this same distinction as between knowledge of God's 'existence' and God's 'providence', the latter including 'all those things which God dispenses in time for human salvation', notably the redemption wrought by Christ's incarnation and passion (II-II.1.8, *resp.*). There is obvious resonance here with Calvin's distinction, also seen in Hooker, between knowledge of God as Creator and as Redeemer.

While, through the *triplex via*, we can discern genuine knowledge of God, it is limited both by the inherent need to refine reasonable language so it applies to the Creator as opposed to a creature and is also limited to rather generic truths about God, not the specific Christian truths such as the Trinity and Christology. Such 'propositions that belong uniquely to revealed theology's subject matter' are 'not available to unaided reason'; 'divine mysteries' must be discovered other than by natural reason.[29] As Kretzmann writes, 'reason unsupported by revelation could have come up with many' of those generic propositions about God, but only 'up to the point at which the theism being argued for begins to rely on propositions that are initially accessible to reason only via revelation and becomes distinctively Christian'.[30] This is far from the expansive optimism which Harrison and others attribute to Aquinas. We will see the contours of Aquinas' account of the natural knowledge of God are broadly the same as Calvin's. Before turning to revelation in more detail, though, we need to examine further the ways Aquinas considers reason to be limited, as these relate to two themes where he is often contrasted with Calvin: the Fall, and philosophy.

---

27. Cf. Davies, *Thought*, 188–90.
28. Davies, *Thought*, 298.
29. Brian Davies and Elenore Stump, 'Introduction', in *The Oxford Handbook of Aquinas*, ed. Brian Davies and Eleonore Stump (Oxford: Oxford University Press, 2011), 7, 8.
30. Kretzmann, *Metaphysics of Creation*, 7, 8.

Reason and its limitations

The circumscribed capacity of reason in Aquinas' account of the natural knowledge of God already undermines the notion that he has an expansive view of reason contrasted with a more limited one in Calvin. But on two further specific questions many scholars suggest Aquinas and Calvin differ. These are (1) the effects of the Fall on human reason and (2) the place of philosophy in theology. Each is analysed in turn, showing (1) Aquinas believes the Fall seriously impairs humanity's ability to reason about God and so cannot be said to diverge dramatically from Calvin on that point; and (2) Aquinas is quite discriminating in his use of philosophy in theology which is always governed by theological concerns, such that he cannot plausibly be characterized as giving philosophy and therefore reason excessive weight in theological method.

The Fall

Among Harrison's central contentions is that Calvin believes the Fall radically diminishes human reason's capacity, whereas Aquinas believes the impact of the Fall on reason is considerably less. Harrison argues that Calvin 'reject[ed] the Thomist idea that the Fall only entailed a loss of supernatural gifts', believing that the natural gifts of reason were also lost, such that 'the mind lost the capacity to acquire true knowledge'.[31] By contrast, says Harrison, Aquinas

> insist[s] that our inherent capacity for knowledge – our 'natural light' – had survived the Fall intact. Adam, in his innocence, he explained, had been possessed of both 'natural gifts' and 'supernatural gifts'. Only the latter had been lost as a consequence of the Fall. Crucially, reason was one of the natural gifts that remained.[32]

Harrison's characterization of Aquinas and Calvin is already thrown into doubt by the rather limited capacity of reason in Aquinas we have outlined. We will later see his characterization of Calvin is wrong because the latter did not believe that reason's light was totally extinguished by the Fall; and readings of Aquinas like this are off the mark.

Harrison begins by citing Aquinas' distinction between the natural and the supernatural gifts of humanity, arguing only the latter were lost at the Fall, leaving the natural gifts (notably reason) unimpaired.[33] But the passage in question does not quite say that, as Aquinas is not talking about the natural gifts. Aquinas' point is that the 'subjection of the body to the soul and of the lower powers to reason was not from nature; otherwise it would have remained after sin'; and, later, 'the primitive subjection by virtue of which reason was subject to God, was not merely a natural

---

31. Harrison, *Fall and Science*, 61, 60.
32. Harrison, *Fall and Science*, 43.
33. Harrison, *Fall and Science*, 43.

gift, but a supernatural endowment of grace' (*S.Th.* I.95.1 *resp.*). This article, in other words, does not deal with reason's *natural* operation at all, only its (now lost) *supernatural*, pre-Fall operation; it cannot help Harrison's argument that the *natural* abilities, which the article does not treat, were not lost at the Fall.

If this passage does not help Harrison's case, the next two passages he cites positively hinder it. While Aquinas does say 'the light of natural reason ... is never forfeit from the soul', he immediately adds, '[Y]et, at times, it is prevented from exercising its proper act'. Aquinas seems to have in mind where the mind is either 'deliberately turned away' or 'busy about things which it loves more' (II-II.15.1, *resp.*). As Aquinas goes on to say, 'lust gives rise to blindness of mind'[34] while 'gluttony ... makes a man weak in regard to the same intelligible things' (II-II.15.3, *resp.*). So Harrison is right to argue that sin cannot remove the natural operation of reason ('never forfeit from the soul') but wrong that reason is not severely affected. Indeed, he himself seems to concede that Aquinas *does* think the natural operation of reason *is* diminished by the Fall; in a footnote, Harrison says, '[T]he intellectual faculties are not "altered", but are merely "impeded."'[35] The relegation of this inconvenient point to a footnote illustrates the problem Harrison's argument faces here; for it is clear from the passage Harrison quotes that, for Aquinas, reason loses its supernatural powers, and its natural powers are diminished. Even to call the intellectual faculties 'impeded' is to say that they do not function as intended.

The next passage Harrison cites in this confused footnote also undermines his assertion that Aquinas considers the Fall has little or only minimal impact on reason's natural operation. Aquinas says, '[B]ecause of sin the reason, *especially with regard to moral decision*, is blunted' (I-II.85.3, *resp.*). Harrison emphasizes those words in his footnote to argue that the effects of sin are primarily on reason's moral rather than intellectual abilities. Quite how such a clear distinction can be drawn on the basis of Aquinas' text is unclear. This article is about the widespread effect of sin on reason's abilities. Sin affects reason so it cannot function properly and this in turn causes humanity to sin further because it is less able to reason to proper moral decisions. So it is implausible to suggest that sin affects moral decision in a worse way than it does intellectual capacity; the whole point of the article is that sin affects all aspects of reason. Indeed, in the preceding article, Aquinas sets out the basic point: 'sin cannot entirely take away from man that he is a rational being', but 'the good of nature ... is diminished by sin' (I-II.85.2, *resp.*).[36]

Harrison defends the distinction (that reason, being natural, is unaffected by sin because only the supernatural gifts were lost at the Fall), arguing reason 'was insulated from the supernatural privations that had followed the Fall'.[37] This

---

34. This metaphor of the mind as blinded, of course, is also crucial to Calvin; see p. 78.

35. Harrison, *Fall and Science*, 43 fn.109. The source of these two terms is unclear; Harrison does not cite a source, but it is certainly not *S.Th.* II-II.15.3.

36. Cf. A. N. Williams, 'Argument to Bliss: The Epistemology of the Summa Theologiae', *Modern Theology* 20.4 (2004): 508–9.

37. Harrison, *Fall and Science*, 44.

distinction is untenable, as seen by reading on in the same question (I-II.85). Aquinas goes on to other effects of sin such as death. Very strictly speaking, it might be possible to argue that death is a supernatural rather than a natural feature of humanity because human beings *in their created nature* should not die, and they only do so after the Fall because God removed the supernatural incorruptibility which prevented death (I-II.85.6, *resp.*). Yet it would be strange to assert that death leaves the natural sphere unaffected; death clearly has an effect in the natural sphere because it robs the natural person of their life. So, returning to article 3, reason's natural operation is clearly impeded by the loss of its supernatural gifts; from this come ignorance and concupiscence, for example (I-II.85.3, *resp.*).[38]

Similarly, Aquinas' discussion of what the first human knew emphasizes the Fall's consequences for reason. So, 'in the state of innocence there could be not only no error but not even false opinion of any sort' (*de ver.* 18.6, *resp.*). Thus, 'by the strength of his own reason … he was protected from the deception which comes from within, as when someone reasons incorrectly, but it was by the divine aid, which he had at that time for all necessary matters, that he was protected from deception' (*ad.* 7.). Error and confused opinion, for Aquinas, are evidence of reason's fallen state; as, for instance, where he cites a range of Jewish, Greek, and pagan authors on the question of whether God has a body and labels them all as wrong (*SCG* I.20.34-6; cf. I.4.3).

Sin's effects on reason are also identified as a key factor in the need for divine revelation. Thus, McInery asks whether Aquinas, 'in speaking so confidently of reason, overlook[s] the consequences of sin?' No: 'if the only way open to us for the knowledge of God were solely that of the reason, the human race would remain in the blackest shadows of ignorance'.[39] We need revelation to teach us because in our fallen state we struggle to reach even those truths about God we could in principle attain naturally. So 'the truth about God such as reason could discover would only be known to a few, and that after a long time, and with the admixture of many errors' (*S.Th.* I.1.1, *resp.*; cf. *SCG* I.4.1, 2).[40] Similarly, at the very point where Aquinas praises reason's capacity to discern divine truths ('most knowable by nature') this is immediately qualified (such truths are 'owing to a deficiency on our part … not apparent to us', *de trin.* III.1, *resp.*).

This 'diminishing' of the power of natural reason is also obvious, as Whidden highlights, from Aquinas' insistence that natural reason has to be redeemed by Christ: one of the 'aspect[s] of sin' is 'the loss of the light of reason'.[41] Our minds as

---

38. Cf. Williams, 'Argument to Bliss', 514.

39. Ralph McInery, 'On Behalf of Natural Theology', *Proceedings of the American Catholic Philosophical Association* 54 (1980): 71; cf. Angus Brook, 'Thomas Aquinas on the Effects of Original Sin: A Philosophical Analysis', *HJ* 59.4 (2018): 725–9.

40. F. C. Bauerschmidt, *Thomas Aquinas: Faith, Reason, and Following Christ* (Oxford: Oxford University Press, 2013), 56–7.

41. Whidden, *Christ the Light*, 205.

well as our bodies need to be healed by divine grace; for example, 'the end for which Christ's miracles were worked was the health of the rational part, which is healed by the light of wisdom'[42] and 'Christ, when he willed, changed the minds of men by his divine power' (*S.Th*. III.44.3, *ad*. 1). Again, Aquinas says that reason must be restored by grace since 'it is not entirely subject to God, [so] the consequence is that many disorders occur in the reason' (I-II.109.8, *resp.*).

Moreover, Aquinas explicitly *rejects* the assertion there is no sin in reason (*de ver*. 15.3, *objj*. 1, 2, 4). Insisting 'there is sin in reason', Aquinas says that sinful actions result from sinful choices; a choice needs reason to present the will with different options from which to choose: 'sin comes not only from passion, but also from choice. But choice consists in an act of reason' (*s.c.*). A flawed action, he says, can be traced back to flawed reasoning (*resp., ad*. 7). Elsewhere, Aquinas says that the intellect moves the will (*S.Th*. I-II.9.1, *resp.*) and concedes that 'sometimes … the reason is not entirely engrossed by the passion' (I-II.10.3, *resp.*), indicating reason often *is* engrossed by passion and then moves the will in the wrong direction. As Oliver concludes, 'because of humanity's fallen state, even the achievement of that which is proportionate to our nature is beyond our grasp'.[43]

For sin further diminishes reason which is already limited by finitude: reason is unable to reach many truths about God; sin exacerbates this condition by making it harder for reason to reach those truths it could naturally attain. As Marshall says, 'sin makes this problem much worse, but since we are creatures, finite and contingent … we would have this problem without the burden of sin'.[44] The inherent limitations of reason's capacity caused by human finitude already act as a caution against arguments which assert Aquinas is over-optimistic about reason's capacity. While Harrison is right that the power of reason is not entirely removed, it is severely impeded, and, as we will see, far from distinguishing Aquinas from Calvin, this is a point of convergence between them.

Philosophy

The previous section argued that Aquinas is not as optimistic about the Fall's effect on human reason as some theologians, arguing he is different from Calvin, have supposed. This section argues the same is true on a second topic where they are often thought to diverge: whether and how philosophy can be used in theology. Again, Harrison's argument will be used as an example of a wider tendency which depicts Calvin and Aquinas diverging on this point.

---

42. Whidden, *Christ the Light*, 205–6.

43. Simon Oliver, 'The Parallel Journey of Faith and Reason: Another Look via Aquinas's *De Veritate*', in *Faithful Reading: New Essays in Theology in Honour of Fergus Kerr*, ed. Simon Oliver, Karen Kilby and Tom O'Loughlin (London: T&T Clark, 2012), 124.

44. Marshall, '*Quod scit una uetula*', 4; Williams helpfully delineates the respective problems caused by finitude and by sin for our knowledge of God in *Architecture of Theology*, 8–9.

Harrison posits a pre-reformation 'concord' between philosophy and theology, lauding the 'masterful synthesis' of the two he sees in Aquinas compared with what he sees as the reformers' tendency to resist the use of philosophy.[45] Similarly, 'Protestant critics often regard [Aquinas] as simply too philosophical to be a faithful theologian'.[46] Indeed, in his commentary on Aristotle's *Metaphysics*,[47] Aquinas makes what seems like a startlingly audacious claim about philosophy. He says that the terms *metaphysics, first philosophy*, and *divine science* or *theology* refer to the same discipline (*metaphys.*, Prologue; cf. VI.1.1167-8). But challenging those who hold 'philosophy plays a dominant role in the thought of Thomas', Kilby rightly insists that any 'impression of philosophical dominance ... begins to wobble under closer scrutiny'.[48] This is not to say that Aquinas does not use philosophy, which he clearly does. Indeed he wrote widely on the work of Aristotle and other philosophers and drew on philosophical concepts or writings in his more overtly theological works. The key issue, as Kilby identifies, is *dominance*, that is, whether convictions held on some philosophical ground (perhaps, for instance, because they were advanced by a favoured philosopher like Aristotle) ever unduly condition or even distort Aquinas' theology. Moreover, simply citing or being influenced by a philosophical source does not necessarily connote agreement to it in every particular.

This section argues Aquinas draws on philosophy in theology but in a careful, circumscribed way. Even the highest form of philosophy, first philosophy or metaphysics, is limited in what it can yield. Aquinas is quite careful to say there is more to theology than even first philosophy can *naturally* attain: we must avoid 'including the contents of faith within the bounds of philosophy' (*de trin.* II.3, *resp.*). To demonstrate the limited capacity of philosophy for Aquinas' method we can identify two ways Aquinas thinks philosophy is useful in theology by distinguishing its use as a *source* and as a *tool*, before considering how it is limited by Aquinas' wider methodology.

As a *source*, philosophy can yield real, but tightly circumscribed, knowledge of God and in particular cannot attain to those truths which are beyond natural reason. It is thus distinct from the knowledge of God which comes from revelation and does not carry the same kind or level of authority.[49] This distinction is elided by Harrison in his assertion that

---

45. Peter Harrison, *The Bible, Protestantism, and the Rise of Natural Science* (Cambridge: Cambridge University Press, 1998), 70.

46. Svensson and VanDrunen, 'Introduction', 3.

47. On this work see Leo Elders, *Thomas Aquinas and His Predecessors: The Philosophers and the Church Fathers* (Washington, DC: Catholic University of America Press, 2018), 54–9.

48. Karen Kilby, 'Philosophy', in *The Cambridge Companion to the* Summa Theologiae, ed. Philip McCosker and Denys Turner (Cambridge: Cambridge University Press, 2016), 62; cf. Mark D. Jordan, *Rewritten Theology: Aquinas after His Readers* (Oxford: Blackwell, 2006), 60–88.

49. Per Erik Persson, *Sacra Doctrina: Reason and Revelation in Aquinas*, trans. Ross Mackenzie (Oxford: Basil Blackwell, 1970), 151.

until the end of the sixteenth century ... 'Authority' extended not only to ecclesiastical councils, the Doctors of the Church, and the deposit of scripture, but encompassed Aristotle, Galen, and other ancients. To a large extent, then, the secular writers of antiquity came to share the privileged status accorded to scripture and the Fathers.[50]

This broad formulation risks the inference that theological authority is a singular, undifferentiated entity incorporating scripture as one 'privileged' source among many which include not just what might be described as tradition (councils and doctors) but also philosophy (Aristotle, Galen, *et al.*). It also does not reflect Aquinas' careful account of different kinds of authority and the use that can be made of them in theology. In a pivotal passage Aquinas contrasts scripture with all other forms of authority. So while theology 'makes use of these authorities' (which includes philosophy and the doctors of the church) they yield only 'extrinsic and probable arguments'. By contrast, theology 'properly uses the authority of the canonical scriptures as an incontrovertible truth' (*S.Th.* I.1.8, ad. 2).

Again, speaking of metaphysics, Aquinas says, '[S]ince this science is about first causes and principles, it must be about God; for God is understood in this way by all inasmuch as he is one of the causes and a principle of things' (*metaphys.* I.3.64). For Aquinas 'some things may be learned from philosophical science' because 'they can be known by natural reason' (*S.Th.* I.1.1, *ad.* 2). Theology 'makes use also of the philosophers *in those questions which they were able to know by the truth of natural reason*' (I.1.8, *ad.* 2, my emphasis). Aquinas gives philosophy some authority, but it is far from accorded 'privileged status' alongside scripture. For all its real usefulness, philosophy is severely restricted in what it can yield in precisely the same way that all knowledge generated by human reason alone is. Thus, it is at best a 'handmaiden' to theology, a lesser science supporting a greater (I.1.5, *ad.* 2), the connection between the Latin *ancilla* and our adjective *ancillary* usefully illustrating philosophy's secondary and subordinate place. Likewise, Aquinas says that some 'truths about God have been provided demonstratively by the philosophers, guided by the light of natural reason' (*SCG* I.3.2) (he identifies God's existence and his unity) while other 'truths about God ... totally surpass man's ability' (I.3.3).

Indeed, and ironically, Aquinas here uses a definitely Aristotelian concept, the subalternation of the sciences, to demonstrate the *limits* of philosophy in theology.[51] Subalternation, broadly, is where one discourse borrows its principles from another. Thus, says Aquinas following Aristotle, some disciplines (he names geometry and arithmetic) rely on self-evident principles which are evident to all. But others must borrow the principles of another discipline (he names optics borrowing from geometry and music from mathematics). Likewise, says Aquinas,

---

50. Harrison, *Bible and Science*, 69.

51. On subalternation and theology see te Velde, *Aquinas on God*, 25–7; Rik van Nieuwenhove, 'Assent to Faith, Theology, and *Scientia* in Aquinas', *New Blackfriars* 100 (2019): 415–16.

sacred doctrine ... proceeds from principles established by the light of a higher science, namely, the science of God and the blessed. Hence, just as the musician accepts on authority the principles taught him by the mathematician, so sacred science is established on principles revealed by God.

(*S. Th.* I.1.2, *resp.*; cf. *de trin.* I.2, *ad.* 5)

Again, we revert to the foundational dichotomy in Aquinas' theology between the truths of God which are knowable by human reason and those which are not; philosophy can teach the former truths but not the latter. Sacred doctrine receives its principles *not* from human reason, but the knowledge of God which only God and the blessed know; here Aquinas uses Aristotelian philosophy to define philosophy's limits.

Philosophy's limits are further demonstrated by the difficulty of learning even the truths of natural reason philosophically. Aquinas writes,

> [O]ur manner of knowing is so weak that no philosopher could perfectly investigate the nature of even one little fly. We even read that a certain philosopher spent thirty years in solitude to know the nature of the bee. If, therefore, our intellect is so weak, it is foolish to be willing to believe concerning God only that which man can know by himself alone.[52]

Elsewhere, Aquinas points out that to reach philosophically even these natural truths is a painstaking task which only those with the time, training and inclination for advanced philosophical study could accomplish. Moreover, metaphysics is the last philosophical discipline to be learned, requiring mastery of lesser sciences first. Thus,

> to know the things that reason can investigate concerning God, a knowledge of many things must also be possessed ... metaphysics, which deals with divine things, is the last part of philosophy to be learned. This means we are able to arrive at the ... aforementioned truth only on the basis of a great deal of labour spent in study.

(*SCG* I.4.3; similarly *de trin.* III.1, *resp.*)

So 'the divine mercy provide[d] it should instruct us to hold by faith even those truths which the human reason is able to investigate' such that 'all men would easily be able to have a share in the knowledge of God, and this without uncertainty and error' (*SCG* I.4.6; cf. *S. Th.* I.1.1, *resp.*). Aquinas then beautifully asserts that because of this divine mercy instructing us, 'one old woman knows more about these things that pertain to the faith than heretofore all philosophers.'[53] Aquinas, then,

---

52. Thomas Aquinas, *The Apostles' Creed*, trans. Joseph B. Collins, ed. Joseph Kenny, accessed 28 November 2019, https://dhspriory.org/thomas/english/Creed.htm.

53. Sermon 14 in *Thomas Aquinas: The Academic Sermons*, ed. Mark-Robin Hoogland (Washington, DC: Catholic University of America Press, 2010), 202. On this image see Marshall, '*Quod Scit Una Uetula*', 1–2.

considers philosophy as a *source* to be useful but limited. It can help us understand some truths about God, but only very limited ones, and only rather unreliably. This indicates the difficulty of saying Aquinas is over-indebted to philosophy.

Philosophy, of course, is also a useful *tool* for Aquinas who often uses philosophical concepts or terms to clarify or explain a doctrinal truth. He says that philosophy can 'throw … light on the contents of faith' by offering elucidations or clarifications (*de trin.* II.3, *resp.*). A single example will suffice. The principal reason Aquinas asserts that God is love is that he is called this in scripture (I Jn 4.16) (*S. Th.* I.20.1, *s.c.*). Having established the scriptural source of this truth, Aquinas further justifies it using philosophical terms (appetite, motion and so on) (*resp.*) and then uses philosophical concepts (such as effects resembling causes) to explain how we love only because we are enabled by God (I.20.2, *resp.*). Here philosophy is used to elucidate truths already held on scriptural grounds. But, in using philosophy as a tool in this way, Aquinas is doing nothing other than what Christian theologians and councils had done since at least the second century (and, arguably, only what many of the authors of the Bible did, such as St John's appropriating the concept of the *logos* to articulate Christ's identity). Notably, the Nicene Creed appropriates the term *homoousios*, which appears nowhere in scripture, to say that the Son and the Father are both divine.[54] Calvin follows this logic in justifying the use of terms like *homoousios* drawn not from scripture but from philosophy (*Inst.* I.13.3-5). To use philosophy as a tool, then, does not mark Aquinas out from the tradition generally, including the reformed tradition represented by Calvin.

So far, we have shown, far from being over-reliant on philosophy, Aquinas asserts it has only limited theological capacity. It can be used as a tool to elucidate or articulate things which are known by other means (notably the truths of revelation). It can certainly yield truth about God, but only within limits. Yet a further argument could be advanced against Aquinas: that, for all his conceptual distinction between what philosophy can and can't yield, he nonetheless fails in practice to distinguish adequately between the two and gives philosophy an excessive priority in his thought. To rebut this accusation we consider three ways Aquinas safeguards against over-reliance on philosophy: firstly, Aquinas' use of Aristotle as perhaps the most notable test-case for his wider views; secondly, the way philosophy generally must be subordinated to basic Christian doctrinal truths; and, finally, the context in and purpose for which the theologian draws on philosophy.

Firstly, Aquinas is certainly indebted to Aristotle; frequently he refers to 'the Philosopher' and appropriates his arguments. Aristotle is the first (*S. Th.* I.1.2, *resp.*) and most frequently cited philosophical authority in the larger *Summa*. So, for instance, Elders argues Aquinas is heavily indebted to Aristotle and adopts his philosophy almost entirely.[55] But this is misleading. For Aquinas,

---

54. On its meaning and possible provenance see P. F. Beatrice, 'The Word "Homoousios" from Hellenism to Christianity', *Church History* 71.2 (2002): 244–72.

55. Elders, *Aquinas and His Predecessors*, 24.

philosophy must be handled with care. After all, he says, '[T]he philosophers themselves … in their rational search for the goal of human life and the means to attain it fell into many shameful errors' and 'disagreed with each other so much that scarcely two or three were of the same opinion' (*de trin.* III.1, *ad.* 3). Sometimes this means Aquinas will favour Aristotle. For example, as Kretzmann notes, Aquinas rejects several Stoic and Platonist accounts of 'natural theology' (*S. Th.* II-II.94.1, *resp.*) while noticeably not rejecting the views of Aristotle on this point.[56] Again, as Elders says, Aquinas carefully prefers Aristotle's account of the 'first good' to that of Plato's (*de ver.* 21.4, *resp.*).[57]

Nonetheless, Aquinas does not follow Aristotle inevitably or invariably; he was 'not an uncritical reader of Aristotle's works'.[58] For instance, there is arguably a clear contrast between Aristotle and Aquinas in their conceptions of the distinction between essence and existence.[59] Kilby charts how Aquinas pulled away from some of his contemporaries such as Sieger of Brabant who were thought to be 'wholly committed Aristotelians'.[60] And even Elders notes that alongside such rather niche issues as whether they considered virginity is desirable,[61] there is some tension between them on more vital issues.[62] For instance, while Aristotle believes there is 'an orderly cosmos which has no beginning'[63] Aquinas believes only God is without beginning.[64] Aquinas holds this on the basis of scripture, articulated in the Athanasian Creed and the teaching of St Jerome (*S. Th.* I.10.2, *s.c.*; I.10.3, *resp.*). The precise details of these disagreements are less important than the fact of their existence; it is clear Aquinas does not follow slavishly everything Aristotle said simply because Aristotle said it.[65]

Moreover, Elders' insistence that Aquinas 'was well aware of the difficulties which the introducing of Aristotelian doctrines in philosophy and theology would bring'[66] also risks misrepresenting how Aquinas thought Aristotle (and philosophy in general) could be used. Aquinas did *not* introduce Aristotelian doctrines into theology, at least not in the sense of believing things solely on the basis that Aristotle did. We show below that, for Aquinas, the sole source of our distinctively Christian knowledge of God was revelation; any form of natural knowledge of

---

56. Kretzmann, *Metaphysics of Theism*, 40–1.

57. Elders, *Aquinas and His Predecessors*, 21, 24.

58. Simon Oliver, 'Reading Philosophy', in *The Routledge Companion to the Practice of Christian Theology*, ed. Mike Higton and Jim Fodor (London: Routledge, 2015), 80.

59. Joseph Owens, 'Aristotle and Aquinas', in *The Cambridge Companion to Aquinas*, ed. Norman Kretzmann and Eleonore Stump (Cambridge: Cambridge University Press, 1993), 38–40.

60. Kilby, 'Philosophy', 67.

61. Elders, *Aquinas and His Predecessors*, 27.

62. Elders, *Aquinas and His Predecessors*, 23.

63. Oliver, *Creation*, 36.

64. Cf. Jordan, *Ordering Wisdom*, 190.

65. Cf. Denys Turner, 'How to Be an Atheist', *New Blackfriars* 83 (2002): 332.

66. Elders, *Aquinas and His Predecessors*, 28.

God by reason, including philosophy, could not attain distinctively Christian truths about God such as his trinity or incarnation or passion.[67] As Kilby puts it, Aquinas has 'theological reasons for granting a certain role to philosophy, [rather] than philosophical reasons for taking theological positions'.[68]

Secondly, Aquinas holds wider doctrinal commitments which regulate the use of philosophy in theology. Returning to the *triplex via* shows philosophy can only be used if its conclusions are refined and, one might say, purified by doctrinal commitments. There is a lot more that must be said about God than that he is the first cause, for example; so to say we can trace from effects to causes must emphasize ways in which the cause differs from the effects. The ways of remotion and eminence are in some sense an intrinsic safeguard against any language about God, including philosophical language, which makes excessive claims for itself.[69]

Similarly, Jordan cites the term *verbum* or *logos* ('word') as a good example of Aquinas adapting the meaning of a philosophical term in response to a scriptural or doctrinal principle.[70] Christianity shares with its philosophical antecedents the use of this term to mean something like the principle or cause which underpins and generates all things. But in the hands of St John and his Christian successors its meaning is radically shifted, not least because the Word becomes embodied in human flesh and dies in the person Jesus of Nazareth. So although Aquinas like many Christian theologians draws on philosophical terms or concepts their meaning is often redefined in the light of revelation, and this is a key safeguard in preventing philosophy having an unduly influential effect. Similarly, as Jordan puts it, 'no Christian should be satisfied to speak only as a philosopher'[71] because there is so much more to theology than simply philosophy.[72] Indeed, Aquinas also says explicitly that 'if philosophy is contrary to faith, it must not be accepted'.[73] So Aquinas says more about God than just what philosophy yields, and where a philosophical concept conflicts with a theological one he adapts or rejects it.

We see this by framing this question of whether Aquinas is unduly indebted to philosophy within the broader debate about philosophy in theology. It can be asserted that early and/or medieval theology is distorted by its debt to pagan philosophy. Barth's rhetoric, for example, is very suspicious of philosophy; 'the Christian Church certainly does not number Aristotle among its ancestors' (*CD* I/1, §1.11).[74] But Williams identifies a wide range of Christian convictions which are simply inconsistent with elements of the Platonic world view which

---

67. See, e.g., Persson, *Sacra Doctrina*, 228.

68. Kilby, 'Philosophy', 66.

69. Te Velde, *Aquinas on God*, 80; Davies, *Thought*, 42–4.

70. Jordan, *Ordering Wisdom*, 33–9.

71. Mark D. Jordan, 'Theology and Philosophy', in *The Cambridge Companion to the* Summa Theologiae, ed. Philip McCosker and Denys Turner (Cambridge: Cambridge University Press, 2016), 233.

72. Jordan, 'Theology and Philosophy', 235.

73. Sermon 14, *Academic Sermons*, 203.

74. For an overview, see James Kincade, 'Karl Barth and Philosophy', *The Journal of Religion* 40.3 (1960): 161–9.

prevailed through the patristic period.[75] Similarly Stead, while more willing than Williams to adduce philosophical influence on early theologians, also identifies fundamental points of difference between theology and pagan philosophy. For Stead, 'Christianity borrowed largely from philosophy' in developing *structures* of belief but 'there are relatively few points at which philosophical work is incorporated into the accepted structure of Christian teaching', not least because of Christianity's 'commitment to the Bible as a sacred book'.[76] Many theologians, including Aquinas, drew on philosophical concepts or language, but the nuance of their appropriation shows they did not imbibe pagan philosophical world views wholesale or uncritically. In, for instance, asserting the divine creation of a material world, the 'First Cause' taking on flesh in the Incarnation, and the redemption of human bodies as well as souls or minds, they were relying on the truth of revelation and differing in some key respects from elements of pagan philosophical perspectives.

Thirdly, what Aquinas is doing in using philosophy has a very different context and goal to what is often understood by philosophy now or as conceived by some of his critics. Aquinas could not really conceive of a philosophy which did not somehow point to the divine; the notion of a free-standing system of philosophy, unrelated to the truths of revelation, was alien to the philosophy he encountered and appropriated. Metaphysics, for Aquinas, reached great heights yet was always lacking; it could gesture at that which was beyond itself but only barely, and it could give little insight into it. Our ultimate end cannot be reached 'through a speculative science, it will come through the light of glory' (*de trin.* 6.4, *ad.* 3).[77] Theology in some sense can be seen as the completion or extension of metaphysics, discerning by God's revelation that which could be hinted at (but no more) by human reason.[78] Theology alone 'will satisfy the thwarted inquiry of the metaphysician', and while it might 'very difficult to distinguish textually between … metaphysics and theology' in a writer like Aquinas, 'of course, spiritually, there is every difference between a philosophy pursued according to nature and the divine gift of grace'.[79] Aquinas' deployment of philosophy in theology is regulated by a distinctively Christian purpose: to draw out the truths of Christian faith so that the believer may grow in faith towards that ultimate destination of union with God which will be granted to the blessed.

---

75. A. N. Williams, *The Divine Sense: The Intellect in Patristic Theology* (Cambridge: Cambridge University Press, 2007), 6–18.

76. G. C. Stead, *Philosophy in Christian Antiquity* (Cambridge: Cambridge University Press, 1994), 79, 93. That Williams will admit much less influence of philosophy on early Christian theology and explicitly criticizes elements of his account (Williams, *Divine Sense*, 8 fn.7) adds weight to the significance of their convergence on the methodological point.

77. Cf. Whidden, *Christ the Light*, 207–11.

78. Jordan, *Ordering Wisdom*, 170.

79. Jordan, *Ordering Wisdom*, 178.

Summary

Oliver rightly concludes, '[T]he Church's teaching was to be preferred [to philosophy] because it was based on the witness of Scripture, the teaching of the tradition, and wider doctrinal concerns regarding the nature of God's grace and freedom.'[80] Aquinas does use philosophy, in the sense of first philosophy or metaphysics, as part of his theology. He thought philosophy could, with some difficulty and for some people, yield genuine knowledge of God. But it is always limited in what it can deliver; while not separate from, or opposed to, *sacra doctrina*, philosophy is a different mode or kind of knowing.[81] So Aquinas does not accord philosophy the same status as distinctively theological sources such as scripture, and he is always discriminating and critical in its use. In many ways he is simply doing what many theologians (including Calvin) do in appropriating philosophical concepts or terms to draw out a theological truth derived from another source (revelation, scripture, tradition). And, as we will see more fully when we consider Calvin's use of philosophy in Chapter 3, arguments like Harrison's wrongly characterize Calvin too: philosophy is not a significant point of disagreement between Calvin and Aquinas.

Reason and revelation

So far, we have established that, despite characterizations of his thought as excessively indebted to reason, Aquinas has a clearly circumscribed account of reason in his methodology. Even on key issues like the effects of the Fall and the usefulness of philosophy he is not as optimistic about reason as often supposed. As well as the real but limited possibility of knowledge by the natural illumination of reason, there is a need for a different source of knowledge of God, the supernatural illumination of God's revelation: 'for Aquinas … faith includes believing some truths that God has revealed which we humans would be unable to grasp on our own.'[82]

A helpful starting point is the opening article of the larger *Summa* which establishes the distinction between *theologia* and *sacra doctrina*, which we might render 'theology' and 'holy teaching', respectively. As Davies highlights, *theologia* (literally, 'talk about God') is a broader category than *sacra doctrina*. *Theologia* 'includ[es] natural theology as practised by people such as Aristotle, whom Aquinas certainly did not think of as being in receipt of *sacra doctrina*.'[83] The distinction between *theologia* and *sacra doctrina* is essentially that between the knowledge of God which comes, respectively, from reason and from revelation.

80. Oliver, 'Reading Philosophy', 82.

81. Nieuwenhove, 'Assent and *Scientia*', 423–4.

82. C. Stephen Evans, 'Faith and Revelation', in *The Oxford Handbook of the Philosophy of Religion*, ed. William Wainwright (Oxford: Oxford University Press, 2005), 330.

83. Davies, '*Sacra Doctrina*', 141.

The difference can be conceived in three ways: the two kinds of knowledge are distinct in their *sources*, their *contents* and their *effects*. To chart the distinction we begin with a point Aquinas in the first article of the larger *Summa* (*S.Th.* I.1.1) before examining other texts which further illustrate his view.

So, firstly, the two kinds of knowledge of God differ in their *source*. In the opening article of the *Summa*, Aquinas contrasts 'knowledge revealed by God' with 'philosophical science built up by human wisdom' and says we must 'be taught divine truths by divine revelation' (*S.Th.* I.1.1, *resp.*). Elsewhere, Aquinas states,

> There is a twofold mode of truth in what we profess about God. Some truths about God exceed all the ability of the human reason … But there are some truths which the natural reason also is able to reach … In fact, [while] such truths about God have been proved demonstratively by the philosophers, guided by the light of natural reason, there are certain truths about God which totally surpass man's natural ability.
>
> (*SCG* I.3.2-3)[84]

Some truths are knowable naturally by human reason; some truths are not. The source of this second kind of truth is not human reason but divine revelation. 'Those things which are beyond man's knowledge may not be sought for by … reason' but 'they are revealed by God' (*S.Th.* I.1.1, *ad.* 1). Again, 'sacred doctrine derives its principles not from any human knowledge, but from the divine knowledge' (I.1.6, *ad.* 1).

The distinction in the sources of our knowledge of God is further borne out by in Aquinas' image of our need for God to teach us some truths we cannot discover by reason. Aquinas says that 'revelation elevates us to know something of God of which we should otherwise be ignorant' (*de trin.* VI.3, *resp.*).[85] Again, in his account of the gifts of the Holy Spirit, Aquinas writes that for some matters 'reason does not suffice, unless it receive in addition the prompting or motion of the Holy Ghost' (I-II.68.2, *resp.*). The image of God teaching us what we need to know recurs elsewhere (e.g., II-II.2.3, *resp.*). We need to be *taught* something we do not already know;[86] Aquinas in the same passage uses the analogy of the medical student who lacks knowledge and must be instructed in their work by a senior physician who has the necessary knowledge.

Again, as Hahn demonstrates, Aquinas sees Christ as our principal teacher. This becomes clear in his treatment of the Lord's work in the *tertia pars* of the larger *Summa* which reaches its climax in question 42. Christ comes, that question says repeatedly, among other things to teach us *doctrine* (see, for instance, *S.Th.*

---

84. Bauerschmidt, *Thomas Aquinas*, 77–9.

85. See, e.g., Pim Valkenberg, 'Scripture', in *Cambridge Companion to the* Summa, ed. McCosker and Turner, 50; Persson, *Sacra Doctrina*, 35.

86. See e.g., Whidden, *Christ the Light*, 27–31.

III.42.2, *ad.* 2).[87] The distinction of sources shows us that reason cannot teach us *sacra doctrina*, for which we need the knowledge of revelation or divine illumination, the teaching which comes from God through Christ.

Secondly, the two kinds of knowledge of God are distinct not just in their *sources* (reason and revelation) but in their *content*. Aquinas writes, '[T]heology included in sacred doctrine differs in kind from that theology which is part of philosophy' (*S.Th.* I.1.1, *ad.* 2). As we have seen, the knowledge of God attainable by natural reason is circumscribed; it yields real, but limited and rather generic, insights. The knowledge the philosopher and the theologian could achieve by natural reason is the same, but only the recipient of revelation can attain vital further knowledge. 'The human mind', says Aquinas, 'does not reach a knowledge of what God is (*quid est*) but only that he is (*an est*)' (*de trin.* I.3, *resp.*). Aquinas thinks some truths, such as God's existence and God's unity, are demonstrably provable by reason (*SCG* I.3.2). But for Aquinas, truths about what God is (*quid est*) cannot be proved demonstrably by reason and come only by revelation. These include, for instance, the doctrine of the Trinity ('that God is both threefold and one is solely an object of belief. There is no way of proving it demonstratively', I.4, *resp.*; cf. *SCG* I.3.2-3; *S.Th.* II-II.2.8).

As well as the understanding that God is Trinity, the doctrines of the person and work of Christ are, for Aquinas, received only by revelation and not reason. This is clear from Aquinas' stated structure in the *Summa Contra Gentiles*. He says that Books I–III consider 'divine things according as the natural reason can arrive at the knowledge of divine things through creatures. This way is imperfect, nevertheless, and in keeping with reason's native capacity'. In Book IV, Aquinas says he will turn to 'those divine things that have been divinely revealed to us to be believed, since they transcend the human intellect' (*SCG* IV.1.9). Aquinas then specifies that these 'things about God Himself which surpass reason and are proposed for belief' include 'the confession of the Trinity … the work of the Incarnation and what follows thereon … the ultimate end of man, such as the resurrection and glorification of bodies, the everlasting beatitude of souls' (IV.1.11). The same doctrines are enumerated in the larger *Summa* (*S.Th.* II-II.2.7-8).

The same point is emphasized in a much less well-known work than either *Summa*, Aquinas' commentary on a late-fifth- or early-sixth-century work attributed to Pseudo-Dionysius, *On the Divine Names*. Here, Aquinas says, '[I]n the teaching of faith we are not able to rely on the principles of wisdom' but can only rely on revelation (*Div. nom.* I-1, 279). While Aquinas does not list clearly what teaching can be found only by revelation it would be consistent with his enumerations elsewhere to identify the unique doctrines of the Christian faith. This interpretation is also consistent with other parts of the same text; for instance, Aquinas later identifies the teachings that God is triune, he can be called Father and he became incarnate (I-2, 283-5). Aquinas explicitly states, '[I]t is in itself

---

87. Michael Hahn, 'Thomas Aquinas's Presentation of Christ as Teacher', *The Thomist* 83.1 (2019): 78–81.

not possible to us either to speak or think' of the Trinity and of the equality of the Father and the Son (I-3, 290). From these texts we can therefore see the distinctive Christian doctrines of God can, for Aquinas, only be delivered by revelation, and this sets apart those doctrines derived from the generic truths about God accessible to reason.

The third distinction between the two sorts of knowledge is that they can be distinguished not just by their *source* (reason and revelation) or *content* (generic truths and Christian doctrine) but by the purpose or *effects* of the knowledge. Here we draw particularly on two analyses advanced by Simon Oliver.[88] At the opening of the larger *Summa* Aquinas writes,

> [M]an is directed to God, as to an end that surpasses the grasp of his reason … but the end must first be known by men who are to direct their thoughts and actions to the end. Hence it was necessary for man's salvation that there should be a knowledge revealed by God, beside philosophical science built up by human wisdom.
>
> (*S.Th.* I.1.1, *resp.*)

Our ultimate end or goal is beatitude, union with God in blessedness (*S.Th.* I-II.1.7, *s.c.*), and blessedness 'can consist in nothing else than the vision of the Divine Essence' (I-II.3.8, *resp.*).[89] Aquinas writes in the same passage, 'The human intellect knows no more of God than that He is.' To attain this vision of the divine essence is not something we can achieve by our intellect alone: 'man cannot attain happiness by his own powers' (I-II.5.5, *s.c.*, *resp.*). So to know our end, never mind how to reach it, we need revelation: 'the natural power of the created intellect does not avail to enable it to see the essence of God … it is necessary that the power of understanding should be added by divine grace' (*S.Th.* 1.12.5, *resp.*).[90] Something must be added which the human cannot naturally attain. Sometimes this is called grace and/or illumination (as in this article); sometimes revelation (as in I.12.13, *add.* 1-3). However described, it comes from a source other than reason.[91] Aquinas repeats the point elsewhere; for instance, 'sacred scripture is divinely ordered to this: that through it, the truth necessary for salvation may be made known to us' (*de trin.* VI.3, *resp.*).

---

88. Oliver, 'Faith and Reason'; and Simon Oliver, '*Salus* and *Sanctus*: On Salvation as Health and Well-Being', Durham University Catholic Theology Research Seminar, 10 October 2019.

89. 'Happiness' is a widespread but weak translation of what Aquinas calls *beatitudo*. It is considerably more than simply feeling good. Te Velde, for example, revealingly puts happiness in speech marks – *Aquinas on God*, 155-6. Good discussions of what Aquinas means by *beatitudo* are te Velde, *Aquinas on God*, 155-60; Davies, *Thought*, 227-30; Jean Porter, 'Happiness', in *Cambridge Companion to the* Summa, ed. McCosker and Turner, 181-93.

90. Davies, *Thought*, 252-3.

91. Whidden, *Christ the Light*, esp. 32-5; cf. Rogers, *Aquinas and Barth*, 45.

Thus, 'in respect of our last end' Aquinas says that even the wisest person must be 'moved by the yet higher promptings of the Holy Ghost' (I-II.68.2, *ad.* 1) and that our journey to blessedness needs the Spirit to guide us (*resp.*). Again, as Hahn shows, the principle purpose of Christ's doctrine is to teach us salvation. For example, Aquinas says that Christ's doctrine 'was the only way to salvation' (III.42.2, *resp.*). So Hahn rightly characterizes 'Christ's human task of teaching about God and himself through the use of words and images, which task has as its end the bringing of other human beings to salvation'.[92] As Aquinas concludes, our ultimate happiness cannot be attained by natural reason, only when we are taught it by God (II-II.2.3, *resp.*), and 'in order that a man may arrive at the perfect vision of heavenly happiness, he must first of all believe God, as a disciple believes the master who is teaching him' (*ad.* 1). In this image of the divine teacher, all three features which distinguish revelation's knowledge from reason's are clear: source (we must believe something beyond our reason which is taught by God), content (we believe that doctrine which God teaches), effects (this teaching the necessary gift which leads us to salvation).

The distinction between the effects of reason's knowledge of God and revelation's can also be couched in terms of what belief is generated by each route. Aquinas distinguishes between three different kinds of belief (II-II.2.2, *resp.*). As Kerr explains, reason may lead us to believe that God exists, what Aquinas calls *credere Deum* (a basic belief, for example, that God exists; the generic level of this belief being evident from the translation in the Dominican edition of 'believing in *a* God'). But there is then *credere Deo* (believing God, something more akin to believing what God communicates); and then *credere in Deum* (believing in God, which entails trust and faith).[93] This latter sort of belief entails not just knowing something but an act of the will in assenting to it.[94] And, crucially, as Rogers points out, this act of will is made possible only by God's revelation which exceeds the natural cognition of our reason.[95]

So unlike the knowledge of God conferred by reason, that conferred by revelation brings *salus* or salvation,[96] which, as Oliver points out, may in both Latin and Greek refer to salvation, health, healing or wholeness.[97] As Oliver goes on, this for Aquinas is beyond natural human capacity, hence the need for divine revelation.[98] Indeed, Aquinas writes that 'the perfection of the rational creature' entails 'a supernatural participation in the divine goodness' we 'cannot attain unless … taught by God' (*S.Th.* II-II.2.3, *resp.*). Rejecting the view that it is 'unnecessary for salvation to believe anything above the natural reason' (*obj.* 1), Aquinas insists

---

92. Hahn, 'Christ as Teacher', 62; Hahn cites a range of other texts to the same effect.
93. Kerr, *After Aquinas*, 67; Oliver, 'Faith and Reason', 136–7; Bruce D. Marshall, 'Aquinas as Postliberal Theologian', *The Thomist* 53.3 (1989): esp. 379–87.
94. Oliver, 'Faith and Reason', 140–4; see also Nieuwenhove, 'Assent and *Scientia*', 420–3.
95. Rogers, *Aquinas and Barth*, 179–80.
96. Persson, *Sacra Doctrina*, 35.
97. Oliver, '*Salus* and *Sanctus*', 5.
98. Oliver, '*Salus* and *Sanctus*', 14–15.

that 'natural knowledge does not suffice for its perfection, and some supernatural knowledge is necessary' (*ad.* 1). The fact that this question follows immediately from a discussion of the articles of faith set down in the creeds (II-II.1.6-10) further supports the case that, for Aquinas, revelation alone can yield the distinctively Christian knowledge of God necessary for redemption and lead us *credere in Deum* which results ultimately in blessedness.

We see here a clear distinction in the content of the knowledge of God delivered by natural reason and by divine revelation, with the distinctive doctrines of Christian faith delivered only by the latter and unknowable to the former. They are distinguished by source (revelation and reason), content (generic concepts of God and specific Christian doctrines) and effect (only the latter brings salvation). The clear distinctions in Aquinas' account undermine arguments he is excessively indebted to reason since he is so clear about its function and limits.

However, further attention must now be given to the relationship between reason and revelation in Aquinas' thought to establish clearly that they are not to be conceived in tension. This is a risk of accounts like Harrison's which understate the distinctive centrality of revelation in Aquinas' thought by over-emphasizing the authority of reason and tradition. Such views, in turn, exacerbate an over-reaction by others who feel that, despite all the conceptual nuance in Aquinas (or perhaps because of it), he nonetheless still leans too far towards reason. There is more than a hint of that accusation in Barth, for example, when he is adamant about the independence of revelation from reason. For Barth, it is essential that we consider 'the Word of God as the act of God's free love and not as if the addressed and hearing man were in any way essential to the concept of the Word of God'. Barth feared that in the anxiety to avoid one side of the debate on the reason-revelation dialectic 'we throw ourselves into the arms, e.g., of Aristotle or Thomas', since he is 'suspicious of the other side too' (*CD* I/1, §6.2)![99] To conclude our discussion of reason and revelation we now set out some further considerations which safeguard the centrality of revelation for Aquinas, who, notwithstanding the substantial if limited place for reason he sets out, can be defended against the kind of challenge Barth seems to be making here. This section will examine three related points: whether revelation and reason risk being set against each other; understanding reason as created rather than autonomous; and the implications of distinguishing how reason operates under the conditions of faith. In each case, the conclusions drawn about Aquinas' method will be set alongside considerations advanced from a reformed perspective by John Webster. This will show how, if understood in this way, Aquinas' account converges with some key reformed concerns rather than being inimical to them.

First we can draw on the helpful distinction, identified by Turner, between a *diversitas* and an *oppositio*.[100] Briefly, *diversitas* considers different aspects of

---

99. Cf. Kerr, *After Aquinas*, 24–5.

100. Turner's mature statement of his position on this distinction – and how it has evolved in dialogue with Fergus Kerr from his initial critique of Kerr – can be found in Denys Turner, 'Reason, the Eucharist, and the Body', in his *God, Mystery, and Mystification* (Notre Dame, IN: University of Notre Dame Press, 2019), 45–68.

something or refers to two different kinds of thing, whereas *oppositio* considers something from the same angle or on the same basis or refers to two kinds of the same thing.[101] Consider (my example, not Turner's or Oliver's) the drink I will pour at the end of writing this chapter. If I say 'this drink is gin' and you say 'this gin is in an Ikea glass' we are talking about fundamentally different things; there is a *diversitas*. The truth of one statement does not affect the truth of the other (it would still be gin were it in a Dartington crystal glass rather than a cheap Ikea one). But if I say 'this drink is gin' and you say 'this drink is whiskey' this is an *oppositio*: we are drawing a conclusion about the same thing (this drink) in the same way (what kind of drink it is). And the two things cannot both be true at the same time: if it is gin, it is not whiskey.

Apply this distinction to the present discussion of scripture and reason; we conceive the distinction as a *diversitas* rather than an *oppositio*. Admittedly, we are talking in both cases about a mode of knowledge and, indeed, knowledge of the same (divine) subject. *But* the way we come to this knowledge, its purpose and effects are fundamentally different. And the end result of the knowledge of God yielded by each route is also fundamentally different. Unaided by revelation, reason alone would reach only to the notion of a creative and providential divine being; it could not tell us of God's triune nature, his love for the world in redeeming it through the life of Christ and so on. *But*, crucially, these two kinds of truth run (to adopt Oliver's phrase) in parallel. It is *not* that the more I know of God by reason the further I move from the God of revelation, and vice versa; they are just not comparable in that sense.

Once we understand reason and revelation are different kinds of thing, rather than opposite kinds of the same thing, that we are dealing with *diversitas* rather than *oppositio*, it becomes much easier to preserve the centrality of revelation. For it is not the case that the more reason there is the less revelation there must be (or, indeed, the more weight we give to reason the less we give to scripture). Rather, it is that we need to understand the distinct, co-operative ways reason and revelation work in our knowledge of God.

While not (so far as I am aware) couching the dialectic between reason and revelation as a *diversitas*, Webster uses different language to the same effect. For Webster, both reason and revelation have their proper place in theology, and, crucially, these must be understood alongside each other, not as competitive or even as separate. His good short account of revelation is clear that it is revelation which saves us.[102] But he cautions us against 'a competitive understanding of the transcendent and the historical'[103] which can readily map on to these debates about revelation and reason by seeing them as contradictory or in tension. Indeed, he explicitly identifies the 'temptation to magnify grace by eliminating the work of

---

101. Oliver, 'Faith and Reason', 133–4.

102. John Webster, *Holy Scripture: A Dogmatic Sketch* (London: Bloomsbury, 2003), 12–16.

103. Webster, *Scripture*, 21.

reason as if reason were by nature an aggressor'.[104] The grace of revelation, though, is not contradictory to the nature of reason; both have their function in the economy of grace.[105]

Secondly, it is essential to recognize that, for Aquinas, reason is *not* some autonomous human faculty or capacity. This is, at root, the simple product of our being created. Reason, like revelation, comes from God; it is a divine gift we have it at all. This becomes clear, for instance, at the outset of Thomas' discussion of grace (*S. Th.* I-II.109-14). Thus, while 'without grace, man of himself can know truth' (I-II.109.1, *s.c.*), the existence and operation of this faculty requires divine action: 'the act of the intellect or of any created being whatsoever depends upon God ... as it is from him that it has the form whereby it acts ... as it is moved by him to act' (*resp.*). Thus, Aquinas continues, 'Every truth by whomsoever is spoken from the Holy Ghost as bestowing natural night' (*ad.* 1; cf. *ad.* 3). The natural light of reason, just as much the supernatural light of revelation, is a God-given gift, dependent on the action of the Holy Spirit both to confer it on us and to move it to any right knowledge at all. Note that Aquinas does not here say that we need the Spirit to guide our reason only in supernatural matters, but in *all* matters: that is, we need God's help to know natural as well as supernatural truths. So Whidden says that the natural light of our intellect 'is not an autonomous light, but one implanted in us by God'.[106] Similarly, 'all our knowing and reasoning, inasmuch as they are acts, owe a great deal, and in some sense all, to God's action in us'.[107] This insistence on the divine provenance of reason goes a considerable way to justifying its place in theological method, for it is not a possession or capacity we own or can control; like revelation, albeit in a different way, our reason is itself a gift from God. This is a much richer (and more overtly theological) account of reason than simply an individual human capacity.

Webster also emphasizes reason's createdness. Defining and justifying the place of reason in theological method in the face of some reformed critique, Webster argues, '[R]eason is created, fallen, and redeemed ... because creatures are *creatures*, they have reason because they have God ... Creaturely reason is contingent. It is not original or self-founding after the manner of the uncreated divine reason.'[108] This is no more or less than Aquinas' position: our reason differs

---

104. John Webster, *The Domain of the Word: Scripture and Theological Reason* (London: Bloomsbury, 2013), 129.

105. Webster, *Scripture*, 123.

106. Whidden, *Christ the Light*, 23, cf. 65.

107. Williams, 'Argument to Bliss', 509; similarly, 'in any knowledge of truth ... the proximate and principal cause of knowledge is the ... intellect. But God alone bestows this power, and he alone moves it', Matthew Cuddeback, 'Thomas Aquinas on Illumination and the Authority of the First Truth', *Nova et Vetera* 7.3 (2009): 591.

108. Webster, *Domain of the Word*, 124.

from God's in many ways, and we have it only because he gives it to us. Both are 'a sphere of God's activity'.[109]

Thirdly, reason for Aquinas appears to operate in a slightly different way when it is moved by faith in God. In a remark which has caused some controversy, Aquinas says that the atheist does not believe in God in the same way a Christian believer, 'for they do not believe that God exists under the conditions that faith determines' (*S. Th.* II-II.2.2, *ad.* 3).[110] Kerr is certainly right to say that Aquinas here envisage reason operating differently for the believer; for *credere in Deum* requires an act not just of the intellect but of the will.[111] This act of will, an act of faith, then opens up new truths to the reason (II-II.2.3, *add.* 2-3). One of the principal effects of faith is enlightening the mind with the truths of doctrine, such as the Trinity and Christ's incarnation, and Aquinas gives a strong hint that this includes an ability for the believer to properly construe the meaning of scripture (II-II.8.2, *s.c., resp.*). Our union with God, Aquinas adds, relies on the gift of knowledge (II-II.9.2, *ad.* 1). In short, reason when exercised by the believer, exercised in faith, allows the supernatural enlargement of our understanding so that we may see the truths necessary for salvation.[112] Reason under the conditions of faith is directly dependent on God who infuses it with grace through faith, while reason more generally is indirectly dependent on God as created and moved by him.

Thus defined, reason's use in theology – or, better, in *sacra doctrina*, that specific element of theology which cannot also be called metaphysics – can only be practised by the believer and not the mere philosopher. And this finds resonance with what Webster calls 'theological reason', which always 'is subject to the divine calling and the divine assistance'.[113] Indeed, Webster explicitly prays Aquinas in aid of this notion of reason, noting how Aquinas always conceives *sacra doctrina* as an exercise of creaturely reason but reliant always on divine grace.[114] Reason then in this sense is God-given and God-guided, far from the caricature of reason as some confident expression of autonomous human capacity against which many reformed writers (such as Barth) understandably react.

---

109. Webster, *Scripture*, 127.

110. There is an interesting debate about whether 'God' as known by natural reason alone is the same subject as 'God' as known by natural reason plus revelation – is the 'god of the philosophers' the same thing as the 'Christian' god? Te Velde (*Aquinas on God*, 3) and Turner (e.g., *Faith, Reason, and the Existence of God*, 17–20) seem to say 'yes'; Kerr seems to say 'no' (*After Aquinas*, 67). Oliver offers a mediating reading of Turner and Kerr in 'Faith and Reason', 135–7. We need not settle that question here, since whether or not both routes yield knowledge of the same divine being, our point is that reason operates differently in theology when it is practised under the condition of faith.

111. Kerr, *After Aquinas*, 66–7; cf. Victor Preller, *Divine Science and the Science of God: A Reformulation of Thomas Aquinas* (Princeton, NJ: Princeton University Press, 1967), 228–30.

112. Cf. Williams, 'Argument to Bliss', 10–11; Oliver, 'Faith and Reason', 142–4.

113. Webster, *Scripture*, 127; cf. *Domain of the Word*, ix.

114. Webster, *Domain of the Word*, 137–42.

The reason-revelation dialectic is crucial to Aquinas. The reading of that dialectic offered in this section shows the centrality of revelation in Aquinas' account of the knowledge of God, in that revelation alone yields the saving truth which God alone can teach us, while preserving a real if limited place for human reason within its natural sphere of teaching us generic truths about the divine. The coherence of this account is further demonstrated when we understand its richness. So the two sources of knowledge of God are not in competition but complementary; ultimately God is the author of our reason (created gift) as he is of revelation (supernatural gift), and reason in *sacra doctrina* operates in a distinct way. We can already see how this richer account would go some way to answering the reformed critique (or challenging arguments like Harrison's) that reason is somehow independent of, or undermines, revelation. Developing this argument alongside Webster's account of theological reason shows how Aquinas can be interpreted as congenial to reformed concerns about the centrality and uniqueness of revelation without undermining the real function reason has in his method. To address where this revelation is now found, the next section moves from one theological warrant, *reason*, to another, *scripture*.

Scripture in Aquinas' theological method

Introduction

A key concern of reformed theological method, as we saw in the concerns of Barth, is to maintain the unique centrality of scripture. This section traces Aquinas' account of scripture. Firstly, it shows (because this will become a key point in suggesting parallels with Calvin) how Aquinas sees scripture as correcting our natural knowledge of God. Then, secondly, we return to the question of where we find revelation, showing for Aquinas revelation is closely identified with scripture. Finally, and here congruence with Calvin seems harder initially to demonstrate, it discusses how scripture is held to be authoritative.

Scripture corrects the natural knowledge of God

Before turning to the question of scripture's sufficiency (thereby returning to the crucial relationship of revelation and scripture), note that Aquinas thinks scripture also works in our natural reason's sphere. This is further evidence that Aquinas does not conceive the theological warrants as somehow in competition or tension.

At the outset of both *Summae* Aquinas insists it is safer and quicker to learn by revelation even things we can know by natural reason because if left to reason alone, only a few humans would find out the necessary truths about God which reason can yield, and then only slowly, partially and with many errors (*S. Th.* I.1.1, *resp.*, *ad.* 1; *SCG* I.4). Later, Aquinas reminds us that 'human reason is very deficient in things concerning God', so we should 'accept by faith not only those things which are above reason, but also those which can be known by reason' (*S. Th.* II-II.2.4, *resp.*). For example, consider the second question of the *Summa*. Aquinas discusses what we can know about God by nature. The basic, simplest reason for believing we can know God is not that this can be said naturally by reason about itself (though Aquinas clearly thinks that) but because St. Paul writes in the Bible that we can know God naturally in that now-familiar text, Rom. 1.20 (I.1.2, *s.c.*). And even where Aquinas is sometimes thought to be very confident about reason's powers, in offering through the 'Five Ways' a rational demonstration of God's existence, his initial basis for believing God's existence is again, revealingly, a scriptural one, 'I am that I am' (Exod. 3.14, quoted in I.2.3 *s.c.*).[115]

So scripture for Aquinas can correct or even supplant reasoned inferences; we can learn by revelation in scripture what we could also learn in principle by reason – hence the old lady who knows God's revelation having more awareness of the truth than the philosopher, even though the latter's natural reason is much more sophisticated. This, as we will see, is a key element of Calvin's account, who thought scripture corrected the defective sight of reason even with its natural sphere. But scripture and reason play different roles in the sphere of the saving knowledge of God which comes to us only by revelation. In the natural sphere of reason, both reason and scripture can serve as sources of knowledge. But in the sphere of revelation, while reason is useful, it cannot function as a source of knowledge; scripture alone (*sola scriptura*) is that source, as we now see.

Scripture's sufficiency

We have seen throughout this chapter that Aquinas has a clear methodological distinction between natural knowledge of God, accessible in principle to all human beings, yielding through reason a substantial but generic account of God, and that knowledge of God which tells us the saving truths of faith comes only by divine revelation. Yet this at once begs a further question: *where* is this saving knowledge found?[116] The previous section showed a fuller understanding of reason and revelation in Aquinas goes a considerable way to demonstrating his congruity with reformed perspectives which insist on revelation alone as the distinctive source of our saving knowledge of God. But this congruity would be undermined if Aquinas thought there were many media of this revelation, where the reformed tradition has emphasized scripture as sole source of this knowledge.

We can contrast three kinds of account here. Harrison, as we saw, thought Aquinas gave privileged status in theology to a range of sources[117] and this would appear to undermine the centrality of revelation (and certainly of scripture).

---

115. Thus Bauerschmidt, *Thomas Aquinas*, x.

116. Leo Elders, 'Aquinas on Holy Scripture as the Medium of Divine Revelation', in *La Doctrine de la Revelation Divine de Saint Thomas D'Aquin: Actes du Symposium sur la Pensée de Saint Thomas d'Aquin* (Vatican City: Libreria Editrice Vaticana, 1990), 133.

117. Harrison, *Bible and Science*, 69.

O'Collins, while not directly analysing Aquinas, nonetheless from a Roman Catholic perspective argues that revelation is in some sense ongoing and may include revelation through for instance art and music[118] and that in particular revelation specifically requires the papal magisterium to authoritatively pronounce on it.[119] But this is a much broader definition than Aquinas'. A second kind seen, for instance, in Valkenberg, adopts a more limited but still fairly wide view of authority in Aquinas. After commenting briefly on why *sola scriptura* is a not unproblematic maxim, we will challenge Valkenberg's account of Aquinas in some detail and thereby (by implication) also contest the wider view of Harrison and O'Collins. Instead, by drawing on a third kind of reading of Aquinas articulated by Davies, we will see how, provided this is understood carefully, Aquinas can be said to adopt a *sola scriptura* view of theological method.

Immediate problems, of course, arise with *sola scriptura* approach if this is taken to mean scripture needs no other theological warrant alongside it. Three can be identified straight away. Firstly, there is a complex history of the church deciding what counted as scripture; in some sense, the *tradition* of the church chronologically precedes scripture, so an account of scripture which gives no place to tradition at all will fall down on those simple historical grounds.[120] Secondly, even to receive the revelation of scripture requires *reason*. As Oliver indicates, 'revelation always has to have something to do with our reasoning, otherwise how could we recognise revelation and make sense of it?'[121] Thirdly, the meaning of biblical passages is contested; both those who asserted that the Son was subordinate to the Father and those who insisted that they were equal could claim support from texts in John's Gospel, a debate Aquinas traverses in *SCG* IV.1-15.[122] In some sense, therefore, other theological warrants are needed alongside scripture; the key issue is tracing the function and authority of each warrant.

A fourth difficulty is that the category of *revelation* cannot be entirely equated with scripture, if only because Jesus of Nazareth was himself God's revelation to us. Barth, with all his strongly reformed emphasis on scripture, insists as much when

---

118. Gerald O'Collins, *Revelation: Towards a Christian Interpretation of God's Self-Revelation in Jesus Christ* (Oxford: Oxford University Press, 2018), 66–73. O'Collins seems alert to the danger of this definition, in insisting that such contemporary revelation by a range of media 'does not essentially bring anything essentially new' to the faith (*Tradition: Understanding Christian Tradition* (Oxford: Oxford University Press, 2018), 45. But from a reformed perspective it would still be a concerningly wide definition.

119. O'Collins, *Revelation*, 132. This is rightly criticized by Andrew Loke, 'Review of Gerald O'Collins *Revelation: Towards a Christian Interpretation of God's Self-Revelation in Jesus Christ*', *JTS* 69.1 (2018): 385–6.

120. Williams, *Architecture of Theology*, 80–2.

121. Oliver, 'Reading Philosophy', 79; cf. Williams, *Architecture of Theology*, 89.

122. As he does with the question of whether the Holy Spirit is divine, *SCG* IV.15–23; see Williams, *Architecture of Theology*, 85–7.

he talks about 'the revelation attested *in* scripture' (*CD* I/1, §8.1); the category of 'revelation' is clearly in some sense broader than scripture. We can, of course, exclude for us today the revelation of the physical, personal presence of Christ in history which the apostles experienced, though for those who *did* encounter the physical Jesus of Nazareth this encounter itself was (at least potentially) revelatory.[123] Nonetheless, identifying these four factors helps locate the key problem of any account of scriptural sufficiency: it cannot be taken to be entirely identical with revelation, nor can any plausible account be offered which does not at least include some place for the other theological warrants. So what is Aquinas' view of scripture's sufficiency? This helps frame the question in the language of the debate about revelation: does anything apart from scripture now reveal the saving knowledge of Christ essentially for our redemption? What is (are) the source(s) for what Aquinas calls *sacra doctrina*? Davies wryly notes that anyone asking that is 'very likely to feel short of an answer', for Aquinas, 'does not have much to say about which enunciations count as *sacra doctrina*'.[124]

In contesting the moderate formulation of Valkenberg we will also see the weakness of the more expansive view of Harrison and O'Collins. Valkenberg adopts a more moderate view than Harrison of what 'enunciations' for Aquinas carry such authority. Valkenberg cites Aquinas' comment that 'individual facts are treated of in sacred doctrine … to establish the authority of those men on whom this sacred scripture or doctrine is based' (*S.Th.* I.1.1, *ad.* 2). Valkenberg says Aquinas'

> reference to divine revelation serves mainly to support the authority of holy men – to whom Aquinas sometimes adds women – as witnesses and transmitters of revelation. This indicates how the authority of textual sources (*auctoritates*) in holy teaching (*sacra doctrina*) proceeds from the authority of teachers who have received a special ability to explain God's revelation to us. These teachers are the prophets and the Apostles from the Bible, but also the Bishops, the Saints and the Doctors of the Church. For Aquinas, they are all included in Holy Scripture.[125]

Indeed, though Valkenberg does not quote it, Aquinas' commentary on Dionysius also suggests scripture requires some additional authorities. There, Aquinas says the truths of the incarnation are 'understood through the divine benignity' in scripture 'but also any deifying lights, i.e., any other divine verities, the hidden tradition of our leaders, namely of the other apostles and other doctors after them' (*div. nom.* I-2, 285). Later, Aquinas refers to the necessity not just 'of things which

---

123. Hahn, 'Christ as Teacher', 77–80.
124. Davies, '*Sacra Doctrina*', 143.
125. Valkenberg, 'Scripture', 51; similarly, Piotr Roszak, 'Revelation and Scripture: Exploring the Scriptural Foundations of *Sacra Doctrina* in Aquinas', *Angelicum* 93.1 (2016): 204–5.

are handed down in sacred scripture, but also things which were said by the holy doctors' (II-1, 304).

Unlike Harrison (who, recall, included extra-Christian sources in his list of Aquinas' theological authorities), Valkenberg at least limits the scope of revelation to Christian authorities. Valkenberg comes closer to conceiving a *sola scriptura* view in Aquinas, but there is still a question about how elastic the definition of 'scripture' is here. For example, there might be considerable disagreement between denominations about who counts as a 'saint' or a 'doctor' and on what criteria. Furthermore, neither the specific text that Valkenberg cites nor similar texts from the *Divine Names* which might be prayed in aid quite argue for that broad an interpretation of scripture.

In the text from *S. Th.* I.1.2, Aquinas nowhere uses the words 'authorities' or 'teachers'. The reply to the second objection which Valkenberg draws on is clearly referring to *those persons who are named in scripture*. Indeed, the objection it rejects is that sacred doctrine cannot be a science because it treats of individual persons. Aquinas' claim for authority here is for the *scriptural texts themselves*; facts about individuals are included 'to establish the authority of those men through whom the divine revelation is based' (I.1.2, *ad*. 2). It is not a wider, generic claim about the authority of subsequent teachers but a narrow, specific claim about the authority of figures named in the scriptural texts. This article cannot ground a general claim that authoritative revelation can be found other than in the scriptural texts.

Turning to the passages from *Divine Names*, again, Aquinas' definitions are narrower than might first appear. The first passage limits 'deifying lights' to what 'has been given to us clearly along with the succession of divine expressions, i.e., insofar as it is handed down in holy scripture' (*div. nom.* I-2, 285). The second likewise ends on a restrictive note, considering authoritative only those 'who preserved sacred scripture unspotted' (II-1, 304). What emerges from these passages is a sense that the authority of subsequent teachers is derivative, dependent on their preserving the teaching of scripture.

To understand Aquinas' account more fully, moreover, we must consider the vital passage where Aquinas discusses the sources of theological authority. He writes, '[O]ur faith rests upon the revelation made to the apostles and prophets who wrote the canonical books and not on the revelations (if such there be) made to other doctors' (*S. Th.* I.1.8, *ad*. 2). Now, Valkenberg argues that this simply excludes as authoritative pre-Christian philosophical texts but includes 'teachers of the church' who 'may be said to be part of scripture'.[126] But this is not what the passage says. It insists that *all* authorities outside of the canonical texts are secondary. 'The authority of the doctors of the church' just as much as 'the authority of philosophers' is *at best* 'probable'.[127]

---

126. Valkenberg, 'Scripture', 54.

127. See Kilby, 'Philosophy', 63; cf. Nicolas M. Healy, 'Introduction', 1–20, in *Aquinas on Scripture: An Introduction to His Critical Commentaries*, ed. Thomas G. Weinandy, Daniel A. Keating and John P. Yocum (London: T&T Clark, 2006).

A similar theme emerges elsewhere, for example, in Aquinas' discussion of whether, in the state of perfection before the Fall, a child immediately after birth would be perfect such that it possessed the full bodily strength of an adult.[128] This may not seem an obvious topic for revealing Aquinas' theological method, but there is a little nugget there. Aquinas writes, '[B]y faith alone do we hold these things which are above nature, and what we believe rests on authority', and he then defines this as 'the authority of scripture' (I.99.1. *resp.*; cf. I.101.1, *resp.*).[129]

So, as Davies rightly argues, a clear pattern emerges in Aquinas' thought which restricts *sacra doctrina* or revelation to a very narrow definition which is almost entirely scriptural. For the most part *sacra doctrina* is almost entirely interchangeable conceptually with *sacra scriptura*; that is, sacred doctrine and sacred scripture are almost entirely coterminous.[130] There is no real distinction in the opening questions of the larger *Summa* between *revelation*, *scripture* and *sacred doctrine* (they are used interchangeably in S. *Th.* I.1.3, *resp.*, for instance, and elsewhere).[131]

Elsewhere, Aquinas writes, '[T]he principles from which this teaching proceeds are those which are received through the revelation of the Holy Spirit and handed down in holy scripture' and 'divine revelation is contained in sacred scripture' (*Div. nom.* I-I, 271). He speaks of 'revelation proceeding from the Holy Spirit in the apostles and prophets' (I-1, 279). A plain reading, in the light of Aquinas' wider account just discussed, clearly indicates he means only those writings which derive from the apostles and prophets, namely scripture.[132] Moreover, the close connection between *sacra doctrina*, revelation and scripture is further emphasized by the emphasis on *teaching*. Scripture alone is the source of Christ's teaching; 'access to revelation is given in the words of canonical scripture and especially in the teaching of Christ contained there'.[133]

Aquinas' repeated emphasis on revelation being something which comes through prophets and apostles, and the clear distinction he makes between those persons and all later doctors of the church (S. *Th.* I.1.8, *ad.* 2), underscores the point. Scripture alone is the means God has chosen to deliver this saving knowledge,[134]

---

128. Incidentally, Aquinas says not – before the Fall, we would have perfectly only those abilities appropriate to our age.

129. Elders, 'Aquinas on Scripture', 137–8.

130. Davies, *Thought*, 12; see also Rogers, *Aquinas and Barth*, 42.

131. Roszak, 'Revelation and Scripture', 209; cf. Davies, '*Sacra Doctrina*', 144; Marshall, '*Quod Scit Una Uetula*', 6; Valkenberg, 'Scripture', 48. A fuller treatment is Christopher T. Baglow, 'Sacred Scripture and Sacred Doctrine in Saint Thomas Aquinas', in *Aquinas on Doctrine: A Critical Introduction*, ed. Thomas Weinandy, Daniel Keating and John Yocum (London: T&T Clark, 2004), esp. 1–6.

132. Davies, '*Sacra Doctrina*', 145; Davies also cites in support of Aquinas' maxim that *canonical scripture alone is the rule of faith*: 147 fn.10; see also Elders, 'Aquinas on Scripture', 137.

133. Davies, '*Sacra Doctrina*', 144; similarly Marshall, '*Quod scit una uetula*', 6.

134. Cf. Bauerschmidt, *Thomas Aquinas*, 66.

though this does not mean it stands completely alone. As Persson concludes, while for Aquinas 'scripture is both normative, clear, and sufficient', its meaning is not always immediately apparent or readily accessible.[135] So a clear account of scriptural sufficiency can be traced in Aquinas, but something more needs to be said; some other warrant is needed to draw out scripture's meaning.

Here we must distinguish between a *source* in theology and a *tool*. We can, returning to Turner's analysis, consider the difference between scripture and reason as a *diversitas* rather than an *oppostio*: the two warrants have very different functions in theological method, so need not be conceived as in tension. Aquinas, as we have seen, considers that the only *source* of divine revelation is the sacred scripture. Williams helpfully highlights that many discussions of the warrants seem to assume they

> function in relation to a theological argument or conclusion in comparable ways. That is, scripture grounds claim X while reason grounds claim Y. The oddity of this assumption emerges when one begins to seek examples of reason's deliverances: exactly where has a Christian doctrine been asserted on the basis of reason alone?[136]

Scripture alone, as the record of God's revelation, can ground a true doctrinal assertion.[137] This is Aquinas' position; doctrine comes from scripture and nowhere else.[138] Similarly, from a reformed perspective Ballor speaks of Aquinas holding the view that scripture is materially sufficient (i.e., that everything needed for our salvation is contained therein; it is sufficient as a *source* of saving knowledge).[139]

This is not to deny reason's legitimate use in clarifying or expressing scriptural truths. As Aquinas writes, 'nothing is handed down in this doctrine other than what is found in holy scripture', but with this crucial qualification, 'he [i.e., Denys] does not say *in* holy writings but *by* holy writings, since whatever can be elicited from these things which are contained in holy scripture are not foreign to this doctrine, although they themselves are not contained in holy scripture' (*div. nom.* I-1, 280). There is, then, need for other warrants: but as tools, not sources. So Williams concludes of Aquinas, even where 'this supposedly rationalistic theologian is supposedly most confident of the reach of human reason, Aquinas actually gives it a straitened role, and one which is almost entirely regulatory'.[140] That is to say, reason can help us articulate scripture and show which kinds of doctrinal inference from scripture are and are not permissible for sacred doctrine.

---

135. Persson, *Sacra Doctrina*, 58.
136. Williams, *Architecture of Theology*, 87.
137. Williams, *Architecture of Theology*, 83, cf. 94.
138. Cf. Baglow, 'Scripture and Doctrine', 3; Persson, *Sacra Doctrina*, 83.
139. Jordan J. Ballor, 'Deformation and Reformation: Thomas Aquinas and the Rise of Protestant Scholasticism', in *Aquinas among the Protestants*, ed. Svensson and VanDrunen, 59.
140. Williams, *Architecture of Theology*, 107.

A parallel can be seen in Lash's notion of the need for 'a set of protocols against idolatry'.¹⁴¹ Reason can help us test a reading of scripture and ensure that reading is consistent with its scriptural source, that the subject of our discourse really is the Christian God there revealed. Reason can adjudicate, but it cannot ground, doctrinal claims; it is a tool, not a source.

But, of course, we might immediately ask how we judge which exercise of reason does this or rather *whose* exercise of reason. Here again we are led to the question of tradition. Harrison and O'Collins, and to a lesser extent Valkenberg, define this quite broadly, suggesting a range of reasoning authorities of the past might be counted as authoritative; we must defer fuller argument to the discussion of tradition. For now, it is clear Aquinas could not support a notion of *sola scriptura* in the sense that scripture stood alone theologically and required no other warrant or tool, but he could support a notion of *sola scriptura* in the sense that scripture was the sole *source* of our saving knowledge of God, albeit one which requires additional tools to interpret. Scripture is sufficient in the sense that all we need to know for our salvation is contained therein, and Aquinas could be said to hold a *sola scriptura* view thus defined.

Scripture's authority

If the unique authority of scripture is affirmed by Aquinas, a more complicated question centres on where scripture's authority is derived. Calvin (in)famously appeared to assert that scripture's authority derived from itself, that it was *autopistis*. Before turning to Calvin's account in Chapter 3 we briefly trace Aquinas' view, to show how it is not necessarily inimical to Calvin's.

For Aquinas, 'holy scripture ... has strength and power in that the apostles and prophets were moved to speak by the Holy Spirit revealing to them and speaking in them' (*div. nom.* I-1, 279). And 'since holy scripture is all wise and most true sincere revealed and handed down by God who is all truth and all knowledge, holy scripture is maximally to be believed' (283). *Sacra doctrina*'s knowledge of God comes only from God, 'as he is known to himself alone and revealed to others' (*S. Th.* I.1.6, *resp.*; cf. *add.* 1, 2). And, as we have seen, scripture alone is the source of this revelation.

Yet how are we to know that scripture is the source of divine revelation? Again, some of that discussion must be deferred until Chapter 5. But how in general might one know what scripture is?

Here we are left with an apparent gap in Aquinas' reasoning. Aquinas' belief in the authority of scripture seems to be a matter of assumption rather than argument.

141. Nicholas Lash, *The Beginning and End of Religion* (Cambridge: Cambridge University Press, 2006), 194; on this concept see Paul D. Murray, 'Theology "Under the Lash": Theology as Idolatry Critique in the Work of Nicholas Lash', *New Blackfriars* 88 (2007): 17–18.

> Sacred scripture ... can dispute with one who denies its principles only if the opponent admits some at least of the truths obtained through divine revelation; thus we can argue heretics from texts in Holy Writ ... [but] if our opponent believes nothing of divine revelation, there is no longer any means of proving the articles of faith by reasoning.
>
> (*S. Th.* I.1.8, *resp.*)

Here we can draw again on Turner, who similarly argues that on questions of faith a Thomist cannot really argue with an atheist, at least not a coherent atheist, because there simply is no common point of departure to argue from.[142] By analogy, the question of scripture's authority, being essentially about whether there is God with such authority in the first place, is not something which can be argued for but can only be accepted and then subsequently interrogated. Thus, Rogers concludes,

> [S]acred doctrine primarily communicates the authority of those individuals from whom we receive divine revelation; it does not try to establish rationally this authority ... the knowledge that is most proper to sacred doctrine ... only comes through a person's belief in divine revelation that has been entrusted to prophets and apostles.[143]

Essentially this is an act of the will rather than the persuasion of the argument; here we return to Kerr's analysis of *credere in Deum*. One accepts as true that these persons received divine revelation, it cannot be argued for, and then, having accepted that principle, begins to reason from the texts they wrote.

This case for scripture as not needing any investigable grounds for its authority may be buttressed if we recall the concept of subalternation. For Aquinas 'subalternate sciences employ principles that are presupposed and believed on the authority of higher sciences' and those principles 'are believed on the word of him who reveals them to us through his witnesses, in much the same way as a physician accepts the testimony of a scientist when he says that there are four elements' (*de trin.* II.2, ad. 5). Applied to this question, Aquinas' view of sub-alternation would suggest that scripture's authority cannot be rationally grounded or argued for it simply must be accepted by faith in the one whose utterance it is.[144]

While (so far as I know) Aquinas does not use the language of *autopistis*, he comes quite close in effect (if not in terminology) with Calvin's position that scripture needs no other source to authenticate itself but is itself the ground of its own authority. Aquinas' refusal to justify the authority of scripture on solely rational grounds points towards an understanding not too dissimilar from Calvin's.

---

142. Turner, 'How to Be an Atheist', 317–25; Turner, *Faith, Reason, and the Existence of God*, 254–9.

143. Paul M. Rogers, 'Thomas Aquinas, Prophecy, and the "Scientific" Character of Sacred Doctrine', *New Blackfriars* 100 (2016): 93; cf. Williams, *Architecture of Theology*, 83.

144. Cf. Nieuewnhove, 'Assent and *Scientia*', esp. 423–4.

Summary

To conceive the purpose of scripture and reason in Aquinas' method, therefore, we must move away from the idea that they are somehow two kinds of the same thing which could in principle be opposed to one another. Aquinas *does* give reason a substantial place in his theological method, but this need not be at the expense of God's revelation, and in particular, the revelation in scripture. While reason may properly lead us to know that God exists, it is scriptural revelation, as expounded by the church, which is the sole ground of our saving knowledge of the Christian God. And in that sense Aquinas has a *sola scriptura* theological method. But this immediately gives rise to a further question. To say that revelation is 'scripture as expounded by the church' raises the issue of what exposition of scripture is considered definitive and authoritative. And that means we must interrogate the function of the third theological warrant, only briefly alluded to so far, *tradition*. We return to that question in Chapter 5, but ensuing chapters will test whether this account of *scripture* and *reason* in Aquinas converges with that of Calvin and of Hooker. Before that, the final part of this chapter asks: if Aquinas conceives only a limited function for reason and believes in the unique authority of scripture, why has this so often been overlooked?

Obscuring Aquinas' method

This chapter argues characterizations of Aquinas as somehow inimical to a reformed position because Aquinas attaches too great a weight to reason and too little to scripture are flawed. Three related reasons why Aquinas' position has been misinterpreted are now adduced. These are (1) misunderstandings of the significance of the *structure* of Aquinas' works with a resulting over-emphasis on some of Aquinas' more philosophical themes (notably the 'Five Ways'); (2) misunderstandings of the meaning of *scientia*; (3) a widespread failure to understand Aquinas' commitment as a *scriptural* teacher and theologian. This section traces how Aquinas' method has often been misinterpreted as excessively indebted to a narrowly defined view of reason at the cost of scripture in each of these ways. This reading finds particular support in some of the twentieth-century interpretations of Aquinas re-evaluated some of his views which demonstrate a theological method like his may not be as opposed to reformed concerns as sometimes supposed.

In the wake of the First Vatican Council (1869–70), Pope Leo XIII wanted to 'organise the course of philosophical studies' in universities and named Aquinas 'a singular safeguard and glory of the Catholic church'.[145] Leo thought a Thomist philosophical curriculum would help resist the threat of modernist thinking and restore the physical and natural sciences (as well as philosophy and theology) to

---

145. Leo XIII, 'Encyclical Letter on the Restoration of Christian Philosophy', in the English Dominican *S.Th.*, I.ix, xv.

a proper footing. The co-option of Aquinas as official Roman Catholic teaching, associated with resistance to new questions and a strong emphasis on the transmission of propositional formulae, alongside the identification of Aquinas as a philosopher, resulted in 'a monolithic neo-Thomism which had become as remote from contemporary concerns and the needs of the twentieth-century church as it was arguably distant from the spirit of Thomas himself'.[146]

By the mid-twentieth century, notably in the Low Countries and France, a theological sensibility called the *nouvelle théologie* emerged which challenged the prevailing interpretations of Aquinas. It called for greater emphasis on the laity in worship and mission, a renewed concern for the study of scripture and, crucially, an urgency to read the texts of key thinkers themselves rather than subsequent manuals or commentaries. Alongside the *nouvelle théologie* was an Anglophone strain of Thomism, influenced by Anglo-American Dominican thought, identifiable in the works of Preller and Turner. While not endorsing the *nouvelle théologie* on every point,[147] this interpretation of Aquinas also emphasizes his theological character, not least by a strong emphasis on the place of faith in theological reasoning and a vision of Aquinas as far more than just a philosopher.[148] While not necessarily an aim of such movements, their readings of Aquinas reveal him to be broadly congenial to key reformed concerns and indicate why this convergence has often been overlooked.

Firstly, the structure of both *Summae* sometimes misleads readers into assuming philosophy is both more important and more autonomous for Aquinas than it actually is. Both works begin with substantial discussions of what can be known of God by natural reason before moving on to specifically Christian account of God. Twenty-five of the first twenty-six of the larger *Summa*'s opening questions are not distinctively Christian in either content or grounding. Only in I.27, turning to the Trinity, is Aquinas dealing with a distinctly Christian element of the doctrine of God reliant explicitly on revelation. From the reformed perspective, Barth, for example, was uneasy about this kind of structure, opting to begin his dogmatics with a discussion of the Trinity – as he says, an unusual structural move (*CD* I/1, §8.1). The risk of doing otherwise, and beginning with generic discussion of the one God, was for Barth too great; it meant that one might end up talking about something other than the Christian God. Barth is rather censorious not only of all the medieval tradition (apart from Lombard

---

146. A. N. Williams, 'The Future of the Past: The Contemporary Significance of the *Nouvelle Théologie*', *IJST* 7.4 (2005): 349; see also Jordan, *Rewritten Theology*, 1–16; Gabriel Flynn, 'Introduction: The Twentieth-Century Renaissance in Catholic Theology', in *Ressourcement: A Movement for Renewal in Twentieth Century Catholic Theology*, ed. Gabriel Flynn and Paul D. Murray (Oxford: Oxford University Press, 2013), 1–22.

147. Turner, for example, believes it has not adequately understood the pronouncements of the First Vatican Council on theological method – see his *Faith, Reason, and the Existence of God*, 14–17.

148. Turner, *Faith, Reason, and the Existence of God*, ix–xv.

and Bonaventure) but also of Calvin and Melanchthon for beginning with the one God and only later in their systems discussing God's triunity. Connected with this structural criticism is the notion that Aquinas' emphasis on the rational demonstrability of God's existence somehow suggests he has a theological method heavily influenced by philosophy at the expense of scripture. The so-called Five Ways in I.2.3 are sometimes cited as 'purely philosophical chains of inference'.[149] Some commentators and many textbooks assume that Aquinas' principal purpose is to demonstrate that God's existence can be proved without recourse to distinctively Christian theological truths.

Whether or not Aquinas thought it could be,[150] it is increasingly accepted that rational demonstration of God's existence is not Aquinas' main concern. Nor is Aquinas trying to establish a set of propositional, philosophical truths about God on the basis of reason alone.[151] In this, Kerr and Turner (who disagree on the question of whether Aquinas thought God's existence must be rationally demonstrable) concur: Kerr cautions against reading the Five Ways 'extracted from their theological context';[152] Turner agrees that they 'could not fairly be conceived as intended to stand on their own' except 'within that wider philosophical and theological context'.[153] This tendency to isolate philosophical proofs from theological context is dated by Edwards not to Aquinas but to subsequent interpreters.[154] And on the reformed side, Eugene Rogers reads the *Summa* as far more congenial on the knowledge of God to a reformed perspective than often supposed;[155] Sudduth, like Kerr and Turner, cautions against reading the Five Ways in 'unfair' isolation from their broader context,[156] namely Aquinas' very limited account of reason in the opening articles of the *Summa* and his consistent emphasis that there are truths about God only revelation yields. Moreover, the backdrop of the richer and more thoroughly theological account of reason advanced in this chapter tells against seeing Aquinas as primarily a philosopher or as having an excessive place for reason in his theological method. The tendency (at least since the First Vatican Council onwards) to wrench specific discussions from Aquinas' wider scheme means the philosophical aspects of his work are excessively heightened; putting those aspects in their wider context helps retrieve an Aquinas who is far from uncongenial to reformed concerns (in this case, about the limits of philosophy's usefulness and the need for revelation).

149. Kerr, *After Aquinas*, 64.
150. Turner, *Faith, Reason, and the Existence of God*, esp. 16–17 (who thinks Aquinas does believe that) with Kerr, *After Aquinas*, esp. 64–6.
151. Jordan, *Rewritten Theology*, 87.
152. Kerr, *After Aquinas*, 64.
153. Turner, *Faith, Reason, and the Existence of God*, 241.
154. Daniel Edwards, 'Catholic Perspectives on Natural Theology', in *OHNT*, ed. Re Manning, 183.
155. Rogers, *Aquinas and Barth*, esp. 183–202.
156. Sudduth, *Reformed Objection*, 186.

Secondly, Aquinas insists that *sacra doctrina* can be called *scientia*, which to modern and post-modern ears may sound rather cold, as though it is largely a set of propositions generated by rational observation or experiment; Barth (while arguing theology could be called *scientia*) is aware of this problem (*CD* I/1, §1.1). But *scientia*, as Burrell says, does not readily translate into its 'current modern language cognates'.[157] We have already seen how this knowledge does not derive from autonomous human reason but ultimately only from God's sharing God's knowledge of himself with us. *Scientia* is not just a body of propositional knowledge, autonomous from divine revelation or the experience of the believer, which must be 'downloaded'. As one of Aquinas' editors puts it, it has *ontological* as well as *epistemological*[158] effects; it is something which, to paraphrase another commentator, 'beds in' to the mind and affects the believer's life, rather than being a static body of knowledge.[159]

In fact, when we consider Aquinas in the round we might see that this *scientia* goes far beyond cognitive propositions. Some commentators do emphasize his work as a preacher himself and as a *teacher* of preachers.[160] But it is rarely mentioned, for example, that he was a poet and hymn-writer.[161] Read Aquinas' apparently 'philosophical' work alongside his sermons or poetry and there might appear to be a tension; certainly the styles are different. But to see these aspects of Aquinas' works as separate, or to ignore one at the expense of the other, is to divide what Aquinas unites.[162] Aquinas would not have seen a contradiction between talking about God on the basis of reason and on the basis of revelation, any more than he would have seen a contradiction between speaking about God in the language of Aristotelian philosophy or the language of the liturgy. An Aquinas whose philosophy is seen against this wider backdrop would be far from the champion of autonomous reason that many of his interpreters and critics have suggested.

---

157. David B. Burrell, 'Aquinas's Appropriation of *Liber de causis* to Articulate the Creator as Cause-of-Being', in *Contemplating Aquinas*, ed. Kerr, 83.

158. Introduction to *The Division and Methods of the Sciences: Questions V and VI of Aquinas's Commentary on the* de Trinitate *of Boethius*, trans. Armand Maurer (Toronto: Pontifical Institution of Medieval Studies, 1986-7), x.

159. Bauerschmidt, *Thomas Aquinas*, 54–5; cf. Williams, 'Argument to Bliss', 510–11, 518–19.

160. Vivian Boland, 'Truth, Knowledge, and Communication: Thomas Aquinas on the Mystery of Teaching', *Studies in Christian Ethics* 19.3 (2006): 294–6.

161. Exceptions are rare, such as Paul Murray, 'Aquinas on Poetry and Theology', *Logos* 19.2 (2013): 68–9, 71; on his hymns, T. F. Tout, 'The Place of St Thomas in History', in *St Thomas Aquinas*, ed. Aelred Whitacre (Eugene, OR: Wipf&Stock, 1926), 16–17.

162. Cf. Nieuwenhove, 'Assent and *Scientia*', 423, arguing that Aquinas does not embody a post-Kantian or post-Barthian separation of faith and reason, or of theology and philosophy or, we might add, of poetry and prose.

2. Knowledge of God in Aquinas

Finally, the *nouvelle théologie* and subsequent writers have helped recover an understanding of Aquinas as a *biblical* theologian as well as (perhaps more than) a philosopher.[163] This can be seen clearly in the recovery of Aquinas' trinitarian thought. Emphasis on what can only be learned about God through revelation in scripture is helping us see Aquinas for the scriptural theologian and teacher he really was,[164] not merely a philosopher or dealer in abstract arguments.[165] Attending, for example, to the significance of the Trinity in Aquinas' theology, as a doctrine inaccessible to reason alone, further emphasizes both the use of and the constraints on reason in his method.[166] And greater attention to Aquinas' biblical commentaries is helping see his use of philosophy in a clearer perspective by calling attention to the governing scriptural focus of his thought.[167]

Summary

Williams rightly challenges 'the fiction of an Aquinas serenely confident of the powers of natural human reason'.[168] Aquinas certainly believes natural reason has powers; it can teach that God exists, and identify many divine attributes. But these powers are God-given and God-guided, even within their natural sphere. And alone reason can teach us nothing of the saving knowledge of God, the truths particularly about the Trinity and the Incarnation. Such knowledge only comes from God by revelation. The source of this revelation is scripture, and only scripture (though that does not mean no other tools are needed to draw out scripture's meaning; hence there is a need for tradition and for reason in theological method). Aquinas therefore can be said to have a *sola scriptura* method in that sense and so is far from uncongenial to reformed concerns on that point, as Ballor and Webster

---

163. E.g., Kilby, 'Philosophy', 67; Valkenberg, 'Scripture', 60; the connection with Aquinas' own work as teacher is highlighted by Peter M. Candler, 'St Thomas Aquinas', in *Christian Theologies of Scripture: A Comparative Introduction*, ed. Justin S. Houlcomb (New York, NY: New York University Press, 2006), 63–4.

164. A good example is Jean-Pierre Torell, *Saint Thomas Aquinas*, 2 vols, trans. Robert Royal (Washington, DC: Catholic University of America Press, 2003, 2005), I.55–74.

165. For instance, Matthew Levering, *Scripture and Metaphysics: Aquinas and the Renewal of Trinitarian Theology* (Oxford: Blackwell, 2004), esp. 23–7.

166. Kerr, *After Aquinas*, 182–3; Joseph Wawrykow, 'Franciscan and Dominican Trinitarian Theology (Thirteenth Century): Aquinas and Bonaventure', in *The Oxford Handbook of the Trinity*, ed. Gilles Emery and Matthew Levering (Oxford: Oxford University Press, 2011), 190–4.

167. Thus Thomas Prügl, 'Thomas Aquinas as Interpreter of Scripture', in *Theology of Aquinas*, ed. Van Nieuwenhove and Wawrykow, 399, 405.

168. Williams, 'Argument to Bliss', 505–6.

among others have recognized. And even on supposedly divisive issues such as the effects of the Fall, the place of philosophy, or the way scripture's authority is established, we have shown there is far less distance between Aquinas and the reformed perspective than often supposed.

Reasons why this convergence has often been overlooked can be readily identified, notably failure to see Aquinas' use of reason in the context of his wider theological commitments as a biblical teacher who believed that scripture alone taught us the divine truths of Christian faith. This has been exacerbated by the tendency of subsequent interpreters (not least since Vatican I) to over-emphasize, without sufficient context or nuance, the function of reason in Aquinas' thought. Read in the light of the *nouvelle théologie* and others, Aquinas can emerge as someone with a strong biblical and spiritual flavour who is not the champion of reason or philosophy as such but conceives them in a wider pattern of God's gift of reason and God's grace of revelation.

The first limb of many characterizations of Hooker and Anglicanism, that Aquinas gives a much greater capacity to reason than the reformed, has been contested in this chapter by a close reading of Aquinas. Chapter 3 turns to challenge the second limb of those characterizations, arguing, conversely, that Calvin attributes a much greater capacity to reason than often supposed.

Chapter 3

KNOWLEDGE OF GOD IN CALVIN

Introduction

Where Aquinas ended up in France having grown up in Italy, Calvin was born in France but ended up in Geneva; where Aquinas' career ended in Paris, Calvin's career began there. As well as these international connections, both had complicated family backgrounds. Initially intended by his father to train as a priest, Calvin studied scripture and the liberal arts in Paris before his father changed his mind and decided his son should go into the law. During the 1530s, the young lawyer was exposed to reformers' ideas in Orleans, while Calvin's father was excommunicated after a cathedral chapter accused him of shady dealings. Calvin increasingly spoke and published in favour of reform of church doctrine and practice. Calvin then accepted an invitation to become a 'reader' in the church in Geneva where he became a pastor, and polemicist in the reformed cause, until his death. Calvin's great systematic theology, the *Institutes of Christian Religion*, was first published in 1536 and went through several French and Latin editions before the final Latin text of 1559. Alongside the *Institutes* we also consider other works such as his polemic tracts against Roman Catholicism, his instructions about church structure and ritual, and his biblical commentaries.

On one familiar reading, 'Calvin fundamentally disagreed with the great medieval Dominican Thomas Aquinas on the nature of theology'.[1] This assessment by one of Calvin's more thoughtful recent biographers reflects an earlier historiographical trope which characterized Calvin as fundamentally in tension with Aquinas, embodying a long-standing view that catholic and reformed theologies are divergent, perhaps even irreconcilable.[2] If accurate, this would

---

1. Bruce Gordon, *Calvin* (London: Yale University Press, 2011), 62.

2. For good accounts of the changing reception of Aquinas by Protestant thinkers, see Christoph Schwöbel, 'Reformed Traditions', in *The Cambridge Companion to the Summa*, ed. Philip McCosker and Denys Turner (Cambridge: Cambridge University Press, 2016), 319–42; Manfred Svensson and David VanDrunen, 'Introduction: The Reception, Critique, and Use of Aquinas in Protestant Thought', in *Aquinas among the Protestants*, ed. Manfred Svensson and David VanDrunen (Oxford: Wiley-Blackwell, 2018), 1–23.

render implausible the claim that Anglicanism could be coherently catholic and reformed, and its (and Hooker's) theological identity was either incoherent or must be positioned on a catholic-reformed spectrum.

However, a few pages before, the same biographer rightly emphasizes Calvin's initial definition of theology as 'knowledge of God and of ourselves' (*Inst.* I.1.1).[3] This misses the obvious echo of Aquinas' similar phrase, at the outset of his great work, of theology's subject, namely God and everything else in relation to God (*S.Th.* I.1.3 *ad.* 1, I.1.7 *resp.*).[4] This obvious resonance in their opening discussions of theological method should alert us to the possibility the two theologians might have more in common than often supposed.

Chapter 2 demonstrated such congruence by showing Aquinas' theological method was far from uncongenial to reformed concerns; in particular, he is much less optimistic about the role of reason in theology than often supposed. This chapter, turning to Calvin, applies the converse argument to the reformer: that, far from being in tension with Aquinas, his reformed account of theological method is substantially similar to Aquinas' catholic one, not least because Calvin, while aware of its limitations, was much less pessimistic about reason's role in theology than often supposed. Such convergence would help ground a reading of Hooker and an account of Anglicanism as both catholic and reformed.

While this chapter can be somewhat shorter than the last, which has already covered many of the general questions about definitions and problems, it follows the same structure. It begins by demonstrating that Calvin believes humans can naturally know something of God by their reason, although this is limited to generic truths such as God's existence. In this respect, and on the effects of the Fall and using philosophy in theology, we next see that Calvin does not substantially differ from Aquinas. Turning then to revelation shows Calvin, again like Aquinas, conceives revelation as the sole source of our saving knowledge of God and of Christian doctrine. We then discuss the role of scripture in more detail, examining its sufficiency and its authority, showing that, some differences of terminology notwithstanding, on these points too there is no significant difference between the two. Reasons why this convergence has been obscured by misreadings of Calvin are then adduced. A shared theological method emerges as plausible and coherent, conceiving scripture as the sole source of our distinctly Christian knowledge of God and reason as having a real but limited role; this shared theological method could undergird the possibility of a catholic and reformed reading of Hooker and of Anglicanism.

---

3. Gordon, *Calvin*, 59.

4. Others have, such as McNeill's edition of the *Institutes*, I.37 fn.3. Calvin uses the phrase *sacra doctrina* ('holy teaching') in the 1536 edition but *sapientia* ('wisdom') in the final 1559 edition. It is beyond our present scope, but it would be interesting to explore whether this was a significant change. That Gordon cites the 1536 wording makes it even odder that he immediately moves on to argue that Calvin fundamentally disagrees with Aquinas without even pausing to note the echo of Aquinas' language here.

Natural knowledge of God in Calvin

Introduction

An earlier generation of commentators held Calvin thought human beings could naturally attain only little or no knowledge of God and thus diverged sharply from Aquinas. So Niesel wrote that anyone who thought that Calvin could be called a natural theologian 'can hardly be regarded as a serious scholar'.[5] Niesel continued, any 'knowledge of God we may acquire from his works and deeds is subjective and unreal' and a 'monstrous deception'.[6] In less strident terms Wendel agrees, writing of Calvin's 'categorial refusal to admit any positive knowledge of a God in fallen man'.[7] More recently, Harrison, asserting a sharp distinction between Calvin and Aquinas on this point, conceives Calvin as dismissive of human reason's natural powers.[8] Harrison says Calvin thinks the Fall meant our 'mind lost the capacity to acquire true knowledge'.[9] But Chapter 2 showed Aquinas was not unduly optimistic about human reason's capacities. He thought it yielded some knowledge of God but not the distinctive knowledge of salvation which comes only by revelation. To challenge further those accounts which contrast Calvin and Aquinas, we first examine Calvin's positive treatment of reason's natural knowledge of God and then his account of its limitations.

The possibility of natural knowledge of God

'Ever since the world began, God's invisible attributes, that is to say his power and deity, have been visible to the eye of reason, in the things he has made' (Rom. 1.20, Revised English Bible). Glossing this passage, Calvin in his 1539 commentary[10] writes, '[S]ince [God's] majesty shines forth in all his works and creatures', they 'clearly demonstrate their creator', and the mere existence of anything is 'a demonstration of God's existence' (*Rom.* 31). Calvin continues, 'God has put into the minds of all knowledge of himself ... he has so demonstrated by his works his existence as to make men see clearly that there is a God' (32). Rom. 1.20 is for Calvin, as it was for Aquinas, a vital text demonstrating humanity can naturally infer the existence of a creator from the creation.

---

5. Wilhem Niesel, *The Theology of Calvin*, trans. Harold Knight (London: Lutterworth, 1956), 48.

6. Niesel, *Calvin*, 43, 46.

7. François Wendel, *Calvin: The Origins and Development of His Thought*, trans. Philip Mairet (London: Collins, 1963), 163. Cf. 'God can now be known only by the special, redemptive illumination' of revelation: T. H. L. Parker, *Calvin's Doctrine of the Knowledge of God* (Edinburgh: Oliver & Boyd, 1969), 48.

8. Peter Harrison, *The Fall of Man and the Foundations of Science* (Cambridge: Cambridge University Press, 2007), 7; likewise Charles Partee, *The Theology of John Calvin* (Louisville, KY: Westminster John Knox Press, 2010), 308.

9. Harrison, *Fall and Science*, 60.

10. For background to Calvin's biblical commentaries, see Gordon, *Calvin*, 103–20.

Calvin makes the same point at the outset of his great systematic theology, the *Institutes*. 'No one can look upon the world without immediately turning his thoughts to the contemplation of God', he says, 'for quite clearly the mighty gifts with which we are endowed are hardly from ourselves'. Not only our awareness that we do not generate our own capacities, though, prompts us to infer the existence of a deity: our 'miserable ruin … compels us to look upward' because we are 'so stung by the consciousness of our own unhappiness' (*Inst.* I.1.1). At the start of his great work, then, Calvin clearly sets out the possibility that we could, on the basis of reasoned reflection on our own situation, conclude there is a God.[11]

Later, Calvin describes this instinctive awareness of God's existence as a *sensus divinitatis* or 'awareness of divinity': 'there is within the human mind, and indeed by natural instinct, an awareness of divinity … God has implanted in all men a certain understanding of his divine majesty' (I.3.1).[12] The phrase recurs in I.3.3 and I.4.4, for instance, denoting a general ability among humans to know by reason that God exists.[13] In these opening chapters, as Adams concludes, 'Calvin argues that there is a knowledge of God accessible to all human beings'.[14]

Indeed, were Calvin sceptical about any natural knowledge of God, it would be hard to explain why he consistently insists that knowing naturally God's existence is not only possible but widespread: 'there is no nation so barbarous, no people so savage, that they have not a deep-seated conviction that there is a God' (I.3.1). The *sensus divinitatis* 'can never be effaced and is engraved on men's minds'. It does not have to be taught but is innate, 'not a doctrine that must first be learned in school' but 'naturally inborn in all, and is fixed deep within, as it were in the very marrow' (I.3.3).[15] Some 'seed remains which can in no wise be uprooted' (I.4.4), the *semen religionis* which remains implanted in all human hearts.[16]

---

11. This reading of Calvin is found, for instance, in W. J. Bouwsma, *John Calvin: A Sixteenth Century Portrait* (Oxford: Oxford University Press, 1998), 71, 103–4; Susan E. Schreiner, *The Theater of His Glory: Nature and the Natural Order in the Thought of John Calvin* (Durham, NC: The Labyrinth Press, 1991), esp. 2–3; Michael Sudduth, 'Calvin, Plantinga, and the Natural Knowledge of God: A Response to Beversluis', *Faith and Philosophy* 15.1 (1998): 93, 99; Paul Helm, *John Calvin's Ideas* (Oxford: Oxford University Press, 2004), 218–22.

12. Paul Helm, 'John Calvin, the "*Sensus Divinitatis*", and the Noetic Effects of Sin', *International Journal for Philosophy of Religion* 43.2 (1998): esp. 89–97.

13. Helm, '*Sensus Divinitatis*', 91.

14. Edward Adams, 'Calvin's View of Natural Knowledge of God', *IJST* 3.3 (2001): 280; cf. *PRRD*, I.276.

15. Parker, discussing the *sensus divinitatis*, makes much of the phrase 'God has implanted' to say there is no natural knowledge of God because it shows that the knowledge is put in our minds by God – *Knowledge of God*, 32–6. That misses the point. What is crucial for the argument is not that this awareness is God-given – Aquinas would hardly have disagreed that we have reason only because God gave it to us – rather, it is that this awareness resides in the reason of all human beings, without requiring access to a specifically Christian source of revelation.

16. Nicholas Wolterstorff, 'The Reformed Tradition', in *A Companion to Philosophy of Religion*, 2nd edn, ed. Charles Taliaferro, Paul Draper and Philip L. Quinn (Oxford: Blackwell, 2010), 204.

Natural reason then, unaided, can certainly demonstrate the existence of a deity. However, Warfield notes, the knowledge it yields is 'far from a mere empty conviction that such a being as God exists'.[17] For as Aquinas demonstrates through the *via causalitatis*, the fact that something exists which did not make itself immediately suggests the existence of a creator. We can, for Calvin, know naturally that God not just exists but that God creates. Humanity can naturally 'perceive that there is a God and that he is their maker' (V.3.1). And then a number of other attributes of this God can be found out by reason. God's 'eternity, power, wisdom, goodness, truth, righteousness and mercy' are obvious for Calvin because (for example) he bears with us despite our sins so must be merciful (*Rom.* 32). Again, 'no long or toilsome proof is needed to elicit evidences that serve to illuminate … that divine majesty' (*Inst.* I.5.9).

More than God's creativity can be known by reason from the creation, though. The beauty and wonder with which Calvin depicts the material world suggest he is a far cry from the rather dry, systematizing figure in some characterizations.[18] Creation, for Calvin, is 'this most beautiful theatre', and 'although it is not the chief evidence for faith, yet it is the first evidence in order … wherever we cast our eyes, all things they meet are works of God' (I.4.20). Calvin lifts up his eyes beyond earth, seeming particularly interested in astronomy, pointing to the heavenly bodies as witnesses of a creative power.[19] So he reflects on 'the greatness of the Artificer who stationed, arranged, and fitted together the starry host of heaven in such wonderful order that nothing more beautiful in appearance can be imagined' (I.4.21). Later, Calvin highlights the beauty of colour and scent in the material world (III.10.2).[20]

Sticking with the astronomical theme, Calvin next argues reason delivers still more than the knowledge of divine creativity; it teaches us providence, too, God's energy sustaining and upholding the creation. Calvin's discussion of providence indeed begins with 'the presence of the divine power shining as much in the continuing state of the universe as its inception'; even the 'unwilling', says Calvin, acknowledge a guiding hand, not just a creative one, at work (I.16.1). Similarly, in his *Genevan Catechism*, Calvin explained that calling God creator 'did not merely imply that God so created his works once that afterwards he took no care of them', but also entailed understanding 'the world … is preserved by him', and that God was wisdom and goodness as well as power (*Treatises*, 94). The harmony and order which governs the stars and the planets demonstrates some divine providential ordering (*Inst.* I.5.2).[21]

---

17. B. B. Warfield, *Calvin and Calvinism* (New York: Oxford University Press, 1931), 36–7.

18. Such as by Newman; see J. Todd Billings, 'The Catholic Calvin', *Pro Ecclesia* 20.2 (2011): 130.

19. Helm, *Ideas*, 23–4.

20. A. N. Williams, *The Architecture of Theology: Structure, System, and Ratio* (Oxford: Oxford University Press, 2011), 196.

21. Bouwsma, *Calvin*, 104 emphasizes Calvin's fascination with the celestial bodies.

As McGrath concludes, 'a general knowledge of God may be discerned from his creation', without 'appeal to specifically Christian sources of revelation'.[22] The older notion of Niesel and Partee, or its more recent instantiation in say Harrison, is hard to justify after even a cursory reading of these opening chapters of the *Institutes* and associated texts. Far from believing our reason useless in theological method, Calvin repeatedly asserted all humans have in principle a *sensus divinitatis* which yields not just awareness of God's existence but can also demonstrate a range of divine characteristics.[23] Yet the knowledge yielded by unaided reason is nonetheless firmly limited, as we now see.

The limits of natural knowledge of God

The limitation of our natural knowledge of God is underpinned, early on in the *Institutes*, by Calvin's account of God's infinity and of divine accommodation. He writes, God's 'infinity ought to make us afraid to try to measure him by our own senses' so God chooses to 'descend' to our low state and accommodates knowledge about him to our very limited capacities (*Inst.* I.13.1).[24] There are obvious resonances here with Aquinas. Calvin is highlighting the strict ontological divide between the human knower and the divine subject; our limited minds lack the loftiness to truly know the infinite divine. All our reason's knowledge of God is going to be inherently limited by 'our slight capacity' (I.13.1). Moreover, Calvin says, 'the poverty of human speech' (I.13.5) means we must find terms to use of God even though they are inadequate to their subject and must be used cautiously. Thus, the term 'person', when applied to Father, Son, and Holy Spirit, must be used so we are not silent, but even so it is still an 'improper expression' (I.13.5). This sounds akin to the *via remotionis*; we must subtract a good deal of what we mean by 'person' if we are to apply it to God, and even then our speech will remain inadequate.

Not least because of the gap between human mind and divine subject, all natural knowledge of God is inherently limited in *scope*, *clarity* and *effects*. On each of these points, addressed in turn, we see Calvin's account closely matches Aquinas'.

Firstly, the natural knowledge of God is always limited in *scope* for Calvin; the truths yielded by reason alone are fairly generic and there is nothing distinctively *Christian* about them. Most obviously, adherents of Islam or Judaism, and a number of pre-Christian philosophers, might say the same about God as the account Calvin has, by reason alone, sketched. Cicero, as Calvin noted, believed pagans could by reason conceive a deity in broadly similar terms (I.3.1). This is only a 'slight taste' (I.5.15) of what we need to learn about God. There is much more knowledge of God beyond what reason can naturally attain. So, says Calvin,

---

22. A. E. McGrath, *A Life of John Calvin: A Study in the Shaping of Western Culture* (Oxford: Blackwell, 1990), 152–3.

23. Helm, '*Sensus Divinitatis*', 92–3.

24. Cf. Williams, *Architecture of Theology*, 156.

even 'Adam, Noah, Abraham, and the rest of the patriarchs' grasped only partial insights, knowing that 'kind of knowledge by which one is permitted to grasp ... that God is who founded and governed the universe'. But, says Calvin, 'I am not yet speaking of the proper doctrine of faith whereby they had been illumined unto the hope of eternal life.' There is, says Calvin, that 'other inner knowledge ... whereby God is known not only as the Founder of the universe and the soul Author and Ruler of all that is made, but also in the person of the Mediator as Redeemer' (I.6.1). This is the beginning of Calvin's account of the *duplex cognitio Dei*: the twofold knowledge of God, the knowledge of God as Creator (which is accessible to reason alone) and the knowledge of God as Redeemer (which is not).[25] Recall Aquinas' insistence on another kind of knowledge of God alongside that which philosophical knowledge could yield and we see the emerging convergence between his and Calvin's thought.

Moreover, the knowledge of God attainable naturally is limited in its *clarity*. At the outset of the *Institutes* Calvin sets out the possibility of natural knowledge of God, but he immediately continues with a cautionary note. As Steinmetz points out, Calvin distinguished sharply between what natural knowledge of God could offer *in principle* and what humanity tended to gain from it *in practice*.[26] Calvin believed natural reason could yield much truth in principle, but in practice it did so only imperfectly: 'because all of us are inclined by nature to hypocrisy, a kind of empty image of righteousness itself abundantly satisfies us' (I.1.2). He adds, 'if men were taught only by nature, they ... would be so tied to confused principles as to worship an unknown God' (I.15.12). So, says Calvin, even in this sphere of that knowledge we can attain naturally, 'it is needful that another and better help be added to direct us aright' to God (I.6.1), who 'foresaw his likeness imprinted upon the ... universe would be insufficiently effective' (I.6.3). Even at its best, then, natural reason's operation is always confused and unclear. Recalling Aquinas' insistence that reason's natural knowledge is often hesitant or erroneous makes the convergence with Calvin clearer still.

Thirdly, natural knowledge of God is limited in its *effects* as well its scope and clarity. Natural knowledge of God remains at an earthly level; it cannot reach to the heavenly, supernatural truths which are connected with Christ.[27] We cannot be saved by this natural truth; rather, for Calvin it serves to make us *inexcusable*, to

---

25. This characterization of Calvin's thought as shaped by the distinction between knowledge of God as creator and as redeemer can be traced back to Edward A. Dowey, *The Knowledge of God in Calvin's Theology* (New York: Columbia University Press, 1952), esp. 41–9. It now pervades the scholarship; see for instance I. John Hesselink, 'Calvin's Theology', in *The Cambridge Companion to John Calvin*, ed. Donald McKim (Cambridge: Cambridge University Press, 2004), 78; R. A. Muller, '*Duplex cognitio Dei* in the Theology of Early Reformed Orthodoxy', *Sixteenth Century Journal* 10.2 (1979): 54; Helm, *Ideas*, 7.

26. David C. Steinmetz, *Calvin in Context*, 2nd edn (Oxford: Oxford University Press, 2010), 29–30.

27. Paul Helm, *Calvin at the Centre* (Oxford: Oxford University Press, 2010), 3.

give us just enough awareness of God to be aware of our sinfulness but not enough to show us redemption. Hence, glossing Rom. 1.20, Calvin says, the divine 'power and deity have been visible to the eye of reason' and our 'conduct, therefore, is indefensible'. He continues, 'the consequence of having this evidence' is that no one can 'allege anything before God's tribunal for the purpose of showing they are not justly condemned' (*Rom*. 31). Calvin returns to the theme in *Institutes* I.5: 'our conscience itself always convicts us of both baseness and ingratitude' (I.5.14; cf. I.5.1, I.3.1). Calvin adds, 'what is … known of God … from the creation of the universe' goes no 'farther than to render them inexcusable' (I.5.14). The natural knowledge of God, then, convicts us of our guilt; it provides no remedy. Natural knowledge of God is distinguished, says Calvin, from that knowledge 'which alone quickens dead souls' (I.6.1; so also *Rom*. 31). At its best, it might prompt us to ponder our situation and, aware of our sinfulness, turn to more moral conduct (*Inst*. I.2.2; I.3.1). It might even prompt us to worship and praise God (I.5.10).[28] But, as Grabill rightly concludes, it remains limited; Calvin never 'den[ies] … a legitimate natural revelation of God', but 'insists rather on its inefficacy with respect to justification'.[29] Recalling Aquinas' view that the knowledge of God gained by reason does not yield the knowledge of salvation, which requires another source, shows the further overlap between his and Calvin's accounts of reason's limitations.

Summary

Postema rightly concludes, 'Calvin's view of God's revelation in nature … is at least rather close to that of Aquinas.'[30] Human reason, unaided, can learn a good deal about God. Yet this knowledge is limited; as Adams, who reads Calvin broadly along the lines outlined here, says, Calvin is 'deeply pessimistic about the outcome of God's natural revelation'.[31] Reason may reveal the existence of a creator, and even some divine attributes, but it does not reveal the doctrines of the Christian God and it cannot bring us salvation. Seeing the convergence of Aquinas' and Calvin's thought on the possibilities and limitations of natural knowledge, we begin to see the wider congruence of their theological method, yet as they are often supposed to differ on two further matters, the effects of the Fall on reason and the role of philosophy in theology, we next address each in turn.

---

28. David C. Steinmetz, 'The Theology of John Calvin', in *The Cambridge Companion to Reformation Theology*, ed. David Bagchi and David C. Steinmetz (Cambridge: Cambridge University Press, 2004), 120.

29. Stephen J. Grabill, *Rediscovering the Natural Law in Reformed Theological Ethics* (Grand Rapids, MI: Eerdmans, 2002), 77; similarly, e.g., *PRRD*, I.274, cf. Wolterstorff, 'Reformed Tradition', 204–5.

30. Gerald J. Postema, 'Calvin's Alleged Rejection of Natural Theology', *SJT* 24 (1971): 426; see also Williams, *Architecture of Theology*, 40–1.

31. Adams, 'Natural Knowledge of God', 290.

Reason and its limitations

Introduction

Characterizations of a reformed-catholic spectrum in theological method often assert that the Fall plays a significantly lesser role, and philosophy a significantly greater one, in catholic perspectives. We have challenged that argument as it might relate to Aquinas, who has a clear sense of the Fall's very serious effects on natural reason and gives philosophy only a limited role in theology governed by clear theological constraints. This section makes the converse argument that Calvin thinks the Fall, though serious, does not completely eradicate reason's capacity and that his conception of philosophy in theology is not dissimilar to Aquinas'.

The Fall

The reformed tradition, emphasizing the effects of the Fall, sometimes gives reason little place in theological method and considers natural knowledge of God to be either unreliable or impossible. Thus, Barth wrote, '[R]eason ... is incurably sick and incapable of any serious theological activity.'[32] More recently, Peter Harrison tries to distinguish Aquinas from Calvin on this point, arguing Calvin, unlike Aquinas, believed the Fall resulted in our total depravity and the loss of natural gifts (such as reason) as well as supernatural gifts.[33] For Calvin, Harrison says, 'human nature was totally depraved' so 'no faculty of the human mind ... retained its prelapsarian perfection'.[34] Harrison describes 'a Calvinist view of human nature, which significantly limited the efficacy of reason and the light of nature'.[35] Chapter 2 contested such readings of Aquinas, while this section challenges similar interpretations of Calvin.

Harrison's reading of the Fall's effects for Calvin begins with humanity's state before the Fall. In that state, reason, Calvin claims, was adequate to all earthly, natural situations; humanity in its 'first condition excelled ... so that its reason ... sufficed for the direction of his earthly life' (*Inst.* I.15.8). The Fall affected both humanity's natural and supernatural operation. 'Man's depravity seduces his mind' (I.2.2), and humanity is 'by nature so blind ... that of himself he has no power to be able to comprehend the true knowledge of God as is proper' (*Treatises*, 27). Our supernatural gifts, says Calvin, including the ability to direct ourselves

---

32. Karl Barth, 'No! Answer to Emil Brunner', in Emil Brunner and Karl Barth, *Natural Theology*, trans. Peter Fraenkel (London: Centenary Press, 1946), 96.

33. Peter Harrison, *The Fall of Man and the Foundations of Science* (Cambridge: Cambridge University Press, 2009), 7.

34. Harrison, *Fall and Science*, 59.

35. Harrison, *Fall and Science*, 65.

to salvation and bliss, were 'stripped' while the natural gifts were 'corrupted' (II.2.12).[36] This passage is vital to Harrison; it indeed says the natural light of reason 'is choked with dense ignorance', so we lost our 'soundness of mind'.[37]

But the key point Harrison overlooks is Calvin's distinction between the supernatural gifts ('lost') and natural ones ('corrupted'). Calvin repeatedly states that what is lost completely is our ability to direct ourselves to salvation. So humanity's 'whole nature is so imbued with depravity that he of himself possess no ability to act upright' (*Treatises*, 198), but this specifically relates to 'the grounds of salvation and the method of attaining it' (197). Again, Calvin's emphasis is that only by divine illumination may we 'come to the right knowledge of our salvation' (27). Total depravity (a phrase which is not at all prominent in Calvin and represents a later development of his thought[38]) is really about *soteriology* not *epistemology*; it is that condition which means we are unable to find our salvation for ourselves, not an assertion we lack any properly human functions at all.

Of course, Calvin, as Helm notes, does think the Fall led to 'a moral rupture between the Creator and mankind with (among other things) noetic consequences'.[39] But generally, Calvin is very careful to stress our natural reason's ability is very seriously impaired rather than lost completely. Returning to the passage Harrison cites in support of his argument that natural reason is destroyed by the Fall, we see Calvin did not say that at all. Calvin explicitly says reason 'could not be completely wiped out' and it was only '*partly* weakened and *partly* corrupted'; while our minds are no longer 'whole and sound', nonetheless 'something of understanding and judgment remain' (*Inst*. II.2.12). Thus, Wendel refers to Calvin's 'discreet formula' which insists on humanity's not-quite-total depravity: the image of God is corrupted and defaced rather than eradicated.[40]

Elsewhere, even where Calvin is describing our depravity rather stridently ('nothing remains after the ruin except what is confused, mutilated, and disease-ridden') he still maintains God's image in humanity was 'corrupted' but 'not totally annihilated and destroyed' (I.15.4; cf. *BLW*, 49). Reason's soundness may be 'gravely wounded by sin' (*Inst*. II.2.4), but it is still 'intelligent enough to taste something of things above' (II.2.13). The light of reason is dimmed but not extinguished; we are short-sighted rather than blind, hence the repeated metaphor of our need of

---

36. There may be an intriguing difference here between the two theologians on the question of humanity's *supernatural* capacity before the Fall. Calvin appears to hold that Adam naturally enjoyed the life of the blessed before the Fall (*Inst*. I.15.3-4, 8), whereas Aquinas holds that Adam did not but enjoyed some intermediate knowledge of God greater than ours but less than the blessed's (*S.Th*. I.94.1, *resp*.). That debate, though, is not germane to our purpose, which is to demonstrate the convergence of their view on humanity's *natural* condition after the Fall.

37. Harrison, *Fall and Science*, 60.

38. For a good discussion and further references, see Partee, *Calvin*, 126–9.

39. Helm, 'Sensus Divinitatis', 100.

40. Wendel, *Calvin*, 185.

spectacles (I.6.1, I.14.1, for instance). Our mind, even 'though fallen and perverted from its wholeness is nevertheless clothed and ornamented with God's excellent gifts' (II.2.15); God's image is defaced but not destroyed.[41] Elsewhere, says Calvin, St John 'denies emphatically the light of the intelligence is entirely extinct'; while 'the light of reason which God gave men is obscured by sin', some sparks remain (*Commentaries*, 131). The effects of sin on reason are clearly serious, for Calvin, but not utterly fatal. There has to be enough reason left to humanity, at least, to realize its own guilt; that is the key point of Calvin's exegesis of Rom. 1.[42]

Harrison's argument that Calvin believes human reason has no capacity at all, and that this distinguishes him from Aquinas' much more positive account, is clearly flawed. We saw Aquinas was quite circumspect in his account of fallen reason, noting the many ways it was now inadequate. This section shows Calvin, similarly, conceives reason as deeply flawed and corrupted (but not completely removed) after the Fall. As Helm says, 'for all his stress on the deep and dramatic effects of the Fall, Calvin does not say that [it] has completely eradicated the *sensus*'.[43] Even Niesel, who does not share Helm's view that Calvin believes there is true natural knowledge of God, agrees that the Fall corrupts rather than destroys reason.[44] The Fall, then, for Calvin as for Aquinas, has seriously debilitating consequences for reason, though it does not remove it from us entirely; there is consensus, rather than divergence, between them on this, as on the role of philosophy in theology we next address.

Philosophy

The previous section demonstrated, despite's Harrison's claim that they differ on the effects of the Fall, in fact Aquinas and Calvin are closely aligned. Turning now to use of philosophy in theology, we now see that Harrison is wrong to suggest substantial divergence between the two. Harrison, recall, held that Calvin and the reformers undid the 'masterful synthesis' of philosophy and theology seen in Aquinas.[45] Indeed, an earlier generation of scholars insisted there is little or no place for human reason and specifically for philosophy in Calvin's thought.[46] And indeed there are a number of points where Calvin appears dismissive of philosophy. For example, several authors cite his rather sweeping declaration that many theologians 'have come far too close to the philosophers', and he names

---

41. J. T. McNeill, 'Natural Law in the Theology of the Reformers', *Journal of Religion* 26.3 (1946): 179.

42. E.g., Steinmetz, *Calvin in Context*, 29; Sudduth, 'Response to Beversluis', 96–100.

43. Helm, '*Sensus Divinitatis*', 89; cf. Schreiner, *Theater of Glory*, 71, 120.

44. Niesel, *Calvin*, 185.

45. Peter Harrison, *The Bible, Protestantism, and the Rise of Natural Science* (Cambridge: Cambridge University Press, 1988), 70.

46. A good (although dated) survey with references is Mary Engel, *John Calvin's Perspectival Anthropology* (Eugene, OR: Wipf&Stock, 1988), 99–100.

'all the ancients save Augustine' as overly accommodating to philosophical ideas (*Inst.* II.2.4).[47]

Calvin, it is true, does not cite philosophers in quite the same way that Aquinas does; there is no real equivalent to Aquinas' frequent recourse to the authority of what 'the Philosopher said'. Nonetheless, Calvin's view of philosophy is rather more nuanced, as a closer look at II.2.4 reveals. Firstly, Calvin is specifically here challenging what he sees as patristic confusion on the particular question of whether the will is free. To say he is cautious about the effects of philosophy on this particular matter is hardly to make a wider case that he is suspicious about philosophy as such. And it was not just philosophy, Calvin thinks, which has caused the problem about free will; it was the patristic authors' fear that insisting the will was not free might result in slothfulness (II.2.4). Moreover, addressing the will's freedom elsewhere, he is quite happy to cite Aristotle to support his argument (*BLW*, 140). In other words, this single passage cannot quite bear the weight Harrison among others wants to put on it as a general dismissal of philosophy.

Secondly, in this same chapter of the *Institutes*, we find Calvin asserting philosophy can be used. For example, human understanding is 'intelligent enough to taste something of the things above' (II.2.13). We can sometimes see 'the admirable light of truth shining' in 'secular writers' because all truth has a single divine source; 'the Spirit of God is the sole fountain of truth, we shall neither reject the truth itself, nor despise it whenever it shall appear' (II.2.15).[48] We can rightly be helped by 'physic, dialectic, mathematics, and other like disciplines, by the work and ministry of the ungodly' (II.2.16). Indeed, we may even discover truths about God in philosophy; 'one can read competent and apt statements about God here and there in the philosophers ... the Lord indeed gave them a slight taste of his divinity' (II.2.18).

More broadly, Calvin clearly knew and made use of philosophy in his work. He was a student of philosophy.[49] He adopted a number of scholastic forms in his writing.[50] As Steinmetz points out, Calvin became familiar with the languages and concepts of ancient philosophy through his study of arts and law at Paris, Orleans and Bourges.[51] So Calvin can, as Raith shows, navigate complicated philosophical terrain, such as his discussion of Plato, Themestius and Aristotle on natural law.[52] But while quoting these debates, Calvin is clear there are governing theological

---

47. Harrison, *Fall and Science*, 60; cf. Parker, *Knowledge of God*, 38.

48. Charles Partee, *Calvin and Classical Philosophy* (Leiden: Brill, 1977), 147, cites further examples.

49. Gordon, *Calvin*, 12, 24.

50. J. Todd Billings, *Calvin, Participation, and the Gift* (Oxford: Oxford University Press, 2007), 35; Helm, *Ideas*, 3.

51. David C. Steinmetz, 'Calvin as Biblical Interpreter among the Ancient Philosophers', *Interpretation* 69.2 (2009): 142.

52. C. D. Raith, 'Calvin's Theological Appropriation of His Philosophical Sources: A Note on Natural Law and *Institutes* 2.2.22-23', *CThJ* 47.1 (2012): esp. 40–3.

concerns against which these philosophical discussions must be tested: notably, as Raith says, Calvin's discussion of natural law is governed by his convictions about sin and grace, which are theological concerns 'outside the realm of philosophy proper'.[53]

Similarly, as Engel,[54] Helm[55] and Partee[56] show, Calvin is both sophisticated and critical in his appropriation of philosophical sources. For instance, even on the question of the will's freedom, he was quite happy to cite philosophers he approved of while a few sentences later condemning theologians who draw excessively on philosophy. His account of the *sensus divinitatis* has overt echoes of Cicero's.[57] Yet his use of Cicero is nuanced: indeed Calvin audaciously first prays Cicero in aid of his view that 'our wicked opinions and evil customs' quench the glimmers of morality in our nature then immediately dismisses Cicero's notion that we can acquire virtue for ourselves (*Inst.* II.2.3). Calvin goes on to explain that we cannot do this 'except by the grace of the Saviour' (II.2.8). Cicero, then, is a philosopher who is a permissible source for Calvin but not one to be used uncritically; Calvin's belief in salvation by Christ means he will not accept elements of Cicero's philosophy which are uncongenial to his wider theological commitments.[58]

Again, as Engel shows, Calvin will draw on Plato or Aristotle, but only where it suits. Unlike Luther, say, Calvin is happy to use Aristotelian categories such as the four causes or the distinction between matter and form.[59] At the same time, he is reluctant to rely too heavily even on Plato, the 'most religious' and 'most circumspect' of the philosophers, who nonetheless still goes awry (getting lost in his discussion of spheres, for instance) (*Inst.* I.V.11), and attempting to impose his philosophically devised category of forms on the divine.[60] Again, like Aquinas, Calvin is also prepared to use philosophical terms where it helps to clarify the meaning of a theological argument. There is, for example, a long justification of the use of the philosophical term *hypostasis* which Calvin says helps articulate the doctrine of the Trinity (I.13.2-5, 20), as well as the use of several other predicates of God using non-scriptural terms such as *infinity*.[61]

---

53. Raith, 'Philosophical Sources', 48.
54. Engel, *Calvin's Anthropology*, 99-110.
55. Helm, *Ideas*, 4.
56. Partee, *Calvin and Classical Philosophy*, esp. 13-22.
57. David C. Steinmetz, 'The Scholastic Calvin', in *Protestant Scholasticism: Essays in Reassessment*, ed. Carl Trueman and R. S. Clark (Carlisle: Paternoster Press, 1999), 25.
58. Helm, *Ideas*, 4; Bouwsma, *Calvin*, 99.
59. Engel, *Calvin's Anthropology*, 94-7; cf. 'Introduction' to *The Bondage and Liberation of the Will: A Defence of the Orthodox Doctrine of Human Choice against the Pelagians*, ed. A. N. S. Lane, trans. G. I. Davies (Carlisle: Paternoster Press, 1996), xxiv-ix.
60. Steinmetz, *Calvin in Context*, 30; cf. Steinmetz, 'Calvin among the Ancient Philosophers', 145-6.
61. Williams, *Architecture of Theology*, 156-7.

But Calvin is reluctant to use the Aristotelian language of first cause and prime mover, 'after the manner of the philosophers', because he thinks this does not accord with belief in divine providence and thereby risks the believer's solace (I.16.3). There is an intriguing combination of pastoral and biblical concerns here which outweighs for Calvin the philosophical conception. The philosophers are lacking, Calvin complains, because 'they never even sensed the assurance of God's benevolence towards us' (II.2.18) and did not have the revelation which comes from Christ and the Holy Spirit (II.2.19-20).[62]

Moreover, like Aquinas, Calvin considers the use of philosophy in theology to be different from the philosophical enterprise as such. At the outset of the second book of the *Institutes*, Calvin writes of 'certain philosophers ... while urging man to know himself, propose the goal of recognising his own worth and excellence', which leads only to 'empty assurance and ... pride' (*Inst.* II.1.1). By contrast, the Christian must consider themselves as wholly dependent on God and utterly unable to boast about their own abilities; such robust self-examination demands humility and a recognition that we can intrinsically know nothing ourselves to elevate us from our fallen state (II.1.2-3). Even the best philosophers, Calvin thought, could not attain knowledge of salvation by their own reason; and indeed their work was wrongly focused inasmuch as it might tend towards human self-satisfaction. Thus, while 'one can read competent and apt statements about God here and there in the philosophers', they nonetheless could not direct their thought rightly to know the truth which only comes from God (II.2.18-19). It is true Calvin is more pungent than Aquinas in his references to philosophers and philosophy, but this should not obscure the fundamental congruity between them: philosophy by itself can yield only partial knowledge, and its usefulness is always limited.

What we see here, then, is Calvin using philosophy but only within limits and constrained by his theological commitments. For example, the pastoral needs of the flock for comfort, and his robust insistence on divine providence, mean Calvin will cite Aristotle on the freedom of the will but resist the language of first cause. Like Aquinas, Calvin does use philosophy, seeing some philosophers on some points as conveying truth to us, truth they only have because of its divine origin (they have drunk from the divine fountain of wisdom, as he puts it).[63] The key point is that he is 'positive, albeit critically so',[64] about many philosophers and does not regard knowledge gained from philosophy to be inadmissible in principle. Rather, it must be tested and weighed against wider theological commitments.

---

62. Unhelpfully, the Battles and Lewis Edition – *Institutes* I.200 – appears to suggest this is Calvin criticizing Aquinas by inserting a reference to *S.Th.* I.19.6. That is not clear in the text; and in any case Aquinas very obviously believes in divine providence, as he says a few questions later (*S.Th.* I.22.1, *resp.*). It may be that he differed from Calvin's assessment of Aristotle, but that is a tangential point. The key issue is that for Calvin and for Aquinas a doctrinal commitment must outweigh any apparent philosophical insight.

63. See Partee, *Calvin and Classical Philosophy*, 91; Helm, *Calvin's Ideas*, 4–5.

64. Raith, 'Philosophical Sources', 44; cf. *PRRD*, I.365.

Summary

This discussion of Calvin's commentary on Romans and the opening chapters of the *Institutes* shows that Calvin clearly believes reason can access by itself some knowledge of God. This knowledge is limited in scope, clarity and effects: it tells us only of God as Creator not as Redeemer; it is often horribly confused, and it does not save us. But it is real knowledge, accessible even to fallen humanity and even to those such as the ancient philosophers who knew nothing of Christianity and can be discerned from looking at the wondrous beauty of the earth and heavens or through the liberal arts. Philosophy is useful as a source and tool for such knowledge, albeit if used critically and within theologically driven constraints; and even after the Fall sufficient capacity remains in reason to discern some truths about God. As Helm concludes,

> Calvin may thus quite properly be said to have a natural theology, so long as one bears in mind the diverse meanings of that expression … innate, properly functioning capacities common (i.e., natural) to all people, which when brought to bear on the common world of sense experience, the natural world, yield a grasp that there is one God and creator of this entire world who is to be worshipped and served.[65]

So the relationship between Aquinas' thought and Calvin's cannot be conceived 'as a matter of championing natural theology versus condemning it'.[66] Approaches to theological method (or Anglican identity) which set them at odds misrepresent them. And, like Aquinas, Calvin believes humanity's natural knowledge of God, while real, is limited, and it does not at all suffice to convey the truths of God as Redeemer necessary for our salvation. That knowledge must come to us from a source other than our own reasoning, hence the need for revelation, to which we now turn.

Reason and revelation

As we have seen, Calvin, like Aquinas, thought that humanity could know naturally many truths about God. But since this knowledge is limited, alongside the knowledge of God accessible to reason must be another source of a different kind of knowledge of God. For Calvin, as for Aquinas, this is revelation.

Calvin believes there is a *duplex cognitio Dei*, a twofold knowledge of God, which has obvious echoes of Aquinas' belief in a 'twofold mode of truth' about God (*SCG* I.3.2-3). Calvin is clear about the limitations of natural reason's knowledge of God; it can only take us so far into the truth. Reason, then, cannot teach us that knowledge of God which only comes from revelation, the illumination of

---

65. Helm, '*Sensus Divinitatis*', 93.
66. Williams, *Architecture of Theology*, 41 fn.21.

the Spirit. As Muller notes, the evidence of the *Commentaries* suggests that long before the final version of the *Institutes* quoted above Calvin was discerning from John's gospel this reason-revelation dynamic, the twofold knowledge of God.[67] Calvin says humans 'above all living beings hav[e] been endowed with reason and intelligence ... some intuition of the eternal light', but this is 'the common light of nature which is far inferior to faith' (*Commentaries*, 133). The knowledge of faith requires a higher illumination than the natural light of reason. So there is a distinction between 'any kind of knowledge of God', which reason may attain, and 'the knowledge which transforms us into the image of God, the beginning and end of which is faith' (*Commentaries*, 137). This knowledge of faith is not accessible to us by reason because it requires knowledge of Christ's divinity, and 'natural reason can never guide men to Christ'; so philosophy cannot lead us to these saving doctrinal truths (*Commentaries*, 132). The knowledge of God attainable by reason does not lead us to understand that Christ is the redeemer or mediator who alone restores fallen humanity; therefore, Calvin says, '[T]he salvation of men is hopeless unless God comes to their add with a new help' (*Commentaries*, 131).

The dialectic between reason and revelation is also obvious when Calvin moves from the generic knowledge of God as Creator in Book I to the knowledge of God as Redeemer in Book II, a move which mirrors Aquinas' progression from generic knowledge of God in the earliest chapters of the *Summae* to the uniquely Christian doctrines of God. In Book I, Calvin writes of the 'kind of knowledge by which one is permitted to grasp ... that God is who founded and governed the universe', but this knowledge is not 'the proper doctrine of faith whereby they had been illumined to the hope of eternal life'. For that knowledge which leads to faith and salvation we need some 'other inner knowledge ... which alone quickens dead souls, whereby God is known not only as the Founder of the universe and the sole Author and Ruler of all that is made, but also in the person of the Mediator as the Redeemer' (*Inst.* I.6.1). As Calvin says elsewhere,

> Our mind is too rude to be able to grasp the spiritual wisdom of God which is revealed to us through faith ... But the Holy Spirit by his illumination makes us capable of understanding those things which would otherwise far exceed our grasp ... by sealing the promises of salvation in our hearts.
>
> (*Treatises*, 105)

So, says Calvin, 'the way to the Kingdom of God is open only to him whose mind has been made new by the illumination of the Holy Spirit'; human wisdom cannot reach such truths (*Inst.* II.2.20). He continues we 'have need of new revelation' and can 'understand God's mysteries only insofar as ... illumined by God's grace' (II.2.21). He quotes Augustine approvingly on 'the inability of the reason to understand the things of God' (II.2.25). And the believer's knowledge of the things

---

67. Muller, '*Duplex cognitio Dei*', 54.

of faith comes only when they are persuaded by the Spirit, not by any exercise of natural reason (III.2.14).[68]

Specifically, Calvin continues, repeating the motif from his commentary on John, 'we cannot by contemplating the universe infer that God is Father', and 'no knowledge of God apart from the Mediator has ... power unto salvation' (II.6.1). Salvation comes only through the revelation of Christ; 'unless God confronts us in Christ, we cannot come to know that we are saved' for 'apart from Christ the saving knowledge of God' is inaccessible (II.6.4). The knowledge of our salvation in Christ can only come by divine revelation;[69] the truth of our redemption is, again, closely connected with the incarnation as the means Christ uses to save us (II.12.4). The saving understanding of God as Trinity likewise only comes by revelation (e.g., I.13.21-2).[70]

It is important to note, though, because much of the debate is couched in terms of tension between reason and revelation (and in particular between reason and scripture) that, while Calvin considers reason and revelation to yield different kinds of knowledge of God, he does not consider them as fundamentally in tension. This is in part because *both* reason and revelation come ultimately from God; there are not two bodies of knowledge of God but two kinds of knowledge of the one God, distinct in their method of transmission and their effects, but not their ultimate origin. As Adams points out, for Calvin, *God* is the author of our natural knowledge of God: it is *God* who has made creation tell of his glory, God who has implanted the seed of awareness of him in human hearts.[71] We are instructed by God in nature (e.g., I.5.15) just as much as by revelation, albeit in a different way and to different effects.

Moreover, what is revealed is more than just doctrinal propositions, a further point of convergence with Aquinas. As Dowey wrote, 'all too often Calvin is dismissed ... as the theologian of an intellectualized and logically severe faith, without appreciation of this inner core of deep Christian experience'.[72] Against such characterizations, two particular features of Calvin's thought can be identified. Firstly, even the *natural* knowledge of God can yield more than propositions: the beauty and intricacy of creation cannot just evoke belief that God exists, nor merely prompt us to guilt, but also result in wonder, praise and even love of God. The display of God's creativity and providence in the beauty and ordering of the cosmos should 'bestir' us 'to trust, invoke, praise, and love' God, and as we are 'invited by the great sweetness of his beneficence and goodness, let us study to love and serve him with all our heart' (I.4.22). The natural knowledge of God, then, includes (but goes beyond) the cognitive.

---

68. Dowey, *Knowledge of God*, 184; cf. Helm, *Calvin at the Centre*, 261–2.

69. Dowey, *Knowledge of God*, 177–9.

70. Cf. Dowey, *Knowledge of God*, 148–50; McGrath, *Calvin*, 155.

71. Adams, 'Natural Knowledge of God', 281–2.

72. Dowey, *Knowledge of God*, 183.

Secondly, if natural knowledge of God yields more than just cognitive truths, how much more does revelation lead us to more than just propositional knowledge? For Calvin, revelation does not just convey doctrines but also shows us our salvation and so can evoke a loving and trusting response to the good news of God's redemptive work for us. Calvin says faith is 'a firm and sure knowledge of the divine favour toward us, founded on the truth of a free promise in Christ, and revealed to our minds, and sealed on our hearts, by the Holy Spirit' (III.2.7). In the same passage, Calvin writes that this revelation is the assurance of God's benevolence towards us such that we find our security in him. It is hardly a purely cognitive or logical or legal mind which reminds us that in response to revelation our love for God is kindled when his 'abundant sweetness' 'utterly ravishes one and draws one to itself' (III.2.41) and refreshing, sustaining, nourishing hope is nurtured in us (III.2.41). Thus, Helm writes of 'Calvin's sustained polemic against faith as mere assent. Faith involves assent, because it has propositional content, but it goes beyond assent, involving trust, reliance upon God's promise, and hence reliance upon God'.[73] This characterization of revelation (whether the generic revelation through creation or the specific revelation in Christ) as being much more than just merely propositional knowledge is of course matched, albeit in different terms, in Aquinas. For Aquinas, we saw, knowledge of God does not just move the intellect or mind, it also moves the *will*.

These passages from Calvin reveal a cluster of concerns, then, which closely mirror Aquinas' account of reason and revelation. Reason may tell us that God created and governs, but only revelation can tell us that he redeems; this knowledge of redemption, attainable only by divine revelation, is what saves us, and it saves us by illuminating the saving truths in particular about the person and work of Christ. But if such truths cannot be found by natural reason, where then are they to be found? Here we must turn from revelation to Calvin's account of scripture.

Scripture in Calvin's theological method

Introduction

The claim reformed theologies can be distinguished from catholic ones by their emphasis on *sola scriptura* is common but misleading.[74] Chapter 2 showed Aquinas believed scripture alone taught us the saving truths of God; while other theological warrants, notably reason, were needed as tools to draw out its meaning, scripture alone could ground doctrinal claims. Now we will see that Calvin broadly shares that view. After examining the role of scripture in aiding *natural* knowledge of

---

73. Helm, *Calvin at the Centre*, 14; see also Dowey, *Knowledge of God*, 183–5.

74. As Williams notes, it is rare to find a serious theologian who actually argues that this means scripture alone may be legitimately used in theological method – and attempts to do so usually falter in the face of inconvenient truths such as the late origin of the canon or the different interpretations of scriptural texts: *Architecture of Theology*, 83.

God, this section considers first the question of scripture's sufficiency, and secondly its authority, showing the broad convergence of Aquinas and Calvin (some differences of language notwithstanding). A shared account of *sola scriptura* emerges, demonstrating catholic and reformed views need not be set in opposition.

Scripture corrects natural knowledge of God

A preliminary point is that for Calvin, as for Aquinas, scripture does not just teach us things we cannot know by reason; it also teaches us things we *could* know by reason. This reminds us the warrants were not separate or autonomous for these authors; while they had distinct roles, and different levels of authority, they were not to be considered in isolation from each other.

Even in its natural sphere, says Calvin near the start of the *Institutes*, human reason does not operate as effectively as it could. So 'although the Lord represents both himself and his everlasting kingdom in the mirror of his works', human dullness and stupidity mean we often do not recognize him (*Inst*. I.5.1). Our reasoning often goes awry, as witnessed by the diversity and error which mar many of our opinions (I.5.12-13). Our eyes cannot always see the 'many burning lamps shin[ing] for us in the workmanship of the universe to show forth the glory of its Author', even though they could in principle; hence God reveals this to us through the illumination of the Spirit (I.5.14).

Calvin continues with the image of scripture as a pair of spectacles which helps us see more clearly what we could, with perfect natural sight, in fact see without it:

> Just as old or bleary-eyed men and those with weak vision … can scarcely construe two words, but with the aid of spectacles will begin to read distinctly; so Scripture, gathering up the otherwise confused knowledge of God in our minds … clearly shows us the true God … besides these common proofs he also put forth his Word, which is a more direct and more certain mark.
>
> (I.6.1)

Foreseeing the marks he had placed in the natural world would prove inadequate, Calvin explains, God implants his Word so we can avoid reading the evidence of reason wrongly and can navigate the labyrinth of the created order so it leads us to him rather than some false deity (I.7.3). So while 'the knowledge of God' is 'quite clearly set forth in the system of the universe', it 'is nonetheless more intimately and also more vividly revealed in his Word' (I.10.1).

Thus, Steinmetz concludes, 'Calvin suggests that creation can be reclaimed as source by believers who view the world with the light of faith and not merely with the light of natural reason.'[75] The book of scripture helps us read the book of nature properly, which our natural reason alone cannot do. Scripture and reason then do not stand separately; there is a relationship or dialectic between them. Scripture can help make up the insufficiency of reason's operation in the sphere of natural

---

75. Steinmetz, *Calvin in Context*, 30.

knowledge of God, bringing correction and clarity to the confused reasoning of the mind. But if scripture corrects what we might in fact know by reason, its principal purpose, as we now see, is to deliver those truths we could not know by reason at all.

Scripture's sufficiency

The previous section emphasized that for Calvin, as for Aquinas, the saving truths of Christian faith come to us only by revelation. This then prompts the question where this revelation is to be found. To provide some manageable way of navigating the terrain we defer until later the role of *tradition*; for now, we ask: for Calvin, does scripture alone reveal this truth to us?

Calvin does not equate revelation and scripture as wholly synonymous. He carefully says the scriptures 'set before us' God's Word, not that they are identical with it (*Inst.* I.13.7).[76] God's revelation to us in the first instance is Christ; the *Genevan Catechism* says we must learn that Christ is revealed to us by God as the means of our redemption (*Treatises*, 92), a point which recurs for instance in the commentary on St John's Prologue.[77] For Calvin, the light which comes into the world (Jn 1.9) is the light of Christ's divinity, knowledge we could never know for ourselves that God has become incarnate and redeemed us in Christ (*Commentaries*, 131–2). For the apostles, access to that revelation came through the personal presence of Jesus; Calvin points particularly to the example of St Thomas as one who encounters that personal revelation.[78]

Of course, in the absence of direct physical access to the historical Jesus, the definition of Christ as revelation still begs the question of where we *now* access that revelation. And, while not collapsing revelation into scripture,[79] Calvin nonetheless holds that scripture alone now constitutes the definitive witness of that revelation, ruling out both tradition and reason as sources of this saving communication: 'we should seek our rule of faith, not from the word of God, but from the tradition of the church, ought not to be accepted' (*BLW*, 52). He condemns 'arrogant pseudoprophetic windbags' who hold there are extra-scriptural sources of doctrine (*Commentaries*, 86). Our own reason is inadequate 'to understand the things of God' (*Inst.* II.2.25). On matters of faith, only the scriptures are 'apt and able to show us the way clearly and certainly' (*Commentaries*, 97). So while Calvin's exegesis of John 1 reminds us that the Word, God's revelation to us, is a broader category than the text of scripture,[80] in practical terms scripture is now our sole source of this revelation.

76. See Partee, *Calvin*, 58–9.

77. On this commentary, see Barbara Pitkin, *Calvin, the Bible, and History* (Oxford: Oxford University Press, 2020), esp. 71–2, 83–94.

78. See Pitkin, *Calvin, Bible, and History*, 86–7, 91.

79. Dowey, *Knowledge of God*, 155.

80. See J. T. McNeill, 'The Significance of the Word of God for Calvin', *Church History* 28.2 (1959): 132–3.

This point recurs in his *Commentaries*; glossing Jeremiah 7, for example, Calvin says the word of God alone points us to 'true religion' (*Commentaries*, 78; so also 79, 82). On I Pet. 1.25, Calvin asks, 'What then is the Word of God which gives us life: what but the law, the prophets, and the gospel?', resisting those who dishonour God's word by turning away from scripture, insisting 'we must not look for the Word of God anywhere except in the preaching of the gospel' (*Commentaries*, 83). So 'scripture is adequate and sufficient for our perfecting. Therefore, anyone who is not satisfied with scripture, hopes to know more than he needs or is good for him' (85). The Word of God is our only 'norm', 'touchstone' and 'source of sound teaching' (86–7), and 'if we would know Christ, we must seek him in the scriptures' (104). The revelation which leads to salvation comes only from scripture; scripture's purpose is to reveal to us the truth of our salvation in Christ.[81]

Turning to the *Institutes* demonstrates the same point. 'Let us not take it into our heads', Calvin cautions, 'to seek out God anywhere else than in his sacred word'; we can only 'conceive him to be as he reveals himself to us, without inquiring about him anywhere else than from his word' (*Inst*. I.13.21). He repeatedly insists on this: for instance, 'the human mind because of its feebleness can in no way attain to God unless it be aided and assisted by his sacred word' (I.6.4). This, of course, does not mean without scripture one can know nothing of God – as we have seen, Calvin thinks we can know much about God by reason alone – but does mean there are some truths we cannot reach without scripture's help.

These truths, as *Institutes* I.6 makes clear, are the saving doctrines of Christian faith. Calvin here considers that knowledge of God 'which alone quickens dead souls' (the link with salvation being traced) and relates particularly to the 'person of the Mediator as the Redeemer' (I.6.1). 'No one', says Calvin, 'can get even the slightest taste of right and sound doctrine unless he be a pupil of scripture' which alone can yield 'the specific doctrine of faith and repentance that sets forth Christ as mediator' (I.6.2). Only the scriptures, Calvin says, can point us towards Christ as our only ground of salvation (this is the theme of II.10.2-23). Scripture 'proclaims that to become our redeemer he was clothed with flesh' (II.12.4). As Murray concludes, 'Christ as the incarnate word is never brought into contact with us apart from scripture'.[82] Similarly, Calvin writes, since reason cannot even know its own nature, so it certainly cannot unaided know the divine nature; hence the doctrine of the Trinity, too, can come only from scripture (I.13.21-22).[83]

To leave the account there, to say that scripture alone was, for Calvin, the ground of our saving knowledge, of the specifically Christian account of God, the doctrines of faith, would be true enough but insufficient. It would expose Calvin to the charge of an unrealistic theological method which can be levelled at many *sola scriptura* accounts. Particularly, on this last point about the Trinity, much of the

---

81. Randall C. Zachman, 'John Calvin', in *Christian Theologies of Scripture: A Comparative Introduction*, ed. Justin S. Holcomb (New York, NY: New York University Press, 2006), 124–5.

82. John Murray, *Calvin on Scripture and Divine Sovereignty* (Welwyn: Evangelical Press, 1979), 40.

83. Helm, *Ideas*, 36 rightly says Calvin and Aquinas agree on this point.

doctrine is couched in language (person, nature, substance) which is clearly not derived from scripture. So some commentators such as van den Belt argue that the phrase itself should be abandoned.[84]

But probing Calvin's account further reveals that, while he does use the phrase 'scripture alone' (e.g., *Inst.* I.7.1, III.17.18), he does not mean scripture is the only theologically authoritative source. Again, Calvin's account of the Trinity in *Institutes* I.13 demonstrates why. Only scripture can be our 'sure rule for both thinking and speaking', but we can, even must, use terms from outside scripture to explain its meaning (I.13.3, 5) and to combat heresy (I.13.4). So, says Calvin, nothing 'prevents us from explaining in clearer words those matters in Scripture which perplex and hinder our understanding, yet which conscientiously and faithfully serve the truth of Scripture itself, and … renders the truth plain and clear' (I.13.3).[85] As Zachman concludes, for Calvin scripture's authority and sufficiency meant that it alone was 'the normative source and limit for the … teaching of the Church in subsequent generations'.[86] Only scripture can ground our knowledge of the saving doctrines of faith, but that does not mean other warrants cannot be used; scripture is, to use later phrases, *materially* sufficient, contains everything needed for salvation, but not *formally* sufficient.

What Calvin is particularly challenging here is the notion that some other source than scripture reveals to us God's saving doctrine. He 'especially repudiate[s] their desire to make certainty of doctrine depend not less on what they call *unwritten* than on the Scriptures. We must ever adhere to Augustine's rule, "Faith is conceived from the Scriptures"' (*Antidote*, 69). We will need to return to this question in discussing tradition, but the essential point here is Calvin is *not* resisting any role for other warrants in theology; rather, he is insisting that outside the text of scripture there can be no legitimate source of doctrine. Calvin is rejecting the notion 'unwritten' traditions of the apostles carried similar authority to the written tradition in scripture. *Sola scriptura*, as Lane says, is therefore in some sense a negative proposition, ruling out the notion tradition (or indeed any other warrant) carries equal weight to scripture and resisting the principle that some other warrant can ground doctrine.[87]

Moreover, Calvin is sensitive to the obvious problem there can be more than one plausible interpretation of a biblical passage. The possibility of plausible but wrong interpretations is evident, for Calvin, in the way many Jews responded to the life of Christ; rightly reading the scripture as saying there was only one God, they then wrongly assumed this meant Christ could not also be God; they were

---

84. Henk van dan Belt, '*Sola Scriptura*: An Inadequate Slogan for the Authority of Scripture', *CThJ* 51 (2016): 204–5.

85. Cf., e.g., Williams, *Architecture of Theology*, 95 fn.18; Helm, *Ideas*, 37–40.

86. Zachman, 'Calvin', 116.

87. A. N. S. Lane, 'Sola Scriptura? Making Sense of a Post-Reformation Slogan', in *A Pathway into the Holy Scripture*, ed. D. F. Wright and Philip Satterthwaite (Grand Rapids, MI: Eerdmans, 1994), 323.

unpersuaded by the possibility that belief in one God could be held alongside belief that Christ was God (*Commentaries*, 89). Calvin's account of how to judge between competing interpretations is revealing. 'Holy Scripture contains a perfect doctrine', he insists; it is the sole and complete record of the revelation of saving truth, but 'a person who has not had much practice in it has good reason for some guidance and direction, to know what he ought to look for'.[88] This guidance comes from testing doctrines, and this 'public testing of doctrines has to do with the common consent and polity of the church' (*Commentaries*, 87). Again, Calvin writes that in cases of uncertainty 'believers should seek a remedy by coming together and reasoning' (88).

This question of the role of the church and its tradition in shaping permissible interpretations of scripture will be considered in Chapter 5. For now, it suffices to say that if we are to speak of Calvin as holding a *sola scriptura* account of scripture this must be carefully defined. Such an appellation does not (as Belt says) need to be rejected, just nuanced. The things of faith can come to us not by our reason but only by revelation, and the only source now available of this revelation is scripture. Scripture is the sole source of our saving knowledge of God, but that does not mean the other warrants have no role in theology; rather, their place is ancillary, in drawing out the meaning of scripture. In that sense Calvin is very similar to Aquinas; for both of them believe in *sola scriptura* if that is understood as scripture being the sole source of our saving knowledge of God. And, on the related question of how we know scripture is authoritative, there is also much more in common between them than often supposed.

Scripture's authority

On the question of how we know scripture is God's revelation to us, our sole source in matters of doctrine, Calvin insists scripture needs no external source (such as tradition) to ground its authority. Famously, he writes,

> Scripture is indeed self-authenticated [*autopiston*], hence it is not right to subject it to proof and reasoning … we believe neither by our own nor by anyone else's judgment that Scripture is from God, but we affirm with utter certainty … that it has flowed to us from the very mouth of God … we seek no proofs … [this] is a conviction which requires no reasons.
>
> (*Inst.* I.7.4)

Having specifically ruled out reason as a basis for determining scripture's authority, he will also explicitly deny tradition such a role. Calvin writes it is 'utterly vain' to 'pretend that the power of judging scripture so lies with the church that its certainty depends on churchly assent' (I.7.2) and it 'never depends upon the definition or decree of men' (I.7.3). Scripture's authority is so self-evident it leaps off the page as

---

88. John Calvin, 'Subject Matter of the Present Work', *Inst.*, I.6; cf. Zachman, 'Cavin', 118–22.

one reads it. The writings of Demosthenes, Cicero, Plato and Aristotle may delight or move us, but when scripture is read, 'such vigour as the orators and philosophers have will nearly vanish'. He adds, '[I]t is easy to see that the Sacred Scriptures ... breathe something divine', and so it is 'vain to fortify the authority of scripture by arguments [or] by the common agreement of the church' (I.8.1).

Thus far, what Calvin says might well thought to be in tension with Aquinas, who did not make a similar claim that scripture authenticates itself. Nonetheless, probing Calvin's view in more detail reveals a curious twist: while he is adamant that neither tradition nor reason grounds scripture's authority, nonetheless he insists that both warrants support that claim.[89] So, he says, 'the best reason agrees' that scripture is divinely authoritative and then adduces a range of evidence (the so-called proofs) such as scripture's antiquity, consistency and so on (this is the thrust of *Institutes* I.8). The authority of the church is evidence for scripture's authority: 'the consent of the church should not be denied its due weight' (I.8.12). So there is something of a tension here; scripture needs no other proof, yet proofs there are.

Further probing, though, will help us see there is no contradiction between the claim of scripture's self-authentication and the existence of proofs of its authority based on the other warrants. Firstly, we consider what 'self-authenticating' means and secondly examine Calvin's distinction between how believers and unbelievers receive scripture.

Firstly, 'self-authenticating' (*autopiston*) is not an easy or obvious term, nor even a common one in Calvin's writings. Van den Belt argues that it has been overstated and misunderstood in the reformed tradition and frequently mistranslated.[90] Reading *Institutes* I.7.5 more closely we see Calvin writes 'those whom the Holy Spirit has inwardly taught truly rest upon Scripture, and that Scripture indeed is self-authenticated'. So here we see Word and Spirit are for Calvin intimately connected. Again, we only believe 'scripture is from God' when we are 'illumined by his power'. Self-authentication cannot just mean the brute assertion that scripture's authority comes only from scripture; rather, it is scripture as illuminated by the Holy Spirit. Thus, for Calvin, 'the Spirit's witness and Scripture's *autopistia* ... are closely related ... Scripture only becomes self-convincing to believers through that witness; the *autopistia* depends on the *testimonium*'.[91] This is a nuanced definition of *autopistis* and crucially it does not mean scripture authenticates itself in some kind of brute autonomous self-attestation. The problem, van den Belt holds, is that subsequently the reformed tradition separated the *autopistia* of scripture from the *testimonium* of the Spirit, attributing self-authentication to the text in itself rather than (as Calvin understood it) the text as received by the Spirit-illuminated believer.[92]

89. *PRRD* II.77, II.258.

90. Henk van dan Belt, 'Scripture as the Voice of God: The Continuing Importance of *Autopistia*', *IJST* 13.4 (2011): 438.

91. Van den Belt, 'Scripture', 438.

92. Van den Belt, 'Scripture', 440–2.

Indeed, to support van den Belt's reading, we see the interconnectedness of the scripture's authority and the spirit's witness recurring frequently in Calvin. For example, Calvin says, '[T]he scriptures obtain full authority among believers only when men regard them as having sprung from heaven as if there the living words of God were heard' (I.7.1), and to be persuaded of this we must 'seek our conviction in a higher place than human reasons ... that is, in the secret testimony of the Spirit'. Calvin continues,

> [T]he Word will not find acceptance in men's hearts before it is sealed by the inward testimony of the Spirit. The same Spirit, therefore, who has spoken through the mouths of the prophets must penetrate into our hearts to persuade us that they faithfully proclaimed what they had been divinely commanded.
> (I.7.4; cf. I.9.3)

The essential interdependence of Word and Spirit is highlighted when Calvin insists that 'without the illumination of the Holy Spirit, the Word can do nothing' (III.2.33) and 'the Word of God is not received by faith' until 'the mind's real understanding is illuminat[ed] by the Spirit' (III.2.36). In other words: *autopistis* does not, for Calvin, means scripture needs nothing else to be held authoritative; we only can accept its intrinsic authority if the Spirit works to reveal it to us.[93]

Secondly, Calvin is emphatic that scripture's authority is revealed by the Spirit only to believers. For the believer, the evidence or proofs for scripture's authority (or 'props', Calvin's word, e.g., I.8.11) serve principally to provide evidence for the believer of things already accepted by faith: 'once we have embraced it devoutly as its dignity deserves', the props are 'very useful aids' which can offer 'wonderful confirmation' of the authority of scripture we have already accepted (I.8.2). By contrast, for the unbeliever, the evidence of the church might lead them to accept scripture's authority; 'the universal judgment of the church ... is of very great value'. Indeed, 'those who have not yet been illumined by the Spirit of God are rendered teachable by reverence for the church so that they may persevere in learning faith in Christ from the gospel' (I.7.3). What we see here is that the testimony of the church cannot render scripture authoritative for the unbeliever, but it can nonetheless render it plausible, worth 'persevering' with.

The claim that scripture authenticates itself is thus rather a difficult one, requiring very considerable nuance if the term is to be applied to Calvin. The text alone can persuade neither the believer nor the unbeliever of its authority; the former requires the illumination of the Spirit to convince them, the latter external evidence to render it plausible. Note the weaker claim made for the 'proofs': they do not persuade someone the scripture is God's word; they merely provide arguments to show such a claim is not implausible.[94]

---

93. E.g., Partee, *Calvin*, 59–62; McNeill, 'Word of God', 133–4; Dowey, *Knowledge of God*, 108.

94. Helm, *Calvin at the Centre*, 69.

Chapter 4 will show this is broadly Hooker's account too, and arguments that Hooker moves outside a reformed perspective on scripture's self-authentication are misguided.[95] It is also broadly consistent with Aquinas' view, as the editor of the McNeill-Battles edition[96] and Helm note.[97] While Aquinas does not (so far as I know) have a word which is similar to *autopistis*, he nonetheless also thought that faith could only be kindled by God's supernatural work in the believer's heart (*S. Th.* II-II.6.1, *resp.*).[98] For Aquinas, that inward conviction is made possible to the believer by trusting the *speaker* of the scriptures. Since only God knows God, only God can reveal God, and scripture is God's revelation of the perfect knowledge of himself. Its authority is therefore not independent but relies on the self-knowledge and authority of the one who speaks it.[99]

This is Calvin's view too; the authority of scripture is precisely not the authority of the written text as such but the authority of its author.[100] He writes we are only persuaded of scripture's authority when 'we are persuaded beyond doubt that God is its author'; 'the highest proof of scripture' is that 'God in person speaks it' (*Inst.* I.7.4; cf. I.7.5, I.9.2). Glossing II Tim. 3.16-17, Calvin says, '[M]any have doubts as to the author of scripture' and 'only those illumined by the Spirit have the eyes to see ... the author of the Scriptures is God' (*Commentaries*, 85). If we can speak of scripture's self-authenticating authority, then, this must mean the authority conferred on it by God who is its author and who by his Spirit inspires the believer to recognize this authority, a point common to Calvin and Aquinas.[101]

Summary

Notions that scripture is sufficient in theology (*sola scriptura*) and is self-authenticating (*autopistis*) lead some to conclude that Calvin's account of the warrant differs fundamentally from Aquinas' and is cited to argue for a reformed-catholic spectrum into which Hooker and Anglicanism must be slotted. But this section has shown how, when Calvin's account is read closely, they in fact have much in common and that both these terms must be applied with careful

---

95. While I broadly agree with Dominiak that Calvin and Hooker are, contrary to some readings, largely in tune on this point, his characterization that for Calvin 'Scripture has ultimate and independent autopistic authority' is infelicitous – P. A. Dominiak, *Richard Hooker: The Architecture of Participation* (London: T&T Clark, 2021), 115.

96. *Inst.*, I.78 fn.11.

97. Helm, *Calvin at the Centre*, 64–70.

98. Thus Helm, *Calvin at the Centre*, 66.

99. Helm, *Ideas*, 247.

100. Cf. Bruce Gordon, 'The Bible in Reformed Thought, 1520–1570', in *The New Cambridge History of the Bible*, 4 vols (Cambridge: Cambridge University Press, 2012–16), III.473.

101. The close connection with Aquinas is identified for instance by Helm, *Ideas*, 248–51; McNeill, 'Word of God', 139.

nuance. Calvin, like Aquinas, thinks scripture is now our only record of God's revelation in Christ and so excludes reason or tradition as *sources* of doctrine, but those warrants are useful *tools* in elucidating scripture's meaning or judging which possible interpretation of scripture is right. Calvin, like Aquinas, thinks scripture's authority is not undergirded by any internal or external evidence but only by the authority of the divine speaker whose speech it is; this insight only comes to the believer and only by the inward witness of the Spirit. The 'proofs', as Calvin calls them, may be useful supports for the argument but they will never persuade someone of the authority of scripture. So Calvin's account of scripture, far from diverging from Aquinas', is broadly in line with it.

Obscuring Calvin's convergence with Aquinas

Introduction

This chapter shows, on the relationship of reason and scripture, Calvin and Aquinas are far from in tension or even opposition. Their accounts of the purpose and relationship of these two warrants are broadly similar. If so, why has this convergence been missed? This chapter demonstrates some of the reasons; in particular, defining phrases like *sola scriptura* and *autopistis* carefully reveal they are not, as commonly supposed, ways in which Calvin differs from Aquinas. Three further factors are now adduced in this section to show how Calvin's own rhetoric, misreadings of Aquinas and the influence of Karl Barth on readings of Calvin have all contributed to the mistaken belief that Calvin's and Aquinas' theological methods are in tension. Identifying these problematic influences will clear space for a convergent reading of Calvin and Aquinas to emerge more clearly.

Calvin's rhetoric

Firstly, Calvin himself is partly responsible for the frequent perception that he is in tension with Aquinas. For example, their common approach to philosophy is masked by their different use of the word. Where Aquinas will cite 'the Philosopher' as a legitimate source, Calvin rails against those who 'philosophise beside the point' (*Treatises*, 94) and parodies 'the giddy imagination of the philosophers' (*Inst.* I.2.18).

The reputation not just of secular philosophers but also of medieval theologians appears to wilt under Calvin's polemical assault. Lane's comprehensive study shows that Calvin treated Augustine in particular and the Fathers in general as authorities while regarding many medieval theologians as opponents.[102] Calvin makes 1,078 references to Augustine and (say) 133 to Ambrose but only six to Aquinas.[103] He makes 'sweeping claims to the support of Augustine'[104] (e.g., 'I have no occasion to

---

102. A. N. S Lane, 'Calvin's Use of Fathers and Medievals', *CThJ* 16 (1981): 161.
103. Lane, 'Fathers and Medievals', 175 fn.16, 180 fn.216.
104. Lane, 'Fathers and Medievals', 171.

use any other words than his', *Inst.* III.22.8) alongside a sweepingly condemnatory characterization of medieval theology as 'mere sophistry ... so twisted, involved, tortuous, and puzzling, that scholastic theology might well be described as a species of secret magic' (*Treatises*, 233). He particularly condemns the 'Schoolmen' who have 'fabricated' a number of doctrines (*Inst.* IV.17.13) (such as transubstantiation, IV.17.14) by being over-indebted to philosophy at the expense of scripture (IV.17.26). This overwhelming preponderance of classical rather than medieval sources, and his rhetoric against medieval writers, can lead to a conclusion that Calvin is antagonistic to medieval theology in general.[105]

However, Calvin's relationship with medieval theology and Aquinas in particular is more complicated than his own sweeping generalizations might suggest. A basic reason why Calvin prefers the Fathers is simply that this was both safe and contested terrain – safe, because all sides of the reformation debates agreed in principle that antiquity represented a period of special doctrinal consensus; contested, because the nub of many arguments was which side could most convincingly claim antiquity's support.[106] By contrast, a major driving force behind the reformation was the belief that the theology and practices of medieval Christianity had seriously distorted key elements of its doctrinal and ritual inheritance from the early church. The medieval period, then, was much more difficult terrain for a reformer like Calvin.[107]

Even so, Calvin is as discriminating in his use of theological sources (of whatever period) as he is of his philosophical ones. For instance, Calvin thought even most patristic writers had inadequately articulated a doctrine of human free will by their desire to sound philosophically coherent (*Inst.* II.2.4). And even Augustine, who Calvin so frequently cites, is sometimes left to one side; Calvin rather sidelines his biblical exegesis, for instance.[108]

Examining Calvin's actual attitude towards medieval theologians reveals the same discriminating approach. For instance, he is sometimes quite critical of Peter Lombard (*c.*1096–1160), yet he complains that after Lombard, 'the schools have gone from bad to worse' (*Inst.* III.11.15). He also, revealingly, distinguishes Lombard as (presumably relatively) 'sane and sober' when compared with 'the later Sophists' (III.15.7).[109] This distinction between the earlier and later medievals is crucial for a proper understanding of Calvin's attitude to Aquinas. For Calvin, even when criticizing Lombard, says he 'disagree[s] with the sounder Schoolmen' but 'differ[s] from the more recent Sophists to an ever greater extent, as they are farther removed from antiquity' (II.2.6). As Muller adds, where criticizing a

---

105. E.g., Dowey, *Knowledge of God*, 10.

106. As they were in the dispute between Hooker and his opponents, see John K. Luoma, 'Who Owns the Fathers? Hooker and Cartwright on the Authority of the Primitive Church', *Sixteenth Century Journal* 8.3 (1977): esp. 49–50, 57, 59.

107. I am grateful to Kenneth Padley for this point.

108. Lane, 'Fathers and Medievals', 172.

109. See Lane, 'Fathers and Medievals', 180.

particular medieval theologian, Calvin usually refers to them with *scholastiques* cognates rather than the *Sorboniques* or *sophistes* cognates he deploys when condemning a generic school or style of theology which he associates with the later medieval period and the schools of the Sorbonne he considers it emerged from.[110] While disagreeing on some specific points with Lombard and Aquinas, then, Calvin nonetheless appears to exculpate them from his sweeping condemnation of later medieval thought.[111] Indeed, the McNeill-Battles edition of the *Institutes* exacerbates the problem by adding footnotes to refer to Aquinas where no such reference is made in Calvin's text, 'leaving the impression that there is more direct engagement and opposition between Calvin and Thomas than the text actually sustains'.[112] So, as Ballor notes, 'recent scholarship has increasingly questioned whether Calvin is directly engaging Thomas's work … rather than versions of Thomism represented by late medieval figures'.[113]

Calvin's rhetoric then has served to mislead; his pungent criticism of specific theological views, and his wider distaste for later medieval theology (particularly that of the Sorbonne), has meant subsequent commentators have failed to see his discriminating approach to his interlocutors. When understood in his broader polemical stance which privileged the patristic over the medieval, and the specific focus of his ire, it becomes clear he is much less antagonistic to Aquinas than some commentators (or indeed his own rhetoric) might suggest.

Misreadings of Aquinas

Ballor's argument connects with a second factor which has led to presumed disagreement between Calvin and Aquinas, namely some of the ways the latter has been (mis)read by subsequent theologians. For if Calvin is reacting against the kind of medieval scholastic theology he saw in the post-Aquinas schools, arguments of a gap between him and Aquinas often also rely on comparing Calvin with the Aquinas of subsequent interpreters rather than Aquinas himself.

Here we can re-emphasize the thrust of Chapter 2, which argued subsequent interpretations of Aquinas had aggravated the suggestion of a divergence between him and Calvin. For example, when read closely alongside each other, Calvin and Aquinas are in fact far closer on a range of controversial topics (such as the effects of the Fall on human reason or the role of philosophy in theology) than often supposed. But the presumption of a gap between them has sometimes been

---

110. R. A. Muller, *The Unaccommodated Calvin: Studies in the Foundation of a Theological Tradition* (Oxford: Oxford University Press, 2000), 38–42.

111. See the editor's comment at *Institutes*, I.263 fn.35.

112. Jordan Ballor, 'Deformation and Reformation: Thomas Aquinas and the Rise of Protestant Scholasticism', in *Aquinas among the Protestants*, ed. Svensson and VanDrunen, 38; cf. Arvin Vos, *Aquinas, Calvin, and Contemporary Protestant Thought* (Grand Rapids, MI: Eerdmans, 1985), 38–40.

113. Ballor, 'Deformation', 37–8; cf. Vos, *Aquinas and Calvin*, 150–7.

exacerbated by failure to attend to Aquinas' text itself and instead is a reaction against certain kinds of Thomism quite removed from Aquinas' own view. In other words, if one compares Calvin's theology with certain kinds of later-nineteenth-century neo-Thomisms, one might conclude that (say) Aquinas was excessively confident in the powers of human reason at the expense of scripture. However, drawing on the insights of Aquinas studies in the wake of the *nouvelle théologie* we see (for example) Aquinas was a much more biblical theologian, and much less confident in reason's powers, than often supposed. Comparing the Aquinas thus retrieved with Calvin reveals considerably less divergence between the two, since they share a real but limited role for reason in theological method and both assert scripture alone is our source of the saving truths of faith.

Barthian readings of Calvin

The effect of Karl Barth on readings of Calvin, thirdly, is a factor which has contributed to the notion of a gap between Calvin and Aquinas and has in particular promoted the misguided view that Hooker must be positioned on a spectrum between them. Thus, Voak argues Hooker steps outside the reformed perspective because, like Aquinas but apparently unlike Calvin, he considered human reason alone could yield substantial knowledge of God.[114] But examining in more detail the effects of Barth on readings of Calvin, we see how the affinity of Calvin's views with Aquinas' on this point has been masked.

This becomes clear when we trace the effects of Barth's view on the reformed tradition's attitude to the possibility of natural knowledge of God. The famous debate between Barth and Brunner is a useful way to navigate the terrain.[115] Brunner was prepared to say that, within circumscribed parameters, there was a possibility of natural knowledge of God accessible to reason: 'God ... leaves the imprint of his nature on what he does. Therefore the creation of the world is at the same time a revelation, a self-communication of God.'[116]

Barth witheringly rejected Brunner's claim with a famous 'No!'. For Barth, any kind of natural knowledge of God would entail 'man himself possess[ing] the capacity ... to inform himself about God, the world, and man'.[117] Barth strenuously rejects such a possibility; for when 'natural theology is allowed to become of

---

114. Nigel Voak, *Richard Hooker and Reformed Theology: A Study of Reason, Will, and Grace* (Oxford: Oxford University Press, 2003), 128.

115. A. E. McGrath, *Emil Brunner: A Reappraisal* (Oxford: Wiley-Blackwell, 2014), 90–132; the length of McGrath's treatment of their dispute rather undermines his assertion that 'it cannot be regarded as a landmark discussion', 91.

116. Emil Brunner, 'Nature and Grace', in Brunner and Barth, *Natural Theology*, 25; cf. McGrath, *Brunner*, 113–21.

117. Karl Barth, *The Knowledge of God and the Service of God according to the Teaching of the Reformation*, trans. J. L. M. Haire and Ian Henderson (London: Hodder and Stoughton, 1938), 9.

interest' then the discussion is 'no longer centred on theology'.[118] For Barth, any starting point other than the concrete revelation of God in Jesus Christ will result in something other than theology; that is, the subject spoken of will no longer be the living God but some human projection or distortion: there can be no 'possibility of reckoning with a knowledge of the God of the apostles and prophets which is not given in and with his revelation', so there can be no '"Christian" natural theology' (*CD* II/1, §26.1).[119] On Barth's account, the reformed perspective is intrinsically hostile to Aquinas who, as we saw, clearly *did* believe there was potential for some natural knowledge of God apart from the specific revelation in Christ witnessed in the scriptures. Underpinning Barth's view is his suspicion of the capacity of human reason to know anything about God at all: it is 'incurably sick and incapable of any serious theological activity'.[120] For Barth, Rom. 1.19-20 indicated only a hypothetical possibility of natural knowledge of God, a knowledge now inaccessible because of sin and the Fall.[121]

Whether Barth's view is in fact so hostile to Aquinas' has been questioned,[122] but his stance that there is no natural knowledge of God now accessible to reason is certainly widespread in the reformed tradition. A typical example is Wolterstorff's assertion that 'a negative attitude to natural theology' is 'one of the most salient features' of the reformed tradition 'going all the way back to its founder, John Calvin'.[123] This is the so-called reformed objection to natural theology.[124]

This reformed objection to the possibility of natural knowledge of God, though, cannot properly be traced to Calvin. The first clue is Barth's own slightly embarrassed reading of Calvin. Barth tries to argue Calvin's failure to reject natural knowledge of God outright is explicable only because of 'the practical non-existence' of Aquinas in the sixteenth century: for that generation, Barth holds, there was not a sufficiently serious Thomist threat which needed to be countered, whereas now 'we are not in a position to repeat their statements without ... making them more

---

118. Karl Barth, 'No!', 76.

119. Cf. John Webster, *Karl Barth*, 2nd edn (London: Continuum, 2004), 76–83; McGrath, *Brunner*, 127–32.

120. Barth, 'No!', 96.

121. Barth, 'No!', 105–6; cf. Karl Barth, *The Epistle to the Romans*, 6th edn, trans. E. C. Hoskyns (London: Oxford University Press, 1968), 47.

122. Notably by Eugene F. Rogers, *Thomas Aquinas and Karl Barth: Sacred Doctrine and the Natural Knowledge of God* (Notre Dame, IN: University of Notre Dame Press, 1995), esp. 182–202.

123. Nicholas Wolterstorff, 'Introduction', in *Faith and Rationality: Reason and Belief in God*, ed. Alvin Plantinga and Nicholas Wolterstorff (Notre Dame, IN: University of Notre Dame Press, 1983), 7.

124. Alvin Plantinga, 'The Reformed Objection to Natural Theology', *Proceedings of the American Catholic Philosophical Association* 54 (1980): esp. 51–3; cf. Parker, *Knowledge of God*, 32–6; Niesel, *Calvin*, esp. 40–6.

pointed'.¹²⁵ Of course, the problem for Barth is not actually that Calvin is unclear or inadequately robust; it is that Calvin would not agree with him. As we have seen, Calvin, like Aquinas, did believe some natural knowledge of God was possible. However, as McGrath notes, the force of Barth's views has led to a 'disturbing tendency to read Calvin through Barthian spectacles' which has 'led to theological prejudices compromising historical scholarship' because of their 'highly selective readings of Calvin'.¹²⁶ By contrast, the argument of this study fits with a broad range of contemporary scholarship which shows Calvin, unlike Barth and the 'reformed objection', asserted natural knowledge of God in his theological method: hence Sudduth, for whom Barth's distorting influence means 'Calvin's positive view of the natural knowledge of God' has been 'marginalise[d] or ignore[d]' within much of the contemporary reformed tradition.¹²⁷ Similar views emerge in, for instance, Muller, Schreiner, Postema and Grabill.¹²⁸

Exploring the Barth-Brunner dispute and its effects thus reveals the distorting influence of Barth's reading of Calvin, a distortion Barth himself appears to recognize in his rather unconvincing attempt to excuse Calvin of the latter's failure to reject with sufficient force and clarity the possibility of natural knowledge of God. Calvin is clear: human reason can know some things about God without additional divine revelation, and reason (though seriously diminished by the Fall) has not lost entirely its natural capacities.

Summary

Taken together, these factors help explain why the presumption of an antagonism between Aquinas and Calvin has emerged. Calvin's rhetoric can sometimes mislead readers into thinking he is generally hostile to medieval theology, when in fact he has good reason for focusing on the contested yet shared territory of patristic witness, and he is usually careful to indicate he is opposing particular theologians or schools (notably the Sorbonne) rather than Aquinas. Subsequent readings of Aquinas have sometimes magnified points of difference when comparing Calvin and Aquinas directly on (say) the role of reason demonstrates congruity. And Barth had a seriously distorting effect on characterizations of Aquinas and Calvin by arguing the reformed tradition was hostile to the idea of natural knowledge of God and (wrongly) characterizing Calvin in that light. Isolating these factors reveals the essential continuity between Aquinas and Calvin on the relationship of scripture and reason in theological method and the possibility of a catholic-reformed consensus.

125. Barth, 'No!', 101.
126. McGrath, *Brunner*, 99.
127. Michael Sudduth, *The Reformed Objection to Natural Theology* (London: Routledge, 2016), 47.
128. See Muller, '*Duplex cognitio Dei*', 51–62; Schreiner, *Theater of His Glory*; Postema, 'Natural Theology', 423–4; Grabill, *Natural Law*, 70–97.

Summary

Characterizations of Anglicanism and of Hooker which rely on presumed antagonism of catholic and reformed perspectives have now been challenged on two limbs of their argument. Chapter 1 contested the first limb of such arguments by showing Aquinas, far from being uncongenial to reformed concerns, gave human reason a much more circumscribed place in his theological method than often supposed, and held to the unique authority of scripture as the source of the saving doctrines necessary for Christian faith. This chapter challenged the second limb of those arguments by showing that Calvin's view is broadly similar. In particular, it demonstrates that Calvin conceives natural reason as yielding real if limited knowledge of God and uses philosophy in theology albeit discriminatingly. It shows that, for Calvin as for Aquinas, revelation is the only way we can know the truths necessary for our salvation, the distinctly Christian truths about God; that these are now found only in scripture; and scripture's self-authentication, far from being an independent assertion that it authenticates itself, is a much more complex concept, reliant on the testimony of the Spirit and the divine authorship rather than the text as such. On reason and scripture, then, Calvin has more in common with Aquinas than often supposed. Reasons why the congruity between Aquinas and Calvin has been frequently overlooked were identified, notably the distorting effects of some readings of Aquinas and Calvin (especially Barth's reading of the latter) and Calvin's own occasionally misleading polemic.

If this account of Calvin and Aquinas is broadly right it has profound implications for how Richard Hooker, and Anglicanism, can be conceived. For if there is no catholic-reformed spectrum in the way many characterizations suppose, we need not place Hooker (or Anglicanism) somewhere on that spectrum but instead see him (and it) as plausibly both catholic and reformed. So the next chapter turns to Hooker's account of the theological warrants scripture and reason, showing how he shares substantially the theological method we have shown Aquinas and Calvin have in common.

Chapter 4

KNOWLEDGE OF GOD IN HOOKER

Introduction

Climbing the steps of his still relatively new pulpit in spring 1586, Richard Hooker, the Master of Temple Church (at the heart of London's legal district), and his deputy, Walter Travers, must have known that Hooker had not been the first choice for the role. Those involved in making the appointment had been unable to agree, a phenomenon not unknown in the Church of England then or now. Hooker had become Master the year before, a compromise candidate between the preferred options of the Archbishop of Canterbury and the courtier Lord Burghley. Burghley had wanted Travers, who was deputy under the previous Master and was a presbyterian: he believed the Bible directed that the church should not be run by bishops who oversaw priests but by a single rank of presbyters. Hooker was a conformist because he did not believe the Bible said any such thing and argued the Church of England should retain bishops; while he did not go so far as to say a presbyterian structure could never be justified, he did not believe there was good reason it should be introduced in England in the 1580s. The question of church governance was one of many where the two disagreed. Parish staff meetings no doubt became rather trying, also a phenomenon not unknown in the Church of England then or now.

The dispute between Hooker and Travers was first private, then public, then political; closeted conversations turned into a war of words from the pulpit and finally a series of appeals to the Privy Council. The key point for our purposes is that the dispute – with Hooker preaching sermons which Travers rebutted later in the day – prompted Thomas Fuller, seventy years later, to write that 'the pulpit spake pure Canterbury in the morning, and Geneva in the afternoon'.[1] Fuller's inference that Hooker, being a conformist, could not really also have been reformed has been a common feature of much of the scholarship since.

---

1. On this quotation, and Fuller's perspective, see Richard Bauckham, 'Hooker, Travers and the Church of Rome in the 1580s', *JEH* 29.1 (1978): 42; Corneliu C. Simut, *The Doctrine of Salvation in the Sermons of Richard Hooker* (Berlin: DeGruyter, 2005), 5–6.

Hooker and Travers certainly disagreed about whether to abandon bishops, and other things beside, but, as this chapter will show, this did not necessarily mean Hooker moved beyond the reformed theological spectrum. Indeed, as we shall see, although Hooker refused to believe what Calvin believed simply because Calvin believed it, there was no fundamental disagreement between Hooker and Calvin on the place of scripture and reason in theological method.

Many characterizations of Anglicanism and of Hooker depict them as essentially reformed or fundamentally catholic or some balancing act between the two.[2] The possibility of a tradition's or theologian's being both catholic and reformed has often been considered incoherent or even impossible because of a widespread presumption that 'catholic' and 'reformed' refer to opposite points on a spectrum. On such accounts, the greater the tradition's or the theologian's catholic affinities, the less reformed they must be and vice versa. However, earlier chapters sought to reframe the debate by advancing the argument that, on plausible readings of one catholic and one reformed theologian, the assertion of such a spectrum is itself wrong. Since on theological method Aquinas and Calvin are broadly convergent, this chapter situates Hooker in the confluence of the theological streams represented by Aquinas and Calvin and thereby shows the plausibility of interpreting him and his tradition as both catholic and reformed.

This chapter follows the pattern of the previous two to excavate Hooker's account of the relationship between two theological warrants, *scripture* and *reason*. It begins by tracing the limited but genuine knowledge of God which Hooker thought available to unaided reason and then turns to the effects of the Fall and the use of philosophy in theology; both examples demonstrate the real but circumscribed place of reason in his theological method. Next it discusses Hooker's account of revelation as the sole source of those truths about God, essential for our salvation and delivering Christian doctrine, which even at its most powerful reason could never discover. Finally, it addresses the sufficiency and authority of scripture. Here, against claims Hooker diverges from the reformed consensus on scripture, we show that (1) Hooker does hold to a *sola scriptura* view if this is understood as meaning scripture is the sole source of our saving knowledge of God, and (2) while Hooker does not say scripture is self-authenticating he is nonetheless congruent with Calvin. Reasons this convergence has been overlooked are then adduced. Throughout, the congruity of Hooker's stance with both Aquinas' and Calvin's will be identified. Hooker emerges as both catholic and reformed with a plausible and coherent theological method.

---

2. Good short surveys of the different characterizations are, e.g., Mark D. Chapman, *Anglican Theology* (London: T&T Clark, 2012), 104–7; W. Bradford Littlejohn, 'The Search for a Reformed Hooker', *Reformation and Renaissance Review* 16.1 (2014): 69–70. Fuller surveys are Michael Brydon, *The Evolving Reputation of Richard Hooker: An Examination of Responses, 1600–1714* (Oxford: Oxford University Press, 2006), 4–15; Diarmaid MacCulloch, 'Richard Hooker's Reputation', *English Historical Review* 117 (2002): 773–812.

Natural knowledge of God in Hooker

Introduction

Hooker's presbyterian opponents thought him dangerously unsound on the capacity of human reason. The *Christian Letter* of 1599 accused Hooker of holding 'in contempt the doctrine and faith' of the Church of England (*ACL* Pref., IV.7.19-20), in particular by believing some 'natural light, teaching knowledge of things necessary to salvation, which knowledge is not contained in holy scripture' (*ACL* 3, IV.11.31-2).[3] Were this true, Hooker would certainly be outside the reformed consensus embodied in the Church of England's Articles of Religion to which all its clergy had to subscribe.

Following Hooker's presbyterian opponents, many subsequent commentators have concluded that the substantial place of reason in Hooker's methodology means he cannot be within the reformed consensus on theological method. Hence, for instance, Voak concludes, 'the degree of knowledge that Hooker ascribes to mere natural persons was ... controversial ... in Reformed England'.[4] However, this section, considering first the possibilities and then the limitations of natural reason's knowledge of God, shows this characterization is wrong and that Hooker is not distant from Calvin. Hooker held reason could know some things, but only within clear limits, about God; in this he is consistent with views of both Aquinas and Calvin already traced.

The possibility of natural knowledge of God

Certainly, Hooker believed that human beings could, by their own reason and without recourse to a specifically supranatural source such as revelation, know some things about God. In 1582/3, in 'the earliest works which remain from Hooker's pen',[5] his two sermons on the letter of Jude, Hooker, describing 'the condition of Pagans and Turks', asserts,

> at the bare beholding of heaven and earth the infidel's heart by and by doth give him, that there is an eternal, infinite, immortal, and ever-living God; whose hands have fashioned and framed the world ... that it must be God which hath built and created all things.
>
> (*Jude* I.9, V.23.21-4, 26-7)

---

3. On the *Letter* and Hooker's response see *FLE*, IV.xiii-xliv.

4. Nigel Voak, *Richard Hooker and Reformed Theology: A Study of Reason, Will, and Grace* (Oxford: Oxford University Press, 2003), 129; similarly H. C. Porter, 'Hooker, the Tudor Constitution, and the *Via Media*', *SRH*, 103–7; A. J. Joyce, *Richard Hooker and Anglican Moral Theology* (Oxford: Oxford University Press, 2012), 72–97.

5. *FLE*, V.1. On Hooker's sermons and notes, which generally receive much less attention than the more famous *Laws*, see *FLE*, V.657-82 and Simut, *Sermons*.

This universal knowledge of God's existence, and key attributes of his infinity and so on, is accessible to those without specific knowledge of Christianity and is accessible by reason ('the light of natural reason hath put this wisdom in his reins', V.24.3-4).

Turning to the larger and later *Laws*,[6] Hooker near the start of his work asserts, as Aquinas and Calvin had, the possibility that, whether or not someone were a Christian, reasoned reflection on evidence accessible to their senses could lead them to conclude that God exists. This shared starting point should alert us to the congruity of their views. Hooker writes,

> The wise and learned among the heathens themselves, have all acknowledged some first cause, whereupon originally the being of all things depends ... They all confess therefore in the working of that first cause, that counsel is used, reason followed, a way observed, that is to say, constant order and law is kept, whereof itself must needs be author to itself.
>
> (*Laws*, I.2.3)

Citing the beliefs of Homer, Plato, Anaxagoras and the Stoics (who of course did not have the benefit of Christian revelation) in some sort of primal agency or first cause, Hooker believes God's existence and creativity can be learned naturally by reason alone. Hooker glosses Rom. 1 to argue for this generic natural knowledge of God accessible to reason: 'by attentive consideration of heaven and earth, we know of mere natural men the Apostle testifies how they knew ... God' (III.8.6; cf. Pref. 3.10). Hooker's interpretation of Rom. 1 echoes Calvin's and Aquinas', both of whom argued for a natural knowledge of God accessible to reason on the basis of the marks of the Creator being implanted in the creation.

But, again like Aquinas and Calvin, Hooker in these opening chapters of the *Laws* also establishes that this natural knowledge attainable by reason goes beyond God's existence and creativity. So reason by itself can discern 'constant order and law' are at work (I.2.3), which hints at a continuously operating divine hand: it can be 'discerned that the natural generation and process of all things receives order', an order called 'Providence' (I.3.4). Again, Hooker says 'the minds, of even mere natural men, have attained to know, not only that there is a God, but also what power, force, wisdom, and other properties that God has, and how all things depend on him' (I.8.6). Even those who are not near to God can discern many truths about God, such as that humans have higher goals than the sensual, inclining or desiring something more (I.5.2-3).[7]

---

6. On the context of the *Laws*, see McGrade, 'Introduction', *Laws*, I.xv-xxviii; on its contents, I.xxxii-cv.

7. Cf. P. A. Dominiak, *Richard Hooker: The Architecture of Participation* (London: T&T Clark, 2021), 127–30.

Thus, Kirby says, '[T]here is a natural knowledge of God as maker of all things, but not as Redeemer'.[8] Reason can know much about God for Hooker, but, in the light of the argument of earlier chapters, this does not distinguish him from Aquinas or Calvin.[9] Next we show Hooker sees this knowledge as circumscribed, as Aquinas and Calvin did.

The limits of natural knowledge of God

For Hooker, natural knowledge of God was seriously circumscribed. Thus, in his 1586 sermon on *Justification*, Hooker says, '[T]he light of nature causes the mind to apprehend those truths which are merely rational', which he contrasts with 'that saving truth which is far above the reach of human reason' (*Just.* 26, V.138.1-4).[10] This, of course, is precisely the distinction drawn by both Calvin and Aquinas: human reason may lead to some genuine knowledge of God but only within limits. For Hooker, natural knowledge of God is limited in its *scope*, its *clarity* and its *effects*.

On the *scope* of this natural knowledge of God, Hooker is clear from the outset that it is genuine but limited. So, for example, Hooker reminds his readers that the gap between divine subject and human knower is so great that our reason is simply inadequate to deliver much knowledge of God:

> Dangerous it were for the feeble brain of man to wade far into the doings of the most High … our soundest knowledge is to know that we know him not indeed as he is, neither can know him … our safest eloquence concerning him is our silence … his glory is inexplicable, his greatness above our capacity and reach.
> (*Laws*, I.2.2)

Hooker here echoes both Calvin and Aquinas in his general assertion that the ontological gap between human and divine results in an epistemological divide which cannot be bridged from the human side. For instance, while God's oneness and simplicity are discernible by reason, the knowledge 'in God a Trinity personal … subsists' is something 'far exceeding the possibility of man's conceit' (I.2.2). The generic knowledge of God's oneness is therefore evident to anyone by reason, but God's threeness cannot be known by reason.

---

8. W. J. T. Kirby, *The Theology of Richard Hooker in the Context of the English Reformation* (Princeton, NJ: Princeton Theological Seminary, 2000), 16.

9. Kirby, *English Reformation*, 14–17.

10. On the 'twofold epistemology' articulated in Hooker's preaching see Simut, *Sermons*, 129, 133–6, 142; though Simut seems at best careless with his terminology, for instance, he incongruously says that for Hooker 'nothing of God's reality can be known by the reason of man' (247), which seems hard to square with the notion of a twofold knowledge with real but different truths yielded by reason and revelation.

Again, Hooker thinks we can discern naturally that something is wrong within the created order; even the heathen can see that there is some 'defect in the matter of things natural'. However, 'the true original cause thereof' is not something that can be discerned by reason; to learn that this defect is the product of 'divine malediction, laid for the sin of man … was above their merely natural capacity and understanding' (I.3.3). Later, Hooker repeats the 'mysteries of our religion are above the reach of our understanding, above the discourse of man's reason' (V.63.1). Here then Hooker crucially distinguishes between the kinds of knowledge of God reason can deliver and those kinds of knowledge of God it is simply inadequate to attain.

On the *clarity* of this natural knowledge of God, Hooker is clear human reason is inadequate to the task of knowing God. Indeed, if Voak were right to parse Hooker as controversially optimistic about reason, it would be hard to account for Hooker's question in his sermon on *Pride*, 'Do we think it so easy for men to define what law doth warrant?' (V.337.16-7). Again, he observes, '[H]ow hard it is oftentimes for even the wisest and skillfullest to see what is justice and what is not' (V.339.7-9). So Hooker says we lack 'right understanding' of divine 'equity and justice' (V.346.19-20). The point recurs in the *Laws*, for instance where Hooker notes, 'so far as the natural understanding even of sundry whole nations been darkened, that they have not discerned … gross iniquity' (*Laws*, I.12.2). These are observations about human reason's power in relation to the *natural* order, the sphere of natural knowledge. Since human reason is so limited in clarity in the *natural* sphere, how much more must it be confused and unclear in the *supernatural* sphere.

On the *effects* of this natural knowledge of God, Hooker also emphasizes reason's limitations. If human reason is insufficient to investigate adequately natural matters, it certainly cannot enquire into supernatural ones (e.g., *Laws*, I.8.1). In particular, reason cannot discern by itself the truths we need for our salvation. Since all human works are impure, Hooker writes, 'what possibility is there … to be saved' by any natural means? Therefore, 'there rests … no way to salvation, or if any, then surely a way which is supernatural' (I.11.5). So 'the light of nature is never able to find out any way of attaining the reward of bliss'; and 'from salvation therefore and life all flesh being excluded' by any natural means, God alone can deliver saving truth (I.11.6). We may naturally desire to overcome our condition, but we cannot naturally discover the means to achieve this.[11]

Summary

Assertions such as Voak's that Hooker is overly optimistic about the possibilities of human reason are therefore questionable. Although Hooker attributes much potential to unaided human reason, it is always limited and can never attain the saving knowledge of God. This account is consistent with Calvin's reformed

---

11. W. J. T. Kirby, 'Reason and Law', *CRH*, 259–60.

views.¹² Despite categorizations of Hooker which assume the more catholic his account of reason is the less reformed he must be,¹³ when the limitations Aquinas places on natural knowledge of God, and the possibilities Calvin attributes to it, are properly understood, Hooker emerges as firmly within their convergence. We next turn to the Fall and to philosophy in theology, showing here too Hooker shares the accounts of both theologians.

Reason and its limitations

Introduction

Chapter 2 showed Aquinas is often considered uncongenial from a reformed perspective because of his supposed failure to give sufficient weight to the effects of the Fall on human reason or by his excessive use of philosophy in theology. Similar arguments are made about Hooker, notably by his presbyterian opponents and those later commentators who characterize him as outside the reformed consensus on these questions. The plausibility of such comparisons has already been severely challenged by showing that Aquinas gives more weight to the Fall than often supposed, and Calvin rather less; and similarly that Calvin, like Aquinas, uses philosophy in theology but only within the limits of doctrinal commitments. Tracing Hooker's view on both questions locates him firmly within that reformed, catholic consensus.

The Fall

Hooker's presbyterian opponents believed he did not give sufficient weight to the Fall's effects on the operation of human reason. The *Christian Letter* accused Hooker of 'pretend[ing] the natural way of finding out laws by reason' could 'guide the will unto that which is good', whereas they thought that humanity 'hath no such reason without the grace of God ... in the state of corruption, as in deed all men naturally now are' (*ACL* 5, IV.19.7-11). This broader view that Hooker gives insufficient account to the effects of the Fall on reason is followed by contemporary commentators such as Voak, who argues it is 'quite mistaken' to see Hooker as within the reformed perspective on this point.¹⁴ Voak adds that 'Calvin and Aquinas disagree' about 'the nature and extent' of the corruption caused by the Fall and that Hooker follows Aquinas against Calvin in holding only a 'relatively moderate conception' of this corruption.¹⁵

---

12. Thus Kirby, 'Reason and Law', 263-4; Nigel Atkinson, *Richard Hooker and the Authority of Scripture, Tradition, and Reason: Reformed Theologian of the Church of England* (Vancouver: Regent College Publishing, 1997), 11-17.

13. For instance, J. S. Marshall, *Hooker and the Anglican Tradition: An Historical and Theological Study of Hooker's Ecclesiastical Polity* (London: A&C Black, 1963), 55.

14. Voak, *RHRT*, 149.

15. Voak, *RHRT*, 144; the unclarity of Voak's assessment is apparent because he almost immediately goes on to say that Hooker and Calvin 'hold similar views on the devastating consequences of the Fall', *RHRT*, 150.

Of course, the notion that human beings could naturally know some things by reason, even about God, does not itself indicate divergence from the reformed perspective since Calvin (as Chapter 3 showed) believed as much. Furthermore, Hooker also believed this capacity was severely diminished by the Fall. Preparing his response to the *Christian Letter*, Hooker wrote,

> There are certain words as Nature, Reason, and Will and suchlike which wheresoever you find named you suspect them presently as bugs words, because what they mean you not in deed as you ought to apprehend. You have heard that man's Nature is corrupt his reason blind his will perverse. Whereupon under colour of condemning corrupt nature you condemn nature.
>
> (*ACL* 5, IV.17.23-9)[16]

Here Hooker is arguing that the presbyterians have thrown the baby out with the bathwater. Hooker would agree that reason does not now operate properly because of the Fall, but this does not mean it is incapable of *any* proper operation at all. Elsewhere he points out that 'to make nothing evident of itself to man's understanding were to take away the possibility of knowing anything at all' (*Laws*, I.8.4). Hooker insists that just because reason is severely limited, it does not mean it should be condemned (III.8.5). If reason really did have no capacity at all after the Fall, humans would literally know nothing at all without revelation – a ludicrous assertion, since even a sixteenth-century presbyterian could think for themselves.

However, as Grislis points out, while Hooker will not condemn nature outright in the way his opponents do, he nonetheless is clear that sin seriously affects the ability of reason.[17] Thus, '[t]here neither is, nor never was any mere natural man absolutely righteous in himself, that is to say, without sin' (*Just.* 1, V.105.24-106.1; cf. *Just.* 7, V.116.5-6). Sin, as Hooker states in an undated funeral sermon,[18] corrupts nature (*Remedy*, V.376.21-3), in particular diminishing reason's ability to conceive good ends or means properly. So, rather than seeking that eternal life which is fear's only true remedy, 'corrupt nature's suggestions are for the safety of temporal life' (V.376.26-7).

Developing this theme elsewhere, Hooker insists reason's capacities in the supernatural sphere were severely diminished by the Fall. Thus, 'the minds of all men being so darkened as they are by the foggy damp of original corruption, it cannot be that any man's heart living should be ... enlightened in the knowledge ... of that wherein his salvation stands' (*Certainty*, V.71.16-20). He says elsewhere, 'all flesh must of necessity fall down and confess, We are not dust and ashes but worse, our minds from the highest to the lowest are not right ... not capable of

---

16. On this passage, see Barry G. Rasmussen, 'Presence and Absence: Richard Hooker's Sacramental Hermeneutic', in *Richard Hooker and the English Reformation*, ed. W. J. T. Kirby (Dordrecht: Kluwer Academic, 2003), 170; Dominiak, *Participation*, 77–80.

17. Egil Grislis, 'The Role of Sin in the Theology of Richard Hooker', *Anglican Theological Review* 84.4 (2002): 882–4.

18. *FLE*, V.263.

that blessedness which we naturally seek' (*Pride*, V.312.24-7). Hooker makes the same point in the *Dublin Fragments*, part of his response to the *Christian Letter*, when he says the 'natural powers and faculties therefore of man's mind are through our native corruption so weakened and of themselves so averse from God' (*DF* 2, V.103.13-7). It is hard to square this emphatic language with the argument Hooker somehow underestimates the effects of the Fall, at least as far as it removes entirely reason's ability to find a way to our salvation.[19]

But it is not just the supernatural possibilities of reason that Hooker believes are affected by the Fall; reason's operation in the natural sphere is also severely impeded. Hooker insists the Fall upends the proper hierarchy in the mind:

> Whereas the orderly disposition of the mind of man should be this, perturbations and appetites all kept in awe by a moderate and sober will; will in all things framed by reason; reason directed by God; this Babylonian had his mind as it were turned upside down ... wilfulness tyrannized over reason, and brutish sensuality over will.
>
> (*Pride*, V.314.15-23)

This disorder in human nature means reason's natural operation is diminished even within its natural sphere: so 'man degenerating and transgressing ... loses the benefit of things which in the world working according to their natures might otherwise have yielded him, and now do not' (*Proverbs*, V.416.20-3). As Almasy says, this insistence on the limitations of fallen reason in its natural sphere is a clear point of convergence between Calvin and Hooker[20] (and, indeed, Aquinas).

Again, precisely at a moment in the *Laws* where Hooker is praising reason's capacity, he simultaneously emphasizes its limits:

> The search of knowledge is a thing painful ... the root hereof divine malediction wherewith the instruments being weakened wherewithal the soul (especially in reasoning) does work ... by reason of that original weakness in the instruments, without which the understanding part is not able in this world by discourse to work.
>
> (*Laws*, I.7.7)

In the same passage Hooker blames Satan, our over-hasty wills and sheer habit as factors which mean we cannot now reason properly. Elsewhere he summarizes this point: our 'evil moral disposition ... permits not the mind to see what does shine before it' (V.63.2). Hooker deploys the metaphors of blindness (I.8.1, III.9.3) and sleepiness (*ACL* 5, IV.18.15-22) to make the same point. In the natural sphere of its own operation, then, the Fall diminishes reason's ability; so, Hooker asserts,

---

19. Cf. R. D. Williams, *Anglican Identities* (London: DLT, 2004), 24-5.

20. Rudolph P. Almasy, 'Richard Hooker's Worries about the Mind: The Path to Certainty', *Perichoresis* 11.1 (2013): 36-7.

'lewd and wicked custom … may be of force even in plain things to smother the light of natural understanding' (*Laws*, I.8.11). Hooker's chastened account of fallen reason is far from the optimism about the warrant many interpretations assert. As Almasy rightly concludes, 'Hooker does indeed worry about the mind, the mind as vulnerable, changeable, deceivable, fragile, and full of curiosity and doubt … easily perplexed, agitated, plagued by too much mental activity'.[21]

Indeed, and perhaps unsurprisingly given Hooker's interest in law,[22] Hooker argues there are specific implications of the Fall for the framing of human law. Even in circumstances where we could have discerned what laws to follow, Hooker says, our fallen minds now cannot readily discover or do the right. So he urges law-makers to remember that fallen human wills are 'obstinate, rebellious' and that laws must be aimed at 'man … in regard of his depraved mind' (I.10.1). He continues, '[E]ven those laws of reason which (man retaining his original integrity) had been sufficient to direct each particular person in all his affairs and duties are not sufficient … now that man and his offspring are grown thus corrupt and sinful' (I.10.13).[23] The need for the establishment of positive human laws to govern natural concourse is, for Hooker, a product of the weakening of reason in its natural sphere attributable to the Fall and is further evidence that he holds a far less optimistic view of reason than often supposed.

So, against Hooker's presbyterian opponents and authors like Voak, Williams rightly contests the depiction of Hooker as diverging from the reformed consensus on this point.[24] Partly, as Bouwsma highlights, this is because scholars have often over-estimated Calvin's pessimism about the fallen mind, in particular because they take 'total depravity' to mean that humanity has no natural capacity at all. But when Calvin's position is understood properly, says Bouwsma, we can see Hooker

> shared Calvin's belief in the total depravity of fallen humanity, which means, of course, not that there is nothing good left in human beings, but that there is no privileged area of the personality left untouched by original sin, notably including the operations of the mind.[25]

For Hooker, the Fall's effect is total, diminishing the whole human person including its reason; so Hooker praises reason but emphasizes repeatedly the problems caused by sin for reason both in the supernatural sphere (it cannot find any way to salvation) and the natural sphere (its ability to regulate human life

---

21. Almasy, 'Hooker's Worries', 46.

22. On Hooker's contribution to legal theory, see Ethan Shagan, 'The Ecclesiastical Polity', in *The Oxford Handbook of English Law and Literature, 1500–1700*, ed. Lorna Hutson (Oxford: Oxford University Press, 2017), esp. 344–7.

23. Cf. McGrade, 'Introduction', *Laws* I.xli.

24. Williams, *Anglican Identities*, 26; cf. Ranall Ingalls, 'Sin and Grace', *CRH*, 152.

25. William Bouwsma, 'Hooker in the Context of European Cultural History', *RHCCC*, 52.

and interaction being much diminished). As Dominiak rightly concludes, 'Hooker retains a sanguine but humble appraisal of the "natural light of reason" because he takes the epistemological limitations of sin seriously'.[26]

Philosophy

Having contested characterizations of Hooker as diverging from the reformed perspective on the effects of the Fall, we now challenge assertions that his use of philosophy in theology diverges from the reformed perspective. Again, the basis of this case is that the catholic and reformed perspectives of Aquinas and Calvin are far more congenial than often supposed. Hooker's approach is now shown to be firmly in keeping with that catholic-reformed consensus.

A surprising but revealing starting point is a disagreement over whether God gives sermons directly to the preacher or whether it is permissible to use other, non-scriptural sources. Hooker thought sermons come from 'the wit of man', human constructions attempting to elucidate divine truth. He recognizes sermons can fall short: 'oftentimes accordingly taste too much of that overcorrupt fountain which they came' (*Laws*, V.22.10), namely the fountain of every human's corrupt mind. Quoting this passage, the author of the *Christian Letter* challenged Hooker, insisting sermons were 'the pure word of God' and 'the seed is the gift of God, and this is done by the grace of God' (*ACL* 12, IV.34.10, 15-6). The relevance of this disagreement is that the presbyterians argued that philosophy could not be used in preaching. They objected to those 'sermons … who instead of the pure Word of God do most curiously bring into the pulpit Poets, Philosophers, Rhetoricians, Physicians, Schoolmen … they think may appear fine and smooth to their hearers' (IV.35.3-6). This was a strand of their broader criticism that Hooker made use of both classical philosophers (especially Aristotle) and medieval scholastics: 'in all your discourse, the patriarch of philosophers … and the ingenious schoolmen, almost in all points have some finger' (*ACL* 20, IV.65.18). Particular ire was reserved for Aristotle, who they considered 'unto divinity [as] is darkness to light',[27] and they accused Hooker of being 'another Aristotle by a certain metaphysical and cryptical method' (*ACL* 21, IV.72.14-5).

Hooker's autograph notes on this passage repeat his assertion that '[s]ermons are framed by the wit of man' (*ACL* 12, IV.34.5). And his reasoning is intriguing: it is that his presbyterian opponents are in fact *undermining* the authority of scripture by elevating the authority of sermons to the same degree. If 'sermons be the word of God in the same sense that the scriptures are his word … then we must hold Calvin's sermons are holy scripture' (IV.32.8-10). By contrast, Hooker asks, '[S]hould we even impart the most peculiar glory of the word of God to that which is not his word?' (*Laws*, V.22.10). Hooker's insistence on the priority of scripture, and his refusal to accord the same authority to sermons, indicates a

---

26. Dominiak, *Participation*, 104.
27. See Rudolph P. Almasy, 'Rhetoric and Apologetics', *CRH*, 145–7.

wider methodological point: while philosophy never carries the same weight as scripture in theology, that does not mean it cannot be useful.

On some points, Hooker certainly does use philosophical sources. For example, he believed that pagan philosophers could have learned of God's existence by natural reason, a belief he shares, of course, with Calvin, so can hardly be said to be diverging from the reformed perspective. Again, he calls Aristotle 'the Arch-Philosopher' and 'the mirror of human wisdom' (I.4.1, I.10.3). So, for example, he cites approvingly Aristotle's account of the good and the beautiful (I.8.1-3).

Hooker also challenges his opponents' exegesis of the New Testament to argue that philosophy is a permissible interlocutor in theology. He depicts his opponents' position as resisting all philosophy on the basis of St. Paul's warning to 'beware of philosophy' in Col. 2.8. But, says Hooker, this misreads the passage which is a warning against 'that philosophy, which to bolster heresy or error casts a fraudulent show of reason', not against 'that philosophy, which is true and sound knowledge attained by natural discourse of reason' (III.8.3). He continues that Col. 2.8 is a warning to be selective in the use of philosophy, 'to be armed with that true and sincere philosophy ... against that deceitful and vain' (III.8.7).

Hooker also cites patristic precedent for the critical appropriation of philosophy in theology; for which 'many great Philosophers have been unsound in belief' yet 'many sound in belief have also been great Philosophers'. For many of the ancient fathers it was 'needful to use the principal instrument' of heretics and pagans, namely 'the light of reason'; hence, 'in the Fathers' writings there are sundry sharp invectives against Heretics, even for their very philosophical reasoning' (III.8.8). So as Kirby says, Hooker appeals to 'the authority of philosophy in general and of Aristotle in particular'[28] adducing both a scriptural basis and the early church to justify this appeal.

But Hooker's relationship with Aristotle and philosophy is more complicated than simple appropriation; as we have already seen, there is a conceptual distinction between philosophy which is useful and philosophy which is not. For instance, he is happy to draw on Aristotle's account of necessary and contingent causes in his discussion of predestination (*DF* 19-23, IV.123-8), but we then hear no more about Aristotle's views on providence and Hooker turns at once to deal at length relevant scriptural passages. Here then is a vital clue: Hooker is happy to draw on Aristotle as a *tool* where his concepts help clarify or elucidate something, but as the *source* for Christian doctrine he turns rather to scripture.

Indeed, as Lane does with Calvin, McGrade points out Hooker makes far more references to patristic literature than either scholastic or classic sources – four times as many, in fact.[29] Moreover, if we consider specifically where references to (say) Aristotle appear, Hooker's appeals to the Philosopher are largely confined to matters other than Christian doctrine. As McGrade goes on to note, Aristotle appears mostly in Hooker's discussions of the natural knowledge of God accessible

---

28. Kirby, 'Reason and Law', 262.
29. A. S. McGrade, 'Classical, Patristic, and Medieval Sources', *CRH*, 52.

to all in Book I, his treatment of honour in Book VII and his discourse on the state and civil law in Book VIII.[30] And, like Calvin, Hooker considered himself on safer ground when appealing to the patristic era. A particular principle from the medieval period is dismissed as simply 'scholastic invention', in part on the grounds that 'the Fathers have it not' (*DF* 17, IV.118-9). And perhaps the single most striking example of Hooker's critical approach to his philosophical and scholastic sources is his outright rejection of transubstantiation in *Laws* V.67. He believes even to discuss transubstantiation or consubstantiation is vain and useless (V.67.6) and neither the witness of scripture nor of antiquity supports either approach (V.67.8-11). The simple words of Christ recorded in scripture suffice for Hooker, to prove that Christ is present in the sacrament, the manner of his presence not being something susceptible to human investigation. The quantitative and qualitative preference for scripture and the patristic era, then, further undermines the notion that Hooker is overly indebted to philosophy.

Furthermore, where Hooker discusses explicitly how the theologian can draw on philosophy, he is at pains to express its limitations. So, in similar terms to Calvin, Hooker cites Homer, Anaxagoras, Plato and the Stoics as evidence that some pagan philosophers rightly inferred the existence of a first cause by reason alone. Yet, he says, those heathens did not know as much about the first cause as a Christian does; their disordered thinking is revealed in the occurrence of polytheism, pantheism or demon-worship (I.3.4, I.4.3). And no pagan philosopher could know by reason the saving truths which were above reason (I.11.5).

And, in similar terms to Aquinas, Hooker points out that even where philosophical learning is possible in *principle* it is a difficult and unreliable way of knowledge in *practice*. So, considering the hereafter, Hooker writes,

> They are, says St Augustine, but a few and they endued with great ripeness of wit and judgment free from all such affairs as might trouble their meditations, instructed in the sharpest and subtlest points of learning, who have, and that very hardly, been able to find out but only the immortality of the soul. The resurrection of the flesh what man did ever at any time dream of?
>
> (*Laws*, I.12.2)

Philosophy, then, is severely limited. It requires effort, intelligence and time to study, which of course few people have. It can only falteringly apprehend truths (such as the immortality of the soul) which are in principle within its reach; it cannot attain at all other truths (such as the resurrection of the body) which are intrinsically beyond its grasp. Part of the need for divine revelation, Hooker says, is that reliance on natural reason alone would lead to 'the certain loss of infinite thousands of souls most undoubtedly now saved' (I.12.2). Indeed, in a passage reminiscent of Aquinas' image of the little old lady, Hooker concludes,

---

30. McGrade, 'Sources', 77-9.

Our Saviour made choice of 12 simple unlearned men, that the greater their lack of wisdom was, the more admirable they might appear, which God supernaturally endued them with from heaven ... They studied for no tongue, they spoke with all; of themselves they were rude, and knew not so much as how to premediate, the spirit gave them speech and eloquent utterance.

(III.8.10)

Philosophy is, then, for Hooker, permissible as a tool in theology. It can reach some useful truths, and it can provide useful language or concepts for theology. But Hooker is far from the uncritical appropriator of philosophy that his presbyterian opponents suggest. He places it within strict limits and its use is always governed by wider theological commitments.

Summary

On these two contested questions, the effects of the Fall on reason and the place of philosophy in theology, Hooker is considerably less positive about reason than many observers assert. Hooker believes in the total depravity of the fallen person, in the sense that all aspects of the person, including the mind, are severely diminished. Hooker's critical and selective use of philosophy is constrained by scriptural and methodological commitments. Hooker's methodological stance puts him firmly within the terrain occupied by both Calvin and Aquinas and so is best depicted as both catholic and reformed in his account of reason. And reason's limitations, both inherent in its nature and because of the Fall, mean that there are truths which humans need to learn which they cannot learn for themselves, hence the need for revelation, to which we turn next.

Reason and revelation

Introduction

A. S. McGrade observes, Hooker 'has the unusual distinction of being severely criticized for both hypo- and hyper-rationalism'.[31] By this he means that some critics fear Hooker elevates human reason over the supra-rational elements of Christian faith, namely those aspects of knowledge which come from revelation; while others contend reason is essentially overwhelmed by Hooker's insistence on the need for some other source of knowledge. The purpose of this section is to challenge both kinds of critic by tracing the sophisticated dialectic of reason and revelation in Hooker, in which each has a distinct (though not separate) purpose in our knowledge of God. By considering first the need for revelation and then the shape of reason, we see how Hooker (like Aquinas and Calvin) believes both that

---

31. A. S. McGrade, 'The Coherence of Hooker's Polity: The Books on Power', *Journal of the History of Ideas* 24.2 (1963): 166.

revelation alone delivers the saving truths of faith which reason cannot attain and also that his account of reason is much richer than often realized.

The need for revelation

The 'hyper-rationalist' position is represented by, for instance, Porter, who categorizes the *Laws* as 'a celebration of "our natural faculty of reason."'[32] Similarly, Munz says Hooker 'established the complete autonomy of reason over the whole of life'.[33] But tracing Hooker's account of the need for revelation belies such characterizations, for Hooker clearly believes reason alone can only reveal certain truths: natural, not supernatural ones. As with Calvin and Aquinas, Hooker's belief in the inherent limitations of reason is closely connected with his assertion that we need revelation for those saving truths of faith. Thus, Hooker writes in an early sermon that the 'doctrine of salvation' must be 'looked for by faith' in Christ, but this is 'a thing improbable to a natural man', so God 'sent immediately from himself to reveal these things unto the world' (*Jude* I.5, V.18.3-5, 12-4, 18-9). As Simut notes, the sermons demonstrate Hooker's insistence that we lack the ability to gain salvation by ourselves as it is beyond our capacity, hence the need for God to reveal it to us.[34]

Elsewhere, Hooker insists there is 'no saving knowledge possible, without the sanctifying Spirit of God ... to find out supernatural laws there is no natural way, because they have not their foundation or ground in the course of nature' (*DF* 7, IV.106.15-17). This supernatural or saving knowledge, says Hooker, is those 'mysteries of our redemption through the blood of Jesus Christ' which could not be discovered 'had not God himself revealed the same' (IV.106.22-6). So in 'matters above the reach of the reason, and beyond the compass of nature ... only faith is to judge, by God's revealed law what is right' (*DF* 9, IV.108.19-20).

Similarly, turning to the *Laws* reveals a clear distinction, a twofold knowledge of God, where reason delivers natural truths about God but only revelation can deliver the supernatural truths needed for salvation. Thus, in addition to 'sensual' and 'intellectual' laws, Hooker conceives a category of 'spiritual and divine' laws which are 'somewhat above the capacity of reason' (*Laws*, I.11.4). This category includes in particular those truths about our redemption through Christ, 'which could not have entered into the heart of man as much as to conceive or to imagine, if God himself had not revealed it extraordinarily' (I.11.5). 'Laws therefore concerning these things that are supernatural ... have not in nature any cause ... but were by the voluntary appointment of God ordained besides nature' (I.11.6). So, Hooker continues, while 'the law of reason does somewhat direct man how to honour God as their Creator', only 'divine law' can teach us there is 'an everlasting Saviour' (I.16.5). The resonance with Calvin's distinction between the knowledge

---

32. Porter, 'Tudor Constitution and *Via Media*', 103.
33. Munz, *Place of Hooker*, 62, cf. 54–5.
34. Simut, *Sermons*, 111, 160, 173.

of God as Creator, accessible to reason, and the knowledge of God as Redeemer, attainable only by revelation, is clear.[35]

Alongside the truths of our redemption, 'articles about the Trinity are matters of faith, and must be believed' (III.3.2, cf. I.14.2); such articles of faith can only reach us by revelation (III.3.3). In these matters of faith, Hooker continues, reason is no source and we rely wholly on revelation. Recall the 'bare beholding of heaven and earth' can, for Hooker, prompt reason to conclude in the existence of a creative God. But, as Hooker explains elsewhere, this 'bare contemplation of heaven and earth' yields only one sort of knowledge of God and is not

> sufficient to give as much as the least spark of light concerning the very principal mysteries of our faith; and whatsoever we may learn by them, the same we can only attain to know according to the manner of the natural sciences, which mere discourse of wit and reason finds out, whereas the things which we properly believe, be only such as are received upon the credit of divine testimony.
>
> (V.22.5)

The distinction is drawn clearly between contemplation of the creation which may yield some knowledge of God and the need for 'divine testimony' to reveal the mysteries of faith which reason cannot grasp.

A useful example of the distinction is Hooker's comparison of Festus and St. Paul, glossing Acts 25.19. St. Paul, inspired by God (by 'the special operation of God's good grace and spirit'), could speak of Christ's passion and resurrection. By contrast, 'Festus a mere natural man, an infidel, a Roman ... heard him, but could not reach to that whereof he spoke; the suffering and the rising of Christ from the dead he rejects as idle superstitious fancies not worth the hearing' (III.8.6). The distinction between the inspired believer's knowledge and the mere natural person's illustrates Hooker's broader concept of the limits of what the intelligent outsider can infer by reason (Festus) when compared with the knowledge available by revelation to the believer (Paul). Voak's assertion that Hooker attributed a controversial degree of knowledge to the natural person is therefore flawed: the natural person, unaided by revelation, can only attain generic and faltering knowledge of God.

The charge of hyper-rationalism, and the attendant characterization of Hooker as outside the reformed perspective, is therefore hard to sustain when his account of revelation is traced. Unlike the wide potential for reason in matters other than those pertaining to salvation, Hooker consistently insists on the need for saving knowledge of God from a source other than human reason and repeatedly emphasizes that we cannot discover the articles of faith or the truths of our redemption from reason alone.[36] To challenge the converse accusation of hypo-rationalism is the next task.

---

35. Kirby, *English Reformation*, 14–17.

36. W. David Neelands rightly critiques Munz's accusation of hyper-rationalism for failing to grasp this distinction – 'The Theology of Grace of Richard Hooker' (ThD diss., Trinity College Toronto, 1988), 120–2.

The shape of reason

If Hooker clearly is not hyper-rationalist because he is adamant about reason's weakness and the need for revelation, neither is he hypo-rationalist, as further probing his account of reason shows. Accusations of hypo-rationalism are levelled, for instance, by Hillerdal, who brands Hooker a 'philosophical failure' who 'failed in his attempt to reconcile reason with revelation', specifically because revelation overwhelms reason and so Hooker 'only seemingly remains the philosopher who uses nothing but reason where all the time he has supposed … the light of revelation'.[37] This is an odd accusation; Hooker, as we have seen, no more tries to be a philosopher who relies only on reason than Aquinas does. On Hillerdal's underlying critique, that reason is somehow supplanted or overwhelmed by revelation, a fuller tracing of the shape of reason will show Hooker has a rich conception of reason. For, like Aquinas and Calvin, Hooker, though aware of reason's limits, grounds its role in theology in a rich theological base, while also emphasizing that revelation and reason, distinct in their function and their authority, must nonetheless not be separated or conceived over against each other.

The most basic grounding of reason's authority and its complementary role to revelation is because both reason and revelation come from God. This principle is established at the outset of the *Laws*:

> There are but two ways whereby the spirit leads men into all truth: the one extraordinary, the other common; the one belonging but to some few, the other extending itself to all that are of God; the one that which we call by a special divine excellence Revelation, the other Reason.
>
> (Pref. 3.10)

Both reason (the ordinary means of natural knowledge, common to all humans) and revelation (the extraordinary means of supernatural knowledge, available only to the believer) are in principle legitimate and complementary sources of divine truth because they both flow from a single divine source. And this gives to both reason and revelation a kind of integrity: divinely given but distinct.

Specifically, as Dominiak's outstanding study demonstrates, for Hooker the legitimate place of human reason in theology is grounded on the theological premise that reason is a created, God-given gift. Following Aquinas, Hooker sees reason as an effect in us which resembles our divine cause (I.5.2, V.56.1) but also one which God must guide if it is to work properly. Thus, glossing Rom. 2.14, Hooker defines 'the light of reason' as the means by which 'God illuminates everyone which comes into the world' (I.8.3). The divine origin of this faculty is made clear. But it is not that reason is given to humanity and then acts as an independent capacity; its abilities are dependent upon the continuous, divine creative gift. Hence, 'concerning the force of man's natural understanding … there

---

37. Gunner Hillerdal, *Reason and Revelation in Richard Hooker* (Lund: CWK Gleerup, 1962), 148.

is no kind of faculty or power in man or any other creature, which can rightly perform the functions allotted to it, without perpetual aid and concurrence of that supreme cause of all things' (I.8.11).[38] As Dominiak concludes, 'gratuitous divine donation and activity are required even for natural knowing'.[39] Indeed, to devalue the potential of human reason, as Hooker's opponents do, is to debase the work of God itself, which in creation bestows and sustains reason, that reason in turn resembling and participating in the divine reason which causes it. The source of reason is 'God himself, who being that light which none can approach to, has sent out these lights whereof we are capable, even as so many sparkles resembling the bright fountain from which they rise' (III.8.9), so it is theologically dangerous to demean those 'sparkles' of reason, as the presbyterians do in reducing the source of knowledge of God to scripture alone (II.1.4).[40]

The divine activity which guides our reasoning is of course the Holy Spirit.[41] Voak and Kirby, disagreeing about Hooker's reformed credentials, both agree on the importance of the pneumatological aspect of his account of reason. Reason requires 'the special grace of the holy ghost' to 'concur … to the enlightening of our minds' (III.8.15), and 'the discourse of reason' must be 'aided with the influence of divine grace' (III.8.18).[42] If the Spirit is needed to guide reason in natural matters, how much more in supernatural ones? Thus, Hooker writes, 'touching the force and use of man's reason in things divine', nothing 'could be done, without the aid and assistance of God's most blessed Spirit' (III.8.18). As Stafford suggests, one of Hooker's key arguments against the presbyterians was they risked separating the Spirit from the operation of human reason;[43] whereas, for Hooker, understanding reason to be a gift in creation and dependent on the Spirit for its operation allows us to see its legitimate, theologically grounded role.

One area where Hooker may be rather clearer than either Aquinas or Calvin is that he insists explicitly that the exercise of reason in shaping doctrine must always be *corporate*, not individual. Hooker expresses a repeated aversion to the attribution of theological authority to any one individual, whether a prominent named individual within a tradition or an individual believer's private conscience.[44] At the outset of the *Laws* he fears that the elevation of Luther and Calvin within their churches 'too much authorised the judgments of a few' (Pref. 4.6). 'Nature', Hooker observes warily,

---

38. For these references and analysis, see Dominiak, *Participation*, 96–7.

39. Dominiak, *Participation*, 97.

40. Dominiak, *Participation*, 145–8; cf. W. David Neelands, 'Hooker on Scripture, Reason, and Tradition', RHCCC, 88.

41. M. E. C. Perrott, 'Richard Hooker and the Problem of Authority in the Elizabethan Church', *JEH* 49 (1998): 49.

42. Cf. Nigel Voak, 'Richard Hooker and the Principle of *Sola Scriptura*', *JTS* 59.1 (2008): 124–5 with Kirby, 'Reason and Law', 269–70.

43. John K. Stafford, 'Richard Hooker's Doctrine of the Holy Spirit', (PhD diss., University of Manitoba, 2005), 115–16.

44. Williams, 'Foreword', xxiii; Perrott, 'Authority', 54–5.

'worketh in us a love of our own counsels. The contradiction of others is a fan to inflame that love' (Pref. 2.6; cf. 5.3). This fear of private judgement suggests that what is needed is public and communal judgement; hence, in Book VIII, Hooker limits even the power of the monarch, who can in many cases only act with the consent of Parliament or Convocation (VIII.3.3, VIII.6.11). Chapter 5 will show the corporate discernment of the church through its councils, particularly the first four ecumenical councils, has special authority in decision-making.[45] Hooker here advances the debate by emphasizing reason's corporate dimension. Chapter 6 will suggest this understanding reason as a corporate act of the church's discernment could be a major benefit of Hooker's approach when considering contemporary debates about faith and reason. But it also further undermines the case that Hooker's conceives reason as excessively autonomous, for it is never the lone act of a thinking individual.[46]

Hooker's account of reason, moreover, cannot be treated in isolation from his wider theological vision. Hillerdal appears to think it can, when he expresses surprise that Hooker can move from discussing the capacity of reason to emphasizing the need for grace, puzzled by Hooker's 'sudden, astonishing references to the grace of God'.[47] But, as Neelands replies, Hooker 'has all along recognized that reason must be aided by faith in matters theological, both because of its disorder through sin, and because of its limitations in approaching the infinite being'.[48] So Hillerdal, as Neelands argues, is identifying a problem (the reciprocal relationship of reason and revelation) which would not have occurred to Hooker, for whom reason and revelation had distinct functions but which, if operating rightly, would be co-operative since both were given to humanity by the same divine source. Reason, in other words, is *never* simply an autonomous human capacity for Hooker precisely because it is created, a gift of God in its origins, and so need not (cannot) be considered in isolation from its divine source.[49] That does not mean Hooker must fall into a hypo-rationalist position because he does have a rich and vibrant account of reason as a distinct human capacity,[50] just not one which is independent

---

45. This might find resonance with Calvin's comments that disputed matters should be settled by believers reasoning together: *Commentaries*, 88–9.

46. Cf. P. A. Dominiak, 'The Logic of Desire: A Reappraisal of Reason and the Emotions in Richard Hooker's Lawes', *Renaissance and Reformation Review* 16.1 (2014): 42; Rudolph P. Almasy, 'Richard Hooker's Of the Lawes of Ecclesiasticall Politie', in *The Oxford Handbook of English Prose, 1500-1640*, ed. Andrew Hadfield (Oxford: Oxford University Press, 2013), 596. This also indicates it differs from that tendency, identified by Simon Oliver, 'Reading Philosophy', in *The Routledge Companion to the Practice of Christian Theology*, ed. Mike Higton and Jim Fodor (Abingdon: Routledge, 2015), 73, to define reason as the mental cogitating of an autonomous individual.

47. Hillerdal, *Reason and Revelation*, 119.

48. Neelands, 'Theology of Grace', 129. Hillerdal, *Reason and Revelation*, 109 is also wrong to say that Hooker believes that the Fall affects human reason but Aquinas does not.

49. Neelands, 'Theology of Grace', 130.

50. Dominiak, *Participation*, 110–12.

of its divine source or guide. In fact, the strands identified here of reason as a corporate act of the church rather than an individual possession, grounded in God's gift and guided by the Spirit, complementary to (and not in competition with) divine revelation, point to a nuanced, sophisticated account of reason and revelation.[51]

Summary

Hooker's account of the reason-revelation dialectic mirrors that we have already demonstrated in Aquinas and Calvin, where revelation is essential as the sole source of saving truth, and so Hooker can be conceived as firmly within that catholic-reformed consensus.[52] At the same time, neither of the twin accusations McGrade identifies as levelled against Hooker is borne out when the shape of his reason-revelation dialectic is understood. Hooker neither gives reason so great a capacity it stands almost independently as a theological source (Munz, Porter), nor gives reason so little value that it is overwhelmed by revelation (Hillerdal). In fact, Hooker has a coherent and nuanced account of reason and revelation which sees them both as necessary, complementary and divinely given.[53] Reason never collapses into revelation, since it remains the act of the creature exercising a natural capacity, but although reason remains distinct it is never separate from revelation because both flow from a single divine source, allowing Hooker to 'yoke the apparently conflicting truths of reason and revelation'.[54] The integrity and mutuality of reason and revelation emerge further in the discussion of scripture where it becomes clear that revelation always needs our reason to be apprehended, so from the broader category of revelation to the more specific question of scripture we now turn.

Scripture in Hooker's theological method

Introduction

Hooker has often been understood as moving away from the reformed consensus on the function of scripture in theology, of rejecting a *sola scriptura* account of theological method. This section challenges that characterization

---

51. A good short account of the complementary, non-competitive relationship of scripture and reason is Almasy, 'Hooker's *Lawes*', 596–7; cf. W. J. T. Kirby, '"The Sundrie Waies of Wisdom": Richard Hooker on the Authority of Scripture and Reason', in *The Oxford Handbook of the Bible in Early Modern England, c. 1530–1700*, ed. Kevin Killeen, Helen Smith and Rachel Judith Willie (Oxford: Oxford University Press, 2015), 165, 172–3.

52. Affinity with Aquinas need not mean divergence from Calvin here; see, e.g., W. J. T. Kirby, 'Grace and Hierarchy: Richard Hooker's Two Platonisms', in *RHER*, ed. Kirby, 34–5.

53. Cf. Andrea Russell, *Richard Hooker: Beyond Certainty* (London: Routledge, 2020), e.g., 104–6.

54. *FLE*, V.673.

by showing his account of scripture is firmly within a reformed perspective. In particular, Hooker thought scripture alone was the ground of our knowledge of God's saving revelation and the essential doctrines of Christian faith. After considering how the function of scripture in the natural knowledge of God shows how the theological warrants should not be conceived as separate or in tension, we then address the sufficiency of scripture to show Hooker shares a *sola scriptura* principle provided this is properly nuanced. In particular, the distinction between *doctrine* and *discipline* emerges as a key concept for Hooker which guarantees the unique sufficiency of scripture within the field of doctrine. Finally the question of scripture's self-authentication is explored to show that, despite assertions of divergence, here too Hooker can be seen as broadly in line with Calvin's reformed stance.

Scripture corrects natural knowledge of God

Before considering the more contested questions of sufficiency and authority, we note that accusations Hooker overestimates reason's theological potential or divides reason and scripture are further undermined when we recall that scripture, for Hooker, plays a helpful part in the sphere of natural knowledge. At the outset of the *Laws* Hooker explains why scripture is 'fraught with the precepts' of laws which could in principle be discovered by natural reason. As we will see, scripture's principal purpose is not to deliver those laws. Nonetheless, it helpfully does so for two reasons: firstly, *clarity*: because some such laws are 'such as we could not easily have found out, and then the benefit is not small to have them readily set down to our hands'; secondly, *certainty*: 'the evidence of God's own testimony added to the natural assent of reason concerning the certainty of them does not a little comfort and confirm the same' (I.12.1).[55]

The complementarity of revelation and reason, indeed, of scripture and reason, is emphasized by Hooker's fairly fluid movement between appeals to each warrant in the natural sphere.[56] Hence, for example, in the middle of a reflection of what may be discerned by natural reason he happily switches to cite Moses and Psalm 19 as evidence for his claims about the natural order (I.3.2). And the ability of scripture to operate in the natural sphere undermines those claims[57] that reason

---

55. Cf. W. Bradford Littlejohn, *Richard Hooker: A Companion to His Life and Thought* (Eugene, OR: Cascade, 2017), 89–90.

56. Neelands, 'Scripture, Reason, and Tradition', 86–90; Peter Lake, *Anglicans and Puritans? Presbyterianism and English Conformist Thought from Whitgift to Hooker* (London: Unwin Hyman, 1988), 151–60.

57. E.g., Peter Munz, *The Place of Hooker in the History of Thought* (London: Routledge, 1982), 54.

and revelation are separate entities operating in separate arenas with reason operating autonomously in the natural sphere and scripture operating without reason in the supernatural sphere.[58]

Scripture, then, for Hooker as for Calvin and Aquinas, is useful in correcting the natural knowledge of God available to reason; the congruence of their thought is further demonstrated by their shared approach to scripture's sufficiency as the sole source of saving knowledge of God, as we now show.

Scripture's sufficiency

A common interpretation of Hooker is that he departs from the reformed perspective because he does not adopt a *sola scriptura* account of theological method. Thus, his presbyterian opponents accused Hooker of moving outside the reformed view embodied in the Church of England's formularies:

> How then agree you with the belief of our Church: which affirms, that holy scripture teaches all things necessary to salvation? ... shew us, whether nature teaching anything touching Christ ... or that cases and matters of salvation be determinable by any other law than of holy scripture?
> (*ACL* 3, IV.13.9-3, 125-6)

Some contemporary writers like Voak agree; 'Hooker was implicitly rejecting the reformed, and more generally Protestant, principle of *sola scriptura* and making reason a necessary addition to Holy Scripture in matters of Christian doctrine.'[59] Others argue that Hooker is firmly within a reformed perspective on this question; thus, LeTourneau insists that on scripture's sufficiency 'Hooker belongs to the reformed tradition'.[60] This section will show that Hooker's theology is rightly characterized by the interpretation represented by LeTourneau, and wrongly by the presbyterians and Voak. Tracing Hooker's account of scripture, both on the immediate dispute in the *Laws* about church polity and his wider theological method, shows that, properly understood, Hooker endorses a *sola scriptura* principle entirely consistent with the reformed view articulated in Calvin and the catholic perspective represented by Aquinas.

The question of whether the Church of England should continue to be led by a threefold order of bishops, priests and deacons or replace it with a single level of

---

58. Here I disagree with Simut, who says that for Hooker 'Christians are not to look to Scripture for answers that belong to reason' (*Sermons*, 206); Hooker is quite clear that scripture also teaches us many things we could know by reason – so, e.g., Joyce, *Anglican Moral Theology*, 113–14.

59. Voak, 'Sola Scriptura', 96; see also Lake, *Anglicans and Puritans?*, 153–5.

60. Mark LeTourneau, 'Richard Hooker and the Sufficiency of Scripture', *JAS* 14.2 (2016): 136; similarly W. J. T. Kirby, 'Hooker as an Apologist of the Magisterial Reformation in England', *RHCCC*, 227–32.

presbyters as in Calvin's Geneva may not be an obvious way to address the question of scripture's function in theological method. But it was the presenting issue of Hooker's dispute with the presbyterians. And just as today Anglican debates about gender and sexuality are in fact much deeper disagreements about the authority and function of the Bible, so in Hooker's day this question of church order was grounded in more fundamental dispute about theological method.

Hooker understood the *Laws* to embody his 'careful endeavour' to uphold 'the present state of the Church of God established among us' (Pref. 1.1). In particular, he opposes those 'persuaded … that every Christian Church stands bound to put down bishops, and in their rooms to elect an Eldership … for the government of each parish' (Pref. 4.6). Underlying this presbyterian demand, says Hooker, is a methodological presumption

> ye suppose the laws for which ye strive are found in scripture … the very main pillar of your cause, [is] that scripture ought to be the only rule of all our actions and consequently that the Church orders which we observe being not commanded in scripture, are offensive and displeasant to God … and therefore That in Scripture there must of necessity be found some particular form of polity Ecclesiastical, the laws whereof admit not any kind of alteration.
>
> (Pref. 7.4-5)

The root of the presbyterian case, therefore, is not a claim about church order so much as a claim about scripture: that the Church of England must abandon bishops because the Bible sets out a presbyteral form of church government which must invariably be followed.

Exploring Hooker's rebuttal can begin by considering possible counter-arguments he does not in fact deploy. So one obvious approach would be to accuse the presbyterians of historical inaccuracy, as indeed Hooker does. The emergence of a presbyteral form of church government can be traced, with some precision, to the particular circumstances of sixteenth-century continental Europe,[61] so Hooker can 'rip up to the very bottom, how and by whom your discipline was planted, at … this age we live in' (Pref. 1.2). Hooker proceeds with that ripping-up exercise by a lively and not entirely complimentary account of Calvin's instituting of presbyterianism in Geneva in the 1530s and 1540s (Pref. 2). He goes on to say that claims of scriptural or still less antique justification for presbyterianism as a binding model are hard to square with the near-universal evidence of episcopal church order dating back over a thousand years: 'a very strange thing, sure it were, that such a discipline … should be taught by Christ and his Apostles in the word of God, and no Church have ever found it, nor received it to the present time'

---

61. See Robert Kingdon, 'The Calvinist Reformation in Geneva', in *The Cambridge History of Christianity*, 9 vols (Cambridge: Cambridge University Press, 2005–9), esp. VI.90–6.

(Pref. 4.1), and he challenges the presbyterians to find an example of non-episcopal church order since the New Testament (Pref. 4.2).

A second, not unconnected approach would be to argue scripture *does* lay down rules about the form of church government and says churches should be led by bishops not by presbyters. Now, Hooker certainly thinks that episcopacy can claim scriptural antecedents. Episcopacy, Hooker says, 'best agrees with the sacred scripture' (III.11.16) and 'the first bishops of the Church of Christ were his blessed apostles' (VII.4.1, cf. VIII.4.3). Yet Hooker consistently and repeatedly refuses to argue that bishops are *demanded* by scripture. He accepts that, given the situation in Geneva, Calvin had some justification in abandoning episcopal order (Pref. 2.1-4). Hooker argues that it is 'altogether too late' to re-impose bishops on the Scottish and French churches (III.11.16). He insists that, even in churches with bishops, that structure could temporarily be dispensed with, for instance, by allowing the ministry of those who were not ordained by priests (VII.14.11).[62] What Hooker denies here is more significant than what he affirms: he refuses to mount a defence of bishops on the basis that they are demanded by scripture.[63]

While Hooker does deploy the historical and scriptural counter-arguments (the presbyterian discipline is relatively recent and is not obviously in the New Testament), in fact his principal ground for opposing the presbyterians is a more fundamental point of theological method.[64] The presbyterian case, says Hooker, asserts, 'Scripture everywhere favours that discipline' (Pref. 3.13), and underlying this is a deeper argument that 'only one law, the scripture, must be the rule to direct in all things' (II.1.3). Thomas Cartwright, quotes Hooker, says 'the word of God contains whatsoever things can fall into any part of man's life' and 'the Word of God directs a man in all his actions',[65] such that 'by scripture we must of necessity be directed in every ... thing which is incident into any part of man's life' (II.3.1).

Now, contends Hooker, this view is unsustainable even when framed in its own terms. If humans could only ever act in ways laid out in scripture, we would sin every time we picked up a straw (Introduction to Book II) or whenever we slept or accepted a drink, since such acts are done by 'natural desire, without ... reference to any commandment of God' (II.2.1). Indeed, the Bible praises figures such as Abraham and Job who followed God before the revelation of Christ: are they to be condemned simply because they lacked the New Testament (II.4.6), along with all those too young or lacking the capacity to know scripture (II.8.6)? Moreover, many aspects of human life, such as the rules of commerce, are not set down explicitly or

---

62. K. P. J. Padley, 'Early Anglican Ecclesiology and Contemporary Ecumenism', *International Journal for the Study of the Christian Church* 9.1 (2009): 6–7.

63. For this reading of Hooker on episcopacy see, e.g., M. R. Somerville, 'Richard Hooker and His Contemporaries on Episcopacy: An Elizabethan Consensus', *JEH* 34 (1984): 183, 187; A. S. McGrade, 'Episcopacy', *CRH*, 486–8.

64. P. P. Hobday, 'Richard Hooker and *Mission and Ministry in Covenant*', *JAS* 18.2 (2020): 223–4.

65. Quoted in *Laws* I.105, I.106.

fully in scripture (Pref. 8.4). It would be a rather cruel deity who gave us such an incomplete account of our duties.

Moreover, since human reason is a divine gift, it demeans or ignores God's graciousness to say he has not communicated with his creatures by media other than religious texts. His opponents, say Hooker, would 'restrain the manifold ways which wisdom has to teach men by', including nature, conscience and experience (II.1.4). But, Hooker adds, '[S]cripture is not the only law whereby God has opened his will' (II.2.2). That God has ordained more than one means of divine self-communication tells against the sufficiency of scripture if the Bible is understood as the sole source of *any* true knowledge, as the presbyterians seem to allege.[66]

Turning to Hooker's positive account of sufficiency, towards the end of Book II he addresses the distinction between the two different kinds of knowledge. In some ways 'the very light of nature alone may discover some truths' (II.8.2). But others require a different source: 'nature is no sufficient teacher what we should do that we may attain to life everlasting. The insufficiency of the light of nature is by the light of scripture … fully and … perfectly herein supplied' (II.8.3). This scriptural light makes good the deficiency of our natural light and is perfect and sufficient for its purpose of supernatural illumination of saving truth, as Hooker expounds poetically:

> The testimonies of God are true, the testimonies of God are perfect, the testimonies of God are all-sufficient to that end for which they were given … God did thereby intend to deliver … a full instruction in all things necessary to salvation, the knowledge whereof man could not by nature otherwise in this life attain to.
>
> (II.8.4)

Here Hooker establishes his *sola scriptura* theological method: scripture alone teaches us the saving knowledge of God which our reason could not attain (so also III.14.3),[67] an account firmly within the reformed perspective. As Voak rightly (but rather surprisingly, given his insistence that Hooker separates himself from the reformed view of scripture) observes, Hooker 'as with the Reformed tradition' asserts 'Holy Scripture is necessary for Christian doctrine'.[68] Grislis makes the point even clearer: for Hooker as for the reformed generally, the Bible was 'the exclusive deposit of divine revelation'.[69]

Hooker's insistence on scripture's sufficiency for its purpose is demonstrated further by his approach not just to his presbyterian opponents but also his catholic ones. For as well as rejecting the presbyterian view that scripture alone was the source of true knowledge of God, Hooker also rejects what he takes to be

---

66. Cf. Chapman, *Anglican Theology*, 115–16.
67. See R. D. Williams, 'Foreword', *CRH*, xix.
68. Voak, '*Sola Scriptura*', 123.
69. Egil Grislis, 'Scriptural Hermeneutics', *CRH*, 274.

the contemporary catholic view that scripture was *insufficient* by itself to reveal the truths necessary to salvation. Hooker contended we ought not to 'seek for any revealed law otherwise than only in the sacred scripture' and should not 'stand bound to yield to traditions ... the same obedience and reverence we do to his written law, honouring equally' both scripture and tradition (I.13.2). So he considers it 'dangerous' to 'add to the word of God uncertain tradition, so the doctrine of man's salvation may be complete ... whatsoever to make up the doctrine of man's salvation is added, as in supply of the scripture's insufficiency, we reject it' (II.8.5). He considers both catholic and presbyterian methodologies 'repugnant to truth' because Rome teaches 'scripture to be so insufficient, as if, except traditions were added, it did not contain all revealed and supernatural truth, which absolutely is necessary for the children of men in this life to know that they may in the next be saved' (II.8.7; cf. III.14.5). Neither sixteenth-century presbyterianism nor sixteenth-century catholicism, says Hooker, properly apprehends sufficiency; the former extends its scope too far and excludes reason; the latter renders it too narrow so as to require tradition.[70] This allows us to see the error of the presbyterians' charge: Hooker did not argue that natural knowledge was needed to supplement or replace scriptural knowledge of the truths of salvation; he did not think the truth of salvation could be found other than through scripture.

Scripture's perfection, its sufficiency for its purpose, is developed in Book III when Hooker turns to the vital distinction between *doctrine* and *discipline*. We can trace this distinction in three ways: the content of each sphere, the source of knowledge within each sphere and whether there can be change in each sphere. We consider each in turn.

The *content* of *doctrine* Hooker defines as 'matters of faith ... necessary to salvation' (III.2.2). Doctrine, Hooker says, covers 'things which supernaturally appertain to the very essence of Christianity' (III.1.4, cf. III.3.3) and includes, for example, the doctrine of the Trinity (I.2.2, III.2.1) and the person and work of Christ (III.1.4; cf. *Jude* I.5, V.17-8). Hooker enumerates the 'points of doctrine, as for example the unity of God the trinity of persons, salvation by Christ, the resurrection of the body, life everlasting, the judgment to come' (III.10.6; cf. *Just.* 16, V.123.1-23).

Such matters are distinct from *discipline*;[71] they are 'of a different nature from Ceremonies, order, and the kind of church government' (*Laws*, III.2.2). Matters of discipline he also calls 'things indifferent' (e.g., II.4.4, from the Greek *adiaphora*), by which he does not mean unimportant but indifferent to salvation; he prefers the term *matters accessory* (cf. II.4.3, III.3.3).[72] The distinction between his view and the presbyterians', Hooker concludes, is that he does not consider church

---

70. Cf. Ranall Ingalls, 'Richard Hooker as Interpreter of the Reformed Doctrine of "Sola Scriptura"', *Anglican and Episcopal History* 77.4 (2008): 360–1.

71. Good accounts of the vital doctrine-discipline distinction are Chapman, *Anglican Theology*, 117–20; Ingalls, 'Reformed Doctrine', 362–5.

72. Chapman, *Anglican Theology*, 117.

government to be a matter of doctrine, but they do; 'matters of discipline and church government are (as they say) matters necessary to salvation and of faith, whereas we put a difference between the one and the other' (III.2.2); for 'there be no necessity' that the Bible should 'prescribe any one particular form of church government' (III.4.1).

A key implication of Hooker's classification of church government differing from the presbyterians' is that doctrine and discipline differ, secondly, not just in content but in *source*. The knowledge of the saving doctrines of Christian faith relies on 'the heavenly support of prophetic revelation, which does open these hidden mysteries that reason could never have been able to find out' (I.11.6). This prophetic revelation is of course a reference to scripture, as Hooker elsewhere makes clear; 'in scripture God ... also reveals whatsoever we neither with safety be ignorant of, nor at all be instructed in, but by supernatural revelation from him'; these 'articles of Christian faith ... if scripture did not comprehend, the Church of God should not be able to measure out' (III.3.3). Again, the description of the articles of faith as 'articles of evangelical doctrine' (III.10.6) emphasizes this close connection between scripture and doctrine. Hooker insists: 'Scripture teaches us all supernaturally revealed truth, without the knowledge whereof salvation cannot be attained ... that saving truth which God has discovered to the world by revelation' (III.8.13).

Later, in Book V, Hooker speaking about worship identifies scripture as God's revelation, insisting on the centrality of reading scripture in church services: 'the Church as a witness preaches his mere revealed truth by reading publicly the Holy Scriptures' (V.19.1). The reading of scripture in worship, says Hooker, is essential and powerful because scripture alone is where we now find the divine revelation:

> The Word of God is his heavenly truth touching matters of eternal life revealed and uttered to men; to prophets and apostles by immediate divine revelation, from them to us by their books and writings ... when we name the Word of God, always to mean the scripture only.
>
> (V.21.1)

The close identification of revelation with scripture, in the sense of where we now find doctrine, also recurs in his other works. Thus, 'that which ties us to' Christ is 'our faith in the promised salvation revealed in the word of truth' (*Jude* I.11, V.25.22-23). Again, the 'simplicity of faith which is in Christ takes the naked promise of God's bare word and on that it rests' (*Certainty* 3, V.77.16-17). Elsewhere, Hooker states that 'the writings of the evangelists and the apostles are the foundation of Christian faith' (*Just.* 15, V.122.28-30).[73]

Doctrine, then, must be grounded on scripture, and scripture alone. By contrast, says Hooker, in matters of discipline scripture is not a clear or binding source. Here the methodological difference between Hooker and his presbyterian

---

73. Simut, *Sermons*, 111.

opponents becomes clear: *sola scriptura* is certainly Hooker's view, in the sense that the truths of revelation needful for salvation are found only there, but this does not mean scripture must regulate all aspects of life. While the presbyterians seek a form of church government in scripture, Hooker does not: 'Scripture does not require of me to make any special choice' (*Laws*, II.4.4) in church government because 'in things indifferent there is a choice' (II.4.3). That choice can certainly be *informed* by scripture, as Hooker says, believing that bishops can claim some New Testament pedigree (VII.4.1-3). Nor is *tradition* binding in matters of discipline, even though Hooker considers episcopacy is 'from ancient times ... universally established' (VII.5.8).

For the government of the church, like all matters of discipline, is not for Hooker determined by scripture or tradition but by *reason*.[74] Matters other than doctrine are 'left ... to the careful discretion of the churches' and 'must by reason be found out' (III.9.1). The continued ordering of the church by bishops, its provenance in scripture and tradition notwithstanding, is 'not absolutely necessary, but of a changeable nature' and 'stand[s] in force, rather by the custom of the church, choosing to continue in it'. For Hooker, in matters of discipline, 'the Church has power to alter with general consent and upon necessary occasion, even the positive laws of the apostles' (VII.5.8). As Graves observes, Hooker rejects both the presbyterian and advanced episcopalian arguments that scripture determined church government and instead insisted church order was justified by 'politic autonomy', that is, the right of each national church to decide its own order.[75] The sufficiency of scripture, for Hooker, meant it was the sole source of matters of faith, but in other matters, reason (drawing on, but not determined by, scripture and tradition) was the decisive source.

Thirdly, doctrine and discipline are distinct because the former may not *vary* but the latter may. Thus, Hooker says doctrines 'have been since the first hour that there was a Church ... and till the last they must be believed', and 'to make new articles of faith no man thinks it lawful' (III.10.6). By contrast, matters of discipline admit of different solutions. Just as what matters is where a path is headed rather than the material it is made from, so too churches can achieve the same goal of order by different means: 'the matter of faith is constant, the matter contrariwise of action daily changeable' (III.3.3). So 'laws (forasmuch as they are not ... necessary to salvation) may ... also be changed as the difference of times or places shall require' (III.10.6; cf. III.10.3-4).

So matters of doctrine and discipline are distinct in their content, source and variability; this distinction underscores the centrality of scripture as the sole ground of saving doctrine. Understood rightly, as Cocksworth highlights, Hooker's account preserves the *sola scriptura* principle by limiting the sufficiency of scripture to doctrine:

---

74. Hobday, 'Hooker and *MMC*', 232.

75. Daniel F. Graves, '"*Iure Divino*"? Four Views on the Authority of the Episcopacy in Richard Hooker', *Anglican and Episcopal History* 81.1 (2012): 55.

Although Hooker was committed to the sufficiency of scripture he was clear that scripture does not claim to be sufficient in all things, just to be sufficient in what it is meant to be – the means by which God speaks of who he is and ... how we can know God and be part of what God is doing.[76]

So Hooker does not, as the presbyterians held and Voak implies, believe that reason is a *ground* of the saving knowledge of God. Nature did not teach anything essential to salvation, for Hooker; this comes only by revelation in scripture. But scripture's sufficiency is bounded; it is the sole rule of faith, containing the deposit of revelation which alone grounds saving doctrine, but it is not the sole rule of life, as though it were the only instruction we needed to live.

Sola scriptura, moreover, does not mean scripture stands alone: as Hooker notes, any theological method would be incoherent if it did. Hooker's opponents demonstrate that themselves; as Hooker observed on the *Christian Letter*, 'they are matters of salvation ... you handle in this book. If therefore determinable only by scripture, why press you upon me so often with human authorities ... why cite you so many commentaries books and sermons?' (*ACL* 3, IV.13.1-4). For Hooker, while scripture is the sole source of saving doctrine it needs other warrants if its riches are to be mined. The presbyterians, Hooker says, believe in crucial doctrines such as the coeternity of the Father and the Son and the procession of the Spirit because such doctrines 'found express literal mention in the scriptures' (*ACL* 2, IV.10.20.25-6). But this, says Hooker, is a puzzling claim. If, for instance, the coeternity of Father and Son was so clearly contained in scripture, it is hard to account for the fourth-century disputes. As Hooker says,

> that ancient strife which was between the Catholic fathers and Arians, Donatists, and others ... the scripture they both believed, the scripture they knew could not give sentence on both sides ... it does not yet appear that an argument of authority of man is in divine matters worth nothing.
>
> (*Laws*, II.7.6)

As Hooker says earlier, the articles of faith are 'in scripture nowhere to be found by express literal mention, only deduced they are out of scripture by collection' (I.14.2).[77] While not very specific about this act of deduction or collection, Hooker does emphasize it is an act of reason: 'Exclud[ing] the use of natural reasoning

---

76. Christopher Cocksworth, *Holding Together: Gospel, Church and Spirit: The Essentials of Christian Identity* (Norwich: Canterbury Press, 2008), 32.

77. A similar observation that such beliefs are not set down 'literally and verbatim' in the Bible so have to be 'deduced' from scripture is cited by Keble (*Works*, I.xc and fn.2). The comment is not included in the Folger edition on the basis that it appears only in the 'less accurate transcription' of the text in the Trinity College Dublin manuscript (*FLE*, IV.xlvii). However, it does reflect Hooker's view; see Grislis, 'Hermeneutics', 280–2; Cocksworth, *Holding Together*, 32–3.

about the sense of holy scripture concerning the articles of our faith' will mean the text 'being misconstrued breeds error: between true and false construction, the difference reason must show' (III.8.16). Hooker stresses we do 'not add reason as a supplement of any maim or defect' in scripture but 'as a necessary instrument without which we could not reap ... that fruit and benefit which it yields' (III.8.10). Reason's use, then, is instrumental and regulatory rather than generative; it does not ground doctrine, which only scripture can, but does guide the church to the proper interpretation of the biblically grounded articles of faith.[78]

The legitimacy of this use of reason can be further seen when we recall reason is not the autonomous thinking of an individual but the corporate, God-given, and Spirit-guided discerning of the church. And 'the guarantor of ... congruence' between scripture and reason's interpretation of it is 'that the same God who inspired Scripture also created the instrumental reason with which we ... comprehend it'.[79] Of course, this prompts the further question of which interpreters or interpretations are permissible in the shaping of doctrine from scripture, a question we defer until the discussion of tradition in Chapter 5. For now, it suffices to say that Hooker clearly does have a broadly reformed account of scripture in which scripture is the sole source of our saving knowledge of God.

Arguments such as Voak's and Gibbs' that Hooker departs from the reformed belief in *sola scriptura* cannot be sustained. For Hooker, scripture's sufficiency or perfection is real, but it is limited to its essential purpose, the delivery of doctrine. As Kirby notes, challenging Voak and defending Hooker's reformed credentials on this point, the key affirmation of *sola scriptura* is not that other theological warrants have little or no authority; rather, it means no warrant other than scripture generates the doctrines of faith, and on that definition Hooker is firmly reformed.[80] Scripture does not deliver the laws of church discipline or everyday life, and the doctrine it contains still needs reason to elucidate and frame in propositional form the saving message it alone delivers. Nonetheless, this is still a *sola scriptura* account, mirroring Calvin's and indeed Aquinas', in the nuanced sense that scripture alone is the source of the saving knowledge of God which reason could never discover. As Kirby concludes,

> Knowledge of God the Creator is not to be confused with the knowledge of the Redeemer ... Hooker's credentials as a reformer stand forth when he maintains that only through the supernatural revelation of the Scriptures is it possible

---

78. Cf. Lake, *Anglicans and Puritans?*, 151.

79. W. Speed Hill, 'Scripture as Text, Text as Scripture: The Case of Richard Hooker', *Text* 9 (1996): 98.

80. W. J. T. Kirby, '"Grace Hath Use of Nature": Richard Hooker and the Conversion of Reason', in *Richard Hooker and Reformed Orthodoxy*, ed. W. Bradford Littlejohn and Scott N. Kindred-Barnes (Göttingen: Vandenhoeck & Ruprecht, 2017), 131–3.

to hope for a participation in the divine nature. Scripture alone can reveal the supernatural way of salvation.[81]

On the question of where we now find the saving knowledge of God, then, Hooker is firmly within the reformed perspective. On a second question, how we know the authority of scripture, Hooker is also thought to depart from it; the next section situates him firmly within the reformed milieu.

Scripture's authority

The presbyterians did not just think Hooker undermined the reformed principle of scripture's sufficiency; they accused him of rejecting the reformers' view that scripture authenticates itself and grounds its own authority. They accused Hooker of believing scripture's authority is dependent upon the church, not its own inherent self-authentication:

> what certainty of salvation can we have ... if the scripture cannot assure us that it is the Word of God? Tells us therefore if your meaning be not that the authority of the church must do that which the scripture cannot do, namely to assure us that they are the Word of God.
>
> (*ACL* 4, IV.15.21-5)

Echoing the presbyterian charge, Voak and LeTourneau among others agree Hooker refuses to say scripture self-authenticates and here 'move[s] decisively outside the boundaries of reformed orthodoxy'.[82]

Certainly, Hooker bluntly asserted scripture did not straightforwardly authenticate itself. Thus, while 'all believe that the Scriptures are sacred, and that they have proceeded from God', he writes, and 'have for this point a demonstration sound and infallible', yet 'it is not the word of God which does or possibly can assure us, that we do well to think it his word' (*Laws*, II.4.2). This seems, at first glance, contrary to Calvin's assertion that scripture grounded its own authority (*Inst.* I.7.4).

However, probing Hooker's account more deeply shows convergence with the reformed perspective even on this point.[83] We begin with the grounding of scripture's authority in its divine authorship, a belief foundational to Aquinas' and Calvin's account of scripture too. Grislis, for example, states, 'Hooker shared with the mainstream of the Church of England ... the central Reformation affirmation

---

81. Kirby, 'Reason and Law', 267.
82. Voak, '*Sola Scriptura*', 127; cf. LeTourneau, 'Sufficiency', 137, 168.
83. See, for instance, W. David Neelands, 'The Use and Abuse of John Calvin in Richard Hooker's Defence of the English Church', *Perichoresis* 10.1 (2012): 15–19.

of the *sola scriptura*', which was founded on 'an unwavering belief that God was the author of the scriptures'.[84]

Indeed, in language reminiscent of Calvin's formulation,[85] Hooker says scripture is a 'means more durable to preserve the laws of God' than pre-scriptural oral tradition, and it was established 'not without precise direction from God himself ... God takes this act to himself' (I.13.1). Again, Hooker insists, 'Scripture being with Christian men being received as the word of God ... we hold that [God's] speech reveals there what he himself sees, and therefore the strongest proof of all' (II.7.5). There is an obvious resonance with Calvin's insistence that the Word's authority flows from the fact it is divine speech (*Inst.* I.7.5). It also coheres with Aquinas' view: 'holy scripture is all wise and most true since revealed and handed down by God, who is all truth and all knowledge' (*Div. nom.* I-1, 283). For all three theologians, then, the initial reason to treat scripture as authoritative is because it is divine speech.

Next, though, it must be asked how we recognize this text is divine speech. Here the presbyterians assert the only ground for this recognition is scripture itself. But Hooker believes this cannot be right. Recognition of scripture's function as the sole source of saving truth requires 'the presuppoal of knowledge concerning certain principles whereof it receives us already persuaded', including 'the sacred authority of scripture', a principle 'which point is confessed impossible for the scripture itself to teach' (*Laws*, I.14.1; cf. II.4.2). We must be 'persuaded by other means that the scriptures are the oracles of God' (I.14.2). The sheer implausibility of the presbyterians' case is obvious, says Hooker. If scripture did authenticate itself, then surely everyone would accept its authority, which is not the case (III.8.13).[86] Moreover, the argument becomes incoherent if pressed. For if scripture authenticates itself, which *part* of authenticates the rest? And that part of scripture itself would need *another* part of scripture to authenticate it, and so on, in an infinite chain of reciprocal authentication (II.4.2).

The recognition of scripture's authority, Hooker identifies, hinges on 'by what means we are taught it' (III.8.14). Voak advances several reasons to argue Hooker diverges from the reformed on this point. Critiquing these reasons shows Voak is wrong and Hooker is clearly within a wider reformed consensus.

Voak concludes Hooker 'rejects the post-Tridentine Roman Catholic solution ... Holy Scripture is authenticated by the Church'.[87] Certainly Hooker rejects the view 'we have no other way but tradition' to discern scripture's authority, but nonetheless 'the first outward motive leading men so to esteem of the Holy Scripture is the authority of the Church' (III.8.14). Indeed, Hooker continues, the 'voice and testimony of the church acknowledging scripture to be the law of the living God is for the truth and certainty thereof no mean evidence' (V.22.2). Likewise, Calvin

---

84. Grislis, 'Hermeneutics', 274.
85. A connection identified by Grislis, 'Hermeneutics', 275; LeTourneau, 'Sufficiency', 141.
86. Speed Hill, 'Scripture as Text', 95–6.
87. Voak, '*Sola Scriptura*', 130; cf. 123–4.

did not think the external 'evidences' of scripture's authority were unimportant or without weight.[88] So while it is true Hooker did not believe tradition was the source of scripture's authority, he does not consider tradition (or indeed other evidence external to scripture) unimportant, and in this he agrees with Calvin, rather undermining Voak's wider argument of divergence between Hooker and the reformed perspective.[89]

Voak's second, third and fourth arguments are that Hooker also rejects 'the Reformed position that Holy Scripture is a self-authenticating first principle', and 'the Reformed view that scripture can be infallibly authenticated ... [by] the internal witness of the Holy Spirit', because for Hooker 'scripture can only be authenticated by inferential reasoning based on objective evidence'.[90]

To counter Voak's arguments we note initially that Hooker distinguishes between what might persuade the sceptic that scripture's authority was at least an intellectually coherent notion from what persuades the believer to accept it as saving truth. So while Hooker believes there is 'a demonstration sound and infallible' which reveals scripture's authority (II.4.2), he is clear this is essentially an argument for justifying scripture's authority to the non-believer: the Fathers 'maintain the authority of the books of God by arguments such as unbelievers themselves must needs think reasonable' (III.8.14). By contrast, for the believer, Hooker is clear there is 'no proof but by the testimony of the Holy Spirit, which assures their heart therein'. What Hooker resists is the notion this can occur other than by the Spirit working through human reason: 'motives and inducements ... are notwithstanding ineffectual of themselves' to prove scripture's authority 'if the special grace of the holy ghost incur not to the enlightening of our minds', and the Spirit directs our reason to accept in faith the scripture's authority (III.8.15).[91] What we see here then is a co-operation of the Spirit and reason to persuade the believer of scripture's authority.[92]

Moreover, as Chapter 3 showed, to say Calvin believed in scripture's self-authentication is a complex claim which needs considerable further nuance. For instance, Calvin was adamant that the witness of the Spirit was essential for recognizing scripture's authority; that authority did not reside in the text itself. Furthermore, Calvin did not separate inner witness from external evidence; as Muller observes, 'Calvin never claimed the internal testimony of the Holy Spirit' operated 'apart from the various external evidences'.[93] What we see in Hooker is

---

88. As Muller notes, 'Calvin, almost paradoxically, devotes more space to a discussion of the external evidences' than to explaining 'why such evidences are unnecessary', *PRRD*, II.258.

89. Ingalls, 'Reformed Doctrine', 359, 366.

90. Voak, '*Sola Scriptura*', 134.

91. See Kirby, '"Sundrie Waies"', 172–3.

92. Ingalls, 'Reformed Doctrine', 368–9; Stafford, 'Holy Spirit', 115.

93. *PRRD*, II.255.

the same; the Spirit moves from the 'inside out' to persuade the believer, while the external evidence may persuade from the 'outside in'. Hence, Kirby rightly criticizes Voak's characterization: '"infallible demonstration" is in fact the inner testimony of the Spirit' and that this 'corresponds to arguments for scripture's authentication ... in Calvin'.[94] As Stafford says, this may be 'a more refined argument than Calvin' but is 'consistent with Calvin's language'.[95]

So far, we have argued suspicion of Hooker's reformed credentials on scripture's authority is misplaced. When Hooker's co-operative account of reason and the Holy Spirit is grasped, and Calvin's nuance on *autopistis* is appreciated, there is in fact no substantial tension between them. But Voak then advances a further claim: that Hooker's approach is 'completely different' from Aquinas' because Aquinas believes scripture's authority is 'incapable of demonstration'.[96] But, of course, Aquinas did not mean there were no rational arguments which pointed to scripture's authority. It is difficult to say precisely since Voak cites the larger *Summa* (I.1.8) but unfortunately does not specify which part of the text he is referencing, but he may be referring to Aquinas' assertion that 'this science does not argue in proof of its principles' (*resp.*). What Aquinas means by this is that unless one's interlocutor will grant something of the possibility of faith – namely, will accept the possibility God exists and communicates – no amount of rational persuasion will convince them of the things of faith: 'if our opponent believes nothing of divine revelation, there is no longer any means of proving the articles of faith by reasoning' (I.1.8, *resp.*). What Voak has failed to see here is the distinction between the believer and the unbeliever; there is the possibility of demonstration but only to the believer (or, at the very least, someone prepared to believe). This, of course, is precisely the point Hooker is making; no amount of rational argument will ultimately persuade the unbeliever unless it is joined to the inward persuasion of the Holy Spirit in that person's heart. Voak's argument that Hooker diverges from Aquinas here is no more convincing than his argument that Hooker diverges from Calvin.[97]

It is certainly true, though, that while in substance he and the reformer converge, Hooker sounds a little more reticent than Calvin about asserting scripture's inherent authority and resists the use of the word or concept *autopistis*.

---

94. Kirby, 'Conversion of Reason', 132.

95. Stafford, 'Holy Spirit', 203; cf. Ingalls, 'Reformed Doctrine', 368–9, who like Stafford sees Hooker as consistent with Calvin but fails to identify as Stafford does the link between the authority of scripture and the witness of the Holy Spirit. LeTourneau, 'Sufficiency', 153–4 tries to argue rather tortuously that Voak is half right because Hooker departs from Calvin in separating the witness of the Spirit from the authenticity of Scripture. (This characterization is also advanced by Lake, *Anglicans and Puritans?*, 154.) But this is precisely what Hooker does not do: Hooker is explicit in III.8.15 that Spirit and reason work together to persuade the believer of scripture's authority.

96. Voak, '*Sola Scriptura*', 133 fn.100.

97. Cf. Dominiak, *Participation*, 119–27.

Two possible reasons for this can be adduced. Firstly, as we saw, Hooker is profoundly wary of attributing too much authority to any individual (*Laws*, Pref. 2.6, 4.6, 5.3).[98] Particularly he condemns the *autokataktritoi* (III.8.8 and *Jude* I.11, IV.26.11), literally those who judge themselves, for setting up their own personal opinion about matters of faith over against the received teaching of the church. This leads to heresy, division and a particular form of circular, insular, exclusive reasoning. It promotes a kind of canon within a canon, an attention to only those aspects of doctrine which the presbyterians wish to emphasize (*ACL* 18, IV.49.6-8, 13). And there were, for Hooker, real dangers in the establishment of this sort of self-selecting, exclusive dogma: 'when the minds of men are once erroneously persuaded that it is the will of God to have those things done which they fancy' the consequences can include polygamy, cruelty, destruction of property and livelihoods, and even the killing of those with whom they disagree (*Laws*, Pref. 8.12).[99] So Hooker is deeply resistant to anything which suggests there is any individual or personal source of authority apart from the formal, public teaching of the church; for a sub-group or individual to establish further tests of orthodoxy is divisive and destabilizing.[100]

Secondly, perhaps part of the problem with asserting scripture's self-authentication is it can sound like the work of a single event or moment. But this is not, for Hooker, how the Spirit normally works in people; it is rarely the case that we immediately accept the authority of scripture in a moment and all else immediately becomes clear. Rather, in *Laws* III.8.13-14, Hooker depicts an unfolding process where we initially accept scripture on the basis of the church's witness, then the Spirit persuades us inwardly of the scripture's inherent authority, before we are further drawn to understand rightly scripture's meaning. This, as Russell notes, is an image which recurs elsewhere, as Hooker's lovely description that 'God does nothing else but lead us along by the hand' from one aspect of scripture to another, so that by seeing one part fulfilled and then others in turn, he 'settled us upon the rock of an assured hope' (*Jude* I.5, V.18.26-8).[101]

---

98. This wariness may also help account for his apparent unwillingness, unlike many of the reformers, to say we can know with certainty we are saved, a question a wider comparison of him and Calvin could usefully explore; see Russell, *Beyond Certainty*, esp. 108–26; Shuger, 'Faith and Assurance', *CRH*, 229–36.

99. McGrade suggests Hooker has specifically in mind Anabaptist-inspired anarchy; *Laws*, I.xxxiv.

100. Joyce, *Anglican Moral Theology*, 55–7 is one of the few contemporary writers to spot this link.

101. Russell, *Beyond Certainty*, 123–4. This may well be a further point of convergence with Aquinas who similarly uses the image of the teacher leading the student by the hand, especially on the reading of scripture: see Peter M. Candler, *Theology, Rhetoric, Manuduction, or Reading Scripture Together on the Path to God* (Grand Rapids, MI: Eerdmans, 2006), 4–5.

Summary

Hooker's presbyterian opponents contended he departed from reformed principles on the place of scripture in theology, an interpretation which is followed by contemporary writers such as Voak and to some extent LeTourneau because Hooker is said to depart from the reformed emphases of *sola scriptura* and scripture's self-authentication. In part, such flawed interpretations arise because they see Calvin and Aquinas as at odds, a premise earlier chapters contested. That characterization becomes less convincing when we trace the common features of Hooker's and Calvin's account of scripture, which include a belief in *sola scriptura* if defined as scripture being the sole source of the saving knowledge of God which reason alone cannot discover, a principle Hooker happily maintains while insisting scripture's sufficiency relates only to doctrine, not other matters such as church order. Hooker converges with Aquinas too; sharing vital elements of his view such as the divine authorship as the ground of the text's authority, and the co-operative roles of the Holy Spirit and human reason in guiding us to recognize the authority and right interpretation of the text. So on the function of scripture in theological method, and indeed on the functions of reason and scripture more generally, Hooker is firmly consistent with both Calvin and Aquinas, sharing a catholic and reformed theological consensus. But if this is so, it prompts the question why this convergence has so often been missed; the final section of this chapter adduces reasons for this failure.

Obscuring Hooker's convergence with Calvin and Aquinas

Introduction

As with previous chapters, a number of reasons can be identified for the failure to see the convergence between Hooker and Calvin and Aquinas. Seven are now adduced to demonstrate that, once a number of misconceptions are corrected, the plausibility of the reading of Hooker advanced here, which characterizes him as both catholic and reformed, can emerge more clearly. These are (1) misreadings of Calvin and Aquinas, (2) distortions of Hooker's views by those appropriating him to advance their own visions of Anglicanism, (3) Hooker's attitude to Calvin, (4) Hooker's attitude to Aquinas, (5) the wider meaning of 'reformed' in sixteenth-century England, (6) Hooker's attitude to Rome and (7) the integrity of Hooker's method.

Misreadings of Calvin and Aquinas

To apply the basic point of this study, many accounts of Hooker rely on the presumed contrast or even irreconcilability of Aquinas' and Calvin's theological methods. For example, they assume Calvin by 'self-authentication' means something which puts him at odds with Aquinas' approach, and therefore Hooker is said to reject the reformed stance (e.g., Joyce),[102] follow it rather than Aquinas' (e.g., Atkinson)[103] or steer some middle way between catholic and reformed extremes (e.g., Gibbs).[104] But, as Chapters 2 and 3 showed, the notion Calvin and Aquinas are opposed on many topics is misplaced and they are in fact more congruent than supposed. What we can see is a process of divergence over the years as Calvin and Aquinas have been appropriated in different ways which have conceived points of difference where the original theologians were not in fact at odds. For example, as Chapter 3 showed, if Calvin's account of reason is read through the prism of Barth's views on natural theology we should certainly think him much more pessimistic about that warrant than Aquinas. Again, as Chapter 5 will demonstrate, if Aquinas' account of tradition is read through the later sixteenth-century interpretation of the Council of Trent then we would conclude it was very uncongenial to reformed concerns. What then happens is Hooker is located against a backdrop of later (mis)readings of Calvin and Aquinas which may be quite distinct from those theologians' original texts. Recovering (say) a pre-sixteenth-century account of Aquinas on tradition, or a pre-twentieth-century account of Calvin on reason, allows us to see the greater congruity of their theological methods and removes the need to situate Hooker on a presumed spectrum between them.

Anglican appropriations of Hooker

Just as Calvin and Aquinas have been interpreted in ways which suit other agendas (e.g., Calvin by Barth, Aquinas by Trent), so too Hooker. Almost certainly the most egregious and successful of these appropriations, which Chapter 5 will discuss, is John Keble's, who depicted Hooker as essentially a forerunner of the Oxford Movement.[105] For now a simple comparison will suffice. Atkinson, for example, is an Anglican evangelical who wants a recovery of Hooker's 'explicitly reformed outlook' to 'lead to a rediscovery of the Church of England's true theological heritage'.[106] But to assert a reformed Hooker, for Atkinson, seems to entail rejecting any notion of congruity with Aquinas.[107] Conversely, Joyce rightly identifies a tendency in some evangelical appropriations of Hooker to over-emphasize his connections with the reformed (for example, she rightly sees him as quite suspicious of the congregationalism which marked many continental reformed churches).[108] Yet in turn she appears to appropriate Hooker for a reading of Anglicanism which is much less sympathetic to the reformed, for instance by

102. Joyce, *Anglican Moral Theology*, 116, 146; against Joyce, see Littlejohn, 'Reformed Hooker', 76–8.

103. Atkinson, *STR*, 93, 108–9.

104. Lee W. Gibbs, 'Richard Hooker's *Via Media* Doctrine of Scripture and Tradition', *HThR* 95.2 (2002): 230.

105. See Brydon, *Evolving Reputation*, 199–201; MacCulloch, 'Reputation', 809–10.

106. Atkinson, *STR*, xii.

107. Atkinson, *STR*, xviii.

108. Joyce, *Anglican Moral Theology*, 13–14.

highlighting his affinity with Aquinas while failing to identify his congruence with Calvin.[109] When the intention of those appropriating Hooker can be identified, some of the imbalances in their accounts can be demonstrated, and characterizing Hooker need not be seen as a competitive exercise.

Hooker's attitude to Calvin

However, it is not just later appropriations which have contributed to misreadings of Hooker; his own prose can sometimes mislead the reader. This may be particularly true of Hooker's attitude to Calvin, which is nuanced in detail but sometimes rather spicy in tone.

The *Christian Letter* accused Hooker of 'singling out' Calvin as an 'adversary' of the Church England (*ACL* 19, IV.57.18-9) and departing from the respect in which Calvin had been held by Hooker's patrons, Bishop Jewel and Archbishop Whitgift (IV.55.1-2). It is certainly true that Hooker was sometimes rather rude about the Genevan reformer; he is somewhat dismissive of Calvin's education (as trained in law but self-taught in theology), and his unflattering description of Calvin as 'incomparably the wisest man that ever the French Church did enjoy' (*Laws*, Pref. 2.1) is a barely concealed jibe.[110] Nonetheless, the *Letter* misses the nuance of Hooker's treatment of Calvin, as does Joyce. She argues that Kirby and Atkinson are wrong to see Hooker as advancing a theology 'wholly consistent' with Calvin's.[111] Yet Hooker is very precise in what he opposes in the Preface: what 'Calvin did for the establishment of his discipline, seems more commendable than that which he taught for the countenancing of it' (Pref 2.7). Hooker does not think the establishment of a presbyterian polity unjustified; he does think the insistence after the fact that such a polity was established because it was required by scripture an unacceptable methodological move since (for Hooker) scripture regulates only matters of doctrine, not discipline.[112] Joyce does not appear to grasp the nuance of Hooker's discriminating attitude to Calvin and so fails to see his wide (though not complete) convergence with the Genevan.

Indeed, as Bauckham argues, focus on the rhetoric of the Preface obscures the many ways Hooker actually agrees with Calvin. In twelve of the fifteen direct references to Calvin through the *Laws* Hooker claims to be endorsing the reformer's views.[113] Of course, it might be possible that Hooker is misreading or

---

109. Joyce, *Anglican Moral Theology*, 52–66 (on Calvin), 238–40 (on Aquinas).

110. Here I agree with Joyce, *Anglican Moral Theology*, 53–4, who argues that many analyses have missed the irony of Hooker's account of Calvin – including, for instance, P. D. L. Avis, 'Richard Hooker and John Calvin', *JEH* 32.1 (1981): 23–4.

111. Joyce, *Anglican Moral Theology*, 60; though she rightly notes that Kirby and Atkinson underestimate the sardonic elements of Hooker's depiction of Calvin, 59 fn.68.

112. Cf. Avis, 'Hooker and Calvin', 26–7.

113. Richard Bauckham, 'Richard Hooker and John Calvin: A Comment', *JEH* 32 (1981): 29; see also Avis, 'Hooker and Calvin', 25–6.

misappropriating Calvin, and this relatively small number of direct references to Calvin proves little by itself.[114] Nonetheless, Bauckham's argument should point us beyond the polemic of the Preface to examine in detail the nuance of Hooker's theology and (as this chapter argues) its broad convergence with Calvin's.

Hooker's attitude to Aquinas

If Hooker's attitude to Calvin can easily be read wrongly, so too his attitude to Aquinas. The *Christian Letter* had famously brandished Hooker as overly indebted to scholastic theology, which 'hath banished from us the true and sincere divinity' (*ACL* 20, IV.65.5,13). Certainly Hooker owes much to Aquinas, who he calls the 'greatest of the school divines' (*Laws*, III.9.2). Hooker's account of law (especially I.3)[115] and his Christology (especially V.51-6)[116] can be convincingly shown to echo Aquinas'.

However, Hooker did not adopt Aquinas' positions simply because they were Aquinas' and was quite happy to reject Aquinas' views where they were uncongenial to his reformed commitments. Hooker rejected what he took to be the scholastic position on habitual grace (a 'new Scholastic invention' ... vain, and unnecessary' (*DF* 17, IV.119.1-2)) as a principle deriving from 'the Schoolmen who follow Thomas' and not from scripture (IV.118.23-4, 29-31).[117] Hooker also thoroughly rejected the doctrine of transubstantiation, which he says is nowhere justified by scripture (*Laws*, V.67.9, cf. *Just*. 11, V.119.25-9) or tradition (*Laws*, V.67.11-2).[118]

Moreover, whereas the presbyterians seemed to treat scholasticism as a single category to be rejected (e.g., *ACL* 20, V.65-8), Hooker (as Simut notes) appears to be alert to the distinction between Aquinas' views and those doctrinal developments of the later scholastic period or the sixteenth century focusing most of his ire on the

---

114. See Bauckham, 'Hooker and Calvin', 30.

115. McGrade, 'Sources', 60; W. J. T. Kirby, 'Richard Hooker and Thomas Aquinas on Defining Law', in *Aquinas among the Protestants*, ed. Manfred Svensson and David VanDrunen (Oxford: Wiley-Blackwell, 2018), 91-2.

116. W. David Neelands, 'Christology and the Sacraments', *CRH*, 369-73.

117. On the ambivalence of Hooker's attitude to Aquinas on justification see Debora K. Shuger, 'Faith and Assurance', *CRH*, 236-42, though she also argues he diverges from the reformed tradition on this point too, 221-2; cf. Simut, *Sermons*, 298-308, who locates Hooker among the reformed on this point.

118. The simplicity and bluntness of Hooker's rejection of transubstantiation is clear, so I follow J. R. Parris, 'Hooker's Doctrine of the Eucharist', *SJT* 16.2 (1963): 156-7 and Bryan D. Spinks, *Two Faces of Elizabethan Anglican Theology: Sacraments and Salvation in the Thought of William Perkins and Richard Hooker* (Lanham, MD: Scarecrow Press, 1999), 153-4. Consequently I disagree with Neelands' assertion that Hooker's opposition to it was 'minimalist' and that the presbyterians' suspicion of him justified; 'Christology and Sacraments', 376.

latter.[119] Chapter 3 demonstrated Calvin takes a similarly discriminating approach. Hooker's clear rejection of key tenets of Roman Catholicism demonstrates he is wrongly characterized if his broad use of Aquinas is taken to infer a general adherence to scholastic theology or Aquinas specifically.

The meaning of 'reformed'

Connected with the failure to examine the nuance of Hooker's relationships to Calvin and Aquinas is a more fundamental mischaracterization of 'reformed' which is now being corrected by several strands of contemporary scholarship.

R. A. Muller has been pivotal in demonstrating that 'reformed' was a much broader and more fluid category than often understood.[120] In relation to Reformation England, as Hampton's crucial study reminds us, 'the Reformed tradition was a broad church, encompassing a wider range of views than it has often been given credit for', and so 'identifying a writer as Reformed does not mean they will hold all and only those theological views' held by a particular other reformer or reformers,[121] hence the need to read alongside each other and in detail the specific authors being compared.[122]

Hooker's reformed character has also been obscured by failure to grasp what it meant to call the sixteenth-century Church of England 'reformed'. Milton rightly delineates the Church of England's of the 'unambiguously reformed character',[123] but this can easily be obscured by its retention under the Elizabethan settlement of elements of pre-reformation order. As Hampton writes, the reformation Church of England was 'committed to a range of liturgical practices and ecclesiological claims that appeared decidedly eccentric from the perspective of the wider European Reformed movement'.[124] The reformation Church of England, of course, retained government of the church by bishops, some pre-reformation clerical garments, cathedrals, kneeling to receive communion, and invented Choral Evensong; with rare exceptions such practices were largely abandoned elsewhere in reformed

---

119. Simut, *Sermons*, 237–9, 261.

120. *PRRD*, I.28; cf. R. A. Muller, 'John Calvin and Later Calvinism: The Identity of the Reformed Tradition', in *The Cambridge Companion to Reformation Theology*, ed. David Bagchi and David C. Steinmetz (Cambridge: Cambridge University Press, 2006), esp. 130–2.

121. S. W. P. Hampton, *Anti-Arminians: The Anglican Reformed Tradition from Charles II to George I* (Oxford: Oxford University Press, 2008), 7–8.

122. Hampton, *Anti-Arminians*, 8.

123. Anthony Milton, *Catholic and Reformed: The Roman and Protestant Churches in English Protestant Thought, 1600–40* (Cambridge: Cambridge University Press, 1995), 12. See also, e.g., Patrick Collinson, *The Elizabethan Puritan Movement* (Oxford: Clarendon Press, 1990), 13–15; Nicholas Tyacke, *Anti-Calvinists: The Rise of English Arminianism c. 1590–1640* (Oxford: Clarendon Press, 1987), 1–8; S. W. P. Hampton, 'Confessional Identity', *OHA*, I.210-1.

124. Hampton, *Anti-Arminians*, 8.

churches.[125] The idiosyncrasies of England's reformation, however, as MacCulloch and Quantin remind us, should not blind us to the emphatically reformed character of the Church of England.[126] The recent contemporary scholarship of Milton, MacCulloch and Hampton, against the backdrop of Muller's expansion of 'reformed' as an historical and theological category, helps us see that just because Richard Hooker was clearly a conformist – the *Laws* is a substantive theological defence of the polity and practices of the Church of England in his day – does not mean he could not also be reformed.

Similarly, recent scholarship is belying the presumption that, in the sixteenth century, to be reformed was to be not catholic. Certainly the reformers rejected a range of teachings and practices associated with the sixteenth-century Roman Catholic Church. But these do not mean they were rejecting outright the theology of, say, Aquinas; Chapter 3 showed Calvin's thought, consciously or not, has clear points of convergence with Aquinas. So, for example, where Atkinson and Joyce essentially argue that the more Thomist we conceive Hooker the less reformed he must be, and vice versa, it is now becoming clearer that Hooker can be situated within 'the Reformed tradition' which was 'often Thomistic virtually from its outset'.[127] Thus, for example, Dominiak shows considerable congruity between Aquinas and Calvin on the controversial topic of whether scripture is self-authenticating,[128] and Kirby the convergence of their accounts of a twofold knowledge of God.[129]

This retrieval in recent scholarship of the complexity of the definition of 'reformed' and its application to sixteenth-century England, as well as the debt of the reformed tradition to Aquinas, yields a broader definition of 'reformed', making it more plausible to situate Hooker within it while showing how he could be simultaneously catholic and reformed.

Hooker's attitude to Rome

A further factor obscuring Hooker's reformed credentials is his attitude to the Roman Catholic Church. Hooker's deputy and sparring partner at Temple Church, Walter Travers, accused Hooker of failure to condemn Rome (*Suppl.*, V.208.8-10), while the *Christian Letter* said Hooker 'would be glad to see the backsliding of all

---

125. Rare but not unheard of: see Hampton, 'Confessional Identity', 220–1.

126. E.g., Diarmaid MacCulloch, 'Putting the English Reformation on the Map', in his *All Things Made New: Writings on the Reformation* (London: Penguin, 2017), 209–15; Jean-Louis Quantin, *The Church of England and Christian Antiquity: The Construction of a Confessional Identity in the 17th Century* (Oxford: Oxford University Press, 2009), 88–9.

127. W. Bradford Littlejohn and Scott N. Kindred-Barnes, 'Introduction', *RHRO*, ed. Littlejohn and Kindred-Barnes, 25.

128. P. A. Dominiak, 'Hooker, Scholasticism, Thomism, and Reformed Orthodoxy', *RHRO*, ed. Littlejohn and Kindred-Barnes, 116–19; cf. his *Participation*, 149, 195.

129. Kirby, 'Defining Law', esp. 91–5.

reformed churches to be made conformable to that wicked synagogue of Rome' (*ACL* 20, IV.68.1,7).

Indeed, Hooker had preached that 'many of our fathers lying in popish superstitions yet by the mercy of god to be saved' (*Just.* 10, V.118.21-2; cf. *Just.* 9, V.118.4-6),[130] which was the cause of Travers' complaint (*Suppl.*, V.200-2).[131] Moreover, Hooker resisted those who 'make the Church of Rome utterly no church at all' because of its serious doctrinal errors (*Laws*, III.1.10, cf. V.68.5-9). This insistence Roman Catholics might be saved, and that Rome was still a genuine Christian church, prompted Travers and other opponents to challenge Hooker's reformed credentials.

In fact, though, while Hooker was certainly pastorally generous towards Rome and its adherents, he was adamant in his reformed convictions about its fundamental doctrinal flaws. Thus, he condemned its doctrine of justification ('the doctrine professed in the church of Rome does bereave men of comfort', *Just.* 9, V.117.25-6) and so breaking from it was entirely proper ('corrupted as she is and refusing to be reformed … we are to sever ourselves from her', *Just.* 9, V.117.29-118.1). Standard reformation polemic about the Israelites departing from Babylon as a metaphor for the reformed's departure from Rome followed (*Just.* 10-11, V.118-9).[132] Even as Hooker insists that Rome is still a genuine church he is blistering about its doctrinal faults ('gross and grievous abominations') (*Laws*, III.1.10). We saw how Hooker roundly rejects Roman Catholic teaching about transubstantiation and Chapter 5 will show how he condemns what he sees as accretion of papal power and the methodologically flawed scriptural exegesis which underpins it. Hooker's generosity towards Roman Catholicism and its adherents, then, should not mislead us into thinking Hooker departed from the substance of the reformed consensus.

Hooker's theological integrity

A final factor which may account for some misreadings of Hooker is that he is a writer of considerable integrity whose nuanced positions are easily misunderstood or distorted. For instance, while he is entirely happy to say scripture is the sole source of doctrine he is unwilling to say that scripture needs no other warrant to draw out its meaning; the nuance of his *sola scriptura* convictions means he is open to being interpreted in different ways. He rejects the argument of his presbyterian opponents that scripture alone is theologically authoritative not just because he thinks they are wrong but because he thinks they are dishonest, accusing him of relying on sources other than scripture even as they cite extra-scriptural sources against him (*ACL* 3, IV.13.1-6).

---

130. Simut, *Sermons*, 184–90.

131. Bauckham, 'Hooker and Rome', 41–4; see *FLE*, V.261-69 for background on the controversy.

132. Bauckham, 'Hooker and Rome', 40–1.

Again, Hooker accepts the legitimacy of both presbyteral and episcopal forms of church government while being unwilling to insist that either is mandated perpetually by scripture or essential to the church but also because he does not believe those claims can be honestly grounded methodologically or historically (*Laws*, Pref. 4.1, 4.4). This nuance can be lost by those who say he is an advocate of one form of church government, when in fact he makes only the fairly restrained claim that episcopacy is not an illegitimate form of church polity and so should not lightly be cast aside,[133] or allows him to be depicted a champion of reason over against scripture when actually he simply asserts, as Calvin and Aquinas do, that reason has a legitimate theological function which does not diminish the centrality and uniqueness of scripture. Hooker's integrity, then, leaves him open to misunderstanding or attack, and this has helped generate contradictory interpretations of his thought which make locating him theologically a difficult matter of navigating contested terrain.

Summary

Cumulatively, this section demonstrates a range of reasons why Hooker's theological identity has been misunderstood. The nuances of the appellation 'reformed' and of Hooker's attitude to Calvin, Aquinas, and Rome, along with the tendency to compare him with subsequent interpretations of Aquinas and Calvin rather than those authors directly, combine to obscure his congruity with both those theologians and the possibility, even plausibility, of a sixteenth-century Church of England conformist adopting a theological stance which was both catholic and reformed. Moreover, Hooker's integrity means he is not always easy to situate in a debate where (for instance) he at least appears much more realistic than some of his interlocutors. Subsequent appropriations of Hooker to justify contemporary accounts of Anglicanism, moreover, have often heightened points of tension between the catholic and reformed traditions and diminished the possibility of seeing them as congruent. Identifying these factors helps us see the plausibility of relocating Hooker not as the defender of any one type of later Anglicanism, nor as uncritically following either Aquinas or Calvin, but emerging as within a firmly catholic and reformed consensus they both share.

Summary

Richard Hooker's reputation has been contested territory since the presbyterians accused him of departing from the reformed consensus and subsequent Anglicans have appropriated him in aid of their own versions of Anglicanism.[134] This chapter closely reads his texts, building on the readings of Aquinas and Calvin in earlier

---

133. Hobday, 'Hooker and *MMC*', 225–6.
134. For example, see Brydon, *Evolving Reputation*, 5–18.

chapters, demonstrating the possibility of reading Hooker as both catholic and reformed on his account of scripture and reason. The investigation shows Hooker follows both Calvin and Aquinas in attributing real but limited capacity to reason as a source of some knowledge of God but maintains a *sola scriptura* view of theological method because scripture alone is the source of God's revelation, which is the only source of that knowledge of God which generates Christian doctrine and yields salvation. Reasons this convergence has been overlooked were adduced, including failure to see Hooker's nuanced approach to his interlocutors or to recognize that nuance in pursuing a partisan reading of his theology. On *scripture* and *reason*, then, Hooker, Calvin and Aquinas have much more in common than often supposed, and the next chapter will test whether this is also true of their accounts of a third warrant, *tradition*.

Chapter 5

TRADITION IN HOOKER, CALVIN AND AQUINAS

Introduction

Was the sixteenth-century Church of England catholic or reformed or something in between, and which should Anglicanism be today? The question itself, as this study argues, needs to be reframed, since no such choice is needed, but for some at the time and since, it was presumed that it did. So, as the last chapter demonstrated, by the late 1590s Richard Hooker was already skating on thin theological ice with his presbyterian opponents, who already suspected him dangerously unsound because of his views on two of the theological warrants, *scripture* and *reason*. They accused him of he was moving away from the reformed tradition and in a more catholic direction and sought to reclaim what they thought was the Church of England's reformed and therefore less catholic identity.[1] By 1599, Hooker was also in the presbyterians' sights for his account of a third warrant, *tradition*.[2] That year, the author(s) of the *Christian Letter* complained that his account of tradition would 'disgrace … the English Church' (*ACL* 4, IV.16.3-4). In particular, they 'suspect[ed] the underpropping of a popish principle concerning the church's authority above the Holy Scripture' (IV.16.2-3). The presbyterians accused Hooker of departing from the reformed *sola scriptura* principle by making scripture reliant on tradition.

Chapters 2 to 4 demonstrated that, despite the presbyterians' accusations and many subsequent interpretations, Hooker's theological method need not be characterized on a reformed-catholic perspective because, at least as related to Aquinas and Calvin, those theological methods are fundamentally congruent

---

1. See Lee W. Gibbs, 'Life of Hooker', *CRH*, 11-13; Richard Bauckham, 'Hooker, Travers, and the Church of Rome in the 1580s', *JEH* 29 (1978): 37-50.

2. On tradition, see Mike Higton, 'Tradition', in *The Routledge Companion to the Practice of Christian Theology*, ed. Mike Higton and Jim Fodor (London: Routledge, 2015), 192-202; A. N. Williams, 'Tradition', in *OHST*, 362-76; A. N. Williams, *The Architecture of Theology: Structure, System, and Ratio* (Oxford: Oxford University Press, 2011), 84-7; Richard Bauckham, 'Tradition in Relation to Scripture and Reason', in *Scripture, Tradition and Reason: A Study in the Criteria of Christian Doctrine: Essays in Honour of R.P.C. Hanson*, ed. Richard Bauckham and Benjamin Drewery (Edinburgh: T&T Clark, 1988), 117-45.

in their accounts of scripture and reason. This chapter advances the argument by demonstrating the convergence of their accounts of tradition, challenging characterizations of Hooker and of Anglicanism which rely on the presumption the catholic Aquinas articulates a more positive view of tradition and the reformed Calvin a more negative one.

An initial discussion of Aquinas highlights some of the questions which generate a debate about the role of tradition in relation to scripture, not least the problem that scripture is not always clear, and indeed did not even exist (in the sense of a fixed collection of texts attributed special authority) until the fourth Christian century. Then for each theologian in turn, the relationship of scripture and tradition in their method is examined before the role of church councils is explored. A key, shared conceptual distinction emerges, as Oberman and Bauckham argue, between the operation of tradition in the earliest Christian centuries and thereafter, a distinction adduced in the Anglican tradition by a seminal work of R. P. C. Hanson. This distinction offers the basis of a shared account of tradition which brings Anglican and reformed perspectives in line with pre-reformation catholic ones. Finally, reasons this convergence has been overlooked are adduced, notably (1) the catholic definition of tradition endorsed by the sixteenth-century Council of Trent embedded a divergence between catholic theology and reformed thought which was not indicated by Aquinas' method, and (2) John Keble's appropriation of Hooker, misleadingly but successfully, portrayed him as pulling away from the reformed on this question. The chapter therefore traces a clear catholic-reformed continuity articulated by Aquinas and Calvin while yielding a theological method which accommodates the historical realities of doctrinal development.

Tradition in Aquinas' theological method

Introduction

Valkenberg contrasts 'the Catholic methodological principle of scripture and tradition as more or less separate sources of revelation' with 'the Reformed methodological principle of scripture being the sole critical norm in theology'.[3] At first glance, this distinction seems justified, given the assertion of official Roman Catholic formularies that 'Sacred Tradition and Sacred Scripture comprise a single sacred deposit of the Word of God entrusted to the Church' (*Fides et ratio*, 46). Claims that scripture and tradition are somehow jointly or autonomously authoritative would be suspicious from a reformed perspective, which emphasis the uniqueness of scripture as the sole source of our saving knowledge of God. However, as we will see, neither the tendency to separate nor the tendency to elide the two warrants is Aquinas' view, so he need not be read as uncongenial to reformed concerns.

---

3. W. G. B. M. Valkenberg, *Words of the Living God: Place and Function of Holy Scripture in the Theology of St Thomas Aquinas* (Leuven: Peeters, 2000), 215.

Aquinas on scripture and tradition

Turning to Aquinas' view of the relationship between scripture and tradition, an initial problem, as Persson notes, is that Aquinas never describes precisely what he means by tradition or how it functions in theological method; at one point, he even writes of the 'tradition of sacred scripture',[4] which might (as the *Fides et ratio* definition seems to) elide the distinction between the two. But Aquinas, as Persson continues, is both sparing and casual in his use of the word 'tradition': it can refer to human traditions such as the canons, say, or even his own teaching.[5] So we need to probe Aquinas' writing more deeply to reveal his underlying account of the warrant, which is both consistent and congenial with reformed concerns.

The key dialectic in the opening chapters of the larger *Summa* was between reason and revelation. Reason can know naturally some truths about God ('the existence of God and other like truths can be known by natural reason': *S. Th.* I.2.2, *ad.*1), but revelation alone delivers the saving truths of the Christian faith ('certain truths which exceed human reason should be made known to us by divine revelation': I.1.1, *resp.*). Harrison, as we saw, attributed Aquinas a fairly expansive account of tradition's scope and authority to include in the category of revelation a range of extra-scriptural and indeed non-Christian sources; Valkenberg, while restricting the range to Christian sources, still suggested an expansive definition of what counted as authoritative tradition.[6] In fact, as Chapter 1 argued, Aquinas effectively restricted revelation almost entirely to scripture, hence the contrast between the knowledge of 'philosophical science' and 'other knowledge – i.e., inspired of God', namely 'scripture' (I.1.1, *s.c.*).

The discrimination between scripture as the locus of revelation and all other, and therefore lesser, sources of authority is clear in what I think is the single instance where Aquinas treats all three warrants and their relationship (*S. Th.* I.1.8). Aquinas begins, '[S]acred scripture has no science above itself' (*resp.*), asserting the clear priority of scripture over all other sources of knowing.[7]

Then, in his dense but crucial reply to the second objection (I.I.8, *ad.* 2), Aquinas explains that sacred doctrine

> is especially based on arguments from authority, inasmuch as it principles are obtained by revelation … Nor does this take away from the dignity of this

---

4. Per Erik Persson, *Sacra Doctrina: Reason and Revelation in Aquinas*, trans. Ross Mackenzie (Oxford: Basil Blackwell, 1970), 45.

5. Persson, *Sacra Doctrina*, 47.

6. Cf. Peter Harrison, *The Bible, Protestantism, and the Rise of Modern Science* (Cambridge: Cambridge University Press, 1998), 69; Pim Valkenberg, 'Scripture', in *The Cambridge Companion to the* Summa Theologiae, ed. Philip McCosker and Denys Turner (Cambridge: Cambridge University Press, 2016), 51.

7. Brian Davies, *The Thought of Thomas Aquinas* (Oxford: Clarendon Press, 1992), 10–14; Rudi te Velde, *Aquinas on God: The Divine Science of the* Summa Theologiae (Farnham: Ashgate, 2006), 19–20.

doctrine, for although the arguments from authority based on human reason is the weakest, yet the argument from authority based on divine revelation is the strongest.

Next, Aquinas simultaneously establishes an ancillary but substantial role for another warrant: reason. Thus, 'sacred doctrine makes use even of human reason' but only 'to make clear other things that are put forward' by revelation. Here, Aquinas explicitly distinguishes the function of the two warrants: revelation alone is the *source* of our doctrine; reason has a role in interpreting or clarifying it but does not itself ground doctrinal claims.

It may be significant that it is only after establishing *reason's* secondary and ancillary authority to revelation does Aquinas turn to *tradition*. Having explained that the authority of revelation is stronger than that of reason, Aquinas then establishes where this revelation is to be found; any authority other than revelation can only carry 'extrinsic and probable arguments' because the church accepts

> the authority of the canonical scriptures as an incontrovertible proof, and the authority of the doctors of the church as one that may properly be used, yet merely as probable. For our faith rests upon the revelation made to the apostles and prophets, who wrote the canonical books, and not on the revelations (if any such there be) made to other doctors.

By saying 'the argument from authority based on divine revelation is the strongest', Aquinas is establishing scripture's primacy because only the divine speech, and no merely human utterance, can carry the authority of the divine speaker – hence, only 'the authority of the canonical scriptures' can undergird 'an incontrovertible proof'.

The 'authority of the doctors of the church', by contrast to the authority of scripture, is 'merely probable'. This is the single reference to what might be called tradition in the opening questions of the larger *Summa*; the uniqueness of the mention alone should raise a question about whether the warrant has significant weight in his theological method. Its 'merely probable' authority is a significant qualification, as is the restrictive formulation that faith rests on the canonical scriptures authored by 'apostles and prophets', not on the teachings of 'doctors of the church'. Valkenberg and Harrison have not grasped the tight definition of the warrants here, where Aquinas very clearly establishes the absolute priority of revelation and equates it almost entirely with scripture (cf. I.1.2, *ad*. 2).[8]

---

8. David S. Sytsma, 'Thomas Aquinas and Reformed Biblical Interpretation', in *Aquinas among the Protestants*, ed. Manfred Svensson and David VanDrunen (Oxford: Wiley-Blackwell, 2018), 60; cf. Nicholas M. Healy, 'Introduction', in *Aquinas on Scripture: An Introduction to his Critical Commentaries*, ed. Thomas G. Weinandy, Daniel A. Keating and John P. Yocum (London: T&T Clark, 2006), 18; Persson, *Sacra Doctrina*, 51–3, 79–80.

This insistence, that scripture alone is the warrant which grounds matters of faith or doctrine, recurs elsewhere. For instance, Aquinas says that 'Holy Writ is the rule of faith, to which no addition or subtraction can be made' (II-II.1.9, *obj*. 1). Similarly, glossing Gal. 1.8-9, Aquinas writes, 'nothing is to be taught except what is contained, either explicitly or implicitly, in the Gospels and epistles and Sacred Scripture' (*in Gal.*, 10).[9] The 'implicitly', of course, begs the question (to which we must return) of who determines what is implicit: even so, the key principle is that scripture alone grounds doctrine. Hence, as Davies concludes, '*sacra doctrina* and *sacra scriptura* can be used interchangeably ... access to revelation is given in the words of canonical scripture and especially in the teaching of Christ'.[10]

Part of the key to understanding tradition's function as a warrant, then, is to contrast it with the function of revelation, of which scripture alone is the source; in other words, we define tradition by first defining revelation and, specifically, conceiving the scriptural deposit of revelation as the sole source of saving truth. Read this way, Aquinas begins to sound congenial to the reformed concerns about the priority of scripture and the dangers of tradition. Indeed, Sytsma cites Hooker's contemporary, the reformed theologian William Whitaker (Regius Professor of Divinity at Cambridge, 1558–95), who 'appealed positively to Aquinas's opinion on the canonical authority and perfection of scripture'.[11] Sytsma highlights numerous examples of Whitaker quoting Aquinas, including the scriptural commentaries, to support this reading.[12]

Nonetheless, even this moderately framed version of *sola scriptura* – scripture as the sole source of saving doctrine – poses further questions, as Williams reminds us. First is the *historical* problem. We need not investigate in detail the questions of when and how the canon was formed[13] to realize that, as a matter of brute historical fact, the Bible did not exist as a collection of texts, to which definitive and unique authority was attributed, for several centuries after Christ. Thus, 'the lateness of any attestation of the ... canon ... pose[s] serious questions to the notion of scripture as solely authoritative'. Moreover, the question of what was and what was not scripture was decided by the church; this 'ecclesial determination' of the canon 'is already evidence that scripture has never and can never ... stand alone'.[14]

Secondly, as Aquinas' phrase 'contained implicitly' hints, some vital questions of faith are not set out clearly in scripture. For example, Williams observes that the Bible 'did not make the spirit's identity clear' so 'one cannot construct any coherent pneumatology solely' from it.[15] The early church only came over time to attribute divinity to the Holy Spirit, ruling out interpretations of scripture which

---

9. Sytsma, 'Biblical Interpretation', 59.

10. Brian Davies, 'Is Sacra Doctrina Theology?' *New Blackfriars* 71 (1990): 144.

11. Sytsma, 'Biblical Interpretation', 58.

12. Sytsma, 'Biblical Interpretation', 57–61.

13. See, e.g., Joseph Verheyden, 'The New Testament Canon', in *The New Cambridge History of the Bible*, 4 vols (Cambridge: Cambridge University Press, 2012–15), I.389–411.

14. Williams, 'Tradition', 366.

15. Williams, *Architecture of Theology*, 86.

suggested he was subordinate to the Father. This attribution relied heavily on extra-scriptural practices (notably the glorification of Father, Son and Spirit in the liturgy).[16] And Aquinas himself recognized that scripture does not stand entirely alone; for while 'the truth of faith is confessed in Holy Writ', it is 'diffuse … under various modes of expression, and sometimes obscurely' (*S. Th.* II-II.1.9, *ad.* 1). For Aquinas, the Spirit's divinity was clearly one of those things implicit in scripture, but how to know what's implicit, and who decides?

The twin problems of the formation of the canon and of defining 'implicit' doctrine lead some theologians to argue for a fairly broad interpretation of what is 'implicit'. For instance, Elders (like Sytsma) asserts that Aquinas sees scripture as the sole source of doctrine, but he argues that this cannot for Aquinas mean *sola scriptura*, for otherwise some later doctrinal developments such as the assumption of Mary would be unscriptural.[17] This, of course, would be very problematic from a reformed perspective; for how are we to judge which doctrinal developments are faithful to scripture, and is there any limit to the possible developments?

This study follows Sytsma rather than Elders, arguing that Aquinas *does* have a *sola scriptura* view of theological method, but Elders (and indeed Williams) is right to be cautious about that formulation, for scripture does not operate alone; it is not that Aquinas thinks only scripture has theological weight, but that its function in shaping doctrine is unique. A closer study of the role of councils and creeds in Aquinas will reveal the possibility of a very precise account of tradition which recognizes the problems of canon-formation and interpretation while maintaining a form of the *sola scriptura* principle.

Councils and creeds

To be plausible, a *sola scriptura* view of theological method has to account for these twin problems: the formation of doctrine before the canon of scripture was formulated and the possibility of reading different 'implicit' doctrines from the same text. Turning to Aquinas' account of the creeds and councils will show that certain kinds of tradition – but only certain kinds – could be said to operate in doctrinal formation.

Initially, we note that Elders' account of tradition gives greater capacity to the warrant than Aquinas himself. The authority of the doctors of the church is merely probable. There is also a distinction – which becomes clearer in Hooker and Calvin – between tradition in grounding practice and in grounding doctrine. For example, Elders holds that Aquinas' arguments to justify veneration of images are entirely grounded in the practice of the early church, not in scripture, and that this represents the breadth of Aquinas' appeal to tradition.[18]

16. Williams, *Architecture of Theology*, 86–7.
17. Leo Elders, 'Aquinas on Holy Scripture as the Medium of Divine Revelation', in *La Doctrine de la Revelation Divine de Saint Thomas d'Aquin: Actes du Symposium sur la Pensée de Saint Thomas d'Aquin* (Vatican City: Libreira Editrice Vaticana, 1990), 138–9.
18. Elders, 'Aquinas on Scripture', 138.

Now, Aquinas does say that the lack of scriptural evidence for the practice is no reason why images cannot be venerated; since 'scripture does not lay down anything concerning the adoration of images' (III.25.3, *obj.* 1), citing the teaching of John Damascene and Basil as sufficient grounds to justify the practice (*s.c.*). He continues, '[T]he apostles, led by the inward instinct of the Holy Ghost, handed to the churches certain instructions which they did not put in writing' which were 'followed by the faithful as time went on' (*ad.* 4).

However, it is important to note precisely what Aquinas is arguing here. Firstly, a tradition not in the Bible may be followed here because there is no biblical evidence either way; so this is not about drawing a doctrine from scripture, which is silent on icons. Secondly, veneration of images is essentially a ritual practice not a doctrine. As Persson rightly infers, Aquinas distinguishes between unwritten tradition's legitimate use in 'the sphere of the activity and outward ordering of the church' and 'specifically scriptural tradition', the latter having its 'primary reference to the substance of faith'.[19] In other words, tradition here is not being used to ground a doctrine but to undergird a ritual.

Aquinas is, as Davies notes, clear that scripture needs authoritative interpretation, and here he turns to the ancient creeds. Thus, Aquinas writes that because scripture's meaning is sometimes 'difficult' and 'obscure', believers need 'a clear summary from the sayings of Holy Writ' which is not an 'addition' but 'something taken from it' (II-II.1.9, *ad.* 1). This collects the truths of faith so they can more conveniently be presented to the believer (*resp.*) and also helps combat heresy by clarifying contested points of doctrine (II-II.1.9, *s.c.*). And Aquinas tightly defines this kind of spiritual 'collection': only the symbols of faith, the creeds, endorsed by the decision of general councils (II-II.1.9 *s.c.*; II-II.1.10, *s.c.*). This brief but significant pair of articles provides a crucial insight into Aquinas' view: special authority is accorded only to the creeds as formulations of ancient councils which clarify the permissible interpretation of scripture. Hence, Davies concludes,

> [S]*acra doctrina* is, for Aquinas, the content of scripture. And for him it is also the content of the creeds since, in his view, all the creeds amount to a restatement of what is in scripture – a pocket Bible, so to speak … To make the truth of faith quickly accessible to everyone, so he continues, the creeds are needed. But these add nothing to what is already contained in scripture. They merely summarise or highlight with a view to the needs of those who hear them.[20]

Aquinas, then, methodologically constrains tradition, conceiving it as dependent on, and ancillary to, scripture. It cannot be a source or ground of doctrine and cannot operate autonomously; it can only (like reason) be accorded instrumental

---

19. Persson, *Sacra Doctrina*, 45–6.
20. Davies, '*Sacra Doctrina*', 144.

use in drawing out scripture's meaning. Revelation is found in scripture, as interpreted by the creeds of the ancient church.[21]

Such a tighter definition would go some way to meeting reformed concerns about the authority of scripture but not wholly so; for it still leaves open to a question about what doctrines are implicit in scripture, and whether *new* fundamental doctrines, or new aspects to fundamental doctrine, can be discovered – or, as some reformed critics of the Council of Trent and later Roman Catholic formulations might say, invented. Key reformed concerns, as the discussion of Calvin will show, were to stop the articulation of new doctrines which might have little or no apparent scriptural grounding and to end rituals or practices which undermined key doctrines.

Part of the answer – as Bauckham identifies – is to assert a point of break or change in theological method.[22] Before the creeds and the canon were fixed, there was a more fluid period of doctrinal development where tradition (in the sense of widespread practice) did have a greater role: for example, arguments that the Son and the Spirit were both divine relied on a crucial appeal to the ritual practice of baptizing in the name of the Father, Son and Spirit. So an account of tradition which limited this broader functioning of the warrant to the specific period where the conciliar formulations of the key doctrines of faith and the canon of scripture were being fixed might meet those reformed concerns about the potentially dangerous malleability of tradition as a warrant while also reflecting historical reality.

Such an account would not be inconsistent with Aquinas' views, but we do need to consider two further questions: the question of error and the question of definition. A first question is whether a church council can err. A key principle of the reformation was that they can; articulated in Articles XXI–XXII of the Church of England's Articles of Religion (*DER*, 296–7), and in Calvin's insistence on the fallibility of all human institutions including church councils (*Inst.* IV.8.11-12). Yet Aquinas insists that 'the universal church cannot err' (*S. Th.* II-II.1.9, *s.c.*). Here then is an apparent tension between the reformed and catholic accounts. A second question is which church councils are considered authoritative.[23] Aquinas does not explicitly tackle this question, though a set of criteria can be drawn from Calvin, as we will see.

Probing the meaning of 'universal' may offer a way forward. A minimalist construction might allow us to define 'universal' as those councils which command widespread support – that is, the first four councils, those which agreed the limits of the canon and the doctrinal definitions about Christ and the Trinity. Such a definition finds some support in Aquinas, where he insists that no new creed can be formulated (II-II.10, *obj.* 1), and that any formulation of faith must be consistent with the creeds already agreed (*ad.* 2). Since the reformed tradition in general does accept the formulations of the first four councils, and indeed accords

---

21. Cf. Bruce D. Marshall, 'Aquinas as Postliberal Theologian', The Thomist 53.3 (1989): 376.
22. Bauckham, 'Tradition', 127.
23. Williams, 'Tradition', 373–4.

them elevated authority, this might provide the practical and theological basis to resolve the problem of tradition.

This might also help resolve the first question of whether a council can err. Aquinas says the creed is 'published by the authority of the universal church and therefore contains nothing defective' (II-II.1.9, *s.c.*). If 'universal' authority were restricted to the first four councils, it might render irrelevant the question of potential error: a narrow construction, that the first four councils did not err *in fact*, would avoid the question of whether they could have erred in principle.

Such a minimalist account of tradition, which conceived a fundamental change in theological method after the first four councils, could accord with Calvin's and Hooker's. It would maintain the principle, important to the reformers, that scripture alone grounds doctrine, while giving due weight to the historical reality that what we call the Bible did not exist for several centuries and that some key questions about faith were not resolved for some time.

Summary

This account would represent a striking departure from what appears to be the contemporary position of the Roman Catholic Church. And it does, in some senses, represent at least an advance on, or interpretation of, Aquinas' views; for he does not specify which councils are authoritative, and he does not always make clear what is and is not a matter of doctrine which can only be grounded in scripture (though, as we will see, Calvin and Hooker also assert this distinction without making it entirely clear which matters are and are not covered by it). But it would not necessarily be inconsistent with Aquinas' views; for, as we will see, the idea of some sort of equality between scripture and tradition, or the idea that tradition can ground doctrine, is not his. Moreover, this reading of Aquinas on tradition does find support from some Roman Catholic theologians. Wood and Valkenberg, for instance, argue there is some distance between contemporary official Roman Catholic teaching on tradition and Aquinas' views.[24] This point is also made by Healy, who concludes Aquinas

> does not anticipate the later Roman Catholic doctrine of two sources of revelation, Scripture and church tradition ... Scripture alone is the basis of our faith, and of itself gives us knowledge sufficient for our salvation, to which nothing new can or need be added.[25]

Where arguments of a reformed-catholic spectrum attribute to Aquinas a notion of tradition akin to that of later Roman Catholic theology, they are clearly flawed.

---

24. Andrew Wood, 'Thomas Aquinas and Joseph Ratzinger's Theology of Divine Revelation's Transmission: A Comparative Study' (MPhil thesis, Australian Catholic University, 2015), 15; Valkenberg, *Words of the Living God*, 15.

25. Healy, 'Introduction', 18.

Identifying this gap opens up the possibility of conceiving tradition in a way the reformed and the Thomist could share by reading Aquinas' account in a minimalist way. So Aquinas can be interpreted as affirming a nuanced version of the *sola scriptura* principle and only an ancillary, constrained role for tradition. This, as the next section shows, converges with Calvin's reformed perspective, allowing us to conceive the possibility of a catholic theological method, drawing on Aquinas, which was not hostile to reformed concerns.

Tradition in Calvin's theological method

Introduction

Showing the limited appeal to tradition in Aquinas, the previous section contested the first limb of many arguments of a divergence between catholic and reformed perspectives, by showing that tradition in Aquinas is far more constrained than often supposed. This section turns to contest the second limb of those arguments, by tracing Calvin's account of tradition which, as well as a sharp critique of the warrant's abuses, also affords it a positive role in theological method. After sketching the general features of Calvin's account, including his fears about the warrant and its potential misuse, it turns to identify the strong similarity of Calvin's and Aquinas' views notably on the creeds and the councils.

Calvin on scripture and tradition

Some earlier generations of scholarship conceived Calvin as attributing little or no capacity to tradition in theology in conscious opposition to the catholic perspective. Thus, Tavard (a Roman Catholic) feared Calvin's emphasis on scripture 'destroy[ed] all tradition'.[26] Warfield (a Protestant) agreed, arguing Calvin 'repudiates ... the entire Romish argument' about the relationship of scripture and tradition, in particular by rebutting 'the Roman controversialists ... endeavouring to prove that the authority of scripture is dependent upon the church's suffrage'.[27] But reading Calvin more carefully shows both are wrong: for, as Balserak notes, it is not a question of whether or not Calvin appeals to tradition; the question is in what ways and within what parameters.[28] We begin by tracing Calvin's sometimes

---

26. G. H. Tavard, *Holy Writ or Holy Church: The Crisis of the Protestant Reformation* (London: Burns & Oates, 1959), 107.

27. B. B. Warfield, *Calvin and Calvinism* (New York: Oxford University Press, 1931), 94, 93.

28. Jon Balserak, 'The Authority of Scripture and Tradition in Calvin's Lectures on the Prophets', in *The Search for Authority in Reformation Europe*, ed. Helen Parish, Elaine Fulton and Peter Webster (Farnham: Ashgate, 2014), 37; cf. J. P. Mackey, *The Modern Theology of Tradition* (London: DLT, 1962), 174.

pungent polemic about tradition, which reveals two particular concerns: the risk of undermining scripture and the risk of attributing too much power to humans.

Firstly, Calvin fears attaching too much weight to tradition risks undermining scripture's unique authority. Hence the *Genevan Confession* asserts the church 'follow[s] scripture alone as rule of faith … without mixing it with any other thing that might be devised by the tradition of men' (*Treatises*, 26). Similarly, Calvin describes the reformer's task as restoring the church 'to the exact standard of the Word of God' (*Treatises*, 187).

Likewise, in the *Institutes*, Calvin insists that only the revelation in scripture conveys divine communication because it alone is divine speech. Hence, Moses and the prophets speak only what is divinely given (*Inst*. IV.8.2-3, 5-6). Superlatively, Christ speaks with the divine voice: 'it is not written of any other but him only, "Hear him!"' and there is a finality to this speech: 'God deprives men of the capacity to put forth new doctrine', because 'Christ alone is our schoolmaster' (IV.8.1, 9). God 'has fulfilled all functions of teaching in his son that we must regard this as the final and eternal testimony from him' (II.8.7). Since only Christ knows the Father's mind ('to whom alone all the secrets of the Father are revealed'), it is to him we must listen; those who 'would attain knowledge of God should always be directed by that eternal Wisdom' (IV.8.5). And, of course, it is only in scripture that we find the saving words of Christ.[29]

The words of scripture, therefore, as uniquely the words of Christ and therefore of God, are the defining authority in theology, to which all other authorities can only be ancillary, hence Calvin's accusation that his

> opponents locate the authority of the church outside God's Word, but we insist that it be attached to the Word, and … the church should … not devise anything of itself but should set the limit of its own wisdom where Christ has made an end of speaking.
>
> (IV.8.13)

As Helm notes, the Word in scripture alone is invested with the authority of being God's own speech; for 'Calvin doctrine is essential to religion, and true doctrine is to be found in Scripture'.[30] Calvin's concern for the priority of revelation, then, leads him to suspect any theological method which appears to attribute too great an authority to sources other than the definitive witness of that revelation, the words of Christ recorded in scripture.

This unease is, secondly, magnified by Calvin's fear that tradition as a warrant is open to serious abuse by flawed and fallible human institutions and individuals. This is one of the key reasons Calvin is adamant that councils can err. Attribution

---

29. Randall C. Zachman, 'John Calvin', in *Christian Theologies of Scripture: A Comparative Introduction*, ed. Justin S. Houlcomb (New York, NY: New York University Press, 2006), 124–5.

30. Paul Helm, *John Calvin's Ideas* (Oxford: Oxford University Press, 2004), 247.

of too great an authority to councils, Calvin fears, can easily slip into a claim of authority for those who constitute them: 'since these men ... constitute the councils, they actually claim for themselves' the power to shape doctrine; this in turn risks church leaders who 'coin dogmas after their own whim' (IV.8.11).[31] Calvin continues, '[T]he riches of the church are always far from that supreme perfection of which our adversaries boast', and 'sensible people see how perilous it is if men once be given such authority' (IV.8.15).[32]

Importantly, there is also a *pastoral* dimension to Calvin's unease about tradition; it is not just a concern about theological method as such but about the effects of too high a conception of tradition on the believer.[33] The believer's firmness in faith, their conviction about their relationship with God, will be undermined if it rests on something mutable or manipulable. After all, Calvin thought, Christ had warned that 'those who boast the title of pastors and teachers' would cause the greatest injury to the faithful (IV.9.4). This is a key concern in his 1543 attack on the Dutch theologian Pighius, *The Bondage and Liberation of the Will*.[34] If key beliefs cannot be identified with certainty, Calvin asks, or shift as the result of church leaders' decisions, 'what will be the stability of faith ... if it should depend on the approval and decisions of human beings?' (*BLW*, 53). Calvin contrasts tradition, a 'weak and shady ... foundation for faith' (52) with scripture's 'solid and constant reliability' (57). As Balserak concludes, Calvin's anxiety about tradition flows in part from his fear of the consequences of putting doctrine into the hands of humans, where it becomes 'insecure, malleable, and liable to abuse'.[35]

Nonetheless, Calvin's very real concerns about tradition should not obscure the appeal he makes to it. After rejecting the view he attributes his opponents – that 'God is not to be heard in scripture alone but through the tradition of the church' (*BLW*, 55) – he insists he must not be 'understood as though I leave no place for the agreement of the church in questions about the faith', only that teaching 'must be tested by reference to scripture' (64). The issue is not whether or not tradition has a role; Calvin is clear it does, but he objects to theological methods which appear to 'give scripture second place' after it (65).[36]

Indeed, Calvin's attack on Pighius' use of tradition demonstrates the *importance* of the warrant for Calvin.[37] It is not just that Calvin thinks Pighius has elevated

---

31. There are obvious parallels here in Hooker's fear of individuals' privileging their own judgement: *Laws*, Pref. 2.6, 5.3.

32. cf. Helm, *Ideas*, 269.

33. On the often overlooked pastoral concern in Calvin's writings, see Shawn D. Wright, 'John Calvin as Pastor', *Southern Baptist Journal of Theology* 13.4 (2009): 4–17; cf. Balserak, 'Scripture and Tradition', 40, 46.

34. See Bruce Gordon, *Calvin* (London: Yale University Press, 2011), 62, 162.

35. Balserak, 'Scripture and Tradition', 40.

36. Cf. J. F. Peter, 'The Place of Tradition in Reformed Theology', *SJT* 18 (1965): 295; cf. *PRRD*, II.16-77.

37. A. N. S. Lane, 'Introduction', *BLW*, xxi-xxiv.

tradition over scripture; he believes that Pighius is misreading the tradition. Through Books III and IV of *Bondage*, Calvin seeks to rebut, point by point, Pighius' appropriation of Augustine. Pighius 'proposed to make Augustine his ally', but Calvin argues 'Augustine supported our position' (*BLW*, 87).[38] Calvin is not claiming that Augustine, or the tradition generally, is authoritative as such; rather, he argues that Augustine's interpretation of scripture is right and challenges Pighius' account of it. Even Augustine had to be tested against scripture, though where consistent with scripture could be cited authoritatively.[39] And Calvin's principal charge against Pighius is still one of advancing unscriptural doctrine; the priority of the warrant is clear (50); the assertion Pighius is misreading the tradition is an important but ancillary criticism. Calvin was, in many ways, arguing for 'a new way of reading the tradition',[40] where it was firmly subordinated to scripture, not demanding the abolition of tradition as such.

Importantly, moreover, Calvin is quite prepared to appeal to tradition particularly in the sphere of ritual and custom. Calvin makes this clear in his response to the Council of Trent's formulation which, as we will see, could be read as grounding doctrine both in scripture and unwritten tradition:

> Though we grant that the Apostles of the Lord handed down to posterity some customs which they never committed to writing; still, first, this has nothing do with the doctrine of faith (as to it, we cannot extract one iota for from them), but only external rites.
>
> (*Antitode*, 70)[41]

Indeed, Calvin appeals widely to tradition (or, more usually, to scripture and tradition together) in discussions about church practice. Thus, in his 1539 *Reply to Cardinal Sadolet*,[42] he rejects the practice of auricular confession because 'it was *neither* commanded by Christ *nor* practised by the ancient church' (*Treatises*, 238, emphasis added). He opposes withholding the cup from the laity *not only* because scripture records that Christ gave both bread and wine to his disciples *but also* the earliest centuries of practice attest that the laity received both (*Inst.* IV.10.14; IV.17.45-50). The same twin appeal is made to resist Roman Catholic claims for the papacy and the imposition of clerical celibacy (IV.6.6; IV.12.23-27). Moreover, in the sphere of custom, an appeal to tradition alone could be decisive: hence Calvin opposes keeping holy water in churches throughout the week because there is no evidence from the apostolic period for the practice (IV.10.20).

38. See B. A. Gerrish, 'Calvin in Christian Theology', in *The Cambridge Companion to John Calvin*, ed. Donald K. McKim (Cambridge: Cambridge University Press, 2004), 291–4.

39. Gordon, *Calvin*, 106–8.

40. Jane Dempsey Douglas, 'Calvin in Ecumenical Context', in *Cambridge Companion to Calvin*, ed. McKim, 307.

41. See Theodore W. Casteel, 'Calvin and Trent: Calvin's Reaction to the Council of Trent in the Context of His Conciliar Thought', *HThR* 63.1 (1970): 100–14.

42. On the correspondence with Sadolet, see Gordon, *Calvin*, 96–8.

The reformers, then, conceived themselves as restoring rather than abandoning ancient tradition,[43] and accounts like Tavard's and Warfield's do not adequately capture the nuance of Calvin's position, thereby magnifying the perception of an inevitable divergence between the catholic and reformed perspectives on the warrant. Especially in matters of practice rather than doctrine, Calvin will appeal to tradition, sometimes by itself but more often in combination with scripture. Even on matters of doctrine (the dispute with Pighius centred on salvation and free will) tradition has a place, hence the dispute over how to interpret one author in the tradition, Augustine. Tradition does not communicate revelation, for Calvin, and therefore cannot ground doctrine, but scriptural interpretation attested by early Christian thinkers can be good evidence for the shape of a particular doctrine. So long as the appeal is couched in those more restrained terms, Calvin is happy to draw on tradition. Turning next to Calvin's account of church councils will provide a fuller picture of Calvin's understanding of the warrant and its similarity to Aquinas'.

Councils and creeds

The previous section suggested Aquinas' understanding of the councils and creeds was a potentially fruitful basis for an account of tradition which also accommodated reformed concerns; this suggestion suggests that Calvin's account of tradition will also reveal a sense that a particular form of tradition carries special theological authority.

When turning to discuss church councils in the fourth book of the *Institutes*, Calvin is sensitive to the possibility he may be misinterpreted as giving tradition and church authority short shrift: 'the fact I shall here be rather severe does not mean that I esteem the ancient councils less than I ought. For I venerate them from my heart, and desire that they be honoured by all' (IV.9.1). Indeed, Calvin thought such gatherings necessary to resolve doctrinal disputes: in cases of controversy, 'the best and surest remedy is for a synod of true bishops to be convened' (IV.9.13); these councils have 'determining authority' (IV.9.8) and can determine what is the right application of scripture. Moreover, at least in the early part of his career, Calvin (like Hooker) thought a council would be the obvious way to try and resolve the disputes between the reformers and Rome, though he doubted whether a council called by the Pope would ever move from the Roman position.[44] Nonetheless, certainly the councils of the past have, for Calvin, a key role in theology – though, as Peter notes, this immediately begs the further question of *which* councils might have authority, 'unless one introduces another criterion to

---

43. R. A. Muller, *After Calvin: Studies in the Development of a Theological Tradition* (Oxford: Oxford University Press, 2003), 51, 72–5; R. Ward Holder, 'Calvin and Tradition: Tracing Expansion, Locating Development, Suggesting Authority', *Toronto Journal of Theology* 25.2 (2009): 219–20.

44. Casteel, 'Calvin and Trent', 95–9, 115–17.

determine that only certain councils are true'.[45] While Calvin does not identify explicitly what such criteria might be, we can identify three characteristics of true councils which might help enumerate which ones carry 'determinative authority' in the shaping of doctrine. These are *consonance with scripture, early date* and *widespread recognition*. Each of these is addressed in turn.

The first characteristic of a council, in Calvin's eyes, is *consonance with scripture*. A council may, for Calvin, adjudicate between competing interpretations of the Bible, establishing one interpretation as doctrinally normative. This is clear where Calvin says it is proper to use the term 'consubstantial' to describe both the Father's relationship with the Son, even though the word does not appear in scripture. In accepting that doctrinal formulation, part of what Nicaea was doing was endorsing Athanasius' interpretation of scripture while rejecting Arius'. Calvin argues this is a legitimate move, even though the word itself is not in scripture, because it was the logical consequence of scripture's claims about Christ:

> [W]hen it is so often asserted in Scripture that there is one God, and further, when Christ is called so often the true and eternal God, one with the Father – what else were the Nicene fathers doing when they declare them of one essence but simply expounding the real meaning of scripture?
>
> (IV.8.16)

Councils, then, appear to have the power to adjudicate the 'real meaning' of scripture, although 'scripture would stand out in the higher place, with everything subject to its standard' (IV.9.8). So councils are considered authoritative 'insofar as they agree with the rule of the Word'; this, for Calvin, upholds the unique authority of scripture while still recognizing an appeal to tradition in the form of conciliar decisions: 'we still give to councils … such rank and honour as is their due' (*Treatises*, 255).

Of course, this immediately raises the further question of who judges a council's consonance with scripture and how. As McNeill observes, there was considerable medieval debate about whether councils could err and whether any actually had.[46] Calvin clearly believes a council could propound a false, unscriptural doctrine; 'I deny it to be the case that an interpretation of scripture adopted by a council is true and certain' (*Inst.* IV.9.13, cf. IV.8.10). This risks the charge, levelled by Tavard, of self-contradiction; in attempting to uphold the authority of scripture while insisting that the authority of councils is not guaranteed, does Calvin substitute individual judgement – even his own judgement – for the corporate authority of church councils?[47] This in turn might risk the destabilizing

---

45. Peter, 'Tradition', 297.
46. *Inst.* II.1158, fn.10.
47. Tavard, *Writ or Church*, 109; cf. Eduardo Echevarria, 'Revelation, Faith, and Tradition: Catholic Ecumenical Dialogue', *CThJ* 63.1 (2016): 42–4.

possibility of everyone judging which doctrines to follow on their basis of their own assessment of a council's consonance with scripture.

Certainly some of Calvin's language is vulnerable to that kind of accusation. Conscience, as Bosco shows, plays a significant part in Calvin's thought. He attaches much weight to individual conscience (*Commentaries*, 87–8) and insists that God may be found in small gatherings of believers as much as general councils (*Inst.* IV.9.2).[48] However, Calvin seems alert to the risk of emphasizing personal conscience identified in the last paragraph: 'you will say I degrade everything, so that every man has the right to accept or reject what the councils decide' (IV.9.8; cf. *Antidote*, 74). But Bosco highlights that Calvin's appeal to conscience is in fact more complicated than a simple assertion that a person's thoughts or feelings are an invariable guide to truth.[49] The emphasis on personal judgement is already more guarded than a critic like Tavard seems to imply, and the other two criteria we can identify from Calvin's account safeguards further his theological method from sliding into individualism.

The second characteristic of authoritative councils is an *early date*. Calvin, like many of the reformed, thought that the closer the stream of doctrine was to the spring of revelation the purer its doctrinal water would be. Hence his pungent contention to Sadolet:

> Our agreement with antiquity is far closer than yours ... all we have attempted has been to renew the ancient form of the church which, at first distorted and stained by men of indifferent character, was afterwards criminally mangled and almost destroyed by the Roman pontiff and his faction.
>
> (*Treatises*, 231)

Again, Calvin asks, 'how much corruption could a long succession of years bring?' (*Inst.* IV.9.4). So, methodologically, the earlier councils are to be preferred, and particularly, and revealingly, those he goes on to enumerate: 'we willingly embrace and reverence as holy the early councils, such as those of Nicaea, Constantinople, Ephesus I, and Chalcedon ... as they relate to the teachings of faith'. He considers they meet both criteria, consonance with scripture (they 'contain nothing but the pure and genuine exposition of scripture') and antiquity ('the church has degenerated from the purity of that golden age') (IV.9.8). Here then Calvin at least implicitly asserts a break point in the development of doctrine with the first four councils named as distinctively authoritative.

This sense of a decisive shift in the operation of tradition is reinforced by Calvin's response to Pighius on the interpretation of Gal. 1.9, 'if anyone proclaims to you a gospel contrary to the one you received, let that one be accursed'. Pighius argued this meant unwritten, oral tradition had apostolic status alongside the words of

---

48. David L. Bosco, 'Conscience as Court and Worm: Calvin and the Three Elements of Conscience', *Journal of Religious Ethics* 14.2 (1986): 333–55.

49. Bosco, 'Conscience', 340, 350–1.

scripture, since the Greek παραλαμβανω carries the particular connotation of transmission by oral means. According to Calvin's description, Pighius said this meant unwritten tradition, 'because Paul speaks not of writing but of word of mouth' (*BLW*, 60).

Calvin contests this interpretation, insisting that revelation of doctrine comes only through scripture's text and not any unwritten tradition which sits alongside it. So he agrees that, initially, the transmission of revelation was oral: 'the apostles at first bore witness by word of mouth' (60), but 'the whole of their gospel was faithfully reduced to a summary which could be fully sufficient' (61). Then, 'after it had been reduced to written form God sealed as his word'; this sealing was necessary because humans tend inevitably to 'seek for a new form of religion if they were not held back ... by fixed boundaries of teaching' (61). Calvin's insistence on fixed boundaries is significant because the canon of scripture is just such a boundary. There was, Calvin recognizes, a period where the revelation of doctrine was transmitted orally and not written down in a single collection, but, once it was, the church had settled on the boundary of the deposit of revelation, and this source is in a sense put beyond reach of alteration. This approach resolves the problem of the tradition existing before scripture, by asserting that the more fluid notion of revelation only existed before the canon was fixed. The first four councils, the oldest, would be accorded the 'determinative authority' to settle the bounds of the canon and doctrinal boundaries, but this power then lapsed once the canon was fixed.

Calvin's third criterion, hinted at but not made explicit, is that for a council to have this kind of determinative authority in doctrine it must not only be *ancient* and *consonant with scripture* but also command *widespread recognition*. This might be a way of parsing 'universal church' as, at the very least, consistent with Aquinas' understanding; intriguingly, it definitely links with Hooker's perspective. Calvin, as we saw, singled out the first four councils (*Inst.* IV.9.8; *Antidote*, 58). McNeill, revealingly, makes the connection: 'Calvin names with full authority (as faithful to scripture) the four general councils commonly held of special authority, e.g., by Anglican writers such as ... Hooker.'[50] Calvin, then, like the Anglican tradition, affords doctrinal authority only to the most ancient councils partly because the attribution of that authority to them is widespread.

This reading of Calvin on councils is further reinforced by his criticism of some Roman Catholic councils, where a principal accusation is their lack of representativeness. Thus, he resists claims on behalf of sixteenth-century Roman Catholic bishops, 'since these men constitute the councils, they actually claim for themselves everything they claim due to the councils' (*Inst.* IV.8.10).[51] The unrepresentativeness of councils made up only of Roman bishops was further exacerbated, for Calvin, by the way bishops were chosen; in calling for a 'synod of true bishops' Calvin questions whether they could be authoritative because

---

50. *Institutes*, II.1171 fn.8.
51. Casteel, 'Calvin and Trent', 102, 113.

'the people's right in electing bishops has been taken away' (IV.5.2). By contrast with the unrepresentativeness of councils in his own day, Calvin asserts that the authority of doctrinal formulations of the early church (notably the Apostles' Creed) is grounded in its widespread recognition – it is 'something all Christians hold in common' (*Treatises*, 92). The criterion of widespread recognition, connected with the representativeness of the decision-taking body, suggests a third aspect to the test of which councils have determinative authority.

Calvin's response to the Council of Trent further supports this threefold test. He contrasts it with the first four councils (*Antidote*, 58) and says it cannot claim like authority. Partly this is because he thinks Trent has endorsed a theological method which will give unwritten tradition something like parity with scripture: it 'ordain[ed] in doctrine that we are not to stand on scripture alone, but also on the things handed down by tradition' (67), such that even 'if supported by no authority of scripture' an appeal to a tradition can develop doctrine 'which they insist should have the same authority as the Law and the Prophets' (68).[52] Whether or not this is a fair reading of Trent, it is certainly very different from Aquinas' chastened account of tradition traced earlier.

Furthermore, Calvin continues, Trent cannot claim real authority because it is unrepresentative and thus fails to meet even Rome's definition of a council. While claiming to be universal and ecumenical, Calvin says, '[H]ad it been only a Provincial Synod they should have been ashamed of the fewness of its members. Why, then ... shall we regard this as a Holy Council?' (57). Elsewhere, he asks, '[T]hey contend that a Council cannot err because it represents the Church. What if the latter point were denied to be true?' (33). For Calvin, then, Trent cannot assert determinative authority because its claim to be representative is flawed.

By contrast to Trent, the first four named councils *do* have special authority because they meet the three criteria discerned in Calvin's argument. This becomes clear when Calvin contrasts Nicaea I (325) with Nicaea II (787). The first, says Calvin, meets all three criteria: scriptural consonance ('simply expounding the real meaning of scripture', *Inst.* IV.8.16); early date (IV.9.8); and wide recognition ('its eminence has been recognised by the consent of all', IV.9.10). The second, by contrast, not so: it was 'perverting and mangling the whole of scripture' by authorizing 'not only images but the worship of them': for Calvin, this breach of the second commandment suffices to condemn it as unscriptural (IV.9.9), and nor can it claim antiquity or widespread recognition in the way the first four can. Whether or not Calvin is right about the council's formulation on images, the methodology (which recurs at *Antidote*, 75), is clear.

Above all, the creeds, of course, represent determinative authority for Calvin as doctrinal formulations of the earliest four councils. He explicitly endorses the Apostles' Creed and, in affirming the first four councils, implicitly endorses the Nicene Creed (while querying the complexity of the latter's language).[53]

---

52. Casteel, 'Calvin and Trent', 103.

53. Cf. Stephen M. Reynolds, 'Calvin's View of the Athanasian and Nicene Creeds', *Westminster Theological Journal* 23.1 (1960): 36.

The first councils carry special doctrinal weight for Calvin, then, which the later councils do not.[54]

What emerges from this discussion of Calvin is that closer attention to the role of councils (and the doctrinal formulations they generate) yields an account of tradition which could maintain the reformed emphasis on *sola scriptura* alongside an acceptance of the historical evidence of the early Christian centuries. As Lane said, 'Calvin respected the first four general councils … councils are a good way to settle doctrinal disputes, but they are not given any automatic infallibility'.[55] Calvin indeed calls them the four 'great councils' (*Antidote*, 58) and accords their formal conciliar decisions doctrinal authority. As Bauckham concludes, 'the church's recognition of the canon … created a real break, which gave the origin of the tradition, in its written form, a uniquely normative status in relation to the rest of the tradition'.[56] Calvin appears to cite such a constrained kind of tradition in doctrine while rejecting the notion of other 'traditions' defining doctrine.

While this account might meet both reformed concerns and reflect the historical reality, it would pose problems notably for the Orthodox, who attribute authority to the first seven councils, as Roman Catholics do to twenty-one.[57] But Pelikan's monumental study recognizes that the first four councils are more widely accounted authoritative. He cites Gregory the Great and Justinian as representative figures showing 'both Greeks and Latins' appealing to the criterion of universality in privileging these four.[58] Perhaps, then, the determination of the first four councils might command widespread support, as these councils are specially honoured by the broadest range of Christians, even if there is disagreement about whether and which subsequent ones should be recognized.

Summary

Calvin insisted, '[W]e neither condemn not impair the authority of the church; nor do we give loose reins to men to dare what they please' (*Antidote*, 77). So

---

54. There is, as Reynolds, 'Calvin's View of the Creeds', 33–5 notes, less clarity about Calvin's view of the Athanasian Creed; nonetheless, Calvin concludes that because it lacks conciliar endorsement, assent to it cannot be demanded of the believer. Interestingly, both Hooker and Aquinas seem ambivalent to it too. Hooker acknowledges all three creeds (*Laws*, V.42.6), and argued that the Athanasian Creed should be retained in the liturgy (V.27.1, V.35.1), but, like Calvin, he refrains from claiming conciliar endorsement for it (V.42.2). Similarly, Aquinas distinguishes the Athanasian Creed (an 'explanation of faith') from the other creeds (called 'symbols'). (*S.Th*. II-II.1.10, *ad*. 3). This is an intriguing point of convergence, albeit not vital to the debate.

55. A. N. S. Lane, 'Calvin's Use of Fathers and Medievals', *CThJ* 16 (1981): 173.

56. Bauckham, 'Tradition', 127.

57. Williams, 'Tradition', 374.

58. Jaroslav Pelikan, *The Christian Tradition: A History of the Development of Doctrine*, 5 vols (Chicago, IL: University of Chicago Press, 1971–89), I.335, cf. I.333.

he is far from the critic of the tradition depicted by Tavard and Warfield. He is certainly cautious, even suspicious at times, about the warrant; in particular, Calvin is wary of the assertion of 'unwritten traditions' may be pastorally destabilizing and accrete corrupting authority to individuals or institutions. Calvin is certainly prepared to cite tradition to support or oppose practices and rituals, and on the appeal to tradition in matters of doctrine, his nascent scheme of three criteria to test conciliar authority suggests a historical shift between how tradition operated before and after the fixing of the canon and creeds. Such an account, preserving scripture's material sufficiency as the sole source of doctrine while accommodating the historical reality, might be plausible while commanding widespread ecumenical support. It is at least not inconsistent with Aquinas, who likewise had a constrained place for tradition in matters of doctrine, so the second limb of many characterizations of the debate – that Calvin gives tradition relatively little or no place compared with Aquinas – is also undermined. As we now show, this approach we can see consistently in Aquinas and Calvin is also consistent with Hooker's approach.

Tradition in Hooker's theological method

Introduction

Readings of Hooker on tradition often presume he must be located somewhere on a spectrum between catholic and reformed poles and cite Aquinas and Calvin as representatives of these respective positions. Thus, following Hooker's presbyterian opponents, Marshall asserts a Thomist influence on Hooker which pulls him away from the reformed: 'Hooker, unlike Calvin, does accept tradition.'[59] Rejecting this interpretation, Atkinson conversely contends for a Hooker whose feet are firmly on reformed ground: 'Hooker's view of tradition ... was closer to a Reformed understanding than Marshall was prepared to admit.'[60] Gibbs, meanwhile, presents Hooker as steering a middle course – a 'distinctive *via media*' – in this debate.[61] So far, this chapter has contested the basis of these interpretations by arguing there is little discernible difference between Aquinas and Calvin on tradition, and a theological method consistent with both could be advanced. This section situates Hooker within that catholic-reformed convergence, first by sketching Hooker's appeal to tradition in light of the vital doctrine-discipline distinction before

---

59. J. S. Marshall, *Hooker and the Anglican Tradition: An Historical and Theological Study of Hooker's Ecclesiastical Polity* (London: A&C Black, 1963), 55.

60. Nigel Atkinson, *Richard Hooker and the Authority of Scripture, Tradition, and Reason: Reformed Theologian of the Church of England* (Vancouver: Regent College Publishing, 1997), 75.

61. Lee W. Gibbs, 'Richard Hooker's *Via Media* Doctrine of Scripture and Tradition', *HThR* 95.2 (2002): 228.

secondly demonstrating the coherence of his account of councils and creeds with those of Aquinas and of Calvin.

Hooker on scripture and tradition

Hooker is a defender of the *status quo*. The *Laws*' central argument is precise and minimalist: it is that no further reformation of the English Church is *necessary*: there is 'no law of God, nor reason of man' which *requires* further adjustment of the Elizabethan settlement (Pref. 1.2). Indeed, a substantial part of the *Laws* is an extended defence of continuing specific church practices. Book V justifies retaining rituals or customs the presbyterians wanted reformed or abolished, while Book VII argues for continuing the rule of the church by bishops which presbyterians wanted replaced by a system of local minsters.[62]

An examination of how Hooker defends the government of the church by bishops, though, reveals the limited nature of his appeal to tradition. As Chapter 3 showed, Hooker's defence of the settlement was not based on scripture. While bishops, he felt, were implicit in the New Testament account, Hooker relied on the wider methodological argument that the church's polity was mutable, a matter of *discipline* not *doctrine*.[63] The role of tradition is largely limited to the former; even in this sphere of discipline, though, Hooker does not claim decisive authority for it: so we must be cautious about readings of Hooker (like Marshall's) which appear to say Hooker accords it much more significant authority than the reformed generally.

Hooker's appeal to tradition within this sphere is, in fact, carefully circumscribed. Long-standing use ('the ancienter, the better', Pref. 4.5) is a good argument to continue a practice. Tradition in this sense, says Hooker, is those 'ordinances made in the prime of Christian religion, established with that authority which Christ hath left to his church for matters indifferent' (V.65.2). So, Hooker asserts, episcopacy was 'from ancient times … universally established', claiming it was divinely instituted, coming 'to the Apostles by a very Divine appointment' (VII.5.8), who then transferred that authority to their successors (VII.4.1, cf. VII.4.3). Tradition carries weight; the novelty of the presbyterian polity tells against it ('till yesterday [n]ever heard of'), while the antiquity of the episcopate is a significant factor in its favour ('some wicked thing has undoubtedly bewitched us, if we forsake that government the use whereof has for many years approved', VII.1.4).

Yet Hooker's appeal to tradition is heavily qualified. Tradition is not attributed to Christ, here, nor is the argument an appeal to tradition *as such*: the appeal is really to *reason*, to the discretion of the church to decide, in which long-standing use is a proper factor to be weighed, yet not by itself a decisive one. Moreover, any particular church polity 'is not absolutely necessary, but of a changeable nature … the Church

---

62. Mark D. Chapman, *Anglican Theology* (London: T&T Clark, 2012), 107, 120; cf. Diarmaid MacCulloch, 'Richard Hooker's Reputation', *EHR* 117 (2002): 799.

63. Chapman, *Anglican Theology*, 120–3.

has power to alter with general consent and upon necessary occasion even the positive laws of the apostles' (VII.5.8).[64] And 'the church has authority to establish ... at one time' a form of government 'which at another ... it may abolish, and in both do it well' (V.8.2). Even a tradition with scriptural provenance it has no binding force, so the New Testament evidence for bishops is not 'any reason sufficient wherefore all churches should forever be bound to keep them without change' (III.10.17).[65] So, for Hooker, 'episcopacy was ordained by the Apostles, warranted by scripture, and the best available church government', but this 'did not involve the assertion of its perpetual necessity'.[66]

Indeed, the limited place of tradition is further emphasized by Hooker's insistence that, in matters of discipline, the *status quo* carries significant but not overwhelming weight; existing arrangements are 'requisite to be observed till like authority see just and reasonable cause to alter them' (V.65.4). 'Reasonable cause' is the key appeal for Hooker: for the vital warrant in retaining bishops, as in all matters of church order, is neither scripture nor tradition but reason. Recall that 'in things indifferent there is a choice' (III.9.1); and Hooker states that episcopacy 'stand[s] in force, rather by the custom of the church, choosing to continue in it' (VII.5.8). Now, Hooker thinks there are very good reasons why the church might choose to retain the custom; 'prelacy must needs be acknowledged exceedingly beneficial to the church' (VII.18.4). As McGrade identifies, there are a range of reasons Hooker cites, such as the usefulness of identifiably senior figures to engage with counterparts in the state (VII.18.9) and to care for clergy (VII.18.11-12).[67]

---

64. Here, even in the later Book VII where Hooker offers the strongest case for maintaining bishops, he pointedly refuses to insist they are indispensable. As M. R. Somerville, 'Richard Hooker and His Contemporaries on Episcopacy: An Elizabethan Consensus', *JEH* 34 (1984): 177-80, argues, this tells against the notion that Hooker changed his mind between the earlier and late books. Hooker was quite prepared to claim divine sanction for bishops: e.g., Daniel F. Graves, '"*Iure Divino*"? Four Views on the Authority of the Episcopacy in Richard Hooker', *Anglican and Episcopal History* 81.1 (2012): 47-60. But the claim that bishops are indispensable to church life because of scripture and/or tradition is a demonstrably later development and inconsistent with Hooker's methodological principle that church government was not to be decided conclusively by either of those warrants: see K. P. J. Padley, 'Early Anglican Ecclesiology and Contemporary Ecumenism', *International Journal for the Study of the Christian Church* 9.1 (2009): 6-7; Anthony Milton, *Catholic and Reformed: The Roman and Protestant Churches in English Protestant Thought, 1600-40* (Cambridge: Cambridge University Press, 1995), 450-61.

65. Thus Nigel Voak, 'Richard Hooker and the Principle of *Sola Scriptura*', *JTS* 59.1 (2008): 125-6; Egil Grislis, 'Scriptural Hermenuetics', *CRH*, 289.

66. Somervile, 'Elizabethan Consensus', 183; cf. A. S. McGrade, 'Episcopacy', *CRH*, 485-6.

67. McGrade, 'Episcopacy', 497-501. McGrade's essay is a rare and fine example of a discussion of episcopacy which focuses not on the theological debate about justifying episcopacy but the practical and pastoral reasons for bishops (though it begins with a very unflattering description of the faults of the Elizabethan episcopate).

Note the appeal here is not to tradition as such but to reasoned choice, in which the evidence of long-standing practice is significant but not decisive.[68]

And if Hooker thinks there are good reasons for having bishops, he also thinks there could be good reasons for dispensing with them. Hooker certainly thinks traditional practices can be temporarily set aside if circumstances warrant; for instance, while the church 'has not ordinarily allowed any other than Bishops to ordain', nevertheless 'there may sometimes be very just and sufficient reason to allow ordination without a Bishop' (VII.4.11).[69] More than this, there are circumstances in which Hooker could conceive the outright abolition of the episcopate would be justified. For instance, he can imagine an episcopate so 'proud, tyrannical, and unreformable' its abolition would be justifiable (VII.5.8).[70] He acknowledges that Calvin had a legitimate case for establishing presbyterianism in Geneva, given the disorder in the city after the bishops had fled (Pref. 2.1-7) and accepts it is 'altogether too late' to reintroduce bishops in Scotland and France (III.10.6). The temporary, or even in extreme circumstances permanent, dispensability of the episcopate shows that, for Hooker, tradition's authority is ancillary and advisory to that of reason.

So arguments like Marshall's which characterize Hooker as giving substantial weight to tradition are difficult to square with his circumscribed appeal to the warrant in matters of discipline; and this should alert us to expect that Hooker would give it only the same or even less weight in matters of fundamental doctrine. And indeed, Hooker writes,

> [W]hat scripture does plainly deliver, to that first of place both of credit and obedience is due; the next whereto is whatsoever any can necessarily conclude by force of reason; after these the voice of the church succeeds. That which the Church by her ecclesiastical authority doth probably think and define to be true or good must ... overrule all inferior judgments.
>
> (V.8.2)

Gibbs cites this passage as evidence of Hooker's steering between catholic and reformed extremes, rejecting equally the models of scripture and tradition standing together or scripture standing alone. Moreover, Gibbs asserts that this tradition is essential in doctrine and that tradition includes, without differentiation, the whole of Christian history.[71] But this is not Hooker's understanding. Hooker is

---

68. Here I disagree with W. J. T. Kirby, 'The "Sundrie Waies of Wisdom": Richard Hooker on the Authority of Scripture and Reason', in *The Oxford Handbook of the Bible in Early Modern England, c. 1530–1700*, ed. Kevin Kileen, Helen Smith and Rachel Judith Willie (Oxford: Oxford University Press, 2015), 174–5, who appears to suggest tradition is the principal reason Hooker argues for the retention of bishops.

69. Padley, 'Earley Anglican Ecclesiology', 6–7.

70. Graves, 'Episcopacy', 49.

71. Gibbs, 'Scripture and Tradition', 234.

establishing (in a way strikingly reminiscent of both the structure and the language of Aquinas in S.Th. I.1.8, ad. 2) a clear hierarchy of authority with scripture first and reasoned conclusions from scripture second and tradition in third place carrying only 'probable' authority. What Hooker seems to mean is that an ecclesial decision binds individual judgement only on matters where scripture and reasoned conclusions from it are silent.

Indeed, the limited place of tradition is further reinforced when this passage is considered in the wider context of Hooker's approach. The word 'tradition' is almost always pejorative for Hooker, deployed to contrast human constructions with divine commandments (e.g., *Laws*, II.6.3). Hooker outlines the benefits of a written deposit of revelation and resists the notion of any other source of revelation, asking

> whether we be now to seek for any revealed law otherwise than only in the sacred scripture, whether we do now stand bound in the sight of God to yield to traditions urged by the Church of Rome the same obedience and reverence as we do to his written law, honouring equally and adoring both as Divine: our answer is, no.
>
> (I.13.2, cf. I.4.5, II.8.5-6)

Gibbs appears not to recognize Hooker's clear distinction that tradition is useful (not decisive) in matters of discipline and commands no authority as a source in matters of doctrine, scripture being materially sufficient for the saving truths of faith. The conceptual doctrine-discipline is vital to conceiving rightly Hooker's appeal to tradition. As Luoma says, '[f]or Hooker, tradition is not a body of truths which is a rival to revealed doctrine. It is a body of ordinances established by the authority which Christ has given to his church in things indifferent ... binding until the church has cause to change them'.[72] Tradition, then, has for the most part, only a limited and advisory role in things indifferent. The weight of antiquity and widespread use is significant, but a practice can be adjusted where a reasoned case can be made for change. For instance, the kiss of peace can be abandoned, for although widespread culturally in the first century, it would be scandalous in polite Elizabethan society (Pref. 4.4).

Before turning to Hooker's account of the distinctive appeal that can be made to one form of tradition, the church councils and creeds, tracing the clarity of Hooker's approach helps rebut Fox's critique of inconsistency. Fox, on the reading advanced here, is right that Hooker rules out any decisive appeal to scripture or tradition to justify retaining bishops. Fox then accuses Hooker of a partial reverse course to claim long-standing continuity as an argument for episcopal government. Fox then says Hooker's argument collapses under the weight of its contradictions and his drowning defence of episcopacy has to reach for the

---

72. J. K. Luoma, 'Who Owns the Fathers? Hooker and Cartwright on the Authority of the Primitive Church', *Sixteenth Century Journal* 8.3 (1977): 55.

straw of a brute appeal to the authority of the civil power to justify bishops.[73] Fox concludes, 'Hooker cannot have it both ways. Either tradition is important, or it is not.'[74] But Fox, failing to grasp the nuance of Hooker's method, has missed the point: few plausible theological methods could make *no* use of tradition; the issue is *not* whether or not tradition is important, but *in what ways* and *in what matters* it can be appealed to. And the key here is that whether the church should have bishops is a matter of discipline, where the church should hear any guidance from the past but is not obliged to follow it. Hooker certainly thought the civil power had a role to play in the ordering of the church in a Christian commonwealth, but as part of a wider ecology of church decision-making[75] in which tradition only ever offered guidance, not compulsion. Hooker in fact has a coherent account of tradition which, as we will see, converges with those of Calvin and Aquinas.

This section has challenged Fox's accusation of incoherence in Hooker's appeal to tradition, as well as arguments which rely on a kind of binary approach where the greater the appeal to tradition the less reformed a theologian must be, and vice versa. In fact, Hooker is clear: tradition is a useful guide in matters of discipline (such as ritual and church order) and settled situations have at least an initial presumption in their favour; yet a reasoned case can always be made for change, so there may be diversity over time and place (what was once right may not always be, and not every church must follow the same path). The chastened appeal to tradition in matters of discipline has been sketched already; however, the key distinction between discipline and doctrine means we must also consider how Hooker envisages a role for tradition in the latter sphere; this prompts the question of the role of councils and creeds that the next section now examines.

Councils and creeds

Hooker, we will see, shares a view of tradition which is broadly similar to Aquinas' and Calvin's, in particular, by an emphasis on the first four councils as carrying what Calvin called 'determinative authority' in matters of doctrine. With his emphasis on consensus and fear of private decision-making, Hooker naturally finds the idea of a council an appealing one. However little either expected their hopes would be fulfilled, both Hooker and Calvin envisaged a general council as the best way of addressing contemporary church disputes.[76] So 'recognising the urgent necessity of mutual communion for the preservation of our unity', Hooker thinks it would best fit with 'those heavenly precepts, which our Lord

---

73. Rory Fox, 'Richard Hooker and the Incoherence of "Ecclesiastical Polity"', *HJ* 44 (2003): 57.

74. Fox, 'Incoherence', 52.

75. For a good rejoinder to Fox on the question of the civil power's role in church decision-making, see Daniel Eppley, 'Royal Supremacy', *CRH*, 523-30.

76. W. J. T. Kirby, 'The Doctrine of the Royal Supremacy in the Thought of Richard Hooker', (DPhil thesis, University of Oxford, 1987), 79 fn.1, 195-6.

and Saviour ... gave concerning peace and unity, if we did all concur in desire to have the use of ancient councils again renewed' (I.10.14, similarly *Inst.* IV.9.13). Councils, says Hooker, are the most convenient way to gather the church's wisdom, particularly in matters of worship and order, although there can still be differences between churches in non-essential matters (*Laws*, IV.13.1-4, 18).[77]

On the role of councils in determining doctrine, though, Hooker is more constrained than some have suggested. Luoma and Gibbs argue that Hooker, unlike his presbyterian opponents, gives weight to the sweep of Christian history: 'Hooker is willing to gather his consensus from throughout the history of the church; Cartwright, only from the first five centuries.'[78] This characterization is misleading; we have already noted that the preponderance of references in Hooker prefers the patristic to the medieval by a factor of four to one.[79] More substantially, while drawing on a range of sources, Hooker specifically prioritizes the first five centuries as uniquely authoritative in the formation of doctrine. Thus, he refers to the 'the space of five hundred years after Christ' where the church 'was troubled with nothing else saving only with care ... to preserve this article from the sinister construction of heretics' (*Laws*, V.62.1). The article is belief in Christ's two natures, which is of course the foundation of classic Christology. No other authority is quoted in that chapter except decisions of the first four councils which are cited by name. Similarly, Hooker elsewhere enumerates as decisive for doctrine the 'four most ancient councils' (V.54.10) and the three ancient creeds (V.42), connecting them specifically by the assertion that the Nicene Creed's authority is grounded in its status as a conciliar definition (V.42.6).

What we see at work here is a distinctive emphasis on the first four councils and the three creeds as setting the boundaries of doctrine. They regulate the church's reading of scripture: 'conclusions drawn erroneously', i.e., 'falsely collected out of scripture', can be 'found repugnant to the word of God' by 'the consent of the universal church, in the councils, or in her contrary uniform practice' (VII.9.2).[80] An example of the latter might be, for example, a claim that scripture did not support the Spirit's divinity, which would be ruled out by the uniform practice of trinitarian baptism (as well as by the other criterion of conciliar definition). The connection here is drawn, as it is Aquinas' definition of *sacra doctrina*, with the material sufficiency of scripture as the source of the saving doctrines of the faith, but it is scripture as interpreted by the first four councils which framed the ancient creeds.[81]

---

77. Andre A. Gazal, '"That Ancient and Christian Liberty": Early Christian Councils in Reformation Anglican Thought', *Perichoresis* 17.4 (2012): 82-3.

78. Luoma, 'Hooker and Cartwright', 57; Gibbs, 'Scripture and Tradition', 234.

79. McGrade, 'Sources', 52; indeed, Luoma, 'Hooker and Cartwright', 56, recognizes this emphasis.

80. Gazal, 'Early Church Councils', 83-4; cf. Christopher Cocksworth, *Holding Together: Gospel, Church and Spirit: The Essentials of Christian Identity* (Norwich: Canterbury Press, 2008), 39-40.

81. W. David Neelands, 'Christology and Sacraments', *CRH*, 39-40.

The tighter definition of tradition as the product of the four councils and the creeds is further reinforced, as Neelands observes, when we recall that Hooker is defending the settlement of the Elizabethan church which attributed peculiar doctrinal authority to the first four councils only. Section 20 of the Act of Supremacy 1599, a provision Hooker cites directly (VIII.3.3), limits the church's power to judge heresy to 'only such as heretofore have been determined ... to be heresy by the authority of the Scriptures, or by the first four general councils' (*DER*, 326–7). Indeed, Hooker grounds the claim that the Church of Rome is still a genuine (albeit flawed) church in part on the recognition that it preserves the Christological and Trinitarian doctrines espoused by the first four councils, defending the Church of England's character as a church on the same basis.[82] Again, Article VII of the Articles of Religion held that the three ancient creeds 'ought thoroughly to be believed and received' (*DER*, 289). Indeed, while Hooker certainly does draw on many theologians form many centuries, he attributes determinative doctrinal authority to the creeds as formulated originally; no modern paraphrase of the creeds, still less a new one, would carry the same authority (a 'gloss or paraphrase devised by ourselves ... could not be of the like authority and credit': *Laws*, V.42.6).

Hooker was, like Calvin, adamant that councils could err. This, indeed, is enunciated in the Anglican formularies; Article XXI states councils 'may err, and sometimes have erred, even in things pertaining unto God. Wherefore things ordained by them as necessary to salvation have neither strength nor authority, unless it may be declared that they be taken out of holy Scripture' (*DER*, 297). Hooker makes this point repeatedly; for instance, 'companies of learned men, be they never so great and reverend, must yield to reason' (*Laws*, II.7.6). Hooker condemns the 'grievous abuse which has been of councils' (I.10.14) and insists that even were there universal agreement of 'ten thousand general councils ... yet one demonstrative reason alleged would outweigh them all' (II.7.5). Nonetheless, to sustain an account of tradition drawn from our reading of Aquinas, Calvin and Hooker, we need only make the minimalist claim that the first four councils were *in fact* free from error in their interpretation of scripture to doctrinal debates; not that councils are *in principle* immune to mistakes. This is, in a sense, the practical consequence of Hooker's and the Articles' endorsement of the creeds and Christological definitions of the first four councils.

Summary

It is clear that this kind of approach is consistent with Calvin's; the effective restriction of a formative role for tradition to the first four councils, justified by their early date, widespread recognition, and consonance with scripture.

---

82. Gazal, 'Early Church Councils', 83.

As Dominiak notes, for Hooker (VIII.6.7), as for Calvin, the unrepresentativeness of Trent is a key reason to resist its claims to authority.[83] The period of doctrinal flux ended for them both with the four councils; 'to make new articles of faith and doctrine no man thinks it lawful' (III.10.6).

While Calvin and Hooker agree about this, though, there is a question about whether Aquinas can be characterized in the same way. Certainly, contemporary Roman Catholic thought, which appears to allow for the development of new fundamental doctrines after the fifth century, is difficult to square with the notion of a break or end point in doctrinal development after Chalcedon which the reformed generally assert, and the attribution of determinative authority to later councils sits ill with Calvin and Hooker. However, a more minimalist reading of Aquinas on tradition can be advanced which at least creates a space for an ecumenically minded Thomist today to occupy with the reformed, in which Aquinas' insistence that the universal church cannot err is applied in a limited fashion as a statement of fact rather than principle and applied to the first four councils as the only ones which can genuinely claim to be universal. As the next section will show, there is a strong case that Aquinas' constrained account of tradition is considerably more congenial to the reformed than some later Roman Catholic understandings of the warrant. Hooker could then emerge as a conversation partner who brought Aquinas and Calvin together.

Indeed, Yves Congar, considering ecumenical disputes about tradition, wrote,

> The doctrine of tradition is one of those few points – I consider them to be few – where Anglicanism would be able to play the role of "bridge church" that it dreams of having. For, while it is thoroughly scriptural, it has nevertheless a very positive attitude towards … Tradition and the ministry.[84]

Rather double-edged though it is, Anglicans could appreciate the compliment, while being intrigued about which other points Congar has in mind. In any case, Congar is right to suggest that Anglicanism could be said to comprehend positions which sometimes seem in tension. This kind of account of tradition would address reformed concerns about ecclesial institutions having too wide-ranging or autonomous authority, with the spiritual and pastoral corruption which can result. It might also address the criticism of Tavard and Echevarria that in their criticism of tradition the reformers simply opened the door to an unsustainable diversity of private interpretations of scripture, for scripture as interpreted by the tradition of the first four councils is privileged over all private interpretation and indeed subsequent tradition. The next section addresses why, in readings of Hooker, the presumption of disagreement between Calvin and Aquinas has arisen.

---

83. P. A. Dominiak, *Richard Hooker: The Architecture of Participation* (London: T&T Clark, 2021), 167.

84. Yves Congar, *Tradition and Traditions: An Historical and a Theological Essay*, trans. Michael Naseby and Thomas Rainsborough (London: Burns & Oates, 1966), 465.

Obscuring the convergence of Hooker, Calvin and Aquinas

Introduction

Earlier chapters argued that Hooker's account of *scripture* and *reason* can best be situated within a reformed-catholic consensus embodied in Aquinas and Calvin. Similarly, this chapter argues that his account of *tradition* should be likewise located. As with the first two warrants, this discussion of the third warrant reveals the distorting effects of presuming divergence between Aquinas and Calvin, with the widespread but flawed characterization of Aquinas attributing greater weight, and Calvin lesser weight, to tradition. Two factors can be identified which have obscured that convergence: the effects of the Council of Trent on understandings of the place of tradition in Roman Catholic theology, and the influence of John Keble on how Hooker is read. Each is discussed in turn to show how they have contributed to many misinterpretations of the debate.

The Council of Trent

A major difficulty in many interpretations of all three theologians is the effect of the Council of Trent on understandings of tradition in Roman Catholic theological method. By examining the different ways its formulation of theological method has been received and critiqued, we will see how it has affected readings of the Roman Catholic position and how some theologians in both the reformed and catholic traditions have tackled its deleterious consequences for relations between the two.

On 8 April 1546, leading Roman Catholic bishops at the Council of Trent[85] adopted its Decree on Scripture and Tradition. Considering whether scripture alone sufficed as the source of doctrine – a key plank of the reformers' theological method and their criticism of Rome – the Council concluded,

> [T]he truth of salvation and the rule of conduct ... are contained in written books and unwritten traditions, which were received from the apostles by from the mouth of Christ himself or ... handed on as it were ... at the inspiration of the Holy Spirit ... the council accepts and venerates with a like feeling ... all the books of both the old and the new testament ... as well as traditions concerning both faith and conduct.
>
> (*Decrees*, II.263)

---

85. The Council of Trent met from 1545 to 1563 at Trent and Bologna in Italy, to consider the church's teaching and worship in the light of reformation challenges. The classic account is Hubert Jedin's magisterial survey, *A History of the Council of Trent*, 2 vols, trans. Ernest Graf (London: Thomas Nelson and Sons, 1957–61); John W. O'Malley, *Trent: What Happened at the Council* (London: Bealknap Press, 2013) is a more accessible overview.

Later official Roman Catholic formularies follow similar lines; for instance, Vatican II declared that doctrine 'bas[es] itself on sacred scripture and tradition' (*Lumen Gentium*, 14). They appear to embody what Oberman called a 'Tradition II' view, that scripture and tradition together form the deposit of revelation and are complementary and necessary sources of doctrine. This of course would be very difficult from a reformed perspective, which insisted that scripture alone sufficed as the source of doctrine and was the sole deposit of revelation (what Oberman called a 'Tradition I' view).[86]

One approach to resolving this tension is to contest the common interpretation of the Tridentine decree and assert it does, not in fact, fall into Oberman's 'Tradition II' category because it does not instantiate a two-source theory of doctrine. Geiselmann, notably, advanced a reading of the decree which suggested it need not be uncongenial to reformed concerns. Geiselmann made much of the wording of the final decree because it differed from earlier drafts. The formulation *partim-et-partim* (revelation contained *partly* in scripture and *partly* in tradition) was dropped in favour of an apparently more ambiguous claim that revelation was contained in scripture *and* tradition.[87] Against Geiselmann, though, the weight of scholarship now argues that the key consideration is that the decree was intended, emphatically, to rule out the reformers' 'Tradition I' account of scripture's material sufficiency.[88] In particular, as Jedin observed, the Council rejected the explicit opportunity to endorse a formulation, backed by about a third of the bishops, that was consistent with asserting scripture's material sufficiency.[89] *Et* or *partim*, the key point is that both the text itself and most subsequent scholarship appear, in Bireley's words, to enunciate 'two sources of divine revelation' in response to 'the Protestant notion of "scripture alone"'.[90] The Tridentine decree, then, is hard to read in anything other than a 'Tradition II' way and this causes considerable tension with the reformed.

Calvin, certainly, understood Trent that way; 'nowhere in Reformation tradition', observes Casteel, 'are the essential theological issues which divided Rome from the reformers more lucidly delineated' than in the Tridentine decrees.[91] Commenting on the Decree, Calvin says it makes 'scripture ... a nose of wax, because it can be

---

86. Heiko A. Oberman, '*Quo Vadis*? Tradition from Irenaeus to *Humani Generis*', *SJT* 16.3 (1963): 238–42.

87. See Matthew L. Selby, 'The Relationship between Scripture and Tradition according to the Council of Trent' (MA diss., University of St Thomas, 2013), 5–14; I have not quoted Geiselmann directly as I have been unable to locate a copy of the article Selby cites.

88. Jedin, *Trent*, II.75; cf. Joseph Ratzinger, *God's Word: Scripture, Tradition, Office*, ed. Peter Hunnermann and Thomas Soding, trans. Henry Taylor (San Francisco, CA: Ignatius Press, 2008), 64, 68.

89. Jedin, *Trent*, II.64.

90. Michael Bireley, *The Refashioning of Catholicism, 1450–1700: A Reassessment of the Counter Reformation* (Basingstoke: Macmillan, 1999), 48.

91. Casteel, 'Calvin and Trent', 91; cf. Gordon, *Calvin*, 174–5.

formed into all shapes' (*Antidote*, 69). Calvin particularly rejected its formulation about scripture and tradition: 'we especially repudiate their desire to make certainty of doctrine depend not less on what they call unwritten than on the scriptures' (70). As Casteel explains, while Calvin 'grants some authority to unwritten tradition' (largely on matters of ritual), he could not accept the Tridentine account which appeared to undermine scripture's uniqueness as 'the final and authoritative norm'.[92]

Hooker similarly criticizes Trent.[93] He believed it could not claim to be representative and so had no binding authority.[94] On Trent's substance, Hooker rejected its account of penance in particular (*Laws*, VI.1.3, VI.6.10-14) and more broadly resisted the Tridentine tendency to afford tradition an analogous or equal authority to scripture (I.13.2). So as well as explicitly challenging Trent in general, Calvin's and Hooker's reformed accounts of tradition are difficult to reconcile with the Tridentine formulations. And whatever Trent's precise meaning, as Congar observes, reformed-catholic rapprochement on theological method became considerably harder because of the Decree and its subsequent application, with the 'atmosphere progressively more and more awkward'.[95]

If Geiselmann's attempt to reconcile the Tridentine account and the reformed perspective does not persuade, though, it does point in a more promising direction, indicating there may be Roman Catholic views of tradition more congenial to reformed concerns. For example, several figures associated with the *nouvelle théologie* sensibility grasped those concerns and tried to recover what they saw as a pre-Tridentine account of tradition which had a more constrained account of the warrant. In that way, Congar adopted what he saw as Augustine's distinction between practices and customs on the one hand, where tradition could be decisive, and doctrines, where it could not[96] – the distinction between the two being clearly reflected in Hooker's and Calvin's accounts.

Congar also perceived the danger that tradition might become 'static, mechanical, inert' if considered in isolation from scripture as an almost autonomous or separate warrant; he traced this problem not to Aquinas but to Trent.[97] This problem, the *nouvelle* theologians thought, was exacerbated further in the late nineteenth and early twentieth centuries, where tradition became ossified and dependent on reading secondary textbooks or manuals rather than primary texts. Hence Williams identifies '*nouvelle théologie*'s challenge to

---

92. Casteel, 'Calvin and Trent', 103, 105.
93. Gazal, 'Early Anglican Councils', 84–5.
94. Eppley, 'Supremacy', 527–8.
95. Congar, *Tradition and Traditions*, 145.
96. Congar, *Tradition and Traditions*, 54–5.
97. Congar, *Tradition and Traditions*, 141, cf. 162, 363; see also Peter M. Candler, *Theology, Rhetoric, Manuduction, or Reading Scripture Together on the Path to God* (Grand Rapids, MI: Eerdmans, 2006), 27–8.

a fossilised neo-scholasticism'[98] which it thought imposed a monolithic, stifling space in which tradition could become little more than the repetition of not uncontroversial theological formulae without real reference to their scriptural or historical sources. Moreover, Congar seems to accept the notion of a break in the patristic period after which doctrine was fixed and tradition no longer carried formative weight for doctrine.[99]

Webster, from the reformed perspective, recognizes Congar's reading of tradition as a major step towards meeting reformed concerns.[100] It also chimes with Oberman's view that Trent marked the point at which Tradition II superseded Tradition I as the dominant perspective on tradition in Roman Catholic teaching. Tradition II, for Oberman, gave extra-scriptural unwritten tradition authority alongside scripture, whereas Tradition I saw scripture alone as the materially sufficient source of doctrine.[101] Aquinas, for Oberman, held a Tradition I account.[102] The possibility of reading Aquinas, and the catholic view before Trent, in a Tradition I way suggests the reformed and catholic perspectives could be reconciled, conceiving tradition as an ancillary to the materially sufficient scripture.

Indeed, intriguingly, both Hooker and Calvin appear to distinguish Trent from its antecedents. So while Hooker blames Aquinas' 'scholastical invention' and 'phantasy' for what he considers a dangerous account of penance (*Laws*, VI.4.9, cf. VI.1.2), he nonetheless expresses even more impatience with 'those who pretend to follow Thomas [but] differ from him' (VI.6.10). The distinction recurs in Hooker's discussion of sacraments, where he thinks Aquinas' successors far more at fault than the angelic doctor himself (VI.6.11). Likewise, Calvin, as Chapter 2 showed, drew the same distinction between Aquinas and later medieval and post-medieval theology at a number of points. Greater awareness of pre-Tridentine views of tradition may help further rapprochement on this question; as van den Belt says, 'popular understanding too easily equates Trent's decisions with the much more diverse and complicated positions of medieval theology'.[103] And Congar certainly envisaged the possibility of a shared rediscovery of Aquinas as a ground for possible consensus.[104]

---

98. A. N. Williams, '"The Future of the Past": The Contemporary Significance of the *Nouvelle Théologie*', *IJST* 7.4 (2005): 353.

99. Congar, *Tradition and Traditions*, 25.

100. John Webster, 'Purity and Plenitude: Evangelical Reflections on Congar's Tradition and Traditions', *IJST* 7.4 (2005): 404.

101. Oberman, '*Quo Vadis?*', 234–41.

102. Oberman, '*Quo Vadis?*', 234 fn.1, 240–1.

103. Henk van den Belt, '*Sola Scriptura*: An Inadequate Slogan for the Authority of Scripture', *CThJ* 51 (2016): 205.

104. Yves Congar, 'Saint Thomas Aquinas and the Spirit of Ecumenism', *New Blackfriars* 55 (1974): esp. 198–200.

What is emerging here is the possibility of recovering a shared understanding of tradition which predates the reformation ruptures and could be held faithfully both reformed and catholic traditions. We have already seen how what Oberman called 'Tradition I' could be a reasonable interpretation of a medieval catholic writer like Aquinas, whose limited appeal to the 'probable authority' of the doctors of the church as ancillary and subordinate to scripture has much in common with Calvin's appropriation of earlier theologians as useful but not infallible.

To hone this account further, we have already noted Bauckham's formulation that the earliest Christian centuries are widely accorded 'a uniquely normative status in relation to the rest of the tradition'.[105] And this kind of reformed account, seen in Oberman and Bauckham, is strengthened if we combine it with the distinctively Anglican perspective of R. P. C. Hanson, who argues that precisely such an understanding characterizes the operation of tradition in the patristic period, from the death of the apostles to the fixing of the canon and creeds. Reading Hanson alongside Bauckham and Oberman will help advance an account of tradition which can plausibly be read as both catholic (in the sense of drawn from the pre-reformation church) and reformed (in the sense of affirming the constrained role for the warrant in theological method).

Hanson recognizes the historical reality that there was not a single set of doctrinal formulations in these early centuries: 'between the death of the apostles and the widespread recognition of the New Testament as authoritative, doctrine was indefinite'.[106] But, he argues, this does not mean that oral tradition or custom carried determinative weight. While there may not, in the earliest centuries, have been agreement about what texts constituted scripture, he says, there was widespread suspicion about appeals to 'unwritten tradition', appeals often associated unfavourable with the 'secret customs' claimed by the Gnostics or other heterodox groups.[107] Attempts by one part of the church to gain general support for a practice or custom of local origin were usually resisted.[108]

The very process of trying to identify a canon of scripture, Hanson suggests, was precisely because appeals to custom or tradition were regarded with suspicion and did not provide a stable basis for widespread recognition of key doctrinal truths.[109] Even before the canon was fixed, and even more after it was, a clear patristic distinction was emerging that custom and practice might be local and adaptable, but that scripture was universal and fixed: 'tradition ... the church felt at liberty to tamper with, but the Church did not dare tamper with the Bible'.[110]

---

105. Bauckham, 'Tradition', 127.
106. R. P. C. Hanson, *Tradition in the Early Church* (London: SCM, 1962), 57.
107. Hanson, *Tradition*, 22–7; 50.
108. Hanson, *Tradition*, 105, 155.
109. E.g., Hanson, *Tradition*, 21, 234, 238.
110. Hanson, *Tradition*, 138.

In short, Hanson holds that the patristic understanding of tradition was 'wholly incompatible with the theory that unwritten custom … is binding on all as part of the original deposit, of equal value with scripture'.[111] As well as falling foul of the *theological* objections of the reformers, 'Tradition II' theological methods thus become much harder to justify *historically*, for if Hanson is right they reflect neither how tradition was understood in the earliest Christian centuries and if Oberman is right nor how tradition was understood in a medieval writer like Aquinas. No doubt the details of Hanson's and Oberman's accounts could be challenged, but the thrust is consistent with the reading of Aquinas offered here and further grounds the possibility of a theological method which catholic, reformed, and Anglican perspectives could share.

The Tridentine formulation, then, exacerbated differences between catholic and reformed perspectives, contributing to a sense of inevitable opposition between them on scripture and tradition. Retrievals of an earlier perspective have been part of a wider movement towards greater agreement between reformed and catholic theologians on tradition, which became more pronounced in the late twentieth-century ecumenical dialogue. Thus, a key 1964 conference recognized 'misunderstandings and disagreements' arising from 'our long history of estrangement and division' but pointed to 'possibilities of a new understanding of some of the most contested areas of our common past'.[112]

Nonetheless, even read this way and with the divisive effects of Trent and its subsequent appropriation corrected, problems remain in reconciling the catholic and reformed views. Some of these focus, as Chapter 6 will discuss, on authority in the church. And there remains anxiety that tradition is still conceived as too autonomous; Webster, for instance, feared that Congar had not fully grasped the depth of the divide which opened up at the reformation and, despite moving towards the reformed perspective on scriptural sufficiency, still attributed too great a capacity to tradition.[113] A key Anglican-Roman Catholic report acknowledged that, despite much progress, 'a necessary consensus has not been achieved', particularly on 'the relationship between Scripture, Tradition, and the exercise of authority'.[114]

So Trent's formulation, which could be, and has often been, read as giving tradition similar or equal status to scripture as containing divine revelation and grounding doctrine, caused almost immediate problems for the reformed, including Hooker and Calvin. Subsequently, understandings with the traditions

---

111. Hanson, *Tradition*, 142.

112. *The Fourth World Conference on Faith and Order*, ed. P. C. Rodger and L. Vischer (London: SCM, 1964), 55.

113. Webster, 'Purity and Plenitude', 408–9; see also Hanson, *Tradition*, 239–42.

114. Anglican-Roman Catholic International Commission II, *The Gift of Authority*, accessed 22 August 2020, https://www.anglicancommunion.org/media/105245/ARCIC_II_The_Gift_of_Authority.pdf, paras 1–3.

have diverged further and this has inevitably led to Hooker being characterized on that spectrum. There is a possibility, as Congar, Oberman and others envisaged, that retrieving from Aquinas a pre-Tridentine catholic understanding of tradition might meet many reformed concerns. Nonetheless, for all the potential of such a retrieval and a consequent recalibration of the ecumenical debate about tradition, as Webster observes, and as Chapter 6 discusses, difficulties remain in reconciling catholic and reformed perspectives on the warrant.

John Keble

If the Council of Trent shaped (even distorted) readings of Aquinas by exacerbating the view he was uncongenial to reformed concerns, John Keble's role in the reception of Hooker has had a similar effect on how the latter is perceived. Tracing Keble's influence reveals a major factor in the frequent underestimation, until roughly the late 1980s, of Hooker's reformed credentials.

As Russell notes, Hooker's influence in Anglicanism since the nineteenth century is 'as much an accolade to the Oxford Movement's championing of Hooker as it is to the great man himself'.[115] Keble was one of the Movement's leading lights, asserting a more catholic kind of Anglican identity by emphasizing or recovering ritual and practices which pre-dated the break with Rome.[116] By the mid-1830s, Keble, increasingly disillusioned with the reformers, was scouring Hooker for evidence of such continuity.[117] Keble then produced a major new edition of Hooker's works, penning a prominent Preface which depicted Hooker as the Movement's forerunner and a defender of the Church of England's catholic identity in the face of reformed characterizations.[118] Keble insisted Hooker must be 'rescued from the unpleasant association, and discreditable praise' of his reformed interpreters.[119] The Preface sought to spring Hooker free from the trap (as Keble saw it) of identification with the reformed perspective, establishing an agenda for the 'recovery' of a 'catholic' Hooker who supported the retention of catholic practices in the sixteenth century and thus could undergird their retention or reintroduction in the nineteenth, such as the campaign to restore prayer for the departed.[120] Indeed, Keble portrayed Hooker as an advocate of the ancient church

---

115. Andrea Russell, *Richard Hooker, beyond Certainty* (London: Routledge, 2020), 1.

116. See Peter Nockles, *The Oxford Movement in Context: Anglican High Churchmanship, 1760–1857* (Cambridge: Cambridge University Press, 1994); *The Oxford Handbook of the Oxford Movement*, ed. Stewart J. Brown, Peter Nockles and James Pereiro (Oxford: Oxford University Press, 2017).

117. Nockles, *Oxford Movement*, 125.

118. On Keble's edition, see MacCulloch, 'Reputation', 808–11; P. G. Stanwood, 'Works and Editions I', *CRH*, 33–4.

119. Keble, 'Editor's Preface', *Works*, I.cxv.

120. Keble, 'Preface', I.lxx, I.ci.

and at best a half-hearted child of the reformation: his 'sympathy with the fourth century rather than the sixteenth is perpetually breaking out'.[121]

Keble's edition, and notably his Preface, is one of the most breathtakingly audacious misappropriations of a theologian ever penned. For the problem is that Hooker's real views are, inconveniently for Keble, perpetually breaking out from Keble's depiction of him. The distorting effect of Keble on Hooker's character, the minimizing of reformed elements in Hooker's works, is obvious from the repeated strains both in the Preface and the text itself. So Keble had to admit that he cannot 'affirm … that this view of Church ceremonies is anywhere expressly set down … by Hooker' while insisting that 'surely something like it lies at the root' of Hooker's account.[122] Keble's ingenuity of interpretation, though, cannot in the end be sustained by Hooker's text. Notably, Keble argued that Hooker would 'insist on the divine origin and indispensable necessity'[123] of bishops, but, as we saw, Hooker adamantly refused to insist that bishops were either essential or indispensable. The gap between what Hooker actually said and what Keble might have wished he had said is apparent in the Preface where he went to considerable lengths to try and explain away the large number of passages in the *Laws* which assert the usefulness and divine origin of the episcopate while being adamant that bishops were not mandatory.[124] Keble presents the evidence in a contentious way, for instance by trying to minimize the significance of Hooker's insistence (*Laws*, VII.14.11) that clergy who had not been ordained by a bishop could nonetheless minister in the Church of England. And where a passage cannot be explained away – notably, Hooker's recognition that bishops could not realistically be re-imposed on churches which had abandoned them (III.11.16) – Keble egregiously left out the offending text from his edition.[125] This is not an isolated example; for instance, Keble also questioned the authenticity of Hooker's sermons on *Jude* because he disliked the reformed tenor of their treatment of justification.[126]

While impossible to justify from a plain reading of Hooker's text, Keble's appropriation widely and wrongly influenced the way Hooker was thereafter interpreted. As MacCulloch noted, 'on the whole, the effect of Keble's magisterial edition was to cement Hooker firmly into the Victorian high church tradition'.[127] More particularly, as Nockles concludes, one effect of this appropriation – and the

---

121. Keble, 'Preface', I.cii.

122. Keble, 'Preface', I.ci.

123. Keble, 'Preface', I.lxxvi; for the Movement's view on church structure see Kenneth L. Parker, 'Tractarian Visions of History', in *Oxford Handbook of the Oxford Movement*, ed. Brown *et al.*, 153–6.

124. Keble, 'Preface', I.lxxvi-lxxxv.

125. MacCulloch, 'Reputation', 780.

126. Keble, 'Preface', I.lv; cf. Bauckham, 'Hooker and Rome', 37.

127. MacCulloch, 'Reputation', 811; cf. Michael Brydon, *The Evolving Reputation of Richard Hooker: An Examination of Responses, 1600–1714* (Oxford: Oxford University Press, 2006), 13–16.

Oxford Movement more generally – was to heighten the function of tradition to an extent substantially beyond the constrained appeal to the warrant in the sixteenth century: 'in their hands, antiquity became an absolute standard and court of appeal, rather than ... merely a corroborative testimony to the truth of the Church of England's formularies and the teaching of her standard divines'.[128]

Summary

Keble's magnification of the role of tradition, and the appropriation of Hooker to justify the retention or even reintroduction of pre-reformation practices, contributed crucially to readings of Hooker which sought to distinguish him from the reformers. This in turn misled subsequent readers into the assumption that Hooker to be defined in distinction from reformed concerns. Equally, the Council of Trent and subsequent official Roman Catholic theology made increasingly distant the possibility of reformed-catholic consensus on the relationship of scripture and tradition, in particular because after Trent it became increasingly difficult to square the Roman Catholic Church's view of tradition with the reformed insistence on scripture's material sufficiency. Both these factors combined to separate reformed and catholic perspectives, and to the assumption that Hooker must be read on that spectrum. Isolating the effects of Trent and of Keble, this chapter has shown, reveals the possibility of an account of tradition which a reformed and a catholic theologian might share – a catholic and reformed convergence which is also the best characterization of Hooker's thought.

Summary

For Hooker, with the precise exception of the formative tradition of the first four councils and their doctrinal formulations including the three creeds, which settle the canon of scripture and the framework of permissible interpretations of the Bible on doctrine, tradition is not a source of doctrine, which can be revealed only by scripture. In matters other than doctrine, such as the rituals and structures of the church, tradition does have a wider function, but even here it is ancillary to reason: on such matters scripture and tradition may be drawn on, but a reasoned argument for or against the retention or alteration of something is decisive. This account of tradition is basically the same as Calvin's, and while consonance with Aquinas is a little harder to demonstrate, nonetheless if his references 'universal church' were narrowly construed to the first four centuries and the creeds, an ecumenically minded Thomist position could emerge. The possibility of such a

---

128. Nockles, *Oxford Movement*, 144; cf. James Pereiro, '"A Cloud of Witnesses": Tractarians and Tractarian Ventures', in *Oxford Handbook of the Oxford Movement*, ed. Brown *et al.*, 204–5.

reading of Aquinas, congenial to the reformed insistence on scripture's material sufficiency, will become even more plausible when we consider in the next chapter some of the specific ways that reformed concerns are actually a reaction against later developments in Roman Catholic theology rather than against Aquinas himself.

Failure to grasp the essential congruence of these three theologians on tradition can be traced to two particular factors. The Council of Trent and its successors prompted a very different account of tradition from that found in Aquinas, conferring on it greater capacity and more autonomy, and it is Trent and its successors (rather than Aquinas) which are inconsistent with the reformed principle of scripture's material sufficiency. Readings of Hooker, already skewed by this widespread misunderstanding of precisely where the reformed-catholic faultlines really lie, have suffered further because of Keble's efforts, successful for about a hundred years until they were challenged in the late twentieth century, to characterize Hooker as on the catholic side of the divide.

Yet when contemporary Roman Catholic retrievals of their pre-reformation tradition (for instance by Congar) are brought into dialogue with reformed critics (such as Oberman, Bauckham, Webster and Hanson), possibilities emerge for seeing tradition's role in theology as less of a stumbling block. This would represent some movement from the official understanding of the contemporary Roman Catholic Church (and, as the next chapter will demonstrate, this is far from uncomplicated), but such a shared perspective can claim a genuine historical and theological grounding in the understanding of the early church as well as our three theologians. It could help ground both ecumenical discussion and a view of Anglicanism as catholic and reformed.

What has emerged from these four chapters, then, is a nuanced *sola scriptura* principle which can be seen in Hooker, Aquinas and Calvin, in which scripture is our sole source of the saving knowledge of God and the only source of fundamental doctrines about Christ, salvation, the Trinity and so on. While other warrants are needed to interpret and apply this deposit, its sole source is scripture. Scripture's authority is derived from its character as divine communication, recognition of which may be prompted by reflection on the evidence of the church's witness but must also be evoked in the hearer or reader by the Spirit's witness. Reason cannot ground doctrine, though reason can know some things about God without the aid of revelation, and the Fall diminishes but does not eradicate reason's capacity. This means the fruit of human reason, say philosophy, can in principle be used to clarify or elucidate doctrine, but only within the parameters generated from scripture.

This investigation then has yielded a shared account of theological method which is coherent and realistic (allowing for the fact that the church chronologically precedes the canon and that scripture is capable of more than one interpretation) and could unite on substantial common ground the traditions which Calvin, Aquinas and Hooker embody. Conceived this way, the tracing of the theological methods of our three theologians allows Hooker, and Anglicanism, to be characterized as both catholic and reformed, rather than as one or the other or a *via media* between them. Moreover, as well as relocating Hooker's theology (and that of Calvin and of Aquinas) more precisely, the theological method traced in all three could be applied fruitfully to some contemporary debates, as the next chapter shows.

Chapter 6

POSSIBILITIES AND LIMITATIONS

Introduction

Hooker and Anglicanism, on the reading advanced in the last four chapters, can be coherently characterized as *both* catholic and reformed, rather than one or the other, or some middle way between them. Such an account is possible because, as the exploration of theological method shows, the two characterizations are not necessarily opposites. A theological method can be both catholic and reformed, insisting on the primacy of scripture as our sole source in matters of doctrine while recognizing the historical and theological reality that reason and tradition play a part in both identifying and interpreting scripture. On matters other than doctrine, scripture and tradition can be seen as indicative, with churches using them to inform decisions made by reason. This method can be grounded in readings of Hooker, Calvin and Aquinas which demonstrate their fundamental similarities and could be shared by descendants in their respective traditions.

Where earlier chapters advanced the historical and theological plausibility of this kind of characterization of Hooker and Anglicanism, this chapter suggests possibilities and identifies limitations of applying this kind of perspective to some contemporary debates. While not arguing that it will solve long-standing and often vexed questions, using this shared method as a lens can at least clarify issues, identify real areas of (dis)agreement and reveal possibly surprising but potentially fruitful conversation partners. Two areas of discussion – the relationship of faith and reason, and questions of authority in the church – are explored to demonstrate what might be yielded by applying these insights, although of course these can only be preliminary and indicative explorations which would need further development.

Firstly, we will see this kind of reading of Anglicanism, and the theological method which underpins it, has potential to advance theological and philosophical debates. The current debate about faith and reason is explored, where a number of writers, both some who claim Christian convictions and some who do not, have questioned whether reason is needed or permissible in theology at all. By bringing this method into dialogue with some – perhaps surprising – conversation partners influenced by second-wave feminisms, some important conclusions emerge. For we will see in Hooker, Calvin and Aquinas a much richer account of reason as biblical, theological, communal and embodied than the individual cognition which reason's critics, whether within the Christian tradition or reacting against it, often conceive. An account of faith and reason which Anglican, reformed and catholic traditions could share can be grounded in the shared theological method we have identified.

Then, secondly, the ecumenical possibilities of this approach will be identified by examining the question of authority in the church which remains a stumbling block for official dialogue between the Anglican and Roman Catholic communions. It will trace the welcome progress towards greater understanding, while highlighting reasons why many Anglicans were cautious about the direction of some official reports and tracing the underlying reasons why the question of authority, particularly of the pope's authority, is so problematic. We will see how, on this reading, appeals to scripture and tradition in the sphere of church discipline can only be advisory rather than decisive, which leaves the problematic alternative of grounding papal authority in appeals to reason. Finally, bringing this method, and this characterization of Anglicanism, into dialogue with the contemporary Roman Catholic sensibility known as 'receptive ecumenism', and a shift in focus from some versions of official Roman Catholic teaching to the more chastened account of church authority in Aquinas, will suggest a more realistic and perhaps more sustainable approach to future Anglican-Roman Catholic dialogue.

Of course, applying the theological method we have traced in our three theologians is not going to solve every dispute between or within churches, or every dispute between Christians and others. So the chapter concludes by highlighting some of the limitations of this approach.

Faith and reason

This section brings our three theologians into dialogue with a range of contemporary philosophical and theological discussions on the relationship of faith and reason, particularly by showing their rich account of reason can help address some concerns both about the rationality of faith and about the use of reason in theology.

The place of reason in Christian theology has, most obviously, been challenged from outside the tradition by those (some associated with the 'New Atheist' movement[1]) who consider that faith and reason are either in tension or effectively opposed. On the one hand, Stephen Pinker argues that one of the achievements of the Enlightenment was to 'energetically apply the standard of reason to understanding our world, and not fall back on generators of delusion like faith, dogma, revelation, authority, charisma, mysticism, divination, visions, gut feelings or the hermeneutic parsing of sacred texts'.[2] Pinker thinks that faith is intrinsically *irrational*: 'to take something on faith means to believe it without good reason, so

---

1. See Phil Ryan, *After the New Atheist Debate* (Toronto: University of Toronto Press, 2018), esp. 1–20; Michael Ruse, *Monotheism and Contemporary Atheism* (Cambridge: Cambridge University Press, 2019).

2. Stephen Pinker, *Enlightenment Now: The Case for Reason, Science, Humanism, and Progress* (London: Penguin, 2019), 8.

by definition a faith in the existence of supernatural entities clashes with reason'.[3] Our theologians would contest those definitions of faith and reason; for now, it suffices to note that there is a quite prominent strand of contemporary thought which asserts religion's basic irrationality and therefore could see no role for reason in theology.

On the other hand, and perhaps more surprisingly, some *Christian* accounts appear to reach similar conclusions. Barth, as we saw, expressed some suspicion about attributing excessive capacity to reason, in part because this may result in idolatry and the construction of a theological vision which is distant or even removed from that revealed by God, notably in Christ and the scriptures.[4] So he begins his systematic theology warning that dogmatics is 'not to allow itself to take its problems from anything else but Scripture' (*CD* 1/1, §8.1). This appears to limit theology to working only with the data of revelation, and Barth went as far as asserting that 'reason ... is incurably sick and incapable of any serious theological activity'.[5]

In the face of both internal and external accounts which oppose or separate reason and faith, a more nuanced critique of reason's theological capacity emerges in some theologians who might loosely be described as influenced by second-wave feminism.[6] A frequent and legitimate critique is that too much theology is, or has been, written by men to the exclusion of women's voices and perspectives.[7] Hooker, Calvin and Aquinas cannot really answer that legitimate challenge. Some feminist theologians seem to suggest the tradition is so irredeemable that the only way forward is to more or less completely *replace* it.[8] But others, such

---

3. Pinker, *Enlightenment Now*, 30.

4. See John Webster, *Karl Barth*, 2nd edn (London: Continuum, 2004), esp. 53–4.

5. Karl Barth, 'No! Answer to Emil Brunner', in Emil Brunner and Karl Barth, *Natural Theology*, trans. Peter Fraenkel (London: Centenary Press, 1946), 96.

6. On the links between theology and second-wave feminism see, e.g., Melissa Raphael, 'A Patrimony of Idols: Second-Wave Jewish and Christian Feminist Theology and the Criticism of Religion', *Sophia: International Journal of Philosophy and Tradition* 53.2 (2014): 241–59; Els Maeckelberghe, 'Across the Generations in Feminist Theology: From Second to Third Wave Feminisms', *Feminist Theology* 8.23 (2000): 63–9. For introductory surveys of feminist theology generally see, e.g., *The Cambridge Companion to Feminist Theology*, ed. Susan Frank Parsons (Cambridge: Cambridge University Press, 2002); *The Oxford Handbook of Feminist Theology*, ed. Mary McClintock Fulkerson and Sheila Briggs (Oxford: Oxford University Press, 2012). More detailed treatments include, for instance, *Horizons in Feminist Theology: Identity, Tradition and Norms*, ed. Rebecca S. Chopp and Sheila Greeve Davaney (Minneapolis, MI: Fortress Press, 1997).

7. E.g., Pamela Sue Anderson, 'Feminist Theology as Philosophy of Religion', in *CCFT*, ed. Parsons, 40–1.

8. A tendency recognized by Genevieve Lloyd, *The Man of Reason: 'Male' and 'Female' in Western Philosophy*, 2nd edn (London: Routledge, 1993), xix–x, 2–3. One writer who comes close to this position is Grace M. Jantzen, *Becoming Divine: Towards a Feminist Philosophy of Religion* (Manchester: Manchester University Press, 1998), who appears to argue for a straightforward rejection of much of the classic Christian tradition: 6 fn.1, 21, 25, 31, 255, 265.

as Tanner, suggest that feminist theologies may be most effective at challenging patriarchal dominance of the tradition if they look to *refresh* understandings of that tradition rather than reject them:[9] in this work of retrieval 'the tasks of feminist theology become a specification of the tasks that characterize theology generally'.[10] Moreover, critiques influenced by such feminisms will in fact be seen as converging with some contemporary readings of Hooker, Aquinas and Calvin.

Among the tasks proposed by both feminist critiques and also by an intrinsic desire to understand these three theologians more fully is the need to recover a richer notion of what they understood by 'reason'. We can identify four areas of engagement: these are reason conceived as (1) biblical, (2) experiential/pastoral, (3) corporate and (4) material. In each case we briefly state an aspect of feminist critique and then give examples of how resources to resolve the problem raised can be found *within* the lives and theological methods of Hooker, Aquinas and Calvin.

A first critique concerns the *biblical* nature of reasoning, the fear that the stream of theology can often appear distant from the well of scripture which ought to be its principal source. A recurring example is the accusation that Christian theology has, in pursuit of both philosophical coherence and earthly hegemony, conceived an essentially privileged and male deity, with insufficient attention to the scriptural vision of God.[11] For some feminist theologians, fresh engagement with scripture is a vital task, as attending to the pluriform voice of scripture will expose and challenge the dominance of patriarchal imagery and belief.[12]

The methodological issue here is that reason in theology must be grounded in constant re-engagement with scripture, in the sense that one of the key reasons we have the capacity to think is so that we can reflect on the revelation witnessed in scripture. All three theologians are, in fact, profoundly biblical. Earlier chapters showed the importance of the Bible in their theological methods; moreover, scripture's centrality is further shown by recalling that they engaged with scripture not just for doctrinal or methodological dispute but as part of a pattern of life and work in which they read and expounded scripture in a variety of contexts. For example, Calvin's and Aquinas' commentaries tend to be given much less attention than their systematic theologies, or Aquinas as an interpreter and teacher.[13] Likewise, Hooker's sermons are less attended to than the larger *Laws*, and even where

---

9. Kathryn Tanner, 'Social Theory Concerning the "New Social Movements" and the Practice of Feminist Theology', in *Horizons*, ed. Chopp and Greeve Davaney, 188–90; cf. Pamela Sue Anderson, *A Feminist Philosophy of Religion* (Oxford: Blackwell, 1998), 53, 60.

10. Tanner, 'Practice of Feminist Theology', 184; similarly Anderson, 'Philosophy of Religion', 42.

11. Jantzen, *Becoming Divine*, 255.

12. See Bridget Gilfillan Upton, 'Feminist Theology as Biblical Hermeneutics', in *CCFT*, ed. Parsons, 99–104 for a good introduction and further references.

13. On these two as expositors of scripture, see, e.g., Peter M. Candler, 'St Thomas Aquinas', in *Christian Theologies of Scripture: A Comparative Introduction*, ed. Justin S. Holcomb (New York, NY: New York University Press, 2006), 63–4; *Calvin and the Bible*, ed. Donald K. McKim (Cambridge: Cambridge University Press, 2006).

they are the focus is usually on the sermons which primarily deal with controversies about salvation rather than those with more obviously spiritual or pastoral themes.[14] Recovery not just of the biblical emphases of these theological methods but also their wider scriptural engagement, seen particularly by examining works other than the *Institutes*, *Summae* or *Laws*, will suggest they were operating with a richer concept of reason as constantly engaging with biblical material while handling, say, philosophical or historical sources, or contemporary disputes in the church.

Secondly, alongside renewed attention to the relationship of scripture and reason, feminist theologies often emphasize the place of *experience*. Their most obvious criticism is that the experience of women, along with other historically or currently disempowered groups, is widely under-represented in theological discourses. But this can be broadened into a wider point that there is a danger of seeing reason as somehow divorced from the contexts in which reasoning takes place. Alasdair MacIntyre reinforces this critique; 'what historical enquiry discloses is the situatedness of all enquiry',[15] namely that one cannot abstract some function or capacity called 'reason' from the specific contexts and circumstances in which reasoning takes place.

Attending to the wider circumstances in which our three theologians lived will show how their thought emerges *within* specific contexts and must, to some extent, have been informed by them. In particular, all three had *pastoral* charges, responsibility for nurturing the Christian faith of a particular community. Aquinas was perhaps above all a *teacher* who made the didactic purpose of his great work clear in the prologue to the greater *Summa*.[16] As Candler notes, 'the pedagogical culture in which Thomas studied and taught cannot be abstracted from [his] "form of life"'.[17] Hooker was of course a parish priest, in the rather rarefied atmosphere of Temple Church as well as Buckinghamshire, Wiltshire and Kent.[18] Calvin drafted

14. The one major study of Hooker's sermons, Corneliu C. Simut, *The Doctrine of Salvation in the Sermons of Richard Hooker* (Berlin: DeGruyter, 2005), traces Hooker's account of controversial soteriological issues through the sermons; Andrea Russell, *Richard Hooker: Beyond Certainty* (London: Routledge, 2020), 121–80 also focuses on the sermons about salvation. John K. Stafford, 'Sorrow and Solace: Richard Hooker's Remedy for Grief', in *Richard Hooker and the English Reformation*, ed. W. J. T. Kirby (Dordrecht: Kluwer Academic, 2003), 131–47, is a fine and relatively unusual example of attention to one of the lesser-known and more obviously pastoral sermons, delivered on the occasion of an unnamed woman's funeral.

15. Alisdair MacIntyre, *After Virtue: A Study in Moral Theory* (London: Bloomsbury, 2013), xii.

16. Vivian Boland, *St Thomas Aquinas* (London: Bloomsbury, 2014), 14–17, 39–78 connects both Aquinas' own teaching and his views on pedagogy.

17. Peter M. Candler, *Theology, Rhetoric, Manuduction, or Reading Scripture Together on the Path to God* (Grand Rapids, MI: Eerdmans, 2006), 4–5.

18. See Philip B. Secor, *Richard Hooker: Prophet of Anglicanism* (Tunbridge Wells: Burns & Oates, 1999), 101–14, 199–220, 278–306). Secor's highly idiosyncratic account does include the basic details of Hooker's career and useful further references.

detailed instructions including something like a sixteenth-century ministers' rota setting out the times of sermons and including the instruction of 'little children' in the catechism (*Treatises*, 62).[19] Calvin's great systematic theology includes considerable detail about the practical business of organizing local churches, which occupies most of the fourth book of the *Institutes*.[20] It seems implausible that these three theologians maintained some sort of distinction between the different ways or contexts in which they taught and thought about faith. While the precise influence of that pastoral ministry on their theology cannot of course be identified, the broader point holds; their reasoning was not abstracted from their experience but was worked out in specific locations and communities of learning and pastoral care.[21]

This insistence that reason cannot be abstracted from particular contexts but must be rooted in experience prompts a third point: this experience is not just individual; in theology, reason is never simply the act of the autonomous (usually privileged) individual but something essentially *communal*; it is the reasoning of the church. Some feminist critiques 'protest against the illusion that human beings are separate and separable items, called individuals, merely collected together dispassionately in random groups'.[22] Oliver and Higton also point out the essentially communal context of theological reason.[23] So too MacIntyre, who suggests that reason has too often been defined as the 'ideal rationality' of 'a socially disembodied being' which simply 'ignores the inescapably historically and socially context-bound character' of all reasoning.[24]

One obvious concern in our three theologians is their recourse to the shared reasoning of some corporate body. All three, notably, say that a church council has a particular role in discerning theological truth in the church, however impractical or flawed such a gathering might be in practice. Aquinas, for example, considers it essential to the truthfulness of doctrinal statements like the creeds that they are drawn up 'in the person, as it were, of the whole Church, which is united together by faith' (*S.Th.* II-II.1.9, *ad.*; cf. *s.c.*). This quotation has been drawn on in later Roman Catholic theology to emphasize the corporate element of reasoning and

---

19. Cf. Bruce Gordon, *Calvin* (New Haven, CT: Yale University Press, 2011), 126–8.

20. See Dorothea Wendebourg, 'The Church in the Magisterial Reformers', in *The Oxford Handbook of Ecclesiology*, ed. P. D. L. Avis (Oxford: Oxford University Press, 2018), 233–5.

21. An excellent overview of female and feminist theologies which emphasizes the embedded and embodied practices of reasoning is Elaine Graham, 'Feminist Critiques, Visions, and Models of the Church', in *Oxford Handbook of Ecclesiology*, ed. Avis, 527–51.

22. Susan Frank Parsons, 'Redeeming Ethics', in *CCFT*, ed. Parsons 212.

23. Simon Oliver, 'Reading Philosophy', in *The Routledge Companion to the Practice of Christian Theology*, ed. Mike Higton and Jim Fodor (Abingdon: Routledge, 2015), 73; Mike Higton, 'Reason', in *Routledge Companion*, ed. Higton and Fodor, 11–13, 15–16.

24. Alasdair MacIntyre, *Whose Justice? Which Rationality?* (Notre Dame, IN: University of Notre Dame Press, 1998), 3–4.

decision-making which, since the Second Vatican Council, has become more prominent under the conception of the *sensus fidelium*, the consensus or sense of the faithful.²⁵ This theme is perhaps even more pronounced in Hooker who considers the community's reasoning to be vital.²⁶ He is, notably, determined that the monarch alone cannot make laws; legislation requires the communal consent of the public's representatives, consent which must be given by the whole of the body not just a part (*Laws*, VIII.6.5).²⁷ Calvin, too, his emphasis on personal conscience notwithstanding, also thought there was specific merit in reasoning together (for instance, his call for a 'synod of true bishops', *Inst.* IV.9.13). Calvin hoped, early in his career, that a council might bring reconciliation either with Rome and/or among the reformed.²⁸

It is important not to overstate this case; as McGrade notes on Hooker, for instance, the definition of those whose opinion was sought excluded significant groups including women and those without property.²⁹ One challenge of feminist critiques, among others, is that the church must attend to which voices are being heard and consider more carefully which voices are being overlooked or excluded.³⁰ This was not a particular priority for our theologians, and more work is clearly needed to establish where and how the range of voices is heard. Nonetheless, the broader point is that reason in Christian theology is always exercised communally.

MacIntryre's reference to disembodiment suggests a fourth area where the account of reason needs refining, namely its relation to the *material*. Susan Frank Parsons epitomizes a concern to move beyond narrowly Cartesian notions of being as dependent simply on cogitation to realize that reason is something practiced by persons who, among other things, have bodies.³¹ She asks 'whether this tool of reason, detached as it was from embodiment and place, could ever bring about justice'.³² This reflects a wider concern in feminist theology about the failure to attend to women in particular as having bodies, and a concern that reason is defined

---

25. See Anthony Ekpo, 'The *Sensus Fidelium* and the Threefold Office of Christ: A Reinterpretation of *Lumen Gentium* No. 12', *Theological Studies* 76.2 (2015): 330–46.

26. R. D. Williams, *Anglican Identities* (London: DLT, 2004), 32–5; see also Mike Higton, *The Life of Christian Doctrine* (London: Bloomsbury T&T Clark, 2020), 103–4, cf. 123–5.

27. See Daniel Eppley, 'Royal Supremacy', in *CRH*, 524.

28. Theodore W. Casteel, 'Calvin and Trent: Calvin's Reaction to the Council of Trent in the Context of His Conciliar Thought', *Harvard Theological Review* 63.1 (1970): esp. 116–17.

29. A. S. McGrade, 'Richard Hooker on Anglican Integrity', *Anglican Theological Review* 9.3 (2009): 428.

30. See, for instance, Mary McClintock Fulkerson and Sheila Briggs, 'Introduction', in *Oxford Handbook of Feminist Theology*, ed. McClintock Fulkerson and Briggs, 1–2; Margaret D. Kamitsuka, *Feminist Theology and the Challenge of Difference* (Oxford: Oxford University Press, 2007), 4–18.

31. Frank Parsons, 'Redeeming Ethics', esp. 210–12.

32. Frank Parsons, 'Redeeming Ethics', 211; Anderson, *Feminist Philosophy of Religion*, 127–30.

as something without reference to the physicality of the reasoner; thus, Jantzen criticizes the epitomizing of the self as rational and therefore disembodied.[33] Aspects of her critique would be highly problematic for our theologians, such as her apparent insistence that doctrines of God which assert God is rational and disembodied must be radically overhauled.[34] But Jantzen's criticism, with feminist theologians more generally, of theologies which ignore the embodiment of the reasoner poses further grounds to reconsider the meaning of reason. In fact, as we can see, Aquinas, Calvin and Hooker all conceive reason in material terms – both as an act of an *embodied* person, not just an intellectual one, and also as engaging with a material creation. In other words, contemporary critiques which rightly identify the risk of conceiving reason as merely abstract and intellectual – and thereby privileging some sorts of reasoner over others – might find unexpected resonance with the earlier tradition which Aquinas, Calvin and Hooker represent.

For reason's material dimensions are seen in all three theologians. For Aquinas and Hooker this can be particularly identified in their sacramental theology. So, as Candler highlights in his reading of Aquinas' account of holy communion, one of the effects of the sacrament is that it reorders our minds.[35] For instance, the outstretched arms of the priest teach us, wordlessly, of Christ's love shown in his outstretched arms on the cross (S. Th. III.87.5, ad. 5); the physical movement towards the altar embodies our journey towards holiness (III.87.3, ad. 1).[36] Turner similarly says, '[A]s Thomas sees it, you could not even begin to work out what you meant by "rationality" independent of the conception of bodies' and this in particular means reason has a sacramental 'shape'.[37] Aquinas' emphasis on the sacraments as means of teaching indicates a wider definition of reason than the merely propositional or cognitive.

For Hooker, likewise, the material of the sacraments was instructive. As Neelands notes, Hooker rejects the presbyterian view that teaching can be accomplished solely by instruction and prayer (*Laws*, V.50.1); in fact, to paraphrase Hooker, while the sacraments do more than teach the mind they certainly do not do less than that (V.57.1; V.58.1).[38] And Williams draws attention to a seemingly rather obscure dispute with the presbyterians about whether communicants, particularly those suspected of papist sympathies, should be subjected to some

33. Jantzen, *Becoming Divine*, 31.
34. Jantzen, *Becoming Divine*, esp. 25, 28–30, 274.
35. Candler, *Theology, Rhetoric, Manuduction*, 140.
36. Candler, *Theology, Rhetoric, Manuduction*, 153; similarly Mark D. Jordan, *Teaching Bodies: Moral Formation in the* Summa *of Thomas Aquinas* (New York, NY: Fordham University Press, 2017), 52, cf. 54–6, 60–1.
37. Denys Turner, 'Faith, Reason, and the Eucharist', in *Redeeming Truth: Considering Faith and Reason*, ed. Lawrence Paul Hemming and Susan Frank Parsons (London: SCM, 2007), 17, 25; cf. 26–31.
38. W. David Neelands, 'Christology and the Sacraments', *CRH*, 375–6; similarly, P. A. Dominiak, 'The Logic of Desire: A Reappraisal of Reason and the Emotions in Richard Hooker's *Lawes*', *Renaissance and Reformation Review* 16.1 (2014): 46–7.

kind of examination or test before being admitted to communion. Among the reasons Hooker advances for not imposing such a test is that, if admitted to the sacrament, 'they will learn the mystery of gospel-like behaviour when leisure serves them' (IV.68.8).[39] Hooker saw the sacraments as capable of helping people 'learn', means whereby something of God's truth might be revealed, even in such apparently unpropitious circumstances as the tentative outward conformity of the wavering adherent.

Indeed, not just the sacraments but human bodies themselves were useful for teaching[40] – hence Hooker's poetic defence of singing in worship, and particularly the benefits of singing the Psalms, on account of the 'admirable facility which music has to express and represent' the mind to itself, and which can either confirm or change our thinking (V.38.1). Hooker's emphasis not just on the sacraments but the physical aspects of ritual, and ritual as something which teaches us, indicates, as Dominiak argues, that 'the rational human self does not exist … as an isolated or dispassionate unit'.[41] Hooker's defence of retaining elements of pre-reformation ritual is grounded, in part, on a richer notion of reason than that advanced by his presbyterian opponents, who risked reducing teaching simply to the verbal and cognitive.

Of the three theologians Calvin is perhaps most likely to be suspected of underplaying this material dimension of reason. Since the material aspects are seen most clearly in Hooker's and Aquinas' sacramental theology, this suspicion in part arises because Calvin's sacramental theology is sometimes thought to be less attentive to the material aspects of sacraments. Oliver, for example, fears in Calvin a 'tendency towards a spiritualised and gnostic existence that lacks any genuine notion of corporeality', emphasizing 'purely spiritual and non-corporeal' aspects of Christian life.[42]

This is an understandable concern (in rejecting transubstantiation and consubstantiation, Calvin was certainly ruling out obvious ways to secure the physical importance of the sacraments), but we can refine Oliver's critique following Billings' discussion. For instance, Billings wonders whether Oliver's claims about Calvin might be adjusted when the clear distinction between Calvin and Zwingli is made clear – the former having a much more participatory account of the sacraments than the latter.[43] Specifically, for instance, Calvin warns against 'too little regard for the signs', in language with a physical flavour ('savour', 'relish'), and he insists that we 'should not think that the life we receive from him is received

---

39. See Williams, *Anglican Identities*, 34; cf. Higton, *Life of Doctrine*, 103.

40. Dominiak, 'Logic of Desire', 48. Hooker's understanding of reason as more than cognitive is also emphasized by Russell, *Beyond Certainty*, e.g., 152–67, 179–80.

41. Dominiak, 'Logic of Desire', 42.

42. Simon Oliver, 'The Eucharist before Nature and Culture', *Modern Theology* 15.3 (1999): 343, 347.

43. J. Todd Billings, *Calvin, Participation, and The Gift: The Activity of Believers in Union with Christ* (Oxford: Oxford University Press, 2007), 104.

by mere knowledge' (*Inst.* IV.17.5).⁴⁴ Calvin's sacramental theology, very different from Aquinas' on the means of the change in the elements, also differs from, say, Zwingli in its emphasis that we receive more than just knowledge and that the elements are more than just symbolic. Calvin thus demonstrates a sacramental theology which is not simply cognitive, and indeed we have seen in Hooker that rejecting transubstantiation and consubstantiation need not imply a sacramental theology unconcerned with the physical.

Reinforcing Billings' emphasis on Calvin's view of the materiality of the sacraments is Calvin's very sensuous account of the material creation and its potential for us. So Calvin wonders at 'the greatness of the Artificer who stationed, arranged, and fitted together the starry host of heaven in such wonderful order that nothing more beautiful in appearance can be imagined' (I.4.21). This should result in us 'bestir[ring] ourselves to trust, invoke, praise, and love'; 'invited by the great sweetness of his beneficence and goodness, let us study to love and serve him with all our heart' (I.4.22). What Calvin envisages here is more than just mere intellectual cogitation and something more experiential and emotional in response to the material universe.⁴⁵

The emphasis on the material elements of the sacraments, then, is for Calvin set clearly in a wider context about the potential for matter to do more than just imply cognitive propositions. The capacity of reason, to link back to earlier discussions about creation and the knowledge of God, is only part of a foundational claim about *creation*; for our reasoning is itself a God-given gift. The *triplex via* may achieve something like this for Aquinas; all our abilities are divinely given. The *via causalitatis* frames our understanding of reflecting our rational divine cause in having, among other things, the capacity to think;⁴⁶ the *via remotionis* highlights the context of our thinking is different from the divine, not least because we have *bodies*. And here, as Lewis famously observed of Hooker,

> Few model universes are more filled – one might say, more drenched – with Deity than his ... it is this conviction which enables Hooker, with no anxiety, to resist any inaccurate claim that is made for revelation against reason, Grace against Nature, the spiritual against the secular.⁴⁷

What Lewis sees in Hooker is the refusal to separate different spheres of life or sources of knowledge. They are, rather, fundamentally one because they are *created* and *given* by God; flowing from the same divine source, they cannot, ultimately, be opposed. Here we see the methodology we have traced in Calvin, Aquinas and

---

44. Billings, *Calvin, Participation, and the Gift*, 135.

45. A. N. Williams, *The Architecture of Theology: Structure, System, and Ratio* (Oxford: Oxford University Press, 2011), 196.

46. Williams, *Architecture of Theology*, 17–19, 221.

47. C. S. Lewis, *English Literature in the Sixteenth Century* (Oxford: Clarendon Press, 1954), 459.

Hooker bringing together some perhaps unlikely conversation partners – C. S. Lewis and feminist theologians – to identify a key contribution that our three theologians' theological method can offer, namely a wider and richer definition of reason. This reason is intrinsically not the autonomous thought of a single individual (usually a privileged one, in some way), but a communal effort of engagement with scripture, experience, matter, and (we might add) conducted by Christians in everyday ministry and discipleship of different forms. So reason, in some sense, is an act of the church as it reads scripture together, shares the sacraments and engages with the practical needs of local communities; ecclesial, theological reason is far wider a concept than reason narrowly conceived as intellectual or equated solely with modern scientific method.

Such an account might cohere with philosophical attempts to reclaim a richer notion of reason. If Pinker represents a contemporary thinker who is suspicious of any claim that religion could be rational, a rather different view of reason is advanced by Stephen Toulmin. In many ways Toulmin is, like Pinker, trying to re-establish the benefits of reason in the face of contemporary challenges; he sets out to address the 'sudden loss of confidence in our traditional ideas about rationality' and says reason has been increasingly 'sidelined' in public discourse.[48] Toulmin thinks that one of the key problems with defending reason is that its definition has become narrower and in some circumstances is equated almost entirely with 'scientific method', an 'enthronement of mathematical rationality'.[49] However, as Toulmin notes, such conceptions do not do justice to the range of human experience and we need some broader definition of reason which recovers the complexity and variety of reason, its sources and expressions. Reason, for Toulmin, cannot be reduced simply to that knowledge which is attainable by the methods of mathematics or the natural sciences.[50] The account of reason in Hooker, Aquinas and Calvin likewise emphasizes that variety of sources and shapes of genuine knowledge.

Other contemporary defences of reason also recognize the value of such a broader definition. For example, one theme which emerges is the risk that an excessively abstract notion of reason, detached from individual thinking and feeling persons, can result in a failure to appreciate the dignity of persons and therefore to nurture individuals, communities or the natural environment. Specifically, as one critique of a New Atheist thinker posits, labelling religion as a single and irrational entity may result in the loss of elements of religious tradition which may in fact be very desirable, such as the emphasis on human dignity in some forms of monotheism.[51] Reason, on these views, must take into account more than just abstract cogitation. Such accounts of reason will be deprived of a key ally if religious belief is simply

---

48. Stephen Toulmin, *Return to Reason* (London: Harvard University Press, 2001), 3.
49. Toulmin, *Return to Reason*, 83, 205.
50. E.g., Toulmin, *Return to Reason*, 13, 214.
51. Lynne Rudder Baker, 'Dennett on Breaking the Spell', in *The Philosophy of Daniel Dennett*, ed. Bryce Hubner (Oxford: Oxford University Press, 2018), 335-6, 340-2.

cast aside as intrinsically irrational. In other words, some contemporary defences of reason are, distinct from any Christian doctrinal concerns, urging just such a broader vision of what reason means that we have argued can be found both in some feminist theological critiques and in our three theologians.

Bringing these critiques into conversation with Hooker, Calvin and Aquinas yields a much richer and more theologically grounded account of our reason than is often attributed to those particular theologians – or attributed to reason in theology generally, either by internal critics of reason's role in theology or external proponents of theology's intrinsic irrationality. There remain some quite striking differences; many feminist theologians argue for a very different doctrine of God, say, than Aquinas, Calvin and Hooker would be prepared to countenance; and our three theologians do not attend to the variety of voices or the embodied experience of women as contemporary feminist theologians rightly suggest we should. Nonetheless, conceived in this way, reason and faith will be seen as not so opposed as a contemporary, post-Enlightenment definition of reason (whether advanced by the sceptic or the believer) might suggest. The sceptic may see reason is concerned with the whole of human experience, not just rational cogitation (as if thought ever could be separated from thinker). The believer might grasp that reason has reflection on scripture and the lived experience of the Christian community at its heart. Drawing on some feminist critiques and others, then, we recover more clearly the methodology and practice of reason in our three theologians. This may help resist contemporary tendencies to separate faith and reason and retrieve reason's place in Christian theology. Moreover, the brief reference to contemporary philosophical discussions (Pinker and Toulmin) suggests that there might be allies *outside* the Christian tradition in the task of reclaiming a richer, more nuanced account of reason. Having demonstrated the potential of the theological method we have traced for the debate about faith and reason, we turn next to show its usefulness in considering ecumenical debates about authority in the church.

Authority in the church

Introduction

The middle and late twentieth century saw substantial progress in a range of dialogues between churches on controversial questions.[52] This included formal dialogue between the Anglican and Roman Catholic communions, and this section examines the debates about their work on authority in the church successive bodies called Anglican-Roman Catholic International Commission (ARCIC). It will show how the key stumbling block remains the question of authority in the church and in particular the role of the Bishop of Rome. Using the theological

---

52. See Charlotte Methuen, 'Ecumenism', in *The Oxford Handbook of Anglican Studies*, ed. Mark D. Chapman, Sathianathan Clarke and Martyn Percy (Oxford: Oxford University Press, 2016), 464–77.

method identified in our theologians will help uncover the basic reasons why Rome's authority remains problematic from an Anglican perspective, thus yielding greater clarity about the question – before turning to the 'receptive ecumenism' of more recent years to see what contribution that method might make to ecumenical dialogue today.

ARCIC I and II

Through a series of reports from the 1970s to 1990s, the first two phases of ARCIC's work (ARCIC I and II) raised the prospect of greater institutional unity between the two churches. ARCIC II recognized 'the question of authority … is at the heart of our sad divisions'.[53] To overcome those divisions, ARCIC foresaw a distinctive role for the Bishop of Rome in some form of future, reconciled institution. Thus, *Gift of Authority*, a 1998 ARCIC report, concluded Anglicans could 'be open to … under certain clear conditions … the exercise of universal primacy by the Bishop of Rome'.[54]

This 'open'ness to a role for the Pope in a potentially reunited church highlights the differences between Anglican and the Roman Catholic Church understandings of authority. These focus in particular on two aspects of Roman Catholic teaching about the papacy which were articulated by the First Vatican Council (1868–70): *jurisdiction* and *infallibility*. Firstly, the Roman Catholic Church claims for the Pope 'ordinary … immediate … full and supreme power of jurisdiction over the whole church throughout the whole world' (*Decrees*, II.814). Secondly, the Roman Catholic Church believes that there are certain circumstances in which the Pope can issue a binding declaration about faith[55]: 'when the Roman pontiff speaks *ex cathedra* … he possesses … that infallibility which the divine Redeemer willed his church to enjoy … such definitions are of themselves, and not by the consent of the church, irreformable' (*Decrees*, II.815).

These claims are difficult to square with an Anglican understanding of the church. Firstly, Article XXXVII of the Articles of Religion (*DER*, 308) insists that the Pope has no jurisdiction in England, echoing parliamentary legislation of 1532 and 1534 which broke the link with Rome, and Anglican structures have resisted any tendency to give the Archbishop of Canterbury similiar power. Secondly, asserting infallibility sits uncomfortably with the reformers' clear commitment that the church can err (see Articles XX and XXII (*DER*, 296–7)).

Recognizing the difficulties of these understandings of the papacy for Anglicans, ARCIC attempted some helpful clarifications about the two concepts. Its 1976 statement *Authority in the Church I* discussed jurisdiction using the

---

53. Anglican-Roman Catholic International Commission, *The Gift of Authority* (1998), accessed 28 August 2020, https://www.anglicancommunion.org/media/105245/ARCIC_II_The_Gift_of_Authority.pdf, para. 62.

54. *Gift*, preface.

55. ARCIC, *Walking Together on the Way* (2017), accessed 28 August 2020, https://www.anglicancommunion.org/media/344839/walking-together-on-the-way-spck-2018.pdf, paras 134, 137.

language of pastoral support and challenge rather than control[56] and noted that papal infallibility was 'hedged about with very rigorous conditions'.[57]

Even with these caveats, the work of ARCIC I and II, particularly on papal primacy, was received by both communions with considerable caution. *Authority I* provoked rather hesitant responses from each side – particularly its statement that 'significant convergence' had been reached on 'the basic principles of primacy'.[58] The Church of England's Faith and Order Advisory Group observed that the 'problems should not be underestimated, in particular the issue of infallibility'.[59] The official Roman Catholic response (from the Congregation for the Doctrine of the Faith, CDF) was even more candid. It observed the tension between official Anglican formularies such as the Thirty-Nine Articles and ARCIC's conclusions – 'the assertions of the Final Report seem incompatible with these documents'.[60] In particular, CDF suggested that ARCIC's account of jurisdiction and infallibility was deficient from a Roman Catholic perspective. Whereas ARCIC seemed to suggest a minimalist reading (the papacy was not contrary to scripture, and its infallibility might be seen as conditional on the reception of infallible declarations), CDF pointed out that Roman Catholic teaching was more maximalist (the papacy was directly grounded in the New Testament and its infallibility could not be questioned).[61] CDF concluded that ACRIC's work did 'not yet constitute a substantial and explicit agreement'.[62]

These tensions, identified by both communions in the late 1970s/early 1980s, were clearly not resolved by the time *Gift* was published in the late 1990s. Some Anglicans, conscious of the tradition's reformed heritage, argued that *Gift's* conclusions about convergence between the two communions failed to acknowledge the genuine concerns of many Anglicans about the trajectory of ARCIC's work on papal authority.[63] Likewise, ARCIC II's statement on Mary met

---

56. ARCIC, *Authority in the Church I* (1976), accessed 28 August 2020, https://www.anglicancommunion.org/media/105230/ARCIC_I_The_Authority_of_the_Church_I.pdf, paras. 11–2, 21.

57. *Authority I*, para. 24(c).

58. *Authority I*, paras 25, 24.

59. Faith and Order Advisory Group (1978), *Response by the Church of England to the Agreed Statements by the Anglican-Roman Catholic International Commission*, accessed 24 January 2023, https://iarccum.org/archive/ARCIC/ARCIC-203A.pdf, para. 54.

60. Sacred Congregation for the Doctrine of the Faith, *Observations on the Final Report of ARCIC* (1982), accessed 24 January 2023, https://www.vatican.va/roman_curia/congregations/cfaith/documents/rc_con_cfaith_doc_19820327_animadversiones_en.html, para. (A)(2)(III).

61. *Observations*, paras (B)(III)(1)-(2).

62. *Observations*, para. (D)(1).

63. S. W. P. Hampton, 'Protestants Betrayed', *The Tablet*, 22 May 2009, 727; Martin Davie, '"Yes" and "No" – *The Gift of Authority*', in *Unpacking the Gift: Anglican Resources for Theological Reflection on* The Gift of Authority, ed. Peter Fisher (London: Church House Publishing, 2002), 40, cf. 52–8.

immediate opposition on similar grounds.⁶⁴ Indeed, as Paul Murray, a key Roman Catholic theologian on ARCIC III, pointed out, whereas the 1988 Lambeth Conference (a gathering of global Anglican bishops roughly every ten years) welcomed ARCIC's conclusions on the Eucharist and on ministry, it pointedly did not endorse ARCIC's work on authority.⁶⁵

So by the turn of the millennium, there seemed to be a disjunction between the positive conclusions of ARCIC I/ARCIC II and much less positive responses within both communions. What I now hope to show is that describing and applying some of the techniques of ARCIC III in dialogue with the theological method and the account of Anglicanism traced here will help, at least, clarify and advance the debate.

ARCIC III and receptive ecumenism

Where ARCIC I and ARCIC II had tended towards urging consensus, ARCIC III began by recognizing the reality of continued *disagreement* between the two communions. Its 2017 report *Walking Together in the Way* honestly identifies areas of potential mutual learning but also areas of continuing disagreement: 'the distance to be travelled is considerably greater than the optimism of the early days suggested'.⁶⁶

ARCIC III adopted 'receptive ecumenism' as the basis of its approach. Receptive ecumenism is a theological approach or sensibility which moves from focusing on supposed deficiencies in another tradition to using that other tradition as a lens through which we look at the weaknesses or inconsistences of our own – 'a process of renewal by receptive learning from one's dialogue partner'.⁶⁷ ARCIC III has proceeded in this way, trying to show both Anglican and Roman Catholic

---

64. In particular, the declaration that both the Anglican and Roman Catholic churches could agree that the Marian dogmas are 'consonant with the teaching of the Scriptures and the ancient common traditions' (*Mary*, para. 60) was immediately challenged by some Anglicans. See Martin Davie, 'Mary – Grace and Hope in Christ – An Evangelical Anglican Response', in *Mary: Grace and Hope in Christ (ARCIC II): Essays by the Faith and Order Advisory Group of the Church of England* (London: CHP, 2008), 53–64.

65. Paul D. Murray, 'The Reception of ARCIC I and II in Europe and Discerning the Strategy and Agenda for ARCIC III', *Ecclesiology* 11 (2015): 207. See generally *Receptive Ecumenism and the Call to Catholic Learning: Exploring a Way for Contemporary Ecumenism*, ed. Paul D. Murray (Oxford: Oxford University Press, 2008); *Receptive Ecumenism as Transformative Ecclesiastical Learning: Walking the Way to a Church Reformed*, ed. Paul D. Murray, Gregory A. Ryan and Paul Lakeland (Oxford: Oxford University Press, 2022).

66. ARCIC, *Walking Together on the Way* (2017), accessed 28 August 2020, https://www.anglicancommunion.org/media/344839/walking-together-on-the-way-spck-2018.pdf, para. 5; cf. 134, 137. See Ormond Rush and Jamie Hawkey, *Walking Together on the Way: Anglican and Roman Catholic Commentaries on the ARCIC Agreed Statement* (London: SPCK, 2018).

67. Anthony T. Currer, 'Receptive Ecumenism and ARCIC III', in *Receptive Ecumenism as Transformative Ecclesiastical Learning*, eds Murray et al., 120.

traditions learning from each other. As a kind of worked example of how this kind of receptive learning might be done, I will try and demonstrate the possibility of fruitful engagement by drawing together the insights of this reading of our three theologians and applying them to the debate about papal authority.

Faced with the suggestion of incorporating a role for the See of Rome into some shared institutional future, a straightforward Anglican response might be an outright rejection of the notion drawn on the ample material in the tradition's reformed heritage, including from Hooker and from Calvin.

Hooker's views on the papacy are largely contiguous with Calvin's and it will be convenient first to set them out by examining the three theological warrants in turn – scripture, tradition and reason. So both contested the appeal to *scripture* for the papacy's claims by challenging the exegesis of the key passages in Matthew's gospel, 16.16-8 and 18.18. They argued that these did not confer unique authority on Peter, but to all the apostles and their successors (plural), hence 'the grand original warrant whereof the guide*s* and prelate*s* in God's church, first his Apostle*s*, and afterwards other*s* following *them* successively' (*Laws*, V.4.1, cf. V.77.8, VI.4.15; cf. *Inst.* IV.6.4, IV.6.7, IV.68-13; emphases added).

Both also challenged the papacy's appeal to *tradition*, arguing Rome's power was a later, political construct rather than an unqualified historic right. They do this by charting the emergence of Rome's claim to sole overarching authority from a much more dispersed pattern of authority, spread among several senior and more autonomous bishoprics, in the earlier centuries (*Laws*, VII.8.9, cf. VIII.7.4-5; cf. *Inst.* IV.6.1, IV.6.16, IV.7.1, IV.7.19, IV.7.21).[68]

Hooker in particular also rejected any straightforward appeal to *reason* for papal authority because he considered it dangerous and corrupting, both morally and spiritually, to concentrate such authority in one individual, as we saw in his aversion to the prominence of Luther and Calvin (*Laws*, Pref. 2.7, 4.7). This emerges again in his treatment of penance. Hooker fears that the appropriation of aspects of the power of absolution to the papacy results in both financial and spiritual corruption of the papal court and catastrophic pastoral consequences for the penitent, who may believe their forgiveness and salvation depend on their ability to pay (VI.5.9, VI.6.7). Calvin also contended the unreasonableness of papal claims by highlighting the practical difficulty of one individual overseeing such a wide geographical area (*Inst.* IV.6.2).

While tracing this concern about the papacy may seem to yield a blanket refusal to accept the proposals of ARCIC I and II, it nonetheless does move the debate beyond a straightforward standoff; for it identifies more clearly the reasons *why* Anglicanism might be cautious about a role for the See of Rome because of quite serious disagreements with the arguments used to ground the authority of that See.

But the interpretation of Hooker and Anglicanism outlined in this book can yield more than just a point-by-point explanation of why incorporating the

---

68. Cf. Andre A. Gazal, "'That Ancient and Christian Liberty": Early Church Councils in Reformation Anglican Thought', *Perichoresis* 17.4 (2012): 85.

papacy would be problematic for Anglicans. It can help pinpoint the deeper basis for disagreement by identifying that this is really a dispute not just about specific propositions but about their underlying theological method. For while both Hooker and Calvin contested the specific appeal to each warrant in Roman Catholic claims about the papacy, the more fundamental methodological point is of course Hooker's insistence that no one form of church government is binding perpetually on all Christians.[69] Good arguments, as we have seen, can for Hooker be made for bishops or presbyters leading the church. But as church government is a matter of discipline, not doctrine, no particular form can be demanded. Hooker is unwilling to accept a *necessary* claim to papal authority not just because of (say) specific disagreements about the history of the papacy but because of a more basic disagreement about the basis of authority in the church. For Hooker, *any* claim to authority in the church which insists on a single universal model of church order is bound to fail because it is not the purpose of scripture or tradition to set out a particular form of church government.

Similarly, Calvin is clear that there must be some form of church order, 'this human ministry which God uses to govern his church' (*Inst.* IV.3.2). Calvin appeals to biblical material justifying ministries of preaching (IV.3.3), apostolic or oversight ministries (IV.3.6), pastors and teachers in particular churches who also administer the sacraments (IV.3.7). He even, as Hooker noted, appealed to scripture specifically to justify the establishment of a presbyterian order in Geneva (*Laws*, Pref. 2.7). But Calvin never goes so far as to say that a particular form of church government is universally mandated in scripture.[70] Calvin's draft ecclesiastical ordinances for Geneva only say 'it will be good' to establish this order, not that it is necessary (*Treatises*, 59). In his discussion of different ministries, the titles and roles Calvin adduces from scripture to some extent overlap and are interchangeable (*Inst.* IV.3.8). Calvin is quite happy to respect the institutions of the papacy and episcopate in their ancient (though not their sixteenth-century) forms (IV.4.3, IV.6.16, IV.7.19, e.g.). So Calvin does not lay down one form of church government as scripturally binding and would not disagree with Hooker on that point.[71]

What this reading of theological method suggests, then, is that we need to dig deeper into each tradition to ask *on what basis* particular arguments are being advanced for any particular theological proposal in ecumenical dialogue. What Hooker yields is a notion of *reason*'s decisiveness in matters other than the

---

69. Cf. Daniel F. Graves, '"Iure Divino"? Four Views on the Authority of the Episcopacy in Richard Hooker', *Anglican and Episcopal History* 81.1 (2012): 49.

70. Thus K. P. J. Padley, 'Early Anglican Ecclesiology and Contemporary Ecumenism', *International Journal for the Study of the Christian Church* 9.1 (2009): 5.

71. For Calvin, only preaching the word and celebration of the dominical sacraments were essential to the church, and so varieties of ministry could be allowed: 'ministry itself ... is not a distinguishing mark of the church', A. J. G. van der Borght, *Theology of Ministry: A Reformed Contribution to an Ecumenical Dialogue* (Leiden: Brill, 2007), 53.

essentials of doctrine and these essentials do not include the way the church is governed. Indeed, the young Roman Catholic theologian who would later become Pope Benedict XVI rightly located the problem in the 1960s when he argued it was precisely a question of underlying theological method.[72] As Chapter 5 showed, some theologians such as Geiselmann tried to interpret post-Tridentine Roman Catholic official theology in a way congenial to reformed concerns. But Ratzinger argued that this was an inadequate reading of Trent and its successors because, for him, official Roman Catholic formulations do assert that both scripture and tradition bind the church to a form of papal government. As CDF's response to ARCIC I said,

> the office of conserving, fostering and expressing ... unity in accord with the Lord's will is a constitutive part of the very nature of the Church (cf. Jn 21,15-19). The power of jurisdiction over all the particular Churches, therefore, is intrinsic (i.e. '*iure divino*') to this office, not something which belongs to it for human reasons nor in order to respond to historical needs.[73]

It is hard to see how this formulation, which insists there is a direct divine mandate for papal authority which does not depend on a reasoned choice, can square with Anglicanism's belief that church order can vary with reasoned decision; it relies, in other words, on a theological method which Hooker in particular, and Anglicanism on that reading, would be bound to reject.

But if we consider the problem in the light of the argument of congruity on theological method between our three authors, we can do more than just identify problems more acutely. As receptive ecumenism recognizes, there are differences *within* as well as *between* traditions. As Ryan points out, 'diverse communities of interpretation ... can be found within a tradition, as well as across churches'.[74] And, as the discussion of tradition in Chapter 5 tried to show, the Roman Catholic tradition – though Ratzinger rightly states its contemporary official formulation – offers more than one possible stance. Thus, Aquinas (unlike the reformers) tends to treat the institutional shape of the church as a given and offers no real critique of it. And he certainly gives the pope in the context of a council some definitive doctrinal role (*S.Th.* II-II.1.10, *resp.*) including the possibility of authorizing new definitions of doctrine (*add.* 2, 3). But there remains some ambiguity in his account; for instance, he does not seem to address the possibility that a council and a pope might disagree, and the papacy's authority is very much couched in terms of the operation of councils – which is not easy to square with Vatican I's claim that the pope's ability to declare doctrine infallibly does not require the consent of

---

72. Joseph Ratzinger, in Karl Rahner and Joseph Ratzinger, *Revelation and Tradition* (London: Burns & Oates, 1966), 32–3.

73. *Observations*, para. (B)(III)(2), cf. (B)(III)(1).

74. Gregory A. Ryan, 'The Reception of Receptive Ecumenism', *Ecclesiology* 17.1 (2021): 21; cf. 9.

the church. Moreover, as Horst notes, there is considerable distance between the papacy in Aquinas' day and the later institution, particularly the latter's claim to infallibility.[75] And it might be possible to see this specific problem in the context of Aquinas' wider method, shared (we have argued) with Hooker and Calvin, which does not appear to give scripture a binding role in matters other than doctrine and does not give tradition a binding role at all.

So some tension may be identified between Aquinas' views and the current conception of papal authority.[76] That tension *within* the Roman Catholic tradition, if approached in a receptive ecumenical mood, might be worth exploring further to see whether a pre-Tridentine, pre-Vatican I account of the papacy could be retrieved, drawing on Aquinas' perspective, which yielded a more chastened view of papal authority that could be more congenial to reformed concerns and therefore potentially more likely to be acceptable to Anglicans. That is not to say that such an account *would* be acceptable to the institutions of the Roman Catholic (or indeed Anglican) communions, but that it would be a discussion worth pursuing within and between the two traditions. At least, deploying the kind of reading advanced here within a 'receptive ecumenical' framework might be a fruitful task for ecumenical dialogue between the two communions.

As Aulen noted, papal authority is among the principles which 'have widened the distance between Rome and evangelical Christendom'.[77] But considering a receptive-ecumenical approach of mutual learning, and bringing together our three theologians, can help identify the problem more clearly by identifying what insights in the Anglican tradition – both about how authority is exercised and what theological basis underpins it – need to be heard in the discussion. We can also – as we the debates about faith and reason earlier in this chapter – identify some perhaps surprising conversation partners and at least suggest the possibility that recovering a pre-Vatican I (and pre-Trent) account of the church as might be developed in a way faithful to an earlier Roman Catholic understanding, grounded in a kind of Thomist theological method and therefore genuinely catholic, while also accommodating reformed concerns.

Of course, there would be considerable further work to do. A fuller discussion, on a receptive ecumenical model, would need to include Roman Catholic perspectives to ask what Anglicans might need to learn. But the argument here does try to adopt some of receptive ecumenism's key insights, not least its recognition of the seriousness of the unresolved problems in ecumenical debate, and bringing together

---

75. Ulrich Horst, *The Dominicans and the Pope: Papal Teaching Authority in the Medieval and Early Modern Thomist Tradition*, trans. James D. Mixson (Notre Dame, IN: University of Notre Dame Press, 2006), 2, 19, 21.

76. Indeed, one of Calvin's editors makes an intriguing case that Aquinas and Calvin are closer in their accounts of the papacy than Aquinas and contemporary Roman Catholic thought: *Inst.* II.1105, fn.8.

77. Gustaf Aulen, *Catholicity and Reformation*, trans. Eric Wahlstrom (Edinburgh: Oliver & Boyd, 1962), 17.

thinkers from the different communions, identifying how *difficult* the questions are, and the differences *within* as well as *between* traditions. The kind of honesty about difficulties and differences which receptive ecumenism embodies might at least help avoid the kind of setback where (as with *Gift*) one side appeared to advance a solution which it was entirely predictable a substantial number of its own church would find deeply problematic. And a shared focus on underlying methodological questions can yield greater understanding of *why* these issues and some proposed solutions might be difficult. So while this sketch is necessarily brief and insufficient, it does perhaps highlight the wisdom of ARCIC III in adopting receptive ecumenism as its approach and the potential for reading theologians of different traditions alongside each other to interrogate both their own traditions and each other's.

Summary

This chapter has tried to show there is constructive potential for the kind of method and account of Anglicanism generated by our reading of Hooker alongside Aquinas and Calvin. It could advance key philosophical and theological debates, perhaps finding unexpected allies, for instance by retrieving an account of reason which is richer – more scriptural, more communal, more embodied – than some more sterile accounts, both secular and theological, have presumed. It can help delineate key issues in ecumenical dialogue, showing *why* some problems are problems and uncovering deeper methodological difficulties.

Having identified the potential fruit of this kind of account of theological method and of Anglicanism, it is important to acknowledge potential limitations. Three in particular can be identified immediately.

Firstly, as receptive ecumenism helpfully reminds us, there are tensions *within* as well as *between* traditions. Indeed, not all Anglicans would accept the reading of theological method advanced here. This would merit further exploration, but an inevitably superficial sketch may identify the problem. Some evangelicals, for instance, would hold that scripture governs us in moral and ethical matters as well as matters of doctrine. The Church of England Evangelical Council's 'Basis of Faith' states that the 'Bible has been given to lead us to salvation, to be the ultimate rule for Christian *faith and conduct*'.[78] Exactly what was meant here would need further explanation, but, as we have seen, there is an apparent tension there with Hooker's and the formularies' view that the purpose of scripture was to contain all things necessary to salvation, that is, the things of *faith*, and not to deliver the complete rules of human conduct. On the other hand, some more catholic-minded Anglicans might argue that scripture (or perhaps scripture and tradition) govern not just matters of doctrine but matters of church order.[79] Again, there is more

---

78. Church of England Evangelical Council, 'Basis of Faith', accessed 28 January 2023, https://ceec.info/basis-of-faith/, para. 3 (emphasis added).

79. This seems to be the view, for instance, of Andrew Davison, *Why Sacraments?* (London: SPCK, 2013), 82, 86.

work to do, but we can identify a tension here, given Hooker's methodological stance that scripture and tradition do not regulate church order. So part of the limitation of Hooker's methodology and account of Anglicanism is that not all Anglicans would accept his underlying premises about, say, the function of scripture and/or tradition.

Secondly, even if the theological method advanced here were accepted, its application in particular circumstances might be resisted; in other words, Anglicans might agree there is a distinction between doctrine and discipline but disagree about where to draw the line. For some, say, questions of church order fall on the doctrine side of the divide and must be regulated by scripture and tradition.[80] For others, the definition of marriage might be considered a matter of doctrine, for others not.[81] Again, Hooker's methodology of itself will not solve such problems, but it might at least help yield a clearer understanding of the underlying issues, and the need in Anglican disputes not just to address the specific and divisive *questions* being disputed but have a prior discussion about what *methodology* should be used to address them.

Thirdly, Hooker is in many ways writing for a different world. He wrote, lyrically if perhaps even at the time optimistically, of a church and a nation which were one and the same (*Laws* VIII.6.11), and of an international landscape where each community had one identifiable church, and of a society where (at least in principle) almost everyone professed Christian faith. How Hooker is to be read in a country where not everyone is a Christian, where there are many faiths and none, is a difficult question; not least because part of Hooker's scheme of theological method entails decision-making on some matters by the Crown in Parliament, and that role has been questioned, by both some Anglicans and some in public life, partly because of the growing diversity of English society and the decreasing number of people who cite the Church of England as their spiritual home.

So this view of Anglicanism may not in the end persuade some within or without the tradition. It has considerable limitations. But hopefully this chapter has shown it has considerable potential, both for Anglican dialogue with other denominations, as in its application to the ARCIC debates, and indeed for theological debate more generally, as in the debates about faith and reason. A catholic, reformed Anglicanism of this kind would have much to contribute, even if only in helping to delineate key disputes more precisely and locate their roots more accurately, by identifying and interrogating the methodological questions which underpin those disputes. And this kind of clarity, as well as being a relief

---

80. For a survey of one such debate, see P. P. Hobday, 'Richard Hooker and *Mission and Ministry in Covenant*', *JAS* 18.2 (2020): 215–34.

81. For example, Kathryn Tanner, 'Hooker and the New Puritans', in *Authorizing Marriage? Canon, Tradition, and Critique in the Blessing of Same-Sex Unions*, ed. Mark D. Jordan (Princeton, NJ: Princeton University Press, 2006), 121–38; cf. P. P. Hobday, 'Relocating Richard Hooker: Theological Method and the Character of Anglicanism' (PhD diss., Durham University, 2021), 201–5.

to Anglicanism's ecumenical partners, would also help tackle the recurring Anglican tendency towards equivocation or contradiction (a tendency evident in its dialogue with other churches too[82]). If nothing else, then, approaching Hooker (and Anglicanism) in this way will help Anglicans better identify questions and problems and mitigate the risk that Anglican contributions to ecumenical dialogue might go further than the tradition as a whole would accept. This chapter can only be a brief and indicative sketch of what might be possible, and more work would need to be done, but hopefully at least this chapter has identified the potential for such work and the fruitfulness of deploying this account of Hooker and theological method as a lens to see other debates more clearly. The conclusion now turns to summarize what the argument of this book might yield not just for a catholic and reformed reading of Richard Hooker but also for the Anglican tradition he articulated, defended and loved.

---

82. See K. P. J. Padley, 'Eternal Progression and Temporal Procession of the Holy Spirit', *International Journal for the Study of the Christian Church* 18.4 (2018): 333, 341–2 for another example of Anglican self-contradiction in ecumenical dialogue.

CONCLUSION

This book has sought to trace a plausible and coherent of Anglican identity which is rooted in the theology, and particularly the theological method, of one of the first theologians of the reformation Church of England. This conclusion briefly rehearses the argument of the previous chapters before considering how this account can help relocate Richard Hooker more precisely and how this interpretation of him might contribute to discussions about the contested identify of the Church of England and of Anglicanism (as well as identifying some potential criticisms of this approach).

Anglicanism's claim to be both catholic and reformed has often been considered surprising, incoherent or implausible. Consequently, the tradition and its foremost theologian, Richard Hooker, have usually been categorized as either more catholic, more reformed or steering some path between them. Chapter 1 introduced Hooker, outlined different interpretations and showed why comparing him with the catholic Thomas Aquinas and the reformed John Calvin might be a legitimate and fruitful exercise. That comparison illuminates the fundamental structural problem of many interpretations of Hooker which assume an inevitable opposition or tension between those two theologians and traditions. Through this study, by reading these theologians closely and comparatively on the theme of theological method, the widespread and surprising convergence of their thought emerges which allows us to conceive both Hooker and Anglicanism as thoroughly and coherently catholic and reformed. This conclusion reviews the argument of the study, suggesting ways that reframing the debate in light of that convergence might help us conceive Hooker, and Anglicanism, in a fruitful way faithful to what is at least one vital and early strand of the tradition.

Chapters 2, 3 and 4 explored two theological warrants, *scripture* and *reason*, in Aquinas, Calvin and Hooker, respectively. This demonstrated Aquinas' and Calvin's congruity on several themes where they are thought to differ, and Hooker situated within that convergence. These include grasping their common assumption of real but limited natural knowledge of God and recognizing that Aquinas is less optimistic (and Calvin less pessimistic) about reason than often supposed. All three share the *sola scriptura* principle in the sense that scripture alone is the source of our saving knowledge of God, dependent for its authority on the divine authorship which the Spirit prompts the believer to apprehend, providing knowledge which unaided human reason could never attain. The distinct but complementary roles of reason and scripture as God-given communicators of knowledge emerge, not in tension but performing different functions (scripture as source, reason as instrument).

The discussion of a third warrant, *tradition*, in Chapter 5 advances this reading. Many interpretations of Hooker, focusing on the appearance of equal status given to scripture and tradition at the Council of Trent, have failed to notice Aquinas' much more chastened view of the warrant as having merely probable and ancillary authority. Delineating Aquinas' actual account of tradition, and identifying Trent rather than Aquinas as the real target of reformed polemic, unlocks the possibility of a shared view of that warrant, where all three theologians make a precise and limited appeal to tradition, affording a uniquely authoritative place only to those elements of doctrine attributable to the most widely recognized and oldest ecumenical councils, the four great councils of the first four Christian centuries. This preserves scripture's unique authority while accommodating the historical circumstances of the formation of the canon and creeds. While not arguing that Aquinas, Calvin and Hooker agreed on every particular, this study does demonstrate there is substantial shared ground on which their ecumenically minded descendants in different traditions or denominations might stand.

As Chapters 2 to 5 indicated, notions that a writer like Hooker could be coherently catholic and reformed, and that Anglicanism can plausibly define itself as both, should be much less surprising than they appear to be. Narrow definitions and misunderstandings of these two terms, and failures to grasp the nuance of the theologies of Calvin and Aquinas (nuances often overlooked or marginalized by subsequent interpreters), have contributed to the assumption that Hooker could not be both catholic and reformed. But in fact, as Williams says, often 'it is the very notions that prompted accusations of Catholic sympathies which are most strongly rooted in the concerns of the magisterial Reformation'.[1] The appropriation of Hooker by partisan accounts of Anglicanism has further exacerbated the erroneous presumption of inevitable catholic-reformed tension. Isolating these factors allows a more direct engagement between Hooker, Calvin and Aquinas which emphasizes the fundamental congruity of their theological methods.

Read this way, Hooker emerges as both emphatically reformed and thoroughly catholic, advocating a nuanced *sola scriptura* principle and a rich but carefully circumscribed account of reason, and far from the defender of custom for custom's sake he sometimes appears to be.[2] If nothing else, this study should indicate the need to put a further, final nail in the coffin of accounts of Anglicanism which claim a distinctive 'triple-cord' or 'three-legged stool'

---

1. R. D. Williams, *Anglican Identities* (London: DLT, 2004), 27.

2. Even a sophisticated analysis like MacCulloch's struggles to avoid caricature, as with his amusing aside that 'After reading Book V … one feels that if the parliamentary legislation of 1559 had prescribed that English clergy were to preach standing on their heads, then Hooker would have found a theological reason for justifying it': Diarmaid MacCulloch, 'Richard Hooker's Reputation', *EHR* 117 (2002): 799.

in theological method since the warrants have different roles and authority in theological reasoning, and this method, shared with Aquinas and Calvin, is not distinctively Anglican at all. Its rhetorical cousin, the patronizing assertion of a theologically or temperamentally superior *via media* between reformed and catholic poles, should likewise be laid to rest.

This reading of Hooker also resonates with and reinforces the wider retrieval, notably by Hampton and Griesel, of a vibrant but often overlooked strand of reformed Anglicanism which remained a vital tradition well into the eighteenth century[3] which also had a clear Thomist flavour.[4] At its origins, and for about the first century of its settled existence, Anglicanism was largely clear in its identity not as some middle way between perceived extremes but as both catholic and reformed, and this was possible because catholic and reformed were not opposite points on a spectrum but different expressions of a broadly shared core of theology. This method conceived God's revelation in scripture as the unique source of saving truth, while giving due weight to the need for our God-given reason in the church's theological discerning, and offering a historically plausible reading of tradition's place in theology by prioritizing only the conciliar formulations of the first four centuries as binding doctrinally on all Christians.

This investigation also reinforces those strands in Roman Catholic, reformed, Anglican and ecumenical discourse which increasingly emphasize the historically overlooked convergence between catholic and reformed, especially between Aquinas and Calvin.[5] While this study focuses on theological method, it suggests that other themes where dispute between the two has usually been asserted, notably justification and salvation, should be freshly investigated. It suggests that Hooker, whose views on justification have been interpreted as variably as has his theological method,[6] would be a useful prism for a fresh examination of that problem and hints that a greater degree of convergence between Aquinas and Calvin may be found there also.

The clarity of the theological method which emerges from this account of Hooker's reformed and catholic character could not only offer much-needed

---

3. S. W. P. Hampton, *Anti-Arminians: The Anglican Reformed Tradition from Charles II to George I* (Oxford: Oxford University Press, 2008), esp. 267–74; Jake Griesel, 'John Edwards of Cambridge (1637–1716): A Reassessment of His Position within the Later Stuart Church of England' (PhD diss., University of Cambridge, 2019), 239, 241–2.

4. Hampton, *Anti-Arminians*, 221–7, 272.

5. For instance, *Aquinas among the Protestants*, ed. Manfred Svensson and David VanDrunen (Oxford: Wiley-Blackwell, 2018); P. A. Dominiak, 'Hooker, Scholasticism, Thomism, and Reformed Orthodoxy', in *Richard Hooker and Reformed Orthodoxy*, ed. W. Bradford Littlejohn and Scott N. Kindred-Barnes (Göttingen: Vandenhoeck & Ruprecht, 2017), 116–19.

6. Good overviews of how Hooker can be situated in that debate are W. David Neelands, 'Predestination', *CRH*, esp. 189–219; Debora K. Shuger, 'Faith and Assurance', *CRH*, 221–50.

clarity to Anglicanism's ecumenical posture, which our ecumenical partners would welcome; it could also contribute to some contemporary debates, as the sixth chapter suggested. *Theologically*, areas of real potential emerge; for instance, it could ground a deep theological account of reason which would respond to the challenge of those who are suspicious of reason's place in theology (whether a certain kind of neo-Barthian theologian or a certain kind of contemporary atheist). It also suggests some surprising possibilities for fruitful conversation with unexpected interlocutors: for instance, this account of reason would address aspects of justified critiques, advanced by second-wave feminisms, of some understandings of reason which perpetuate the notion of the warrant as a disembodied, purely intellectual, capacity exercised largely by men. So too *ecumenically*, it would at the very least refine areas of disagreement (notably about the papacy) and clarify the need for considerable further work if Anglicanism is to advance towards greater institutional unity with the Roman Catholic Church while remaining faithful to its grounding in the reformation.

Relocating Hooker also helps relocate Anglicanism's theological identity. At least, it can undergird the historical and theological plausibility of Anglicanism's claim to be both catholic and reformed. But where, if anywhere, can Anglicanism's distinctiveness be located? For if there is (as this study argues) nothing intrinsically distinctive about its theological method since that is clearly shared with theologians of other traditions, so the *via media* falls away, does this mean reverting to what Sykes rightly branded the frustratingly unspecific (and disingenuous) 'no special doctrines' account?[7]

Shortly after being nominated as Archbishop of Canterbury, Rowan Williams (who, like Sykes, highlights the inadequacy of the 'no special doctrines' view[8]) was asked to describe Anglicanism's distinctiveness, and replied:

> Anglicanism is a Church that has tried to find its unity less in a single structural pattern, or even a confession of faith, than in a pattern of preaching and ministering the sacramental action … If you are looking for a Christian identity that is dependent neither on a pyramidal view of authority nor on highly specific confessional statements, there's a lot to be said for Anglicanism.[9]

Williams is not just making a structural or procedural claim but a *doctrinal* one, albeit in some sense a negative one. For it is a *doctrinal* claim to say that the church must be governed by a papal magisterium which has the power to adjudicate questions of doctrine or that such questions must be referred back to some confessional text to which subscription is demanded. The doctrinal claim of Hooker, and of Anglicanism, is by contrast that there is *no* doctrinal necessity for one particular form of church government, and the *only* essential doctrines which

---

7. Stephen Sykes, *Unashamed Anglicanism* (London: DLT, 1995), x–xi, 102–9.
8. Cf. Williams, *Anglican Identities*, 1.
9. 'What We Need Now: Gratitude', *Church Times*, 6 December 2002, 15.

can be demanded of Christians are those grounded in scripture as interpreted authoritatively by the first four ecumenical councils (as the Thirty-Nine Articles say).[10] No particular form of church government, nor subscription to any other articles as doctrinally binding, can therefore be mandated. This yields a tradition which is committed to the shared and fundamental truths (particularly about Christ, the Trinity and human salvation) which almost all Christians have held in common, but which gives a good deal of room for diversity in modes of government, styles of spirituality, preferences in worship and even structures at the local level.

Of course, a possible corollary of this insistence on a few fundamental doctrines and generosity in all else is, as recent experience shows, not just diversity but disagreement and division. But, more positively, Anglicanism's comprehensiveness, as Newey suggestively posits, could lie in the Chalcedonian-like way it can embrace or 'comprehend' distinct traditions without seeing them as inherently contradictory.[11] This need not mean those two elements need to be merged or mixed, or cherry-picked to create a third thing (the *via media* as a sort of ecclesiological equivalent of a Christological *tertium quid*[12]) which is neither catholic nor reformed.[13] Nor need it mean that emphasizing one will inevitably be at the expense of the other (any more than assertion of Christ's humanity *necessarily* entails diminishing his divinity).[14] In the same way, to emphasize the uniqueness of scripture in theological method need not be to the detriment of a significant place for reason. Hooker, whose account of Chalcedonian Christology embodies the best of his poetic, theologically astute, and historically alert writing, would have approved.

On this reading, the Church of England would be at its best if it embraced *both* its catholic *and* its reformed heritage, rather than assuming that closeness to one of these inevitably entailed distance from the other. The frustratingly sterile presumption of an inevitable stand-off between traditional parochial forms of church life and newer 'pioneering' modes might be one debate where it would help to see that more of one does not necessarily mean less of the other, while indicating

10. Cf. Oliver O'Donovan, *On the Thirty-Nine Articles: Conversations with Tudor Christianity*, 2nd edn (London: SCM, 2011), 49.

11. Edmund Newey, 'The Form of Reason: Participation in the Work of Richard Hooker, Benjamin Whichcote, Ralph Cudworth and Jeremy Taylor', *Modern Theology* 18.1 (2002): 19–20.

12. Gibbs attempts a reading of Hooker as propounding a *via media* which creates a *tertium quid* (a third thing mixing two others which blends some but not all of the original characteristics of each) between a kind of reformed view and a kind of catholic view: Lee W. Gibbs, 'Richard Hooker's *Via Media* Doctrine of Scripture and Tradition', *HThR* 95.2 (2002): 229. This reading of Hooker seems rather implausible, given his commitment to a Chalcedonian orthodoxy, on which see Williams, *Anglican Identities*, 27–32.

13. Edmund Newey, 'The Covenant and the *Via Media*: Compatible or Contradictory Notions of Anglicanism?', in Pro Communione: *Theological Essays on the Anglican Covenant*, ed. Benjamin Guyer (Eugene, OR: Pickwick, 2012), 52–6.

14. This is a key argument of Williams' recent monograph on Christology, which identifies the surprising congruity of Aquinas and Calvin on this point: R. D. Williams, *Christ the Heart of Creation* (London: Bloomsbury, 2018), esp. 127–8, 144–50.

that both sides of the argument could deepen their own tradition by learning from the other's. Conceiving Anglican comprehensiveness in this register could also help move beyond other frustrating impasses, as a recent theological account of how cathedrals can faithfully serve potentially competing constituencies has suggested.[15]

Both this account of Hooker as thoroughly grounded in catholic and reformed traditions which converge rather than compete, and the catholic and reformed Anglicanism I argue can be drawn from this reading of him, are clearly open to challenge and certainly prompt some questions which would be worth pursuing.

An obvious challenge might be that this book is merely trying to advance a view of Anglicanism as its author wishes it were, rather than describing something intrinsic to the tradition as such. Inevitably, as someone who worships in, and works for, the Church of England, I bring my own views about my church and my employer. And it is certainly true that I believe an Anglicanism which is faithful to its catholic and its reformed roots, with clear unity on the essentials of Christology in particular but with a generous embrace of diversity on practices and structures, has a lot to commend it. But other versions of Anglicanism are, of course, available! And, of course, such an approach does pose further questions: what is essential, and what is not? Are there kinds of diversity of practice and structure, or particular practices and structures, which might so undermine the coherence of the tradition that they should be resisted?

A connected criticism might be that, having argued that too many writers simply use Hooker as a mirror for their own perspective, seeing in him an Anglicanism they themselves prefer, this work is in fact just one more attempt to read Hooker in a way congenial to my own ecclesiastical preoccupations – in other words, because I wish to think Anglicanism is both catholic and reformed, I inevitably 'discover' that Hooker does too. While acknowledging the force of such challenges, and the risk of my own biases, I believe this reading of Hooker has solid roots: many accounts of Hooker rely on comparison with either Calvin or Aquinas; the attempt to make a sustained, tripartite comparison is much rarer, and I believe it does afford a particularly firm basis for the argument of this book. This reading also sits within a wider and growing body of scholarship which is identifying convergence between Aquinas and Calvin, and the reformed catholic identity of both Hooker and of Anglicanism in its origins, which further advances its plausibility.

A further criticism might be that this work risks being too abstract, in the sense that it tries to distil something called a theological method (in the limited sense of how they conceive the relationship of the three theological warrants) and then identify convergence on that narrow ground, whereas considering the three theologians' work more roundly may in fact reveal much wider and perhaps more significant disagreements. For instance, even if such a substantial measure of convergence were granted on their theological method, would this be sustained if their views of salvation or of the sacraments were compared? I have tried to indicate that there are already a number of writers who are identifying potential

---

15. Simon Oliver, 'The Cathedral and Rooted Growth', in *Holy Ground: Cathedrals in the Twenty-First Century*, ed. Stephen Platten (Durham: Sacristy Press, 2017), 29–33.

convergence on those areas where reformed and catholic traditions have been thought to disagree, and, at the very least, my reading of the three on methodology might suggest Hooker would be a useful prism through which to look at tripartite comparisons on other topics, too.

Having argued the *plausibility* of this kind of reading of Hooker and of Anglican identity does not, of course, answer the question of its *desirability*: whether the Church of England, or the Anglican Communion, is willing to embrace this kind of identity is another question. Certainly the failure of the proposed Anglican Covenant, whatever one's view of that initiative's merit, suggests there is little appetite for wide commitment to any one model of Anglicanism. But if Anglicans are willing to embrace it, there is a rich and potentially fruitful account of the tradition's origins and character to hand in the work of Richard Hooker. It goes beyond stale theological and historiographical tropes such as the *via media* and the 'three-legged stool' to yield a rich account of Anglicanism which could help it handle internal debates and ecumenical dialogue with, if nothing else, a much greater degree of clarity.

Relocating Richard Hooker as a catholic and reformed theologian may help undergird a coherent Anglicanism, resistant to narrowly or competitively partisan interpretations, clearer and more reliable as an ecumenical partner, perhaps even a resource for other traditions who might connect with refreshed readings of Aquinas and Calvin within the contemporary Roman Catholic and Reformed traditions those formative theologians helped shape. The comparison of the three theologians also suggests that – while his achievement is neither as comprehensive nor as influential as either Aquinas' or Calvin's – Hooker can nonetheless be seen as a sophisticated systematic theologian in his own right. Thus, Hooker's theological method in particular is worth study not just as an exercise in denominational apologetics but as a substantial and serious theological enterprise. Read this way, the clarity and coherence of Richard Hooker's catholic, reformed Anglicanism offers something to other Christian traditions, and to Christian theology more generally, as well as the Anglican variety of Christianity which he articulated so poetically and with such poise.

BIBLIOGRAPHY

Primary sources

Aquinas, Thomas. *The Apostles' Creed*. Translated by Joseph B. Collins. Edited by Joseph Kenny. Accessed 28 November 2019. https://dhspriory.org/thomas/english/Creed.htm.

Aquinas, Thomas. *Commentary on Blessed Dionysius's* On the Divine Names. Translated by Harry C. Marsh, 'Cosmic Structure and the Knowledge of God: Thomas Aquinas' *in Librum Beati Dionysii* De Divinis nominibus expositio'. PhD diss., Vanderbilt University, 1994.

Aquinas, Thomas. *Commentary on St. Paul's Epistle to the Galatians*. Translated by F. R. Larcher. Albany, NY: Magi Books, 1966.

Aquinas, Thomas. *Commentary on the* Metaphysics *of Aristotle*. 2 vols. Translated by John P. Rowan. Chicago, IL: Henry Regnery, 1961.

Aquinas, Thomas. *Expositio super librum Boethii de Trinitate* (*Exposition of Boethius' Book on the Trinity*). The edition used is Maurer's two-volume translation: *Faith, Reason and Theology: Questions I-IV of His Commentary on the* de Trinitate *of Boethius* and *The Division and Methods of the Sciences: Questions V and VI of His Commentary on the* de Trinitate *of Boethius*. Translated by Armand Maurer. Toronto: Pontifical Institution of Medieval Studies, 1986–7.

Aquinas, Thomas. *Quaestiones disputatae de veritate* (*Disputed Questions on Truth*). The edition used is the three-volume translation, *Truth*. Translated by Robert W. Mulligan, James V. McGlynn and Robert W. Schmidt. Indianapolis, IN: Hackett Publishing Company, 1994.

Aquinas, Thomas. *Summa Contra Gentiles*. 4 vols. Translated by the English Dominican Fathers. London: Burns & Oates, 1923–9.

Aquinas, Thomas. *Summa Theologica*. 5 vols. Translated by the Fathers of the English Dominican Province. Notre Dame, IL: Christian Classics, 1981.

Aquinas, Thomas. *Thomas Aquinas: The Academic Sermons*. Edited by Mark-Robin Hoogland. Washington, DC: Catholic University of America Press, 2010.

Bray, Gerald, ed. *Documents of the English Reformation, 1526–1701*. Edited by Gerald Bray. London: James Clarke, 2004.

Calvin, John. *Calvin's Commentaries: Romans and Thessalonians*. Translated by Ross Mackenzie. Edinburgh: Oliver and Boyd, 1960.

Calvin, John. 'Canons and Decrees of the Council of Trent with the Antidote'. In *John Calvin: Tracts and Letters*. 9 vols, III.18–188. Translated and edited by Henry Beveridge. Edinburgh: Banner of Truth Trust, 2009.

Calvin, John. *Commentaries*. Translated and edited by Jospeh Haroutunian. London: SCM, 1963.

Calvin, John. *Institutes of the Christian Religion*. 2 vols. Edited by John T. McNeill. Translated by Ford Lewis Battles. Louisville, KY: Westminster John Knox Press, 2006.

Calvin, John. *Theological Treatises*. Edited by J. K. S. Reid. Louisville, KY: Westminster John Knox Press, 2006.

Hooker, Richard. 'A Christian Letter of Certain English Protestants with Richard Hooker's Autograph Notes'. *FLE* IV.1–80.
Hooker, Richard. 'The Dublin Fragments: Grace and Free Will, the Sacraments, and Predestination'. *FLE* IV.99–167.
Hooker, Richard. 'The First Sermon upon Part of St Jude'. *FLE* V.13–35.
Hooker, Richard. *Folger Library Edition of the Works of Richard Hooker*. 7 vols. General editor W. Speed Hill. Vols I–V: Cambridge, MMA: Belknap Press of Harvard University Press, 1977–90; Vol. VI: Binghamton, NY: Medieval & Renaissance Texts and Studies, 1993; Vol. VII: Tempe, AZ: Medieval & Renaissance Texts and Studies, 1998.
Hooker, Richard. 'A Learned Discourse of Justification'. *FLE* V.105–69.
Hooker, Richard. 'A Learned Sermon of the Certainty and Perpetuity of Faith in the Elect'. *FLE* V.59–82.
Hooker, Richard. 'A Learned Sermon on the Nature of Pride'. *FLE* V.309–61.
Hooker, Richard. *Of the Laws of Ecclesiastical Polity: A Critical Edition with Modern Spelling*. 3 vols. Edited by A. S. McGrade. Oxford: Oxford University Press, 2014.
Hooker, Richard. 'A Remedy against Sorrow and Fear'. *FLE* V.363–77.
Hooker, Richard. 'The Second Sermon upon Part of St Jude'. *FLE* V.36–57.
Hooker, Richard. *The Works of That Learned and Judicious Divine, Mr Richard Hooker*. Seventh edition. 3 vols. Edited by John Keble. Revised by R.W. Church and F. Paget. Oxford: Clarendon Press, 1888.
Tanner, Norman P., ed. *Decrees of the Ecumenical Councils*. Vol. II: *Trent to Vatican II*. London: Sheed and Ward, 1990.
Tertullian. *De praescriptione haereticorum*. In *The Ante-Nicene Fathers: The Writings of the Fathers Down to AD 325*. 10 vols, III.243–65. Edited by Alexander Roberts. Edinburgh: T&T Clark, 1986–90.
Travers, Walter. 'A Supplication Made to the Privy Council'. *FLE* V.189–210.

Secondary sources

Adams, Edward. 'Calvin's View of Natural Knowledge of God'. *International Journal of Systematic Theology* 3.3 (2001): 280–92.
Allen, Paul L. *Theological Method: A Guide for the Perplexed*. London: T&T Clark, 2012.
Almasy, Rudolph P. 'Richard Hooker's *Of the Lawes of Ecclesiasticall Politie*'. In *The Oxford Handbook of English Prose 1500–1640*, edited by Andrew Hadfield, 592–610. Oxford: Oxford University Press, 2013.
Almasy, Rudolph P. 'Richard Hooker's Worries about the Mind: The Path to Certainty'. *Perichoresis* 11.1 (2013): 31–49.
Anderson, Pamela Sue. *A Feminist Philosophy of Religion*. Oxford: Blackwell, 1998.
Anglican Catholic Future. 'About'. Accessed 26 May 2020. https://www.facebook.com/pg/AnglicanCatholicFuture/about/?ref=page_internal.
Anglican-Roman Catholic International Commission (ARCIC). *Authority in the Church I* (1976). Accessed 28 August 2020. https://www.anglicancommunion.org/media/105230/ARCIC_I_The_Authority_of_the_Church_I.pdf.
Anglican-Roman Catholic International Commission (ARCIC). *The Gift of Authority* (1998). Accessed 28 August 2020. https://www.anglicancommunion.org/media/105245/ARCIC_II_The_Gift_of_Authority.pdf.

Anglican-Roman Catholic International Commission (ARCIC). *Mary: Grace and Hope in Christ* (2004). Accessed 28 August 2020. https://www.anglicancommunion.org/media/105263/mary-grace-and-hope-in-christ_english.pdf.

Anglican-Roman Catholic International Commission (ARCIC). *Walking Together on the Way* (2017). Accessed 28 August 2020. https://www.anglicancommunion.org/media/344839/walking-together-on-the-way-spck-2018.pdf.

Atkinson, Nigel. *Richard Hooker and the Authority of Scripture, Tradition, and Reason*. Vancouver: Regent College Publishing, 1997.

Aulen, Gustaf. *Catholicity and Reformation*. Translated by Eric Walhstrom. Edinburgh: Oliver & Boyd, 1962.

Avis, P. D. L. 'Richard Hooker and John Calvin'. *Journal of Ecclesiastical History* 32.1 (1981): 19–28.

Avis, P. D. L. *The Identity of Anglicanism: Essentials of Anglican Ecclesiology*. London: T&T Clark, 2007.

Avis, P. D. L., ed. *The Oxford Handbook of Ecclesiology*. Oxford: Oxford University Press, 2018.

Bagchi, David and David C. Steinmetz, eds. *The Cambridge Companion to Reformation Theology*. Cambridge: Cambridge University Press, 2004.

Baglow, Christopher T. 'Sacred Scripture and Sacred Doctrine in St Thomas Aquinas'. In *Aquinas on Doctrine: A Critical Introduction*, edited by Thomas G. Weinandy, Daniel A. Keating and John P. Yocum, 1–26. London: T&T Clark, 2004.

Balserak, Jon. 'The Authority of Scripture and Tradition in Calvin's Lectures on the Prophets'. In *The Search for Authority in Reformation Europe*, edited by Helen Parish, Elaine Fulton and Peter Webster, 29–48. Farnham: Ashgate, 2014.

Barth, Karl. *The Knowledge of God and the Service of God according to the Teaching of the Reformation*. Translated by J. L. M. Haire and Ian Henderson. London: Hodder and Stoughton, 1938.

Barth, Karl. *Church Dogmatics*. 13 vols. Edited by G. W. Bromiley and T. F. Torrance. Edinburgh: T&T Clark, 1956–75.

Barth, Karl. *The Epistle to the Romans*. Sixth edition. Translated by E. C. Hoskyns. London: Oxford University Press, 1968.

Bauckham, Richard. 'Hooker, Travers, and the Church of Rome in the 1580s'. *Journal of Ecclesiastical History* 29.1 (1978): 37–50.

Bauckham, Richard. 'Richard Hooker and John Calvin: A Comment'. *Journal of Ecclesiastical History* 32.1 (1981): 29–33.

Bauckham, Richard and Benjamin Drewery, eds. *Scripture, Tradition, and Reason: Studies in the Criteria of Christian Doctrine: Essays in Honour of Richard P.C. Hanson*. Edinburgh: T&T Clark, 1988.

Bauerschmidt, F. C. *Thomas Aquinas: Faith, Reason, and Following Christ*. Oxford: Oxford University Press, 2013.

Beatrice, P. F. 'The Word "Homoousios" from Hellenism to Christianity'. *Church History* 71.2 (2002): 244–72.

van den Belt, Henk. 'Scripture as the Voice of God: The Continuing Importance of Autopistia'. *International Journal of Systematic Theology* 13.4 (2011): 434–47.

van den Belt, Henk. '*Sola Scriptura*: An Inadequate Slogan for the Authority of Scripture'. *Calvin Theological Journal* 51 (2016): 204–26.

Billings, J. Todd. *Calvin, Participation, and the Gift: The Activity of Believers in Union with Christ*. Oxford: Oxford University Press, 2007.

Billings, J. Todd. 'The Catholic Calvin'. *Pro Ecclesia* 20.2 (2011): 120–34.

Bireley, Michael. *The Refashioning of Catholicism, 1450-1700: A Reassessment of the Counter Reformation.* Basingstoke: Macmillan, 1999.
Boland, Vivian. 'Truth, Knowledge, and Communication: Thomas Aquinas on the Mystery of Teaching'. *Studies in Christian Ethics* 19.3 (2006): 287–304.
Boland, Vivian. *St Thomas Aquinas.* London: Bloomsbury, 2014.
van der Borght, A. J. G. *Theology of Ministry: A Reformed Contribution to an Ecumenical Dialogue.* Leiden: Brill, 2007.
Bosco, David L. 'Conscience as Court and Worm: Calvin and the Three Elements of Conscience'. *Journal of Religious Ethics* 14.2 (1986): 333–55.
Bouwsma, W. J. *John Calvin: A Sixteenth Century Portrait.* Oxford: Oxford University Press, 1998.
Brook, Angus. 'Thomas Aquinas on the Effects of Original Sin: A Philosophical Analysis'. *Heythrop Journal* 59.4 (2018): 721–32.
Brown, Stewart J., Peter Nockles and James Pereiro, eds. *The Oxford Handbook of the Oxford Movement.* Oxford: Oxford University Press, 2017.
Brunner, Emil and Karl Barth. *Natural Theology.* Translated by Peter Fraenkel. London: Centenary Press, 1946.
Brydon, Michael. *The Evolving Reputation of Richard Hooker: An Examination of Responses, 1600-1714.* Oxford: Oxford University Press, 2006.
Candler, Peter M. *Theology, Rhetoric, Manuduction, or Reading Scripture Together on the Path to God.* Grand Rapids, MI: Eerdmans, 2006.
Casteel, Theodore W. 'Calvin and Trent: Calvin's Reaction to the Council of Trent in the Context of His Conciliar Thought'. *Harvard Theological Review* 63.1 (1970): 91–117.
Chapman, Mark D. *Anglican Theology.* London: T&T Clark, 2012.
Chapman, Mark D. '"Homosexual Practice" and the Anglican Communion from the 1990s: A Case Study in Theology and Identity'. In *New Approaches in History and Theology to Same-Sex Love and Desire*, edited by Mark D. Chapman and Dominic Janes, 187–208. Basingstoke: Macmillan, 2018.
Chapman, Mark D., Sathianathan Clarke and Martyn Percy, eds. *The Oxford Handbook of Anglican Studies.* Oxford: Oxford University Press, 2016.
Chillingworth, William. *The Religion of Protestants a Safe Way to Salvation.* London: Henry G. Bohn, 1846.
Collinson, Patrick. *The Elizabethan Puritan Movement.* Oxford: Clarendon Press, 1990.
Chopp, Rebecca S. and Sheila Greeve Davaney, eds. *Horizons in Feminist Theology: Identity, Tradition and Norms.* Minneapolis, MN: Fortress Press, 1997.
Church of England Evangelical Council. 'Basis of Faith'. Accessed 28 January 2023. https://ceec.info/basis-of-faith.
Church Society. 'Objectives of Church Society'. Accessed 26 May 2020. https://churchsociety.org/docs/about_us/CS%20Objectives.pdf.
Cocksworth, Christopher. *Holding Together: Gospel, Church, and Spirit – The Essentials of Christian Identity.* Norwich: Canterbury Press, 2008.
Congar, Yves. *Tradition and Traditions: An Historical and a Theological Essay.* London: Burns & Oates, 1966.
Congar, Yves. 'Saint Thomas Aquinas and the Spirit of Ecumenism'. *New Blackfriars* 55 (1974): 196–209.
Craig, William Lane and J. P. Moreland, eds. *The Blackwell Companion to Natural Theology.* Oxford: Wiley-Blackwell, 2012.
Cuddeback, Matthew. 'Thomas Aquinas on Illumination and the Authority of the First Truth'. *Nova et Vetera* 7.3 (2009): 579–602.

Davie, Martin. '"Yes" and "No" – *The Gift of Authority*'. In *Unpacking the Gift: Anglican Resources for Theological Reflection on* The Gift of Authority, edited by Peter Fisher, 33–59. London: Church House Publishing, 2002.

Davies, Brian. 'Is Sacra Doctrina Theology?' *New Blackfriars* 71 (1990): 141–7.

Davies, Brian. *The Thought of Thomas Aquinas*. Oxford: Clarendon Press, 1992.

Davies, Brian, ed. *Philosophy of Religion: A Guide and Anthology*. Oxford: Oxford University Press, 2000.

Davies, Brian. *Aquinas: An Introduction*. London: Continuum, 2003.

Davies, Brian and Eleonore Stump. 'Introduction'. In *The Oxford Handbook of Aquinas*, edited by Brian Davies and Eleonore Stump, 3–10. Oxford: Oxford University Press, 2011.

Davison, Andrew. *Why Sacraments?* London: SPCK, 2013.

Dominiak, P. A. 'The Logic of Desire: A Reappraisal of Reason and the Emotions in Richard Hooker's Lawes'. *Reformation and Renaissance Review* 16.1 (2014): 46–7.

Dominiak, P. A. *Richard Hooker: The Architecture of Participation*. London: T&T Clark, 2021.

Dowey, Edmund A. *The Knowledge of God in Calvin's Theology*. New York: Columbia University Press, 1952.

Ecchevaria, Eduardo. 'Revelation, Faith, and Tradition: Catholic Ecumenical Dialogue'. *Calvin Theological Journal* 63.1 (2014): 25–62.

Edwards, David L. *What Anglicans Believe in the Twenty-First Century*. London: Continuum, 2002.

Ekpo, Anthony. 'The *Sensus Fidelium* and the Threefold Office of Christ: A Reinterpretation of *Lumen Gentium* No 12'. *Theological Studies* 76.2 (2015): 330–46.

Elders, Leo. 'Aquinas on Holy Scripture as the Medium of Divine Revelation'. In *La Doctrine de la Revelation Divine de Saint Thomas D'Aquin: Actes du Symposium sur la Pensée de Saint Thomas d'Aquin*, 132–52. Vatican City: Libreria Editrice Vaticana, 1990.

Elders, Leo. *Thomas Aquinas and His Predecessors: The Philosophers and the Church Fathers*. Washington, DC: Catholic University of America Press, 2018.

Engel, Mary. *John Calvin's Perspectival Anthropology*. Eugene, OR: Wipf&Stock, 1988.

Evans, C. Stephen. 'Faith and Revelation'. In *The Oxford Handbook of the Philosophy of Religion*, edited by William Wainwright, 323–43. Oxford: Oxford University Press, 2005.

Faith and Order Advisory Group of the Church of England. *Response by the Church of England to the Agreed Statements by the Anglican-Roman Catholic International Commission (1978)*. Accessed 23 January 2023. https://iarccum.org/archive/ARCIC/ARCIC-203A.pdf

Faith and Order Advisory Group of the Church of England, ed. *Mary: Grace and Hope in Christ (ARCIC II): Essays by the Faith and Order Advisory Group of the Church of England*. London: CHP, 2008.

Flynn, Gabriel and Paul D. Murray, eds. *Ressourcement: A Movement for Renewal in Twentieth-Century Catholic Theology*. Oxford: Oxford University Press, 2014.

Fox, Rory. 'Richard Hooker and the Incoherence of "Ecclesiastical Polity"'. *Heythrop Journal* 44 (2003): 43–59.

Frank Parsons, Susan, ed. *The Cambridge Companion to Feminist Theology*. Cambridge: Cambridge University Press, 2002.

Gazal, Andre A. '"That Ancient and Christian Liberty": Early Church Councils in Reformation Anglican Thought'. *Perichoresis* 17.4 (2012): 73–92.

Gibbs, Lee W. 'Richard Hooker's *Via Media* Doctrine of Justification'. *Harvard Theological Review* 74.2 (1981): 211–20.

Gibbs, Lee W. 'Richard Hooker's *Via Media* Doctrine of Scripture and Tradition'. *Harvard Theological Review* 95.2 (2002): 227–35.
Gordon, Bruce. *Calvin*. New Haven, CT: Yale University Press, 2011.
Gore, A. A. *The Assault on Reason: Our Information Ecosystem, from the Age of Print to the Age of Trump*. Second edition. London: Bloomsbury, 2017.
Grabill, Stephen J. *Rediscovering the Natural Law in Reformed Theological Ethics*. Grand Rapids, MI: Eerdmans, 2002.
Graves, Daniel F. '"*Iure Divino*"? Four Views on the Authority of the Episcopacy in Richard Hooker'. *Anglican and Episcopal History* 81.1 (2012): 47–60.
Grislis, Egil. 'The Role of Sin in the Theology of Richard Hooker'. *Anglican Theological Review* 84.4 (2002): 881–96.
Hahn, Michael. 'Thomas Aquinas's Presentation of Christ as Teacher'. *The Thomist* 83.1 (2019): 57–89.
Hamid, David. 'The Nature and Shape of the Anglican Communion Today'. In *Beyond Colonial Anglicanism: The Anglican Communion in the Twenty-First Century*, edited by Ian T. Douglas and Kwok-Pui Lan, 71–98. New York: Church Publishing, 2001.
Hampton, S. W. P. *Anti-Arminians: The Anglican Reformed Tradition from Charles II to George I*. Oxford: Oxford University Press, 2008.
Hampton, S. W. P. 'Protestants Betrayed'. *The Tablet* (22 May 2009).
Hampton, S. W. P. *Grace and Conformity: The Reformed Conformist Tradition and the Early Stuart Church of England*. Oxford: Oxford University Press, 2021.
Hanson, R. P. C. *Tradition in the Early Church*. London: SCM, 1962.
Harrison, Peter. *The Bible, Protestantism, and the Rise of Natural Science*. Cambridge: Cambridge University Press, 1998.
Harrison, Peter. *The Fall of Man and the Foundations of Science*. Cambridge: Cambridge University Press, 2007.
Healy, Nicholas M. 'Introduction'. In *Aquinas on Scripture: An Introduction to His Critical Commentaries*, edited by Thomas G. Weinandy, Daniel A. Keating and John P. Yocum, 1–20. London: T&T Clark, 2006.
Helm, Paul. 'Calvin, the "*Sensus Divinitatis*", and the Noetic Effects of Sin'. *International Journal for the Philosophy of Religion* 43.2 (1998): 87–107.
Helm, Paul. *John Calvin's Ideas*. Oxford: Oxford University Press, 2004.
Helm, Paul. *Calvin at the Centre*. Oxford: Oxford University Press, 2010.
Higton, Mike. *The Life of Christian Doctrine*. London: Bloomsbury T&T Clark, 2020.
Higton, Mike and Jim Fodor, eds. *The Routledge Companion to the Practice of Christian Theology*. London: Routledge, 2015.
Hillerdal, Gunner. *Reason and Revelation in Richard Hooker*. Lund: CWK Gleerup, 1962.
Hobday, P. P. 'Richard Hooker and *Mission and Ministry in Covenant*'. *Journal of Anglican Studies* 18.2 (2020): 215–34.
Holcomb, Justin S., ed. *Christian Theologies of Scripture: A Comparative Introduction*. New York, NY: New York University Press, 2006.
Horst, Ulrich. *The Dominicans and the Pope: Papal Teaching Authority in the Medieval and Early Modern Thomist Tradition*. Translated by James D. Mixson. Notre Dame, IN: University of Notre Dame Press, 2007.
Hoyle, D. M. *Reformation and Religious Identity in Cambridge, 1590–1644*. Woodbridge: Boydell Press, 2007.
Ingalls, Ranall. 'Richard Hooker as Interpreter of the Reformed Doctrine of "*Sola Scriptura*"'. *Anglican and Episcopal History* 77.4 (2008): 351–78.
Jacob, William. *The Making of the Worldwide Anglican Church*. London: SPCK, 1997.

Jantzen, Grace M. *Becoming Divine: Towards a Feminist Philosophy of Religion*. Manchester: Manchester University Press, 1998.
Jedin, Hubert. *A History of the Council of Trent*. 2 vols. Translated by Ernest Graf. London: Thomas Nelson and Sons, 1957–61.
John Paul II, Pope. 'Encyclical Letter on the Relationship between Faith and Reason' (14 September 1998). Accessed 16 August 2020. http://www.vatican.va/content/john-paul-ii/en/encyclicals/documents/hf_jp_ii_enc_14091998_fides-et-ratio.html.
Jordan, Mark D. *Ordering Wisdom: The Hierarchy of Philosophical Discourses in Aquinas*. Notre Dame, IN: University of Notre Dame Press, 1987.
Jordan, Mark D. *Rewritten Theology: Aquinas after His Readers*. Oxford: Blackwell, 2006.
Jordan, Mark D. *Teaching Bodies: Moral Formation in the* Summa *of Thomas Aquinas*. New York, NY: Fordham University Press, 2017.
Joyce, A. J. *Richard Hooker and Anglican Moral Theology*. Oxford: Oxford University Press, 2009.
Kamitsuka, Margaret D. *Feminist Theology and the Challenge of Difference*. Oxford: Oxford University Press, 2007.
Kerr, Fergus. *Contemplating Aquinas: Varieties of Interpretation*. London: SCM, 2003.
Kerr, Fergus. *Aquinas: A Very Short Introduction*. Oxford: Oxford University Press, 2009.
Kirby, W. J. T. *The Theology of Richard Hooker in the Context of the English Reformation*. Princeton, NJ: Princeton Theological Seminary, 2000.
Kirby, W. J. T., ed. *Richard Hooker and the English Reformation*. Dordrecht: Kluwer Academic, 2003.
Kirby, W. J. T., ed. *A Companion to Richard Hooker*. Leiden: Brill, 2008.
Kirby, W. J. T. 'The "Sundrie Waies" of Wisdom: Richard Hooker on the Authority of Scripture and Reason'. In *The Oxford Handbook of the Bible in Early Modern England, c. 1530-1700*, edited by Kevin Killeen, Helen Smith and Rachel Judith Willie, 164–75. Oxford: Oxford University Press, 2015.
Kincade, James. 'Karl Barth and Philosophy'. *The Journal of Religion* 40.3 (1960): 161–9.
Kingdon, Robert. 'The Calvinist Reformation in Geneva'. In *The Cambridge History of Christianity*, 9 vols, VI.90–103. Cambridge: Cambridge University Press, 2005–9.
Kretzmann, Norman. *The Metaphysics of Theism: Aquinas's Natural Theology in* Summa Contra Gentiles I. Oxford: Oxford University Press, 1997.
Kretzmann, Norman. *The Metaphysics of Creation: Aquinas's Natural Theology in* Summa Contra Gentiles II. Oxford: Oxford University Press, 2001.
Kretzmann, Norman and Eleonore Stump, eds. *The Cambridge Companion to Aquinas*. Cambridge: Cambridge University Press, 1993.
Lane, A. N. S. 'Scripture, Tradition, and the Church: An Historical Survey'. *Vox Evangelica* 9 (1975): 37–55.
Lane, A. N. S. 'Calvin's Use of the Fathers and Medievals'. *Calvin Theological Journal* 16 (1981): 149–205.
Lane, A. N. S. '*Sola Scriptura*? Making Sense of a Post-Reformation Slogan'. In *A Pathway into the Holy Scripture*, edited by D. F. Wright and Philip Satterthwaite, 297–327. Grand Rapids, MI: Eerdmans, 1994.
Lash, Nicholas. *The Beginning and End of Religion*. Cambridge: Cambridge University Press, 2006.
Lake, Peter. *Anglicans and Puritans? Presbyterianism and English Conformist Thought from Whitgift to Hooker*. London: Unwin Hyman, 1988.
The Lambeth Conferences, 1867-1948. London: SPCK, 1948.

LeTourneau, Mark. 'Richard Hooker and the Sufficiency of Scripture'. *Journal of Anglican Studies* 14.2 (2016): 134–55.
Levering, Matthew. *Scripture and Metaphysics: Aquinas and the Renewal of Trinitarian Theology*. Oxford: Blackwell, 2004.
Lewis, C. S. *English Literature in the Sixteenth Century*. Oxford: Clarendon Press, 1954.
Littlejohn, W. Bradford. 'The Search for a Reformed Hooker: Some Modest Proposals'. *Reformation and Renaissance Review* 16.1 (2014): 68–82.
Littlejohn, W. Bradford. *Richard Hooker: A Companion to His Life and Work*. Eugene, OR: Cascade, 2015.
Littlejohn, W. Bradford and Scott N. Kindred-Barnes, eds. *Richard Hooker and Reformed Orthodoxy*. Göttingen: Vandenoeck & Ruprecht, 2017.
Lloyd, Genevieve. *The Man of Reason: 'Male' and 'Female' in Western Philosophy*. Second edition. London: Routledge, 1993.
Loke, Andrew. 'Review of Gerald O'Collins' *Revelation: Towards a Christian Interpretation of God's Self-Revelation in Jesus Christ*'. *Journal of Theological Studies* 69.1 (2018): 385–6.
Luoma, John K. 'Who Owns the Fathers? Hooker and Cartwright on the Authority of the Primitive Church'. *Sixteenth Century Journal* 8.3 (1977): 45–59.
MacCulloch, Diarmaid. *The Later Reformation in England*. Second edition. Basingstoke: Palgrave, 2001.
MacCulloch, Diarmaid. 'Richard Hooker's Reputation'. *English Historical Review* 117 (2002): 773–812.
MacCulloch, Diarmaid. *Reformation: Europe's House Divided, 1490–1700*. London: Penguin, 2004.
MacCulloch, Diarmaid. 'Putting the English Reformation on the Map'. In Diarmaid MacCulloch, *All Things Made New: Writings on the Reformation*, 197–217. London: Penguin, 2017.
MacIntyre, Alasdair. *Whose Justice? Which Rationality?* Notre Dame, IN: University of Notre Dame Press, 1998.
MacIntyre, Alasdair. *After Virtue: A Study in Moral Theory*. Third edition. London: Bloomsbury, 2013.
Mackey, J. P. *The Modern Theology of Tradition*. London: DLT, 1962.
Maeckelberghe, E. 'Across the Generations in Feminist Theology: From Second to Third Wave Feminisms'. *Feminist Theology* 9.23 (2000): 63–9.
Marshall, Bruce D. 'Aquinas as Postliberal Theologian'. *The Thomist* 53.3 (1989): 379–87.
Marshall, J. S. *Hooker and the Anglican Tradition*. London: A&C Black, 1963.
McAdoo, H. R. *The Spirit of Anglicanism: A Study of Theological Method in the Sixteenth Century*. London: A&C Black, 1965.
McClintock Fulkerson, Mary and Sheila Briggs, eds. *The Oxford Handbook of Feminist Theology*. Oxford: Oxford University Press, 2012.
McCosker, Philip and Denys Turner, eds. *The Cambridge Companion to the* Summa Theologiae. Cambridge: Cambridge University Press, 2016.
McGrade, A. S. 'The Coherence of Hooker's Polity: The Books on Power'. *Journal of the History of Ideas* 24.2 (1963): 163–82.
McGrade, A. S., ed. *Richard Hooker and the Construction of Christian Community*. Tempe, AZ: Medieval and Renaissance Texts and Studies, 1997.
McGrade, A. S. 'Richard Hooker on Anglican Integrity'. *Anglican Theological Review* 9.3 (2009): 428.

McGrath, A. E. *A Life of John Calvin: A Study in the Shaping of Western Culture*. Oxford: Blackwell, 1990.

McGrath, A. E. *Christian Theology: An Introduction*. Fifth edition. Oxford: Oxford University Press, 2011.

McGrath, A. E. *Emil Brunner: A Reappraisal*. Oxford: Wiley-Blackwell, 2014.

McInery, Ralph. 'On Behalf of Natural Theology'. *Proceedings of the American Catholic Philosophical Association* 54 (1980): 63–73.

McKim, Donald K., ed. *The Cambridge Companion to John Calvin*. Cambridge: Cambridge University Press, 2004.

McKim, Donald K., ed. *Calvin and the Bible*. Cambridge: Cambridge University Press, 2006.

McNeill, J. T. 'Natural Law in the Theology of the Reformers'. *Journal of Religion* 26.3 (1946): 168–82.

McNeill, J. T. 'The Significance of the Word of God for Calvin'. *Church History* 28.2 (1959): 131–46.

Milton, Anthony. *Catholic and Reformed: The Roman and Protestant Churches in English Protestant Thought, 1600–1640*. Cambridge: Cambridge University Press, 1995.

More, P. E. and F. L. Cross, eds. *Anglicanism: The Thought and Practice of the Church of England*. London: SPCK, 1935.

Muller, R. A. '*Duplex cognitio Dei* in the Theology of Early Reformed Orthodoxy'. *Sixteenth Century Journal* 10.2 (1979): 51–62.

Muller, R. A. *The Unaccommodated Calvin: Studies in the Foundation of a Theological Tradition*. Oxford: Oxford University Press, 2000.

Muller, R. A. *After Calvin: Studies in the Development of a Theological Tradition*. Oxford: Oxford University Press, 2003.

Muller, R. A. *Post-Reformation Reformed Dogmatics: The Rise and Development of Reformed Orthodoxy, ca.1520 to ca.1725*. Second edition. 5 vols. Grand Rapids, MI: Baker Academic, 2003.

Murray, John. *Calvin on Scripture and Divine Sovereignty*. Welwyn: Evangelical Press, 1979.

Murray, Paul D. 'Theology "Under the Lash": Theology as Idolatry Critique in the Work of Nicholas Lash'. *New Blackfriars* 88 (2007): 246–66.

Murray, Paul D., ed. *Receptive Ecumenism and the Call to Catholic Learning: Exploring a Way for Contemporary Ecumenism*. Oxford: Oxford University Press, 2008.

Murray, Paul D. 'Aquinas on Poetry and Theology'. *Logos* 19.2 (2013): 63–72.

Murray, Paul D. 'The Reception of ARCIC I and II in Europe and Discerning the Strategy and Agenda for ARCIC III'. *Ecclesiology* 11 (2015): 199–218.

Murray, Paul D., Gregory A. Ryan and Paul Lakeland, eds. *Receptive Ecumenism as Transforming Ecclesiastical Learning: Walking the Way to a Church Reformed*. Oxford: Oxford University Press, 2022.

Munz, Peter. *The Place of Hooker in the History of Christian Thought*. London: Routledge, 1952.

Neelands, W. David. 'The Use and Abuse of John Calvin in Richard Hooker's Defence of the English Church'. *Perichoresis* 10.1 (2012): 3–22.

Nelson, R. David and Charles Raith. *Ecumenism: A Guide for the Perplexed*. London: Bloomsbury, 2017.

The New Cambridge History of the Bible. Edited by James Carleton-Paget, Joachim Schaper, Richard Marsden, E. Ann Matter, Euan Cameron, and John Riches. 4 vols. Cambridge: Cambridge University Press, 2012–6.

Newey, Edmund. 'The Form of Reason: Participation in the Work of Richard Hooker, Benjamin Whichcote, Ralph Cudworth and Jeremy Taylor'. *Modern Theology* 18.1 (2002): 1–26.
Newey, Edmund. 'The Covenant and the *Via Media*: Compatible or Contradictory Notions of Anglicanism?' In Pro Communione: *Theological Essays on the Anglican Covenant*, edited by Benjamin Guyer, 50–65. Eugene, OR: Pickwick, 2012.
Niesel, Wilhelm. *The Theology of Calvin*. Translated by Harold Knight. London: Lutterworth, 1956.
van Nieuwenhove, Rik and Jospeh Wawrykow, eds. *The Theology of Thomas Aquinas*. Notre Dame, IN: University of Notre Dame Press, 2010.
van Nieuewhenove, Rik. 'Assent to Faith, Theology, and *Scientia* in Aquinas'. *New Blackfriars* 100 (2019): 415–16.
Nockles, Peter. *The Oxford Movement in Context: Anglican High Churchmanship, 1760-1857*. Cambridge: Cambridge University Press, 2004.
Noll, Mark A. *In the Beginning Was the Word: The Bible in American Public Life 1492-1783*. Oxford: Oxford University Press, 2016.
O'Collins, Gerald. *Revelation: Towards a Christian Interpretation of God's Self-Revelation in Jesus Christ*. Oxford: Oxford University Press, 2016.
O'Collins, Gerald. *Inspiration: Towards a Christian Interpretation of Biblical Revelation*. Oxford: Oxford University Press, 2018.
O'Collins, Gerald. *Tradition: Understanding Christian Tradition*. Oxford: Oxford University Press, 2018.
O'Donovan, Oliver. *On the Thirty-Nine Articles: Conversations with Tudor Christianity*. Second edition. London: SCM, 2001.
O'Malley, John W. *Trent: What Happened at the Council*. London: Bealknap Press, 2013.
Oberman, Heiko A. '*Quo Vadis*? Tradition from Irenaeus to *Humani Generis*'. *Scottish Journal of Theology* 16.3 (1963): 225–55.
Oliver, Simon. 'The Eucharist before Nature and Culture'. *Modern Theology* 15.3 (1999): 331–53.
Oliver, Simon. 'The Parallel Journey of Faith and Reason: Another Look at Aquinas's *De Veritate*'. In *Faithful Reading: New Essays in Theology in Honour of Fergus Kerr*, edited by Simon Oliver, Karen Kilby and Tom O'Loughlin, 113–30. London: T&T Clark, 2012.
Oliver, Simon. 'The Cathedral and Rooted Growth'. In *Holy Ground: Cathedrals in the Twenty-First Century*, edited by Stephen Platten, 23–40. Durham: Sacristy Press, 2017.
Oliver, Simon. *Creation: A Guide for the Perplexed*. London: Bloomsbury, 2017.
Oliver, Simon. '*Salus* and *Sanctus*: On Salvation as Health and Well-being'. Durham University Catholic Theology Research Seminar (10 October 2019).
Padley, K. P. J. 'Early Anglican Ecclesiology and Contemporary Ecumenism'. *International Journal for the Study of the Christian Church* 9.1 (2009): 3–16.
Padley, K. P. J. 'Eternal Progression and Temporal Procession of the Holy Spirit'. *International Journal for the Study of the Christian Church* 18.4 (2018): 332–43.
Parker, T. H. L. *Calvin's Doctrine of the Knowledge of God*. Edinburgh: Oliver & Boyd, 1969.
Parris, J. R. 'Hooker's Doctrine of the Eucharist'. *Scottish Journal of Theology* 16.2 (1963): 151–65.
Partee, Charles. *Calvin and Classical Philosophy*. Leiden: Brill, 1997.
Partee, Charles. *The Theology of John Calvin*. Louisville, KY: Westminster John Knox Press, 2010.

Pelikan, Jaroslav. *The Christian Tradition: A History of the Development of Christian Doctrine*. 5 vols. Chicago, IL: University of Chicago Press, 1971–89.
Persson, Per Erik. Sacra Doctrina: *Reason and Revelation in Aquinas*. Translated by Ross Mackenzie. Oxford: Basil Blackwell, 1970.
Perrott, M. E. C. 'Richard Hooker and the Problem of Authority in the Elizabethan Church'. *Journal of Ecclesiastical History* 49 (1998): 29–60.
Peter, J. F. 'The Place of Tradition in Reformed Theology'. *Scottish Journal of Theology* 18 (1965): 294–307.
Pinker, Stephen. *Enlightenment Now: The Case for Reason, Science, Humanism, and Progress*. London: Penguin, 2019.
Pitkin, Barbara. *Calvin, the Bible, and History*. Oxford: Oxford University Press, 2020.
Plantinga, Alvin. 'The Reformed Objection to Natural Theology'. *Proceedings of the American Catholic Philosophical Association* 54 (1980): 49–63.
Postema, Gerald J. 'Calvin's Alleged Rejection of Natural Theology'. *Scottish Journal of Theology* 24 (1971): 423–34.
Preller, Victor. *Divine Science and the Science of God: A Reformulation of Thomas Aquinas*. Princeton, NJ: Princeton University Press, 1967.
Quantin, Jean-Louis. *The Church of England and Christian Antiquity: The Construction of a Confessional Identity in the Seventeenth Century*. Oxford: Oxford University Press, 2009.
Rahner, Karl and Joseph Ratzinger. *Revelation and Tradition*. London: Burns & Oates, 1966.
Raith, C. D. 'Calvin's Theological Appropriation of His Philosophical Sources: A Note on Natural Law and *Institutes* 2.2.22-23'. *Calvin Theological Journal* 47.1 (2012): 32–49.
Raphael, Melissa. 'A Patrimony of Idols: Second-Wave Jewish and Christian Feminist Theology and the Criticism of Religion'. *Sophia: International Journal of Philosophy and Tradition* 53.2 (2014): 241–59.
Ratzinger, Joseph. *God's Word: Scripture, Tradition, Office*. Translated by Henry Taylor. Edited by Peter Hünermann and Thomas Söding. San Francisco, CA: Ignatius Press, 2008.
Re Manning, Russell, ed. *The Oxford Handbook of Natural Theology*. Oxford: Oxford University Press, 2013.
Reid, J. K. S. *The Authority of Scripture: A Study of the Reformation and Post-Reformation Understanding of the Bible*. London: Methuen & Co., 1957.
Reynolds, Stephen M. 'Calvin's View of the Athanasian and Nicene Creeds'. *Westminster Theological Journal* 23.1 (1960): 33–7.
Rodger, P. C. and K. Vischer, eds. *The Fourth World Conference on Faith and Order*. London: SCM, 1964.
Rogers, Eugene F. *Thomas Aquinas: Sacred Doctrine and the Knowledge of God*. Notre Dame, IN: University of Notre Dame Press, 1995.
Rogers, Paul M. 'Thomas Aquinas, Prophecy, and the "Scientific" Character of Sacred Doctrine'. *New Blackfriars* 100 (2016): 81–103.
Roszak, Piotr. 'Revelation and Scripture: Exploring the Scriptural Foundations of Sacra Doctrina in Aquinas'. *Angelicum* 93.1 (2016): 191–218.
Rudder Baker, Lynne. 'Dennett on Breaking the Spell'. In *The Philosophy of Daniel Dennett*, edited by Bryce Hubner, 331–44. Oxford: Oxford University Press, 2018.
Ruse, Michael. *Monotheism and Contemporary Atheism*. Cambridge: Cambridge University Press, 2019.

Rush, Ormond and Jamie Hawkey, eds. *Walking Together on the Way: Anglican and Roman Catholic Commentaries on the ARCIC Agreed Statement*. London: SPCK, 2018.
Russell, Andrea. *Richard Hooker: Beyond Certainty*. Routledge: London, 2020.
Ryan, Gregory A. 'The Reception of Receptive Ecumenism'. *Ecclesiology* 17.1 (2021): 7–28.
Ryan, Phil. *After the New Atheist Debate*. Toronto: University of Toronto Press, 2018.
Sachs, William L. *Homosexuality and the Crisis of Anglicanism*. Cambridge: Cambridge University Press, 2009.
Sacred Congregation for the Doctrine of the Faith. *Observations on the Final Report of ARCIC* (1982). Accessed 23 January 2023. https://www.vatican.va/roman_curia/congregations/cfaith/documents/rc_con_cfaith_doc_19820327_animadversiones_en.html.
Schreiner, Susan. *The Theater of His Glory: Nature and the Natural Order in the Thought of John Calvin*. Durham, NC: The Labyrinth Press, 1991.
Second Vatican Council. '*Lumen Gentium*, Dogmatic Constitution on the Church' (21 November 1964). https://www.vatican.va/archive/hist_councils/ii_vatican_council/documents/vat-ii_const_19641121_lumen-gentium_en.html.
Secor, Philip B. *Richard Hooker: Prophet of Anglicanism*. Tunbridge Wells: Burns & Oates, 1999.
Shagan, Ethan. 'The Ecclesiastical Polity'. In *The Oxford Handbook of English Law and Literature*, edited by Lorna Hutson, 337–52. Oxford: Oxford University Press, 2017.
Simut, Corneliu C. *The Doctrine of Salvation in the Sermons of Richard Hooker*. Berlin: DeGruyter, 2005.
Somerville, M. R. 'Richard Hooker and His Contemporaries on Episcopacy: An Elizabethan Consensus'. *Journal of Ecclesiastical History* 34 (1984): 177–87.
Speed Hill, W., ed. *Studies in Richard Hooker: Essays Preliminary to an Edition of His Works*. Cleveland, OH: Case Western University Press, 1972.
Speed Hill, W. 'Scripture as Text, Text as Scripture: The Case of Richard Hooker'. *Text* 9 (1996): 93–110.
Spencer, Stephen. *The SCM Studyguide to Anglicanism*. London: SCM, 2010.
Spinks, Bryan D. *Two Faces of Elizabethan Anglican Theology: Sacraments and Salvation in the Thought of William Perkins and Richard Hooker*. Lanham, MD: Scarecrow Press, 1999.
Steinmetz, David C. 'The Scholastic Calvin'. In *Protestant Scholasticism: Essays in Reassessment*, edited by Carl Trueman and R. S. Clark, 16–30. Carlisle: Paternoster Press, 1999.
Steinmetz, David C. 'Calvin as Biblical Interpreter among the Ancient Philosophers'. *Interpretation* 69.2 (2009): 142–53.
Steinmetz, David C. *Calvin in Context*. Second edition. Oxford: Oxford University Press, 2010.
Strong, Rowan, gen. ed. *The Oxford History of Anglicanism*. 5 vols. Oxford: Oxford University Press, 2016-9.
Sudduth, Michael. 'Calvin, Plantinga, and the Natural Knowledge of God: A Response to Beversluis'. *Faith and Philosophy* 15.1 (1998): 92–103.
Sudduth, Michael. *The Reformed Objection to Natural Theology*. London: Routledge, 2016.
Suggate, Alan. 'The Anglican Tradition in Moral Theology'. In *Worship and Ethics: Lutherans and Anglicans in Dialogue*, edited by Oswald Bayer and Alan Suggate, 2–25. Berlin: DeGruyter, 1996.
Stead, G. C. *Philosophy in Christian Antiquity*. Cambridge: Cambridge University Press, 2007.

Svensson, Manfred and David VanDrunen, eds. *Aquinas among the Protestants*. Oxford: Wiley-Blackwell, 2018.
Sykes, Norman. 'The Religion of Protestants'. In *The Cambridge History of the Bible*. 3 vols, III.175–82. Cambridge: Cambridge University Press, 1963–70.
Sykes, Stephen. *The Integrity of Anglicanism*. Oxford: Mowbray, 1974.
Sykes, Stephen. *Unashamed Anglicanism*. London: DLT, 1995.
Tanner, Kathryn. 'Hooker and the New Puritans'. In *Authorizing Marriage? Canon, Tradition, and Critique in the Blessing of Same-Sex Unions*, edited by Mark D. Jordan, 121–38. Princeton, NJ: Princeton University Press, 2006.
Tavard, G. H. *Holy Writ or Holy Church: The Crisis of the Protestant Reformation*. London: Burns & Oates, 1959.
Topham, Jonathan R. 'Natural Theology and the Sciences'. In *The Cambridge Companion to Science and Religion*, edited by Peter Harrison, 59–79. Cambridge: Cambridge University Press, 2010.
Torrell, Jean-Pierre. *Saint Thomas Aquinas*. Revised edition. 2 vols. Translated by Robert Royal. Washington, DC: Catholic University of America Press, 2003–5.
Toulmin, Stephen. *Return to Reason*. London: Harvard University Press, 2001.
Tout, T. F. 'The Place of St Thomas in History'. In *St Thomas Aquinas*, edited by Aelred Whitacre, 1–32. Eugene, OR: Wipf&Stock, 1926.
Turner, Denys. 'How to Be an Atheist'. *New Blackfriars* 83 (2002): 317–35.
Turner, Denys. *Faith, Reason, and the Existence of God*. Cambridge: Cambridge University Press, 2004.
Turner, Denys. 'Faith, Reason, and the Eucharist'. In *Redeeming Truth: Considering Faith and Reason*, edited by Lawrence Paul Hemming and Susan Frank Parsons, 15–33. London: SCM, 2007.
Turner, Denys. 'Reason, the Eucharist, and the Body'. In Denys Turner, *God, Mystery and Mystification*, 45–68. Notre Dame, IN: University of Notre Dame Press, 2019.
Tyacke, Nicholas. *Anti-Calvinists: The Rise of English Arminianism*. Oxford: Clarendon Press, 1990.
Valkenberg, W. G. B. M. *Words of the Living God: Place and Function of Holy Scripture in the Theology of St Thomas Aquinas*. Leuven: Peters, 2000.
te Velde, Rudi. *Aquinas on God: The Divine Science of the* Summa Theologiae. Aldershot: Ashgate, 2006.
Via Media blog. 'Background'. Accessed 26 May 2020. https://viamedia.news/about-viamedia/.
Voak, Nigel. *Richard Hooker and Reformed Theology: A Study of Reason, Will, and Grace*. Oxford: Oxford University Press, 2003.
Voak, Nigel. 'Richard Hooker and the Principle of *Sola Scriptura*'. *Journal of Theological Studies* 59.1 (2008): 96–139.
Vos, Arvin. *Aquinas, Calvin, and Contemporary Protestant Thought*. Grand Rapids, MI: Eerdmans, 1985.
Ward Holder, R. 'Calvin and Tradition: Tracing Expansion, Locating Development, Suggesting Authority'. *Toronto Journal of Theology* 25.2 (2009): 215–26.
Ward, Kevin. *A History of Global Anglicanism*. Cambridge: Cambridge University Press, 2007.
Warfield, B. B. *Calvin and Calvinism*. New York: Oxford University Press, 1931.
Warwrykow, Joseph. 'Franciscan and Dominican Trinitarian Theology (Thirteenth Century: Aquinas and Bonaventure)'. In *The Oxford Handbook of the Trinity*, edited by Gilles Emery and Matthew Levering, 182–96. Oxford: Oxford University Press, 2011.

Webster, John. *Holy Scripture: A Dogmatic Sketch*. London: Bloomsbury, 2003.
Webster, John. *Karl Barth*. Second edition. London: Continuum, 2004.
Webster, John. 'Purity and Plenitude: Evangelical Reflections on Congar's *Tradition and Traditions*'. *International Journal of Systematic Theology* 7.4 (2005): 399–413.
Webster, John. *The Domain of the Word: Scripture and Theological Reason*. London: T&T Clark, 2014.
Webster, John, Kathryn Tanner and Iain Torrance, eds. *The Oxford Handbook of Systematic Theology*. Oxford: Oxford University Press, 2009.
Wells, Samuel. *What Anglicans Believe: An Introduction*. Norwich: Canterbury Press, 2011.
Wendel, François. *Calvin: The Origins and Development of His Thought*. Translated by Philip Mairet. London: Collins, 1963.
Whidden, David L. *Christ the Light: The Theology of Light and Illumination in Thomas Aquinas*. Minneapolis, MN: Fortress Press, 2014.
Williams, A. N. 'Argument to Bliss: The Epistemology of the Summa Theologiae'. *Modern Theology* 20.4 (2004): 505–26.
Williams, A. N. '"The Future of the Past": The Contemporary Significance of the *Nouvelle Théologie*'. *International Journal of Systematic Theology* 7.4 (2005): 347–61.
Williams, A. N. *The Divine Sense: The Intellect in Patristic Theology*. Cambridge: Cambridge University Press, 2007.
Williams, A. N. *The Architecture of Theology: Structure, System, and Ratio*. Oxford: Oxford University Press, 2011.
Williams, R. D. 'What We Need Now: Gratitude'. *Church Times* (6 December 2002).
Williams, R. D. *Anglican Identities*. London: DLT, 2004.
Williams, R. D. *The Edge of Words: God and the Habits of Language*. London: Bloomsbury, 2014.
Williams, R. D. *Christ the Heart of Creation*. London: Bloomsbury, 2018.
Wolterstorff, Nicholas. 'Introduction'. In *Faith and Rationality: Reason and Belief in God*, edited by Alvin Plantinga and Nicholas Wolterstorff, 1–15. Notre Dame, IN: University of Notre Dame Press, 1983.
Wolterstorff, Nicholas. 'The Reformed Tradition'. In *A Companion to Philosophy of Religion*, edited by Charles Taliaferro, Paul Draper and Philip L. Quinn, 204–9. Oxford: Blackwell, 2010.
Wright, Shawn D. 'John Calvin as Pastor'. *Southern Baptist Journal of Theology* 13.4 (2009): 4–17.
World Council of Churches. 'About Us' and 'History'. Accessed 23 October 2018. http://wcrc.ch/about-us and http://wcrc.ch/history.

Unpublished dissertations

Barczi, Nathan. 'A Light to my Path: Calvin and Aquinas on the Doctrine and Metaphysics of Scripture'. MA diss., University of Nottingham, 2010.
Griesel, Jake. 'John Edwards of Cambridge (1637–1716): A Reassessment of His Position within the Later Stuart Church of England'. PhD diss., University of Cambridge, 2019.
Hobday, P. P. 'Richard Hooker and Anglican Theological Method'. MA diss., University of Nottingham, 2014.
Hobday, P. P. 'Relocating Richard Hooker: Theological Method and the Character of Anglicanism'. PhD diss., Durham University, 2021.

Kirby, W. J. T. 'The Doctrine of the Royal Supremacy in the Thought of Richard Hooker'. DPhil thesis, University of Oxford, 1987.
Neelands, W. David. 'The Theology of Grace of Richard Hooker'. ThD diss., Trinity College Toronto, 1988.
Neish, Jane. 'Reason, Faith, and Religious Unity: A Study in the Thought of William Chillingworth'. MA diss., McMaster University, 2003.
Selby, Matthew L. 'The Relationship between Scripture and Tradition according to the Council of Trent'. MA diss., University of St Thomas, 2013.
Stafford, John K. 'Richard Hooker's Doctrine of the Holy Spirit'. PhD diss., University of Manitoba, 2005.
Wood, Andrew. 'Thomas Aquinas and Joseph Ratzinger's Theology of Divine Revelation's Transmission: A Comparative Study'. MPhil thesis, Australian Catholic University, 2015.

INDEX

adiaphora 118
  see also: things indifferent
Anaxagoras 96, 105
Anglican Communion 1–3, 5–6, 8, 195, 205
Anglican-Roman Catholic International Commission (ARCIC) 170, 188–98
Anglicans / Anglicanism 1–11, 13–15, 58, 60, 73, 84, 91, 94, 128–30, 135, 137–8, 153, 163–4, 169–71, 174, 177–205
Apostles' Creed 30 fn.52, 154
Aristotle 28–35, 40, 70–2, 82, 103–4
Articles of Religion 95, 144, 163, 189–90, 203
Athanasian Creed 32 fn.53, 154, fn.54 155
atheism 43, 52, 178, 187, 102
Augustine, St 12 fn.31, 18, 70, 74, 80, 85–6, 105, 149–50, 167
autopistis / autopistia 51–2, 82–5, 126

Barth, Karl 12, 33, 40, 43–4, 46, 54–6, 67, 85, 88–9, 129, 179, 202
bishops 3, 5–6, 47, 93–4, 114–16, 120–32, 150, 153–4, 157–61, 165–6, 172, 183, 191, 193
Brunner, Emil 88–90, 67 fn.32
Burgley, Lord 93

Cartwright, Thomas 116, 162
church councils 29, 31, 111, 138, 142–56, 161–6, 173, 192–4, 200, 203
  Chalcedon 152, 164, 203
  Constantinople 152
  Ephesus 152
  Nicaea I 151–4
  Nicaea II 154
  Trent 4, 129, 138, 144, 149, 154–5, 164–8, 170–4, 183 fn.28, 194–5, 200

  Vatican I 53–5, 58, 189, 194–5
  Vatican II 166, 181
Church of England 1–8, 11, 93, 95, 114–15, 123, 132–5, 137, 172, 196–7, 199, 203–5
Cicero 64, 71, 82
conformist 3, 14, 93, 133, 135
conscience 3, 66, 110, 117, 152, 183
consubstantiation 105, 185–6
creation 18–23, 34, 61–4, 66, 75–7, 88, 96, 108, 110, 184, 186
creator 17, 20–3, 61–6, 68, 73–4, 96, 107–8, 122
creeds 40, 142–6, 150–7, 160–3, 169, 173, 182, 200

depravity 16, 67–8, 102, 106
duplex cognitio Dei 65, 73–4, 90

Fall 3, 15, 23–7, 35, 49, 58, 60–1, 66–9, 73, 87, 89–90, 94, 99–103, 106, 174
feminism 178–88
'Five Ways' 17, 45, 53–5

grace
  Aquinas on 20–1, 25, 27, 34–5, 38, 41–3
  Calvin on 71–4
  Hooker on 99, 103, 108, 110–11, 124, 131, 186

holy communion / eucharist 184–6, 191
Holy Spirit 36, 42, 46 fn. 122, 49, 51, 64, 72, 74, 76, 82–3, 110, 125–8, 141, 165, 198 fn.82
Homer 96, 105

intellect 20–1, 27, 30, 37–8, 42–3, 76

Jewel, John 7, 130
Job 116

justification 2 fn.6, 66, 97, 131 fn.117, 134, 172, 201

Keble, John 8, 121 fn.77, 165, 171–3

Lambeth Conference 5 fn.1, 191
law
    divine or scriptural 79, 96, 99, 114–18, 124, 154, 157, 160
    human 59, 70, 98, 102, 105, 107, 113, 120–2, 130–1, 158, 183
Leo XIII, Pope 53
Lewis, C. S. 1, 186–7
Luther, Martin 11, 71, 110, 192

Mary 142, 190–1
metaphysics 28–30, 34–5, 43
mind 21, 24–5, 37–8, 43, 56, 61–4, 67–9, 74, 76, 78–9, 97, 101–3, 106, 184–5
Moses 113, 147

natural theology 16, 32, 35, 73, 88–90, 129
neo-scholasticism / neo-Thomism 54, 88, 168
Nicene Creed 31, 151, 154, 162
nouvelle théologie 12, 54, 88, 167–8

Oxford Movement 8, 129, 171–3

papacy 2 fn.6, 149, 189–96, 202
papal infallibility 189–96
Paul, St 18, 45, 104, 108, 153
Peter Lombard 54, 86–7
philosophy 1, 3, 27–35, 37, 53–7, 69–73, 85–7, 103–6, 174
Pighius, Albert 148–53
Plato 32, 70–1, 82, 96, 105
presbyterians 2–3, 8, 93, 95, 99–103, 106, 110, 114–30, 134, 137, 156–7, 159–62, 184–5, 193
providence 23, 63, 72, 75, 96, 104
Pseudo-Dionysius 18, 37, 47

reason 2–4, 178–88, 192, 200–3
    Aquinas on 16–44
    Calvin on 61–76
    Hooker on 95–112

receptive ecumenism 178, 189–96
redemption 23, 34, 40, 47, 66, 75–6, 78, 107–8
revelation 3, 166, 170, 174, 179–80, 186, 201
    Aquinas on 24–44, 138–45
    Calvin on 67–76, 88–90, 147, 152–4
    Hooker on 99–114, 160
Romans 1 17–18, 45, 61, 69, 89, 96

sacra doctrina 35–7, 43–4, 47–51, 56, 60 fn.4, 141, 162
salvation 165, 174, 181, 192, 196, 201–4
    Aquinas on 19–20, 23, 38–40, 43, 50–1, 145
    Calvin on 63–6, 68, 71–6, 79–80, 91, 150
    Hooker on 94–5, 98, 100–2, 107–8, 114, 117–23, 136, 163
scientia 53, 56
scripture 2–3, 10–13, 173–5, 180–5, 190–7
    Aquinas on 44–53
    Calvin on 76–85
    canon of 76, 127, 141–4, 153–6, 169, 171–4
    Hooker on 112–28
    sufficiency 3, 45–51, 78–81, 114–23, 156, 162, 166, 170, 174
    see also: autopistis / autopistia
sensus divinitatis 62–4, 69, 71
sermons 56, 93, 95, 103, 121, 172, 180–2
sin *see* Fall
sola scriptura 3, 137, 141, 174, 199–200
    Aquinas on 15–16, 45–4, 51, 53, 57, 142, 146
    Calvin on 76–7, 79–81, 84–5, 155
    Hooker on 94, 112–13, 117, 120–4, 128, 134, 136
stoics 32, 96, 105
subalternation 29, 52

theological warrants 11, 15, 137, 192, 199, 204
    Aquinas on 44, 46–7
    Calvin on 76
    Hooker on 91–4, 113, 122
things indifferent 118–20, 158–60

tradition 2–4, 11–13, 15, 137–73, 177–80, 192–8, 200
   Aquinas on 138–46
   Calvin on 146–56
   Hooker on 165–73
transubstantiation 86, 105, 131, 134, 185–6
Travers, Walter 7–8, 93–4, 133–4

trinity 15, 23, 33, 37–8, 43, 54, 57, 79–80, 97, 108, 118, 144, 174, 203
triplex via 18–21, 23, 33, 186

will 27, 39, 43, 52, 70, 72, 76, 86, 99–100, 117, 127, 150
Williams, Rowan 6, 13, 102, 184–5, 200–2

www.ingramcontent.com/pod-product-compliance
Lightning Source LLC
Chambersburg PA
CBHW051521230426
43668CB00012B/1691